The Spanish Influenza of 1918–19

The Spanish influenza pandemic of 1918–19 was the worst pandemic of modern times, claiming over 30 million lives around the globe in less than six months. In the hardest hit societies, everything else was put aside in a bid to cope with its ravages. It left millions orphaned and medical science desperate to find its cause. Despite the magnitude of its impact, few scholarly attempts have been made to examine this calamity in its many-sided complexity.

This book begins this process on a global, multidisciplinary scale, seeking to apply the insights of a wide range of social and medical sciences to an investigation of the pandemic. Topics covered include the historiography of the pandemic, its virology, the enormous demographic impact, the medical and governmental responses it elicited, and its long-term effects, particularly the recent attempts to identify the precise causative virus from specimens taken from flu victims in 1918, or victims buried in the Arctic permafrost at that time.

With a range of contributions that span the globe and an extensive bibliography of relevant works, this book will be essential reading for students and academics interested in the history and sociology of illness and medicine.

Howard Phillips, South African by birth, studied at the University of Cape Town and London University before joining the staff of the History Department at UCT in 1974. Since completing his doctoral thesis on the impact of the Spanish flu pandemic on South Africa (which was published in 1990), he has researched, taught and written on the medical history of South Africa. In 1998, together with David Killingray, he organised the first international conference on the influenza pandemic of 1918–19.

David Killingray was born in 1939. He studied at the London School of Economics, the University of York, and the School of Oriental and African Studies where he gained a PhD in African history. He was a school teacher for 12 years in the UK and Tanzania. In 1972 he joined Goldsmiths College, University of London, where he is now Professor of Modern History. He has written books and many articles on aspects of African, Imperial, Caribbean and English local history, and has just completed a book on African soldiers in the Second World War.

Routledge Studies in the Social History of Medicine

Edited by Bernard Harris
University of Southampton

Joseph Melling
University of Exeter

Anne Borsay
University of Wales at Lampeter

The Society for the Social History of Medicine was founded in 1969, and exists to promote research into all aspects of the field, without regard to limitations of either time or place. In addition to this book series, the Society also organises a regular programme of conferences, and publishes an internationally recognised journal, *Social History of Medicine*. The Society offers a range of benefits, including reduced-price admission to conferences and discounts on SSHM books, to its members. Individuals wishing to learn more about the Society are invited to contact the series editors through the publisher.

The Society took the decision to launch 'Studies in the Social History of Medicine', in association with Routledge, in 1989, in order to provide an outlet for some of the latest research in the field. Since that time, the series has expanded significantly under a number of series editors, and now includes both edited collections and monographs. Individuals wishing to submit proposals are invited to contact the series editor in the first instance.

1 Nutrition in Britain
Science, scientists and politics in the twentieth century
Edited by David F. Smith

2 Migrant, Minorities and Health
Historical and contemporary studies
Edited by Lara Marks and Michael Worboys

3 From Idiocy to Mental Deficiency
Historical perspectives on people with learning disabilities
Edited by David Wright and Anne Digby

4 Midwives, Society and Childbirth
Debates and controversies in the modern period
Edited by Hilary Marland and Anne Marie Rafferty

5 Illness and Healing Alternatives in Western Europe
Edited by Marijke Gijswit-Hofstra, Hilary Maarland and Has de Waardt

The Spanish Influenza Pandemic of 1918–19

New perspectives

Edited by Howard Phillips and David Killingray

LONDON AND NEW YORK

First published 2003 by Routledge
2 Park Square, Milton Park, Abingdon, Oxfordshire OX14 4RN

Simultaneously published in the USA and Canada
by Routledge
711 Third Avenue, New York, NY 10017

Routledge is an imprint of the Taylor & Francis Group

First issued in paperback 2011

Typeset in Baskerville by Wearset Ltd, Boldon, Tyne and Wear

British Library Cataloguing in Publication Data
A catalogue record for this book is available from the British Library

Library of Congress Cataloging in Publication Data
The Spanish influenza pandemic of 1918–19 : new perspectives /
edited by Howard Phillips and David Killingray.
     p. cm.
  Includes bibliographical references and index.
  1. Influenza—History—20th century. I. Phillips, H., Ph. D.
  II. Killingray, David.

RC150.4.S66 2003
614.5′18′09041—dc21

                                                  2002037041

ISBN 978-0-415-23445-0 (hbk)
ISBN 978-0-415-51079-0 (pbk)

Contents

Illustrations

Figures

Boxes

Tables

Contributors

Nancy K. Bristow, BA (Colorado College), MA, PhD (Berkeley, California), is a professor in the Department of History at the University of Puget Sound, Tacoma, Washington, USA. She is the author of *Making Men Moral: Social engineering during the Great War* (1996).

Peter Curson is professorial fellow in Human Geography at Macquarie University, Sydney, Australia. He is a population geographer interested in population–environment interactions. He is the author/editor of a number of books on plague, epidemics of infectious disease, population and natural disasters and the human health implications of climate change.

Myron Echenberg, MA (McGill), PhD (Wisconsin), is an professor in the Department of History at McGill University, Montreal, Canada. He has published widely in the history of Francophone West Africa. His *Black Death, White Medicine: Bubonic plague and the politics of public health in Senegal, 1914–1945*, was published in 2001.

Beatriz Echeverri, PhD, Universidad Complutense of Madrid, is associate professor in the Department of Population at the Universidad Complutense. She is the author of *La Gripe Española: La pandemia de 1918–1919* (1992).

James Ellison, BA (Michigan State), MA, PhD (Florida), is an assistant professor in the Department of Anthropology at California State University, Long Beach, USA. In 1999 he was awarded a doctorate in anthropology for a thesis on the making of the Nyakyusa in colonial Tanzania.

Michel Garenne, PhD in Demography, is currently a research director at the French Centre for Population and Development Studies (CEPED) in Paris. He has taught demography in Paris universities and at Harvard. His work has focused on various health issues in Tropical Africa and in the world. He is the author of numerous articles on mortality studies, causes of death, infectious and parasitic diseases, sex differences in cause specific mortality, health systems and reproductive health.

Ann Herring is an associate professor and former chair of the Department of Anthropology, McMaster University, Hamilton, Canada. She is the author of numerous articles relating to the history of disease among Aboriginal people in Canada and co-author of *Aboriginal Health in Canada* (1995) with J.B. Waldram and T.K. Young.

Wataru Iijima is professor in the Department of Economics, Yokohama National University, Japan. He has studied the prevalence of bubonic plague and the development of a public health system in modern China, and his book entitled *Plague and Modern China: The institutionalisation of a public health system and social change* was published in 2000.

Niall Johnson, BSc (Macquarie), MA (Wilfrid Laurier), has recently completed his PhD thesis on the 1918–19 influenza pandemic in Britain at the Department of Geography, University of Cambridge.

Edwin D. Kilbourne, MD, was Professor Emeritus of Microbiology and Immunology at New York Medical, Valhalla, New York, USA. He retired in 2003. Prior to that appointment, he had been professor and chairman of the Department of Microbiology, and later Distinguished Service Professor (without term) at Mount Sinai School of Medicine in New York City, and before that Director of the Division of Virus Research at Cornell University Medical College. He is a member of the National Academy of Sciences, USA. Among his numerous works during a distinguished career as an influenza virologist are *Influenza* (1987), and an edited volume, *The Influenza Viruses and Influenza* (1975).

David Killingray, BSc(Econ), PhD (London), is professor of modern history at Goldsmiths College, University of London. He is the author and editor of *Guardians of Empire* (1999), *The West Indies* (1999), and from 1990–2002 joint editor of *African Affairs*, the quarterly journal of The Royal African Society.

Kevin McCracken is senior lecturer in the Department of Human Geography, Macquarie University, Sydney, Australia, where he teaches population and medical geography. His research in recent years has focused on geographical dimensions of health, historical population studies, community needs assessment and population ageing.

Jürgen Müller, Dipl.-Geogr. (Hannover), is a PhD candidate in the History Department of the University of Hannover. He is working on a comparative regional study of Spanish Influenza in sub-Saharan Africa. As junior research fellow, he taught African history to undergraduates and has written articles on influenza and tertiary education in Africa.

Andrew Noymer, BA (Harvard), MA (London School of Hygiene and Tropical Medicine, University of London), is a PhD student in

Sociology at the University of California at Berkeley. His interests in demography include historical demography, male–female mortality differences, and mathematical models of epidemics.

John S. Oxford is Professor of Virology at St. Barts and The London Hospital, Queen Mary's School of Medicine and Dentistry. His major research area is the origin and spread of the 1918 pandemic virus and he participated in the Spitsbergen exhumations of victims. He is Scientific Director of Retroscreen Virology Ltd (www.retroscreen.com), a virology biotechnology company at the College focusing on the search for new antivirals and vaccines.

Howard Phillips, BA (Cape Town), MA (London), PhD (Cape Town), is an associate professor in the Department of Historical Studies at the University of Cape Town, South Africa. He is the author of *Black October: The Spanish flu epidemic of 1918 in South Africa* (1990).

Mridula Ramanna, MA (Delhi), PhD (Bombay), is reader in the Department of History at South Indian Education Society's College, University of Mumbai, India. Her *Western Medicine and Public Health in Colonial Bombay, 1845–1895* was published in 2002.

Terence Ranger is Emeritus Professor of Race Relations in the University of Oxford and until recently Visiting Professor of History in the University of Zimbabwe. He is the author and editor of numerous books including *Epidemics and Ideas: Essays on the historical perception of pestilence* (1992), *The Invention of Tradition* (1983), *Peasant Consciousness and Guerrilla Warfare in Zimbabwe* (1985), *Are We not Also Men? The Samkange Family and African Politics in Zimbabwe 1920–64* (1995), and *Voices From the Rocks: Nature, Culture & History in the Matopos Hills of Zimbabwe* (1999).

Geoffrey W. Rice, MA, PhD (Canterbury, New Zealand), is associate professor in the Department of History at the University of Canterbury, Christchurch, New Zealand. He is the author of *Black November: The 1918 influenza epidemic in New Zealand* (1988) and is general editor of the second edition of the *Oxford History of New Zealand* (1992).

Lisa Sattenspiel is an associate professor in the Department of Anthropology, University of Missouri-Columbia, USA. She uses mathematical models to study the transmission and spread of infectious diseases. She has studied the spread of hepatitis A among Albuquerque, New Mexico day care centres, the spread of measles within the West Indian island of Dominica, and the effect of non-random interactions among risk groups on the spread of HIV.

Stephen C. Schoenbaum, AB (Swarthmore), MD, MPH (Harvard), practised as a physician and epidemiologist before moving into medical administration. He is currently senior vice-president of the Commonwealth Fund in New York, USA. He has published extensively in scientific journals in the fields of internal medicine, epidemiology and healthcare management, and edited two books.

Jeffery K. Taubenberger, MD, PhD (Medical College of Virginia), is the chief of the Division of Molecular Pathology at the Armed Forces Institute of Pathology in Washington, DC, USA. He is the author of many articles in the field of pathology.

Wilfried Witte, MA (Technical University, Berlin), works as a physician in a hospital in central Berlin and is completing an MD thesis on the 1918 pandemic at the Ruprecht-Karls-University in Heidelberg, Germany.

Patrick Zylberman is senior researcher at the Centre de recherche médicine, sciences, santé et société (INSERM-CNRS-EHESS) in Paris. With Lion Murard he wrote *L'Hygiène dans la République: La Santé publique en France ou l'utopie contrariée, 1870–1918* (Paris, 1996) and with Ilana Löwy edited a special issue of *Studies in History and Philosophy of Biological and Biomedical Sciences, The Rockefeller Foundation and the Biomedical Sciences* (Cambridge, September 2000). He is currently working on the history of public health in France and Europe in the twentieth century.

A virologist's foreword

John S. Oxford

I view 1918 as a pivotal year in human history. Contiguous with the end of the Great War came the huge wave of global influenza. My own father came back from the Western Front that autumn and whilst he only had to travel across the Channel to home and, he thought to safety, many other soldiers filled liners and cargo ships to overflowing as they returned home to Australia, South Africa, New Zealand and the USA. Probably never before, or since, have so many young people travelled together in such over-crowded circumstances. But they had survived the war and were looking forward to family reunion parties, village gatherings and victory marches.

From the point of view of a minuscule virus spread from person to person in droplets from coughs, this was an unprecedented and gloriously unique opportunity – influenza took it. Throughout history, at least after the Ice Age, where there were larger townships and gatherings, micro-organisms have taken advantage of us, as carriers and as a home of replication. Even in this year the number of bacteria and viruses on the planet far exceed our population. So the northern autumn of 1918 witnessed a singular and cataclysmic event, documented so well in this unique volume.

In fact I can think of no more useful exercise than to gather such a diverse group of historians, scientists, geographers and doctors together in one spot to shine a searchlight on the largest outbreak of infectious disease that the world has ever known. But even so, it has to be appreciated that 95 per cent of the world survived, including my own father. But why, with 30 or more million deaths, has knowledge about the pandemic been so hidden in three old but nevertheless fascinating textbooks? In fact the present book to my knowledge is the first comprehensive international anaylsis since a volume published as long ago as 1922. At one stage I had a copy of that book almost to myself. But 10 years ago I received an urgent recall for the book: the librarian seemed slightly breathless and excited. Apparently three people had asked for a viewing. Now three in a population of 50 million in England seemed nothing to get excited about but, as she explained, one was even foreign!

Since then, helped by a few groups of scientists and I suspect by

modern technology giving us the first chance to pursue the genetic structure of the virus, virological interest in the events of 1918–19 has grown. I
sat some time ago with Howard Phillips within view of Table Mountain
and he explained his idea of this international conference. I was
enthralled by the vision but in the event was too preoccupied myself that
year with our exhumation of the Norwegian coal miners who died of
influenza in Spitsbergen near the North Pole and who were buried in the
permafrost. We had permission to exhume them and in August 1998 we
opened the grave site under microbial containment and took samples of
lung, trachea, kidney and brain.

To sample the brain might seem quirky for an international scientific
team from Canada, USA, Norway and the UK interested in a respiratory
virus and its pathology and genetic structure. But Rod Daniels, at the
National Institute of Medical Research, Mill Hill, and I had already
located brains from cases of encephalitis lethargica (EL) who had died of
this sleepy sickness in the ensuing years from 1918.

Several years before, Schoenbaum had published an analysis of the two
pandemics, respiratory influenza and EL and noted a causal relationship.
Around 5 million people died of EL during the 1920s, so we may have to
revise the total mortality even further upwards should this link be proven
by genetic analysis to the influenza pandemic of 1918. More or less at the
same time Johan Hultin had sampled another permafrost victim in Alaska
and was working with Jeffery Taubenberger in the USA to obtain a definite nucleotide sequence of the HA gene. As virologists we had all thought
that this would be the virulence gene of the 1918 influenza virus. We were
to be proven wrong.

A question that struck me as I read the chapters of this book was what
do these cold statistics hide? I feel they strive to tell us about the greatest
endeavour of human history and extolled by every religion that I know –
that of a stretched-out hand to help. The villagers of Eyam, Derbyshire, in
1666 made this sacrifice to combat the further spread of plague to other
villages. Being already infected, they cut themselves off from other families to stop the spread and helped each other. There must have been many
more acts of heroism in homes of the world in the Great Pandemic than
in the Great War as husbands and wives and families strained to cope with
the disease. Indeed, many families died together. Couples even died on
their marriage day. It was Stalin who said that to have 20,000 die is a statis-
tic but to have one person die is a tragedy. I recalled this as I read the
chapters. But I also feel this book can extend to those who all these years
later can remember the events in their own families and wish to better
understand the true nature of this world-wide outbreak.

Finally, as a virologist I would want to know where the virus came from
– from Russia as in 1889, from Asia as in 1957 and 1968? Possibly not.
Even as the conference was proceeding in Cape Town my students had
uncovered a description of an earlier outbreak at Etaples in northern

France in the winter of 1916, and later that year in Aldershot barracks. These wintertime outbreaks of bronchitis or 'epidemic catarrh' struck at young soldiers with high mortality and caused heliotrope cyanosis, a clinical hallmark of the 1918 outbreak. Vera Brittain described in her book *Testament of Youth* the horror of the overcrowded camp at Etaples with 100,000 soldiers daily pouring in and out. I can think of no more likely spot for a virus to mutate and spread. We may have to rename the virus 'French' influenza rather than 'Spanish' influenza, and to re-ascribe the date to 1916 rather than 1918, but there is no disputing two things. First, 1918 saw a wave of infection and respiratory death which no one on the planet would want to live through again, and second, as virologists, we do expect another influenza pandemic to visit and, in our most pessimistic moments wonder whether, in spite of new anti-neuraminidase inhibitors, amantadine and influenza vaccines, we will eventually experience a 1918 scenario of our own. I hope not.

A historian's foreword

Terence Ranger

The brevity of the influenza pandemic of August–September 1918 posed great problems to doctors at the time. They had no chance to try out different remedies or to learn anything about the disease before it was over. It has posed great problems to historians ever since.

Such a condensed event does not allow for conventional vertical historical narrative; it needs rather a lateral, descriptive talent. The last name of the distinguished Zimbabwean novelist, Yvonne Vera, is one of the indigenous terms for influenza. She has said that her own books reflect a particular view of history – not a narrative view but an idea of history compressed into a significant moment. She sees this as a matrilineal vision. African grandmothers, mothers and daughters discuss a particular event, perhaps a death. They describe it and then circle around it, constantly returning to it, widening it out and bringing into it past memories and future anticipations. Her novels deal with such compressed and compacted moments, suggesting how the imagination can comprehend and express them.

Maybe we need this sort of feminised history for the flu epidemic, that widespread but brief moment of death, remembered by hundreds of thousands of grandmothers and mothers and daughters. The main way in which the epidemic is commemorated in African societies seems very appropriate. It is recalled in the names given to the babies born as older people were dying, a birth coming out of death. (The many 'Frazers' in Zimbabwe, for instance, do not commemorate some influential Scottish missionary but 'freza', the flu.)

Poets and novelists were absent from the otherwise impressively interdisciplinary conference on the pandemic in Cape Town in September 1998. But there were plenty of subjective reminders of the context in which the deadly moment of influenza was experienced in the Cape. Delegates were lodged in the Breakwater, now a lavish conference centre, but in origin the sort of crowded prison in which the pandemic could take its greatest toll. The organisers laid on a conference expedition to the graves of unnamed black labourers who died during the pandemic while working at an explosives factory owned by the great mining company, De Beers.

Jails, explosives and diamonds summoned up the context of coercion, violence and unskilled migrant labour in which influenza spread in southern Africa.

Unnamed on their graves, these victims of an incomprehensible disaster are still visited by their descendants – an expression of the tenacity of African memory. Imaginatively the organisers handed each conference delegate flowers to lay on the graves. This evocation and commemoration of the obscure dead seemed one of the most significant moments of the conference.

It seems likely, indeed, that such a process of recall will be one way in which the pandemic figures in future histories, as a shaping episode in the lives of forgotten people, sometimes ending them and sometimes beginning them anew. Thus Robert Edgar and Hilary Sapire have literally exhumed the story of the Cape visionary, Nontetha, whose unknown burial place Edgar discovered. Nontetha, previously a peripheral female elder, survived the influenza, became a prophetess inspired by and interpreting the fever, gained a following, was declared mad by the colonial authorities, and died in the asylum.[1] An accumulation of such private histories will eventually redeem the neglect of the pandemic in official public historiography.

I was very grateful to be at the Cape Town conference where one could combine reflections on small lives with contemplation of future global catastrophes and compare the literal exhumations of historians to the literal digging up of flu victims out of the ice by epidemiologists. I was informed and stimulated by every presentation. I am sure readers of this book will find the same.

Acknowledgements

The editors readily place on record their gratitude to the following for their role in turning into black and white reality an idea first mooted at a seminar at the University of Cape Town in 1993, and subsequently given flesh in a coffee shop in Sevenoaks, Kent:

- all sixty participants in the 'Spanish Flu 1918–98: The Influenza Pandemic of 1918 after 80 years' conference held at the University of Cape Town between 12 and 16 September 1998;
- the World Health Organization, the University of Cape Town and the Wellcome Trust for helping to fund that conference;
- Janet de Waal for her outstanding administrative efficiency, superlative wordprocessing skills and endless patience;
- our respective families, Juelle, Laura and Jeremy Phillips, and Margaret Killingray, for enduring the high social costs of their respective husbands'/fathers' recurrent bouts of Spanish flu all through the 1990s.

Howard Phillips and David Killingray
October 2000

Introduction

Howard Phillips and David Killingray

For much of the last two centuries professional historians have been extremely sceptical about the importance of epidemics in history. Overlooking cataclysmic natural disasters, they have focused, rather, on political, economic and intellectual processes to explain change over time. Until fairly recently they have been reluctant to attribute lasting significance to such disasters or to depict them as of great moment historically, however large they may have loomed to contemporaries. For instance, writing in 1936, E.P. Cheyney concluded that the effects of the Black Death, 'like other catastrophic occurrences in history ... were less important than the workings of more silent and persistent forces'.[1] Such a stance, believed William McNeill, stemmed from a basic tenet of positivist, scientific historiography:

> We all want human experience to make sense and historians cater to this universal demand by emphasizing elements in the past that are calculable, definable, and, often, controllable as well. Epidemic disease, when it did become decisive in peace or in war, ran counter to the effort to make the past intelligible. Historians consequently played such episodes down.[2]

In the last quarter-century, however, that assessment has waned to a degree, with the influence of greater emphasis on social, cultural and environmental historical writing. Perhaps, too, the emergence of AIDS has provided an immediate example of the power of a pandemic to alarm and transform societies.

Yet, for reasons that will be raised later in this Introduction, the influenza pandemic of 1918–19 (inaccurately dubbed the 'Spanish' flu by the non-Spanish European press of the time) has only recently been taken up by historians as an epidemic worthy of their attention. In this regard, despite the unprecedented magnitude and speed of its toll, the 1918–19 flu pandemic stands in marked contrast to the other great global pandemics of the last two millennia: bubonic plague in the sixth, fourteenth and nineteenth centuries, smallpox in the sixteenth–nineteenth centuries, cholera in the nineteenth century and AIDS in the late twentieth century. In recent decades, all of these, along with numerous more local epidemics, have attracted the attention of historians, and our understanding of them – and of epidemics in general – has increased many times over as a result.[3]

Not surprisingly, the reasons why the Spanish flu should have yielded a relatively poor historiographical harvest were a recurrent topic of discussion at the first-ever conference on this pandemic, held in Cape Town in September 1998, precisely 80 years after that city, like others around the globe, was engulfed by the pandemic. The conference itself arose out of a recognition that, if the study of the pandemic was to move beyond its existing, rather limited state, it was imperative first to bring together scholars in the field whatever their disciplinary approach or geographical focus, so that they could take stock of current knowledge, share each others' insights and open up fresh perspectives on the subject. If the greatest pandemic in the world's history – at least in regard to its toll, speed and extent – was to be understood fully, then, of necessity, this had to be done on a global, catholic basis, without artificial academic or national boundaries intruding. As a clear-sighted review essay on epidemics in history recently noted, '[P]ractically speaking, the only relevant point of view for microbial issues is global, since bacteria, parasites, and viruses exploit appropriate ecospheres wherever they find them, regardless of national boundaries.'[4] Accordingly, like the 1918–19 influenza pandemic itself, the Cape Town conference put few bounds on its scope. Not only did the thirty-six papers presented there span five of the six continents hit by the pandemic – regrettably, no papers on South America were offered – but the disciplinary perspectives brought to bear were unusually broad for a single academic conference – virology, pathology, epidemiology, demography, history, anthropology, geography and gender studies were all represented.

The sixteen chapters of this book stem from a selection of these papers, chosen, *inter alia*, with an eye to reflecting this diversity of approach and region, and are organised around six main themes: virological and pathological perspectives; contemporary medical and nursing responses; contemporary responses by governments; the demographic impact; long-term consequences and memories; and epidemiological lessons derived from the pandemic. This thematic arrangement underscores the need to conceptualise the pandemic globally and comparatively too, and not just nationally and locally, if it and its impact are to be adequately understood. By implication the globe-encompassing, multilingual bibliography which concludes the book makes the same point.

Given the diversity of the conference participants' intellectual backgrounds, their different ways of making sense of a past phenomenon meshed surprisingly easily. Though at times it became necessary to stop discussion in a session and define more precisely terms understood differently by medical and social scientists, by and large they did speak clearly to each other and papers attracted discussion from a wide array of disciplinary and geographical perspectives, with comparisons and cross-pollination the order of sessions. C.P. Snow's two-culture divide was little in evidence as participants, their interest united by a tight focus on a single, albeit protean, subject, strained to learn from each other. Tea-breaks quite commonly were marked by invigorating exchanges on the same research topic between, for instance, virologists and historians or geographers and pathologists. It was an unusual academic spectacle, all against the backdrop of blue-etched Table Mountain. Tellingly, attendance flagged little during the conference's four days.

These vibrant discussions also produced the recognition that, compared to all other pandemics except AIDS, the 1918–19 influenza pandemic raises three novel, source-centred issues for those who would write about it today: first, coming in the heyday of the newspaper and printed word, it left behind mountains of written evidence across the world, often in the unlikeliest of places, more so than any pandemic before it – compared to them it is, paradoxically, the best documented but least known pandemic; second, it is still possible, even 80-plus years later, as it slips over the horizon of personal memory for all time, to supplement the extensive written evidence with oral testimony from survivors whose memories can add personal perspectives such as are no longer available for any pandemic before it; third, again uniquely among past pandemics, within the last 5 years, medical scientists have raised the possibility that they may be able to identify the causative virus through state-of-the-art analysis of specimens over 80 years old from a pathological museum or from corpses exhumed from within the Arctic Circle, and thus elucidate the character and lethality of the deadly virus once and for all.

What discussion at the Cape Town conference made clear, however, was that these features were less problems to be overcome than rare opportunities to be exploited to the full so as to grasp the complex totality of the 1918–19 pandemic better; and also that the conference, largely through coincidence, was being held at just the right moment to highlight this fact. Though 1998 had originally been chosen as the year for the conference for no other reason than its octuple neatness, it turned out to have come at a particularly propitious conjuncture, allowing many new strands in Spanish flu research to be drawn together so as to shift discussion and research on the topic onto a new plane. It is hoped that this book will show that full advantage was taken of this unusual opportunity.

What happened in 1918–19?

Although the flu pandemic of 1918–19 was the single worst demographic disaster of the twentieth century, the precise number of those who died, as the virus swept around the world in the space of few months, is not known. A recent calculation is that more than 30 million people died, many more than the total number killed in the First World War, although a lack of contemporary data and of accurate records make that figure no more than an informed estimate.[5] Without doubt the influenza pandemic of 1918–19 was the most devastating infection to strike the world since the Black Death ravaged the population of Asia and Europe in the mid fourteenth century. The influenza outbreak of 1918–19 was pandemic for two reasons: first of all the infection began in a single place and spread throughout the world resulting in very high morbidity and mortality rates; and second, it was a new A virus subtype unrelated to previously known influenza viruses and thus not a mutation of a known virus.[6] In its global reach it was wider than the Black Death, which was confined to the Euro-Asian land mass and North Africa; in speed of transmission it was much more rapid than the serious pandemics of cholera and plague in the nineteenth century. Only isolated places, for example the Atlantic island of St. Helena not visited by shipping during the pandemic, escaped its virulent breath.

The fact that the influenza pandemic of 1918–19, although well recalled in collective memories, is less well recorded by historians in no way reduces the historical significance of the disease and its impact. Epidemic outbreaks of influenza occurred before 1918. The outbreak in England in the 1550s was particularly serious and historians continue to debate the extent to which England's population fell as a result of poor harvests followed by epidemic influenza; figures for mortality vary from 5 to 20 per cent.[7] During the eighteenth–nineteenth centuries epidemic influenza struck repeatedly and regularly in various parts of the world: for example, there were serious outbreaks in Europe in 1732–3, 1761–2, 1788–9, with a pandemic outbreak in 1781–2. Epidemic influenza occurred in Europe in the 1830s and again in 1847–8, but the most serious was the pandemic of 1889–90 which continued to spread or be revived until 1892.[8] After 1918–19 pandemic influenza occurred in 1957, 1968 and 1977, and the threat of a new outbreak is ever present. Despite international monitoring and extensive research on influenza, one expert has written that 'all authorities predict that future pandemics will occur, but are unsure of when or the ability or will to implement measures to prevent the tragedies of the past'.[9] As we stand at the beginning of the third millennium, there is a heightened consciousness about potentially pandemic diseases for two main reasons: first, the mutation of new strains of diseases, such as tuberculosis, which threaten to thwart well-tried antidotes; and second, the outbreak of a disease such as HIV/AIDS for which there is as yet no known cure. HIV/AIDS has spread at an alarming rate in parts of the 'South', where it is mainly a disease among heterosexual people, although the considerable and costly exertions of medical science to find a cure (excessively so, some argue, compared to the research given to tackling more serious diseases) are likely to be devoted to sufferers in the wealthy 'North' where the disease is certainly a threat, but not a direct one to most people. But there is no known prevention if another virulent influenza outbreak occurs with the potential to kill globally on a vast scale. As one scholar commented at the Cape Town conference: 'I know how to avoid getting AIDS, but I do not know how to avoid getting influenza.'

Influenza is ubiquitous, indeed to such an extent that the term 'flu' has become a common synonym for a cold or even a sniffle. In its most common viral forms flu is always present in human populations, regularly killing a small number of vulnerable people, usually the very young and the elderly. Flu is not generally deemed to be a killer disease and thus has rarely been a notifiable disease. Occasionally, for example 1889–90, 1957–8, 1968–9 and 1977–8, a much more virulent flu virus appears, such as the A virus of 1918, resulting in extremely high levels of morbidity which means that, even with a relatively low mortality rate, the overall number of deaths is inevitably large. Attempts to identify a regular pattern in such outbreaks have not been successful. Pandemic influenza appears to originate in a single place; the location is not clear but it is commonly within a large land mass such as Russia, North America or China. Flu has a short incubation period and, as a respiratory transmitted infection, is quickly spread from one person to another, especially in places where people are closely crowded together. No one season more than another seems to be the time for the spread of the infection. Temperature and climate appear to have little effect on the ability of the virus to spread although low temperatures and high relative humidity, or a combination of the two conditions, seem to help spread the infection.

The Spanish influenza of 1918–19 had unique features for sufferers. In serious cases victims experienced severe headaches, body pains and fever; their faces turned blue/black, the marks of cyanosis, and they coughed blood and bled from the nose. Death was usually caused as bacteria invaded the lungs, turning those vital organs into sacks of fluid and thus effectively drowning the patient. For most sufferers the attack lasted for 2–4 days. However, death could be sudden and there were repeated reports of people suddenly collapsing and dying, or being taken ill and succumbing to the infection within a few hours.

The place of origin of the 1918 influenza virus is much debated. Both North America and China have been suggested, although most evidence points to the former where the infection was first recognised in the mid West early in March of that year. From the United States influenza swept around the world in three waves and few areas escaped its malignant effect. The first wave in March and April 1918 spread rapidly to war-ravaged Europe and then on to Asia and North Africa, before reaching Australia by July. The mortality rate was fairly low and the outbreak did not occasion excessive concern. The second and highly lethal wave occurred in late August 1918 and re-appeared as a third and less virulent wave in 1919. The virus spread rapidly along the conduits of war and commerce to engulf the entire world in a matter of a few weeks. A modern system of global communications, of steamships and railways, along with the constant and large-scale movement of men and materials for the war, provided the conditions for the easy and speedy spread of the virus. Military encampments and the close concentration and movement of men provided ideal conditions for the transmission of a respiratory infection.

The medical profession, which had made great strides in epidemiological knowledge and surgery over the previous two decades, found itself unprepared and ill-equipped to deal with the disease and had no effective way of combating or curing it. Since the 1890s it had been believed that influenza was caused by a bacillus, identified as Pfeiffer's bacillus. Little was then known about viruses and much of the research into the epidemiology of influenza was focused in the wrong directions. The micro-organism responsible for influenza was only identified in 1933, as was the isolation of the virus of swine influenza.[10] In 1918–19 many vaccines were hastily developed for use against flu, but with little if any efficacy. At the time of the outbreak many rumours and theories about the origin and spread of the infection abounded. Inevitably the disease was associated with the war: that it resulted from conditions on the war fronts, or that it was being used as a weapon by the enemy, ideas that became part of the propaganda of the belligerents. For example, in Ireland in March 1919, Dr Kathleen Lynn told the rebel Sinn Féin council that

> the factory of the fever is still in full working order in Flanders ... the battlefield. ... The English and French have left millions of men and horses to rot unburied where they fell. ... In France and Flanders the poisonous matter from millions of unburied bodies is constantly rising up into the air, which is blown all over the world by the winds.[11]

In mid August 1918 the influenza virus mutated, and with startling virulence and at great speed spread as a second wave on both sides of the Atlantic and in three continents. In the same week there were outbreaks of flu in three nodal Atlantic ports, in Freetown, Brest and Boston. A British naval vessel, HMS *Mantua*, outward bound from England, arrived at the West African port of Freetown on 15 August with 200 sailors who were sick. Within 2 weeks the virus had been spread to local dock workers who in turn carried the infection into the town and on to other ships which then carried the virus to other African ports and elsewhere. From Freetown the virus was spread inland to the surrounding villages. By the end of September some 3 per cent of Sierra Leone's population was estimated as dead from flu. Brest in western France was a major Atlantic harbour receiving a steady flow of US troops of the American Expeditionary Force, eventually totalling over 790,000 men, bound for the Western Front. By 22 August the second wave of flu had arrived in the town to move rapidly through the barrack accommodation of the large transit camps, the neighbouring

French naval base, and to be carried hither and thither by the constantly mobile population of the bustling town. Within 3 weeks the death toll from influenza had reached 370. A few days after Brest had been infected, flu arrived in Boston, a main embarkation port in New England for American servicemen going to Europe. From June to August the United States had been virtually free of influenza, but now trans-Atlantic and coastal shipping, railways and roads carried with startling speed this more virulent virus into the North American continent.[12]

By September flu had spread throughout much of Europe killing hundreds of thousands of people. Even in well-ordered societies with well-established medical and statistical services, it is difficult to compute the full extent of the pandemic. Individual medical diagnoses varied and in all probability many deaths from influenza were either not reported or recorded as due to other causes. In central and eastern Europe many people were weakened by the long effects of the war and thus more susceptible to diseases, including influenza. All armies, especially those confronting each other on the Western Front, were also hard hit by the disease. In Britain the mortality figures exceeded 200,000;[13] the number of dead in France was slightly higher, and in Germany deaths totalled over 250,000. Russia's vast Euro-Asian land mass was not immune from the virus, although civil war and revolution, and raging typhus, meant that little attention was given to influenza. The movement of refugees undoubtedly helped to exacerbate the transmission of influenza and total deaths there may have reached 450,000.

Throughout Europe the outbreak was widely known as 'Spanish flu' because Spain was neutral in the First World War and, unlike the belligerent powers, news reports were uncensored. In the popular mind calamities often need to have their origin and cause identified and other countries or peoples credited with blame. This xenophobic response has been common in Europe, that impulse to blame others or the silent places of the Asian heartlands for the source of disease. In fact some serious pandemics had emanated from Asia, for example the cholera epidemics of the nineteenth century,[14] and the influenza pandemic of 1889–90 which gained the appellation of the 'Russian flu' and that of 1957 which was dubbed the 'Asian flu'. In 1918 neutral Spain was unjustly blamed for the terrifying outbreak of influenza and the title of 'Spanish Lady' was widely attached to the disease. The literature on the flu pandemic is strangely silent as to why the gender-specific term 'Lady' was so widely used to describe the outbreak.

Within North America, influenza spread across the whole continent from the north-east in the space of 2 months. Major cities suffered unevenly, for example Philadelphia had higher mortality rates than New York, much to the bewilderment of public health officials and later medical researchers. Some 675,000 Americans died in the pandemic and about 50,000 Canadians. By mid September the virus had been carried by ships into the islands of the Caribbean and along land and sea routes to the central American isthmus. Little has been written on the course of the pandemic in the Latin American countries. What is well recorded for North America, and a few areas of South America, is that mortality rates from flu among aboriginal peoples were very high, sweeping through Inuit communities in northern Canada and Alaska, and other Native American groups with disastrous results.

Governments and official organisations were little prepared for an epidemic which, for most industrial countries, occurred when they were involved in the Great War. American troops crossing the Atlantic helped to spread the disease into Europe. International quarantine measures had operated with some success since the mid nineteenth century, but they existed to control the spread of notifiable diseases such as bubonic plague and cholera, which were rightly perceived as major killers and caused real alarm. Influenza was not such a disease. In the aftermath of both the First World War and the pandemic, closer attention was given to how to avoid a future deadly outbreak of influenza. Many states, including several within the British Empire, made flu a notifiable disease. An international intelligence gathering system was created under the auspices of the International Office of Public Health in Paris, which went on to work closely with the League of Nations' International Health Organisation, to monitor outbreaks of influenza. However, it was not until 1947 that a more effective international influenza centre was created in London with nearly 100 bases around the world.

Various methods were used in the industrial states to try and prevent the further spread of the pandemic. Ports were quarantined; public transport, passengers and luggage were fumigated; public buildings – schools and cinemas, but rarely churches or bars – were closed; local legislation instructed people to wear masks and to avoid congregating; advertisements urged the prophylactic values of tobacco and alcohol; many people resorted to prayer and patent medicines. But all measures were seemingly without avail. Hospital wards, doctors' surgeries and clinics were weighed down with patients. Probably the best advice for sufferers, if it could be followed, was the use of aspirin to lower the body temperature, bed rest and effective nursing care. The vast majority of those infected around the world, in a global population which was predominantly peasant and poor, lacked such knowledge and certainly access to easy means of relief.

A surprising feature of the 1918–19 pandemic, compared to all other recorded influenza pandemics, was the high incidence of death universally among those aged between 20–40 years, particularly men, the very group that might be thought to be stronger and thus less likely to succumb to influenza. This was the case whether a country was at war or at peace. This age–gender death pattern still remains something of a mystery. The cause may have been genetic or physiological. Another reason may be due to the tendency of many men, out of necessity or masculine impulse, to continue working rather than resting when they were sick. A cold or a slight feeling of being unwell was not sufficient reason or excuse for a man, who was often the sole or major bread-winner, to stop working. The poor, and those living in over-crowded and insanitary conditions, were also more likely to catch and to die from the virus, although patterns of mortality varied from one place to another around the world. Certainly the poor were rendered more vulnerable due to low levels of nutrition and poor physical health.

The dying and the dead placed heavy burdens on families and social institutions. Bodies remained unburied for days; in many towns and cities coffins were in short supply; many victims were buried in mass graves. And throughout the world the brief rage of flu left in its wake millions of widowed and orphaned, an almost unimaginable burden of personal grief and, of course, poverty.[15] In countries with the highest death rates, future population profiles were affected for the next generation or more.

Influenza moved between countries and continents along the routes of ships and railways. From Freetown the disease moved down the West African coast and from ports into the interior.[16] For example, the *Shango* from Freetown took flu to Cape Coast and Accra by 3 September. Two weeks later the S.S. *Bida*, which had also called at Freetown, carried flu further east along the West African coast to the unsuspecting capital of Nigeria, Lagos. Coastal towns were infected and the colonial railway system, built mainly to export primary products, now transported infected people into the interior where they spread the disease to even remote communities by bicycle, canoe, camel and on foot. The many shipping routes converging on South African ports, and the country's well-developed transport infrastructure, provided for the speedy transmission of the disease throughout the southern half of the continent. Flu arrived in the expanding city of Cape Town on board two troopships which had called at Freetown, the *Jaroslav* and the *Veronej*, both bringing home some 1,300 men of the South African Native Labour Contingent who had served in France. Although the authorities took elementary precautions to isolate men infected with flu, they did not identify all the cases. Men deemed healthy entrained for home and the virus was spread with great rapidity throughout southern Africa and beyond the Zambezi into central Africa.

African death rates were higher than those of Europe, varying between *c*.2 and 5 per cent of the population.[17] In South Africa, the official death toll of *c*.140,000 seriously underestimated African mortality. A recent revised figure suggests that the figure should be doubled.[18] East Africa, already racked by the triple curses of war, famine and disease, experienced death rates from flu higher than other regions of Africa; in Kenya as many as 150,000 people died, 5.5 per cent of the population. Popular responses to a disease which suddenly appeared killed so many and then disappeared took many forms – 'killing by a stroke' as it was referred to in the Ekiti region of southern Nigeria. Religious revivals occurred, a turning to old gods and new; millenarian movements developed in Africa, and elsewhere, in response to inexplicable disease.[19]

Compared to other continents, Asia probably suffered the highest death rates during the 1918–19 pandemic, although predictably morbidity and mortality figures are crude estimates. There are many gaps in Asia's epidemiological history of influenza, most notably for China where little research has been undertaken. Iijima's recent research on influenza in China in 1918–19 suggests a low mortality rate well below 1 per cent, considerably lower than the figure for Japan, although given the conditions for avian flu in China it is difficult to understand why this should be so.[20] Japan suffered during the pandemic,[21] and so also did Indonesia where, it is estimated, some 1.5 million people died.[22] But of all the Asian countries India undoubtedly had the highest death rate during the pandemic. The second wave of the disease came into India via the port of Bombay and then spread across the subcontinent from west to east during September 1918. Mortality peaked in the Bombay Presidency in October, in the central and northern provinces in November, and in Bengal in December where it was reported the 'rivers became clogged with corpses because firewood available was insufficient for the cremation of Hindus'. The official toll, calculated shortly after the pandemic, was 6 million; a recent study by Mills has substantially increased the death rate to a controversially high figure of 17–18 million.[23] Mills argues that the widespread famine-like situation of 1918 might have exacerbated India's influenza mortality, although Wakimura suggests that in northern areas more significant factors were the close links between famine, epidemic malaria, inflation and the lack of public health provision.[24] It is, however, impossible to distinguish between deaths attributable to flu, and those deaths resulting from either other diseases or the social dislocations caused by the flu.[25]

Island communities, unless isolated for the period of the pandemic or able to enforce a stringent system of quarantine, could not avoid infection. Australia imposed a strict maritime quarantine which possibly helped 'to dull the edge of the disease's virulency';[26] nevertheless, the total death toll there in the southern summer of 1918–19 was 12,000. By contrast, New Zealand failed to protect itself or to prevent the spread of the pandemic to island communities in the South Pacific. As the disease moved through New Zealand in November–December 1918 it killed more Maori than *Pakehas* (White Men).[27] The flu entered the Pacific from the east, north and the west. Some islands suffered crushingly heavy mortality rates. The steamer, *Tulane*, left Auckland, New Zealand, with a clean bill of health but was a floating visitor of death to a succession of islands. The results were lethal; in Fiji *c.*5 per cent of the population died, in Tonga the death rate was 10 per cent, while in Western Samoa the figure reached a horrifying 25 per cent. However, in the neighbouring US-administered islands of Eastern Samoa, where a tight naval quarantine was imposed, there may have been no deaths at all.[28]

In its wake around the world the pandemic left a long shadow of suffering and illness, the widowed and the orphaned. In addition many hundreds of thousands of people – in fact, an unknown global number – either died or suffered the effects of diseases that were closely related to influenza such as encephalitis lethargica, and also parkinsonism. Indeed, some authorities argue that many of the diseases of the central nervous system may follow bouts of severe influenza and are closely related to the disease.[29]

What occurred in 1918–19, we are repeatedly told by virologists and epidemiologists, is likely to happen again. Influenza at some time will return in a virulent form and, unless medical science can isolate the virus and produce an effective antidote, there will be no effective protection when it does strike. Thus there have been recent efforts by Hultin, Taubenberger, Duncan and Oxford to seek extant traces of the virus, either from laboratory-preserved tissue of victims or from corpses buried in the Arctic permafrost.[30] The seriousness of the threat is demonstrated by the drastic procedures taken by the Hong Kong authorities and by the global influenza intelligence community in 1997 when that colony experienced an outbreak of flu in its chicken population. Prompt action may have averted a serious outbreak of influenza.[31] In 1918 influenza encircled the world with relative ease in a matter of a few weeks, carried by a mobile population along global transport routes. In the early twenty-first century the economic and physical means for the rapid spread of a lethal disease from one part of the world to another have greatly increased. With the growth in air travel and the larger numbers of people constantly on the move, an infectious disease can occur in any part of the world and, without the knowledge of the person infected, can then be carried across the globe within a few hours.

Given the extent of the death rate from influenza in 1918–19, it is surprising that the history of the outbreak is not better known. Several recent global histories of the twentieth century have either ignored the influenza pandemic altogether or given it but one or two lines, for example Grenville's *History of the World in the Twentieth Century*, and Overy's edited *Times History of the 20th Century*.[32] For people born in the inter-war years of the twentieth century there is likely to be a knowledge of the pandemic from family stories of death, affliction and recovery. This is particularly so in Africa and Asia, where the pandemic hit hardest, and where the period of the outbreak is often known by a specific name.[33] Why, then, has the pandemic been so ignored? It occurred at the climax of the First World War, when there had been mass killing on an unprecedented scale, and as revolution swept across eastern and central Europe. The disaster of war, and the resulting unrest in much of Europe, overshadowed the pandemic and its subsequent inclusion in the history written about the period. In Europe, predictably, it was the 'glorious dead' who were foremost in the public mind and the names of those 'fallen in war' were recorded on national and local war memorials. By its very ubiquity, even when it came in unparalleled force, influenza and its victims were not a subject for public mourning or memorials. And for historians of the time with their agendas of politics and statecraft, disease and its social and economic consequences were not a matter of great immediate concern.

This raises several interesting counterfactual questions: if 1918 had been a year of peace, would the 'Spanish' influenza have spread so rapidly? Indeed, would it have been a lethal pandemic at all? And would the outbreak have been better known to historians? If the major industrial states of the world had not been at war when the flu struck, then the infrastructures of total conflict which so easily encouraged the transmission of the virus would not have been in place. The active intervention of officials and the medical services might have been able more readily to identify and deal with the outbreak and arrest its movement. The business of prosecuting a terrible war diverted official attention from a silent and more lethal killer, as successfully as it has done for subsequent historians of the period. Even without war, because influenza was so common and regularly took an annual toll of the young and elderly, there was no guarantee even when it came in a particularly virulent form and killed large numbers of people, that it would make a special mark in the history books.[34]

The historiography of the 1918–19 influenza pandemic

A graph tracing writing which focused specifically on the pandemic over the last 80+ years would be very uneven in character: a sharply ascending curve indicating the initial flood of contemporary and near-contemporary, mainly medical, accounts in its immediate wake would be followed by a steep descent and a relative lull for almost 40 years, before a series of sharp spikes began to appear in the late 1950s and 1960s, indicating spasmodic bursts of interest. From the mid 1970s these would, in turn, be succeeded by a curve which continued to climb upwards, right up to the present. These rises and falls provide a graphic record of the past being 'discovered' and 'rediscovered' in accord with changing current concerns, a process neatly captured in Croce's maxim that all history is contemporary history.[35]

From this it follows that the way in which the 1918–19 pandemic has been conceived by those who have written about it has not been constant over time – its image has changed, largely depending on the eye, angle and prevailing preoccupation of the individual beholder. Since, according to Müller's bibliography, the total number of such beholders is over 600, then any first survey like this of the historical writing on the topic must resort to broad generalisations about particular genres, limiting references to specific works to a mere handful of significant titles. This is how the overview that follows will proceed, as it plots the graph of the Spanish influenza's historiography and the pandemic's changing conceptualisation and tries to account for these contours.

The initial surge of writing in the immediate aftermath of the pandemic was barely historical in character. Largely recounting what had happened from a medical participant's point of view, these works aimed mainly to make medical sense of the devastating episode so that lessons could be drawn from this experience lest the pandemic return within months, a dire event fully expected. Of historical perspective or approach there was scarcely a hint, nor is this surprising.

What is more remarkable, however, is the almost complete silence of professional historians of the day about the pandemic, in striking contrast to their readiness to tackle as a historical topic, its contemporary, the First World War. Although they had lived through both, it was almost as if they deemed a world war to be suitable as a subject for historians but not a world pandemic. Typically, a historical survey published in 1924 by the Encyclopaedia Britannica, *These Eventful Years: The twentieth century in the making . . . being the dramatic story of all that has happened throughout the world during the most momentous period in all history*, ignored the pandemic entirely.[36] Even as medically aware an historian as Sir Andrew Macphail, professor of the history of medicine at McGill University in Montreal, did no more than lump influenza together with 'other infectious diseases' in his chapter on 'Diseases of War' in the official history of the Canadian medical services in the First World War, while the rest of his chapter dealt with ten other diseases individually.[37] Trumping even this failure to recognise the significance of the influenza pandemic, the *Casualties and War Statistics* volume of Britain's official *History of the Great War*, published in 1931, blithely declared: 'Apart from reproducing . . . the recorded figures for influenza in the British armies at home and abroad during the Great War little need be said about this disease.'[38]

Given the presence of such a blind spot among historical scholars of the day, it comes as no surprise either that, in all the Carnegie Endowment's 208 volumes on the Economic and Social History of the World War, only a few pages were devoted to the 'grippe', and then primarily as a medical or statistical phenomenon.[39]

To such reasons as have already been suggested for this neglect of the pandemic by the historians of that era – that it was subsumed by the First World War, its very rapid passage and non-return, the hard-to-grasp magnitude of its toll which could not be credibly attributed to as everyday a disease as influenza, and the absence of any notable household names among its victims – a historiographical perspective can add two hypotheses: first, that it was overlooked by historians-at-large because its impact was relatively light in Europe and North America, the areas of the world whose academies effectively defined what then constituted 'scientific history'; and second, that, as the Spanish flu amounted to an enormous rout in the war against disease for the medical profession, it was not a subject to hold much appeal for the triumphalist brand of medical history then in vogue, thanks to medicine's stream of successes since Pasteur. Where, for instance, would it find a place in the upbeat chapter in *These Eventful Years* entitled 'Harvest Time in Medicine and Surgery'?

The upshot of this indifference to the pandemic by historians was that, for over 40 years after 1918, historical accounts treating it were, by default, the by-products of investigations into the nature of the pandemic by epidemiologists and virologists, whose prime goal was to discover why it had been so lethal as they sought to find ways to prevent a recurrence of similar proportions. As the British Ministry of Health's comprehensive, multi-authored survey of the pandemic's course and toll around the world put it in 1920:

> There can be no doubt that as an historical survey it [the Report] will prove invaluable for future reference in the event of subsequent epidemics. ... That to understand the aetiology of a disease we must study both its historical and contemporary manifestations is as much a truism to the epidemiologist as the parallel proposition in the science of social and economic institutions.[40]

Seven years later a similar epidemiological overview, this time undertaken for the American Medical Association by a Chicago University bacteriologist, E.O. Jordan, devoted nearly half of its 512 pages to spelling out the pandemic's origin, course, incidence and toll, aspects which, it noted, were 'gigantic but urgent' to unravel 'in the face of the almost certain recurrence some day of another world-wide pandemic'.[41]

In such accounts history was treated as a utilitarian object for quite specific epidemiological investigation and, consequently, in these the pandemic was seen through a narrowly medical science lens, with most attention being given to elucidating its cause, mode of transmission and toll, and practically none to its social and cultural dimensions or consequences. To these authors the influenza pandemic of 1918–19 was one laboratory specimen among several, to be dissected in the interests of preventive epidemiology of the future and not its own historical significance, a perception only intensified by the decisive identification of the causative virus in 1933. Such, for instance, was the perspective of Burnet and Clarke's 1942 survey of the preceding 50 years of influenza 'in the light of modern work on the virus'. To these medical scientists, the 1918–19 pandemic represented primarily the pre-eminent example of 'influenza in its serious form' – that, to them, was its chief claim to significance.[42] Not until the appearance of the second big influenza pandemic of the twentieth century, the Asian flu of 1957, was the 1918–19 pandemic to be perceived in another light, as a topic for historical examination in its own right.

The one-dimensionality of such a medically centred conception of the 1918–19 pandemic was clearly revealed by the Asian flu pandemic of 1957, for this awakened memories of just how socially catastrophic and all-enveloping the 1918–19 calamity had been. Taking his cue from this realisation and recognising in it a gripping story, in 1961 an American popular historian, Adolph Hoehling, produced a lively account of what he called *The Great Epidemic.*[43] Based on contemporary newspapers and published reports, the work focused on the Spanish flu as a historical event in its own right, tracking it primarily through the USA where he highlighted the responses it evoked by means of a rich array of anecdotes, photographs, posters, handbills and cartoons. Though it was largely descriptive, without much understanding of what underlay these responses, it displayed an interest in the pandemic's social side for the first time. To the medically minded reviewer of the *San Francisco Chronicle*, however, this made it 'Fairly superficial as a medical history ... [though] brisk enough reading.'[44]

Across the Atlantic, however, the Asian flu of 1957 had quite the opposite effect on publishers, if one contemporary author is to be believed. In England it aroused such anxiety about a recurrence of a 1918-type disaster that a manuscript giving a global account of the Spanish flu, and intended for publication on its fortieth anniversary in 1958, was put on hold as 'No publisher in his senses would have dared to face charges of frightening the public still further than it had already been by the newspaper reports.'[45] When the work was finally published in 1969, in the wake of the Hong Kong flu pandemic of 1968–9, which had yet again stirred up memories of 1918 (but this time without deterring a publisher), Charles Graves' sensationally titled *Invasion by Virus. Can it happen again?*, provided the first world survey of the 1918–19 pandemic since the epidemiological overviews of the 1920s. Patching together an extensive body of material collected by a small team of researchers from official reports and newspapers of the time, Graves described the pandemic's transmission and toll country by country and the counter-measures it elicited in an uncritical chronicle of events, lacking perspective, analysis or an interest in longer-term consequences. Epitomising his conception of the pandemic as an unfolding drama of how a deadly virus was unwittingly spread world-wide was his line that, 'The story of the 1918 pandemic is really the story of ships sailing the seven seas carrying cargoes of potential death, which were unloaded at ports of debarkation in countries in all parts of the world.'[46]

In this it typified the genre of popular accounts of the pandemic which portrayed it primarily as a dramatic tale of human catastrophe. Publication of such a work soon after a new influenza epidemic had abated held with it the prospect of good sales to a general public whose awareness of the disease had been temporarily raised. From another angle, at least one pharmaceutical company involved in the manufacture of anti-flu vaccine, Philips-Duphar Nederland, presumably saw other marketing possibilities in the story of the 1918–19 pandemic. In 1968 it commissioned a Dutch journalist, A.C. de Gooijer, to write a popular account of the pandemic, to be distributed to doctors in Holland exactly 50 years after the outbreak. Not surprisingly in these circumstances, the richly illustrated *De Spaanse Griep van '18: De epidemie die meer dan 20,000,000 lewens eiste* which resulted did not fail to mention, after graphic descriptions of the pandemic's passage through Holland and Switzerland in 1918, how the development of anti-flu vaccine had subsequently allowed influenza to be far more effectively countered.[47] Nor, it would seem, was it unsuccessful in getting this message across, because in 1978, in the aftermath of yet another international flu scare, the book was republished so as to reach the wider public too.[48]

Undoubtedly the best example of the dramatic genre was published in 1974, 6 years after the Hong Kong flu reminder of 1918. With melodramatic chapter titles like 'Are we going to be wiped out?' and 'Doctor! Doctor! Do something!', Richard Collier's *The Plague of the Spanish Lady* (1974) set out to recount the pandemic's story through the lens of ordinary human experience. However, whereas other popular works with this intention relied largely on the press of the time, Collier drew as well on the personal memories of over 1,700 flu survivors, collected by a large research team around the world via interviews and letters. 'For the first time we have not a medical textbook or the creation of a novelist, but the diverse reactions of ordinary citizens as the disease grew in intensity', clamoured the publisher's blurb.[49]

Yet, how to shape this mass of individual testimony into a coherent account was a problem which Collier did not resolve. As a result, though his book effectively captured the contemporary horror and panic as the 'Spanish Lady' circumnavigated the globe, it failed to grasp the event as a whole or put it into perspective, or even track it chronologically or assess its impact. Its focus is solely the pandemic's course and the human responses it evoked in the short term. Ultimately, the whole is no more than the sum of its many vignettes, which is probably why Collier felt constrained to add a short appendix on some of the basic questions not treated in his text, such as its toll, its causative virus and, inevitably, the likelihood of another such visitation. None of this was original, however. What Collier's book did do very effectively, however, was to highlight most strikingly the value of personal testimony for gaining a full measure of the Spanish flu, a dimension which he actively encouraged later historians of the pandemic to heed by his generosity in making readily available to them his store of letters from flu survivors.

Nevertheless, it was not principally the sales of popular works on the 1918–19 pandemic which drew the attention of academic historians to the topic – they have usually been disdainful of such success – but the changing intellectual climate in universities from the mid-1970s onwards. There, the emergence of social and environmental history and, a little later, of the social history of medicine as academically respectable subdisciplines saw epidemics beginning to be perceived as part of the mainstream of history and not as some quirkish phenomenon in the margins of the past. This meant that a number of historians who had chanced upon the 1918–19 pandemic in the course of their research into more established fields like the history of the First World War, urban and regional history, economic history and administrative history, or who had heard of the pandemic from ageing relatives who had lived through it, were more inclined to pursue their chance 'discovery' than their predecessors a decade or two earlier had been.[50]

A further sign of the gradual recognition of the Spanish flu as an acceptable topic in the historical academy was the trickle of university theses on the topic which began to appear from the mid-1970s. In the 20 years from 1976 fifteen such theses were submitted to universities in countries as widespread as the USA, Canada, Great Britain, Switzerland, Sweden, South Africa, Zimbabwe, New Zealand, Australia and Brazil; in the 20 years before 1976 only four such theses had been submitted.

By far the best-known academic history of the pandemic to appear from these years, Alfred Crosby's *Epidemic and Peace 1918* (1976),[51] fits appropriately into this category of the 'discovery' of the subject as a result of the emergence of a novel approach to history, in this case environmental history – though it is perhaps worth noting that it was not this aspect which ultimately made it historically significant in his eyes, but its impact on the war and the peacemaking which followed it. In regard to the latter, he postulated (without convincing many) that President Woodrow Wilson had been so incapacitated by an attack of Spanish flu at Versailles that his moderating hand was absent from the final treaty – with major long-term results. It was clearly not yet possible for an environmental historian (perhaps responding to his publisher's concerns) to ignore well-established landmarks of traditional political and diplomatic history to give an epidemic meaning.

Having already explored the role of epidemic diseases like smallpox in the European conquest of Latin America and determined it to have been decisive, in *Epidemic and Peace* Crosby sought to extend this line of inquiry to the Spanish flu pandemic. His crystallizing contention, he later reflected, was that 'we need to look at history not only as politics or religion or economics, but as biology'.[52] Focusing on the pandemic in the USA, its troops at home and abroad and its peace negotiators at Versailles, he concluded – somewhat short-sightedly, it turns out – that, except with regard to peacemaking and medical research, it had had its greatest impact at the level of the private individual rather than public policy. For the millions of people who had lost loved ones, Crosby argued, it was clearly a (if not 'the') watershed event in their lives. Though this argument became explicit only in his final chapter, his prior synthesis raised historical writing on the influenza pandemic onto a new plane. He clearly demonstrated that the Spanish flu was far more than just a swiftly passing moment of horror worthy of a good raconteur, but rather a momentous historical event requiring serious scholarly inquiry by virtue of its huge death toll and its extremely disruptive all-round effect. 'It serves a useful counterpoint to the concerns and pretensions of political and diplomatic historians, forcing us to recognize that a single, brief epidemic generated more fatalities, more suffering, and more demographic change in the United States than all the wars of the Twentieth Century', observed one academic reviewer tellingly.[53]

Weaving together a wide range of published and unpublished sources into a coherent and easily accessible narrative which wore its learning lightly – the work won the 1976 American Medical Writers' Association award for the Best Book on a Medical Subject for Laymen – Crosby set on foot this scholarly inquiry, balancing his rich qualitative and quantitative data as he followed the pandemic's course and noted the immediate responses it evoked. Crosby 'deserves plaudits for his provocative specula-tions and for his lively style which makes his solid scholarship eminently readable. His combination of medical, political, and social history is an effective one and should appeal both to professional historians and to general readers' concluded *The American Historical Review*'s reviewer enthu-siastically.[54] As in the case of many 'discovery' works, however, when it came to putting the USA's experience in the pandemic into longer or comparative perspective or tracing the longer-term consequences, the book faltered. 'Too much of this book consists of details without a context', commented one reviewer summarily.[55]

Yet it was not just Crosby's book and the publicity it attracted, or a changing historiographical climate, which brought the Spanish flu more within scholars' purview, particularly in the USA, but also changing viruses. The 1976 swine flu episode in the USA, coming just weeks after the publication of *Epidemic and Peace*, instantly triggered widespread inter-est in the 1918–19 pandemic and made Crosby a much sought-after speaker, while the emergence of AIDS in the 1980s revived dormant memories of the last time the USA had been subjected to an awesome epi-demic. In fact, so striking were the parallels with the Spanish flu that in 1989 Cambridge University Press bought the publication rights of *Epidemic and Peace* from the original publisher and re-issued the work with text unchanged but under a telling new title, *America's Forgotten Pandemic. The influenza of 1918* (1989). In a brief preface to the new edition, Crosby pointed out that 'AIDS is the first killer disease to spread worldwide during most of our lifetimes. ... If we want to know how we react to calamitous surges of disease, we should take a look at the 1918 flu.'[56]

This combination of later epidemics recalling memories of the 1918 pandemic, and a congenial intellectual environment meant that historical studies of the Spanish flu effectively took off all around the world from the mid-1970s. An analysis of Müller's bibliography indicates that nearly 80 per cent of all post-1924 works on the topic were published after 1975. The largest category of these has been local, regional or urban studies of the pandemic, especially in the USA. Typically, such works use a mixture of local newspapers, reports by local authorities and doctors and, sometimes, snatches of oral evidence from elderly residents, to describe the arrival and deadly course of the disease in their locale, the countermeasures taken against it and its ultimate toll. Of consequences, public or private, little is usually said. In a sense, these studies resemble old-style military history, with influenza as the enemy and the battle to defeat it the authors' dominant theme. Though sometimes verging on the antiquarian, these modest works will become the building blocks for broader national histories of the Spanish influenza and, in this regard at least, their timely collection of vanishing personal testimony and local tales is invaluable.

Generally, studies of the 1918–19 pandemic from this period, which began life within university history departments, have provided perspectives which are both longer and broader. A good example is Fred Van Hartesveldt's ambitious edited volume, *The 1918–19 Pandemic of Influenza. The urban impact in the western world* (1992), which examines four themes chosen by the editor – the pandemic's morbidity and mortality patterns, its effects on daily life, the medical and public health response it elicited and its economic impact – in ten Western hemisphere cities, in a bid to 'pull together some of the pieces of what is known about the pandemic and provide some comparative elements for a more general picture'.[57] Adopting an urban focus so as to 'provide manageable units for study and because concentrations of population are natural foci of infectious disease',[58] the chapters have many of the strengths of fine-grained microhistory, but Van Hartesveldt does not adequately weave together their array of local perspectives or draw out their similarities and differences. At the final hurdle, therefore, this potentially exciting attempt at comparative history falters, leaving the book as not much more than the sum total of its individual chapters. In keeping with first forays, these are stronger at tracing the pandemic's progress at the public rather than the private level – noticeably, oral evidence has scarcely been utilised – and pay less attention to its social and cultural sides and its long-term consequences than these merit. It is thus a book whose substantial promise is not fulfilled, providing what the *Bulletin of the History of Medicine* called 'a valuable framework for comparative studies',[59] but not that study itself. Comparative inquiries into the Spanish influenza will have to go a long way to match the insights of Winter and Robert's *Capital Cities at War: Paris, London, Berlin 1914–1919* (1997).

Few comprehensive national histories of the influenza pandemic exist yet. Where they have been attempted, such studies – twelve would be a generous estimate of their number[60] – owe more to the zeal of individual historians than to the impetus imparted by some systematic project. At their best, they weave together a number of local studies of the pandemic into a greater whole, putting the result into a larger national context. This is particularly effective for highlighting long-term national trends and identifying how the Spanish flu either accelerated or redirected these, in keeping with Emmanuel Le Roy Ladurie's judgement that '[T]he best studies of *l'histoire événementielle* ... [look] both backward and especially forward in time, to find out whether the event in question really "made any difference" or not.'[61]

The broad scope of such works and their wide-ranging source material also encouraged them to open up novel angles on the pandemic, such as the social composition of flu victims, popular and religious explanations of the disaster, its social and psychological effects on those who survived and the physical after-effects of a serious bout of the disease, particularly encephalitis lethargica.

Yet, these new perspectives have not been the sole preserve of a handful of national histories. In many cases they were pioneered by scholars with a less ambitious agenda, whose response to the stimuli of the last quarter-century was to focus on one particular feature of the pandemic. For instance, historical geographers have tracked the pandemic's pathways across oceans, continents and even individual towns and suburbs with as high a degree of precision as their often imperfect sources allowed. With an equal zest for exactitude, historical demographers have subjected contemporary statistics to close scrutiny and argued that long-accepted mortality figures seriously underestimate the toll, perhaps by as much as 100 per cent.

Discerning patterns in these mortality figures – for example by age, gender, place of residence and occupation – has as a consequence allowed better-defined questions to be posed about the pandemic's distinctive impact. In turn, such questions have been skilfully used by anthropologists studying first nation populations in North America to explore the experience of those communities in 1918–19.

For their part, historians of medicine and the healthcare professions have moved beyond anecdotal recollections of doctors and nurses to investigate what light the pandemic sheds on the nature of these professions and contemporary medical thinking. Their studies also investigate such public health systems and networks as existed in 1918, both nationally and internationally. In a similar way, using epidemics as 'mirrors reflecting social processes',[62] one or two historians have begun to explore how the pandemic experience illuminates colonialism, although, on the fundamental question in this regard, how traditional medicine and thinking in colonial societies responded to the challenge of the pandemic, little inquiry has yet been undertaken. For that matter, the response of universalist religions has not been much analysed either, which is surprising, given the obvious scope for drawing enriching comparisons with their stance during earlier and subsequent epidemics and thereby plotting their changing ideas on the nature and extent of divine intervention in the world.

Perhaps most unexpected in the historiography of the last 25 years is the absence of any systematic investigation of the connection between the influenza pandemic of 1918–19 and the First World War. That might alter with the growth of a social studies of warfare approach to the conflict, but historians thinking along these lines will, as a first step, have to wrestle successfully with Jay Winter's insistence that 'The flu and its huge death toll were a product not of the war, but of the (then as now) unknown processes of viral morphology.'[63]

Coincidentally, even as Winter was penning his discontent with a war–pandemic link, dramatic and ingenious state-of-the-art virological research was getting under way to try and identify precisely the causative virus of the 1918–19 pandemic through the analysis of tissue specimens taken from flu victims, either in 1918 (and since preserved in a Washington pathological museum) or, more dramatically, from the exhumed bodies of Norwegian and Alaskan victims buried over 80 years ago within the Arctic Circle. These virological ventures of the late 1990s caught a popular imagination already aroused by the drama of the 1997 Hong Kong chicken flu outbreak, and they received extensive coverage in the daily press, in international magazines like *Time* and the *New Yorker*, on television and, to date, in three popular books.[64] All this media attention has served to revive the influenza pandemic of 1918–19 as a topic for discussion, this time, however, as a vehicle for a sensational scientific quest at the end of the second millennium. It is too soon to say whether this episode will prompt even more scholarly research on the Spanish flu but, going by what has happened in the past, it should. Certainly there is no lack of important historical questions and perspectives pertaining to the pandemic still to be addressed.

The contribution of this book

That there are so many unexplored questions was underscored at the 1998 Cape Town conference on the pandemic, from which the chapters in this book derive. Every one of the thirty-six papers presented there broke new ground in some way and, in selecting sixteen of these for inclusion in this book, the editors have sought to strike a fine balance between their wish for wide geographical coverage, a variety of disciplinary approaches and the need for a degree of overall coherence. To secure the latter, the chapters have been organised around the six main themes set out earlier in this introduction. To grasp their inter-relation better, the following paragraphs will briefly sketch their contents and put each chapter into context.

Part I, 'Virological and pathological perspectives', contains two chapters, one by an influenza virologist of long standing and one by a relative newcomer to the field, whose contribution might be labelled that of an archaeological pathologist. Edwin Kilbourne's opening chapter draws on a lifetime of study to assess the 1918–19 pandemic in the light of modern thinking in the field, providing a virological base-line from which its viral essence and, perhaps, its peculiar lethality can be understood. Unprompted by the editors, he firmly asserts that if what happened in 1918 is to be fully comprehended, virologists need historians as much as historians need virologists.

A crucial step in the direction of gaining such understanding is described in Jeffery Taubenberger's chapter which presents preliminary findings on the identity of the 1918 flu virus. The specimens on which his analysis is based come from old tissue samples taken from the lungs of young flu victims and preserved in formalin/paraffin or Arctic permafrost since then. These samples his team, at the Armed Forces Institute of Pathology in Washington, have subjected to the latest biotechnological genetic characterisation, and in this chapter he presents their first findings. It is hoped that these mark the beginning of the ultimate unravelling of the enigma relating to the causative virus – why was it so deadly?

Part II of the book – 'Contemporary medical and nursing perspectives' – pursues the medical theme, but in a more conventional historical way. Wilfried Witte goes back to 1918 to explore the debates among the world's top bacteriologists of the day, in Germany, as to the aetiology of the pandemic, and describes how doubts began to surface about the adequacy of the prevailing belief in Pfeiffer's bacillus as the causative agent of influenza. Perhaps, posited some, an even smaller organism was responsible, a suggestion which neatly encapsulates the process whereby existing scientific paradigms are challenged by events and new explanatory frameworks are put forward to supersede them.

Nancy Bristow's chapter in this section brings to an examination of contemporary medical and nursing responses to the pandemic a gendered reading which allows a clear distinction to be drawn between the reactions of male doctors and those of female nurses in the USA. It offers a sensitive grasp of their different expectations as healthcare professionals and how this shaped their experience, and its perception and portrayal, in 1918. The gendered division of the healthcare profession in early twentieth-century America stands clearly illuminated as a result.

Part III – 'Official responses to the pandemic' – emphasises that there are very different levels of knowledge about the pandemic, depending on the region considered. Whereas in his chapter Geoffrey Rice is able to draw on his own detailed research on the Spanish flu in New Zealand and Japan to juxtapose the responses of two very different Pacific Rim societies, to the considerable illumination of both, Mridula Ramanna's chapter is, astonishingly, the first local study of how colonial Indian officialdom in Bombay (now Mumbai) dealt with the pandemic. When one remembers that the toll in just that Presidency is estimated to have been over one million, and in British India as a whole possibly 18 million, the breadth of the Indian lacuna in Spanish influenza historiography is starkly clear.

Like Part III of the book, Part IV – 'The demographic impact' – drives home how varied is the state of investigation of even crucial aspects of the pandemic. Whereas the achievement of the chapter by Wataru Iijima is just to be able to provide initial estimates of the number of Spanish flu deaths in China, the chapters by McCracken and Curson, Johnson, Herring and Sattenspiel, Echeverri, Zylberman and Noymer and Garenne are able to subject the detailed and reliable mortality figures for six 'developed' countries to demographic analysis of considerable sophistication. Thus, using relatively 'hard' figures for Britain and for Sydney, the historical geographers Niall Johnson, and Peter Curson and Kevin McCracken, are able to chart the pandemic's path and probe its toll for social and spatial patterns in their respective areas with graphic detail, while the analysis of Inuit deaths in the Canadian sub-Arctic by Anne Herring and Lisa Sattenspiel, both anthropologists, fruitfully adds that discipline's insights concerning social organisation and ecology to those of historical geography to produce a fine-grained micro-analysis of the pandemic's varied mortality pattern in one very remote locality.

But such wide variations in mortality were not limited to out-of-the-way localities. Indeed, explaining this feature is another of the conundrums posed by the pandemic. In her chapter on eponymous Spain, Beatriz Echeverri seeks an answer in the differing social conditions and levels of civil organisation prevailing in each province of the country, a hypothesis which researchers elsewhere need to investigate as well. Taking the longer view, she also notes a short-term fall in birth-rates in 1919 as a result of high mortality among mothers-to-be in 1918. The negative effect this trend in maternal mortality had on female:male ratios generally in the post-1918 population is a phenomenon which Andrew Noymer and Michel Garenne also identify in the USA, but, according to the novel analysis in their chapter, the demographic consequences of this fall in 1918 stretched through to at least the 1930s, suggesting the pandemic had a far longer-term impact on population than previously envisaged. If this was also true of other countries, the implications for establishing the total number of flu victims (both direct and indirect) are enormous.

Zylberman's chapter, though focusing just on France, raises two other universal questions which, as noted earlier, have hardly been explored in any depth hitherto. To what extent did civilians in belligerent countries suffer greater mortality than soldiers in the pandemic because medical and nursing resources were directed towards the latter, as a matter of priority, to meet military needs first?[65] And second, and more broadly, what was the relationship between the First World War and the pandemic – cause, complement, or connected only by chronology? If the answer is either of the first two, the number of lives lost as a result of the war could more than triple at a stroke.

The last three chapters are assigned to two parts, but all three deal with the aftermath of the pandemic, though from three different disciplinary perspectives. In Part V – 'Long-term consequences and memories' – Jim

Ellison's chapter uses historical anthropology to make sense of how the temporary role assumed by chiefs in colonial Tanzania to cope with flu-induced famines was permanently inscribed into British colonial policy there by uncomprehending administrators in the 1920s. This is truly an example of discerning a far-reaching consequence of the pandemic through a 'pandemically-informed reading' of the archives, a skill which other historians should learn to cultivate. On the other side of the African continent, in Senegal, one with such skills is Myron Echenberg, who devotes his chapter to interrogating the virtual absence of references to the 1918–19 flu pandemic from both official records and the memories of the elderly informants he interviewed. His answer is one further strand in explaining the peculiar puzzle of the forgetting of the pandemic.

The one field in which the influenza pandemic did leave an indelible mark is, not surprisingly, epidemiology. In his chapter in Part VI – 'Epidemiological Lessons of the Pandemic' – Steve Schoenbaum reviews the first decade of epidemiological investigation into influenza after 1918. This recovers forgotten chapters in the history of epidemic influenza and suggests that there are important lessons still to be learnt today with regard to immunisation from these pre-virology experiments.

Cumulatively, the sixteen chapters and the pioneering bibliography significantly extend our knowledge of the Spanish influenza and its consequences across a broad front, both in anticipated areas like virology, demography and the history of healthcare, but also in less obvious fields like administrative and political history, military history and the nature of memory. With regard to its toll, they begin to point to answers to four of the most crucial questions left by the pandemic: how many died, why were so many of these young adults, why was the mortality so variable geographically, and what were the long-term consequences of the toll for national population structures?

For all this trailblazing, the list of topics above simultaneously emphasises the inchoate state of Spanish influenza historiography by virtue of its omissions. The absence of studies of major regions of the globe, especially Latin America, the Middle East, Russia, south-east Asia and inland China is very noticeable, as are chapters which systematically probe questions which have already been fruitfully discussed with reference to other epidemics by social and cultural historians of disease and medicine – for example, how the Spanish influenza was constructed and understood by contemporaries and what this says about their *mentalité*, both lay and religious, and their prejudices which so readily attributed the outbreak to others; the pandemic's iconography and the literature and poetry which it prompted both in the short and long run – comparisons with the First World War would be very apt here; what light the influenza pandemic experience sheds on prevailing attitudes to death, the body and its disposal, grief, mourning and memorials, again bearing in mind the experience of the First World War; how far the pandemic enhanced or undermined colonial rule and the acceptance of European biomedicine and socio-cultural practices in colonies; what its impact was on the national state and its medical institutions, and their perceptions of their role in securing public health and welfare and how this was translated to the international sphere, particularly via the creation of a global disease intelligence network. For comparative studies on topics like these there is abundant scope.

On an even broader canvas, the Spanish flu as a whole needs to be located in relation to key events and processes which shaped the twentieth-century world, such as the First World War, the process of demographic transition and the advance of medical and virological knowledge and practice; moreover, as a marker of the shrinkage of the globe, the pandemic's speedy and lethal progress is very graphic. At such vast issues this book can only hint.

Part I

Virological and pathological perspectives

1 A virologist's perspective on the 1918–19 pandemic

Edwin D. Kilbourne

Introduction

Although lacking the clear-cut pathognomic stigmata of such plagues as poliomyelitis and smallpox, influenza pandemics of the past can be identified with reasonable certainty as the manifestations of an acute, prostrating respiratory tract disease with a high attack rate. In a careful examination of both primary and secondary sources, Patterson has postulated the occurrence of nine pandemics during the period 1700–1900. These presumed pandemics occurred at irregular intervals and no common factor seemed to be involved in their precipitation.[1] The causative virus of human influenza was first identified in 1933. In the subsequent modern virological period, pandemics have occurred in 1957 and 1968, associated with the introduction, probably from animal or avian sources, of markedly different strains of the influenza A virus, known by their surface antigens as H2N2 and H3N2. The likelihood that the pandemic of 1918 was caused by a similar infectious agent is strengthened by seroarchaeologic evidence that persons exposed to and presumably infected by the 1918 virus have antibodies to the virus of swine influenza – which appeared as a new disease in the American middle west in 1918. Very recently, it has been reported that fragments of the genome of a virus similar to the swine (H1N1) virus have been demonstrated in the preserved lung tissue of human victims of the pandemic.[2] Because influenza pandemics have occurred at intervals of 11 to 39 years, and it is now (2003) 35 years since the last pandemic in 1968, there is increasing concern about the prospect of another pandemic and about its potential severity. This concern is heightened by the recognition that the effective vaccines now available have never been sufficiently utilised to affect significantly the course of any pandemic, and by the increasing number of antibiotic-resistant bacterial pathogens which, as secondary invaders, account for most of the deaths in pandemic periods.[3]

Virus changes that account for pandemics are of two sorts:

1 the principal and essential change is a major change in one or both of the surface viral antigens to create a virus which differs so markedly

from those previously encountered in human experience that people of all ages become susceptible;

2   other changes that influence the intrinsic virulence of the virus are suspected, but as yet unproven, although it has been found in animal influenza that virulence[4] or host range affinity[5] can be greatly enhanced by mutation of a single viral nucleotide.

It is also true that a dramatic vaccine failure and world-wide dissemination of a virus occurred in 1947 without subtype changes in the surface antigens of the human virus.[6] This chapter will address the implications of these findings for putting the 1918 pandemic into perspective and assessing realistically expectations for the dangers of future pandemics.

The literal and figurative exhumation of 1918 influenza by serologic and virologic archaeology

Because the science of virology was in its infancy in 1918, no virus was recovered from victims of the epidemic. Bacteriology at the time was well advanced, and the prevalence of secondary bacterial infections in influenza victims led to the mistaken identification of various bacterial pathogens – notably Pfeiffer's 'influenza bacillus' (*Haemophilus influenzae*) – as causative agents. After influenza viruses were first isolated from mammals, first from swine by Shope in 1931 and later from humans by Smith, Andrewes and Laidlaw in 1933, a retrospective connection was made of these viruses with the virus of 1918 by examining the sera of persons old enough to have been exposed to the 1918 virus. It was found that this cohort of the population carried antibodies reactive with the swine influenza virus, while others did not.[7] When this evidence was coupled with records of swine influenza appearing as a new disease in the north central United States in 1918,[8] it appeared that the primary host for the 1918 virus may have been human.[9] The direction of migration of the virus across species barriers remains moot, however,[10] because the infection can be virtually asymptomatic in swine, and may have escaped recognition prior to 1918.

The previously cited recovery by Taubenberger and his colleagues of remnants of swine influenza virus genes in the lungs of soldiers who died of influenza in 1918 and from the lung of an Inuit woman frozen in the Alaskan tundra, has provided even stronger evidence that a virus resembling contemporary swine influenza viruses was in fact the aetiologic agent of that disaster.

Deductions on the probable virology of the 1918 pandemic from the more recent pandemics occurring within the period of modern virology

Although the clinical picture and epidemiology of the yearly influenza epidemics after the isolation of the influenza virus in 1933 resembled the milder cases of influenza in 1918, no modern epidemics of flu have had the dramatic and lethal impact of that event. Therefore, it has been questioned whether, in fact, the causative agents of 'Spanish' influenza and the modern disease are related. There were, however, hints from the study of serum specimens from people exposed to the 1918 virus that suggested that the 1918 virus (if such it was) was antigenically related to the virus now indigenous to American swine.[11]

No true pandemics of influenza occurred in the interval 1918–57, and therefore there was no opportunity to apply post-1933 technology and science to the study of a pandemic until 1957 when the 'Asian' influenza epidemic moved swiftly from the Far East to encompass the world in a matter of months. This, and a second pandemic following close behind in 1968 – as well as pandemic threats in 1976 and 1997 – are worth examining for the light they shed, retrospectively, on the pandemic of 1918. (See Box 1.1 for a chronology of major epidemics.)

The 'mild' or 'pseudo-pandemic' of 1947

Although vaccine-induced immunity to influenza A virus is continually challenged by progressively selected mutations in the virus's major antigens, (antigenic drift), virus strains within a subtype (e.g. H_1N_1) are antigenically cross-reactive. Cross-*immunity* diminishes as further mutations accumulate, necessitating frequent changes in vaccine strains, although older vaccines are usually partially protective. The post-war epidemic of 1947 is notable for the total failure of a vaccine previously effective in the 1943–4 and 1944–5 seasons. We have combined extensive antigenic characterization of the hemagglutinin (HA) and neuraminidase (NA) antigens of the 1943 and 1947 viruses with analysis of their nucleotide and amino acid sequences and have found marked antigenic and amino acid differences in viruses of the two periods. Furthermore, in a mouse model, vaccination with the 1943 vaccine had no effect on infection with the 1947 strain. These findings are important because complete lack of cross-immunogenicity has previously been found only with antigenic shift, in which antigenically novel surface antigens have been captured by reassortment of human and animal strains, sometimes leading to pandemics. Although the 1947 epidemic lacked the usual hallmarks of pandemic disease, including an extensive increase in mortaliity, it warns of the possibility that extreme intra-subtypic antigenic variation – if coupled with an increase in disease severity – could produce pandemic disease without the introduction of animal virus antigens.[13]

Early chronology

1929 – last evidence (serologic) of circulation in humans of a 'swine'-like influenza virus

1930 – isolation by Shope of an influenza virus from swine

1933 – first isolation of an influenza virus from humans by Smith, Andrews and Laidlaw

Pandemics, pseudo-pandemics and pandemic threats

1947 – influenza 'A Prime' – a global, relatively non-lethal epidemic of a variant virus of the same A subtype that had circulated since 1929. Vaccines made from antecedent (H1N1) strains failed to protect.

1957 – the first true pandemic since 1918. The H2N2 'Asian' influenza virus differed from its antecedents in both major antigens, thus confronting the world's population with an essentially novel virus to which it had no immunity. This epidemic was important in demonstrating that a 'modern' influenza virus could cause pandemic disease and fatal viral pneumonia reminiscent of 1918. Completely replaced all H1N1 subtype viruses.

1968 – in the 'Hong Kong' pandemic only the major haemagglutinin (HA) antigen changed, but change was sufficient to induce a pandemic, modified in severity by population immunity against the minor neuraminidase (NA) antigen. Completely replaced all H2N2 viruses.

1976 – at least 250 recruits at Fort Dix, New Jersey were infected with swine influenza virus. A controversial mass immunisation programme was initiated in the USA for fear of 'another 1918'. With no further cases of disease and complications attributed to the vaccine, programme was cancelled after vaccination of 43 million people.

1977 – the 'Russian' flu (actually originating in China) which produced a global pandemic affecting initially those less than 25 years of age. An early return of a virus (H1N1) last seen two decades before. Unprecedented co-circulation of H1N1 and H3N2 (Hong Kong) subtypes continues to this day.

1997 – H5N1 avian influenza in Hong Kong with sixteen proved infections of humans and six fatalities. Perhaps due to mass destruction of chickens suspected to be the source, the epidemic ceased.

1999 – H9N2 avian virus appeared early in the year, also in Hong Kong, as a brief zoonotic infection without evidence of human to human transmission. As with H5N1 virus, apparent origin in chickens. Apparent cessation of cases without mass slaughter of fowl.

Box 1.1 Major influenza epidemics or pandemic threats since 1918 – every pandemic is different

The 'Asian' pandemic of 1957 – the first modern pandemic

The Asian virus was readily isolated from patients by methods that had become standard in the study of contemporary influenza viruses and it proved to be similar in its biological and chemical properties to modern influenza viruses. However, the surface proteins of the virus – the haemagglutinin (HA) and neuraminidase (NA) antigens – were very different from those of human viruses previously encountered. Most of the population, immunised only by exposure to the H1N1 group of viruses, had no immunity to the new H2N2 'Asian' virus. For this reason, pandemic spread occurred with lethal outcome in some patients, amongst whom the disease was indistinguishable from that seen in 1918.

Three remarkable observations were made during this first modern pandemic and its successor in 1968:

1   the new virus completely and suddenly replaced its predecessor, which was not to reappear until decades later;
2   the magnitude of antigenic change in the virus proteins was unprecedented and differed fundamentally from the gradual and cumulative 'point' mutations that had explained the yearly 'drift' of the virus to partially escape vaccines and rising levels of population antibodies; and
3   antigenic proteins similar to those in the 1957 and 1968 human viruses had been identified previously in nature in avian species.[14] This third observation suggested the possible derivation of perhaps all human influenza pandemics from animal sources.

The 'Hong Kong' pandemic of 1968 – a periodicity of pandemics appeared to be emerging

Taken together, the pervasive but relatively non-lethal pandemic of 1947 and the unequivocal pandemics of 1957 and 1968 seemed to set a roughly decennial pattern of recurrence that was a cause for concern towards the close of the 1970s.[15] It was not surprising, then, that the appearance of an initially untyped influenza virus at Fort Dix, New Jersey, USA in 1976 was greeted with alarm that was exacerbated when person to person transmission of the virus was demonstrated.

The great non-pandemic of 1976 – the abortive introduction of a major new variant into the human population without epidemic spread

The Fort Dix virus was rapidly identified by the Centers for Disease Control at Atlanta as a swine influenza virus, postulated by some to be the agent of 1918. But, remarkably, after infection of some 250 recruits, the virus disappeared and did not spread beyond the confines of the post. In the meantime, a National Immunisation Program was mounted as vaccine was prepared for the immunisation of 'every man, woman and child in the United States', in the words of President Gerald Ford.[16] More than 40 million were vaccinated before the programme was terminated because of the disappearance of the disease and the (rare) occurrence of neurological symptoms in some vaccinated subjects.[17]

Every epidemic of influenza provides new lessons, if only we recognise them. The lessons of the Fort Dix episode are several:

1 an animal influenza virus can cause serially transmissible disease in humans;
2 introduction of a major new antigenic variant into the human population is not necessarily followed by pandemic or even epidemic disease; and
3 mass immunisation against a potential pandemic virus is feasible.

The premature reappearance of a 1947-like H1N1 virus in 1977 – a global pandemic of the young

Originating in mainland China, but recognised and reported first in the Soviet Union, a virus very similar to those circulating in the 1947–56 period emerged and spread rapidly throughout the world, but not as a true pandemic, because this 'Russian' virus affected principally children and young adults who had not had previous exposure to its antigens in the earlier decade. It was noteworthy that the appearance of this H1N1 influenza A virus subtype was not followed by the disappearance of the prevalent subtype as had been seen following the introduction of new subtypes in 1957 and 1968. The subsequent persistent co-circulation of both H1N1 and H3N2 subtypes until the present time was also a new 'lesson' in influenza epidemiology. Furthermore, the return of the H1N1 subtype after only two decades, although in accord with earlier evidence of recycling of influenza A virus subtype antigens, was unexpectedly soon. Earlier circulation of H2 and H3 antigens had preceded their reappearance in 1957 and 1968 by some 60 to 70 years.

The pandemic threats of 1997 and 1999: avian influenza virus in Hong Kong

The occurrence in 1997 of sixteen cases of human influenza caused by an avian influenza virus in Hong Kong is reminiscent of the situation when a swine influenza virus infected recruits at Fort Dix in 1976, in that a viral subtype alien to humans threatened an epidemic or even a pandemic. A major and important difference was the early demonstration that the swine virus had spread from person to person while the avian virus appeared unable to do so. Another difference was the strong circumstantial and genetic evidence identifying chickens as the source of the virus, whereas only the genetic similarity of human isolates in 1976 to contemporary swine influenza viruses[18] suggested an animal source. Different, also, was the precedent of occasional infection of individual farmers and others by swine influenza viruses. With all these factors considered, and in the absence of further cases of H5N1 infection after the destruction of most of the chickens in Hong Kong at the end of 1997, there has been no rush to immunise the human population, although one-third of the infections were fatal. However, other experimental vaccines against the avian virus are still in preparation (March 2000), after initial unsatisfactory attempts to immunise a small group of subjects with an H5 recombinant vaccine, and will be studied in limited trials of their immunogenicity in humans in the near future. With a second series of zoonotic infections, caused by yet another avian influenza virus, occurring in Hong Kong in 1999, and also acquired from chickens,[19] it appears that such abortive cross-species infections may be relatively frequent events that are now emerging to notice because of enhanced surveillance.

Determinants of influenza virus pandemicity

Although influenza pandemics of the more recent past have characteristics in common, one is struck more by their differences than their similarities. In common is the pandemicity by which they are defined – the almost simultaneous involvement of humans on every continent. The magnitude and severity of involvement are influenced by host and environmental factors (see Table 1.1), but key to the event is a sudden and major change in the circulating virus. This is less a change in the immediately antecedent virus than the introduction of a virus almost totally new to recent human experience. The only reasonable explanation of this sudden 'shift'[20] in the surface antigen(s) of the virus has been the capture by the fading, immunologically suppressed human virus of novel antigens from animal

Table 1.1 Determinants of influenza virus pandemicity

Viral	Host	Environmental
Antigenic novelty[a]	absence of specific immunity	animal source[b]
Transmissibility[c]	population density	seasonal factors
Virulence[d]	age, underlying disease, stress	crowding may give higher dose and provide bacterial invaders

Notes

a Greatest when both HA and NA antigens change; degree of difference from immediately antecedent virus.

b Opportunity provided for recombination of animal and human strains and 'capture' of alien animal virus antigens.

c Transmissibility and virulence are not necessarily correlated.

d Intrinsic to the virus but can be influenced by host and environmental factors, as shown.

sources.[21] The degree of virus change associated with classical pandemics cannot be explained as the result of the gradual, sequential point mutations that account for the annual, relatively minor antigenic changes (or 'drift') of influenza viruses.[22] However, it must be kept in mind that global distribution of a 'drifting' H1N1 virus successfully challenged (then) current vaccines and occurred in 1947 as a mild or pseudo-pandemic. Thirty years later, a virus of the H1N1 subtype returned to cause a pandemic of the young. Elsewhere, I have proposed that the H1N1 subtype viruses may in fact be, in the computer sense, the 'default' human viruses.[23] Indeed, included in the H1N1 group is the putative agent of 1918.

It may be significant that the 1918 and 1947 pandemics came at the termination of two world wars – perhaps reflecting crowding, stress and mixing of populations – all allowing for rapid viral spread and multiple opportunities for the generation of mutants and the evolution of a new virus.

In retrospect, which of these determinants of influenza virus pandemicity were operative in 1918?

Box 1.2 attempts an evaluation of the viral, host and environmental factors known to be associated with modern pandemics as they may relate to the situation in 1918. It must be confessed that this analysis is not terribly helpful. Historical records often have been more hyperbolic and dramatic than scientifically helpful, except to verify that a frightening disease with lethal impact occurred. Because we have in hand neither the immediately antecedent virus nor the 1918 virus itself (except as noted previously[24]), the antigenic novelty of the virus cannot be evaluated. The global sweep of its incursions, however, certainly bespeaks a virtual pansusceptibility of the human population.

Mortality from influenza is usually highest at both extremes of age – the very young and the elderly. The uniquely high mortality of influenza–pneumonia in young adults has remained a puzzling feature of the 1918 pandemic. Based on evidence that yet another H1N1 virus circulated in the period 1908–18,[25] I tentatively speculate that children under ten might have been protected from the later assaults of the 1918 agent by earlier exposure to its antigenic cousin in the earlier period. The relatively lower mortality of the elderly is less easy to explain unless they were relatively immune to the secondary bacterial invaders that co-infected most young recruits.

That the 1918 virus was uniquely virulent would seem to be obvious. However, the typical case of flu in 1918 was much like the typical case of influenza today. But historical accounts attest to the sudden deaths and extreme prostration that felled many of its victims. It is difficult, however, to separate the effects of the virus from that of the many bacterial co-invaders documented to be present at the time. Not only may influenza have paved the way for secondary bacterial infection, but such infections (common in military camps) may have directly enhanced viral virulence

Viral

Antigenic novelty. Unclear. There is serologic evidence that H1N1 subtype viruses circulated in humans early in the century (1908–18) prior to the emergence of 'swine-like' H1N1 viruses in 1918.

Transmissibility. Unclear. If the virus prevalent in the northern spring of 1918 was the same virus that had a devastating impact in the northern autumn of that year, its transmissibility was not sufficient to foster summertime epidemics in the United States. Later, transmissibility within households appeared to be high. If, in fact, it spread from man to swine, transcending species barriers, that is another indication of exceptional transmissibility.

Virulence. Intrinsic virulence of the virus was obviously exceptional. Its effects were compounded further by wartime stress and crowding and secondary bacterial infections.

Host

Absent specific immunity. The reciprocal of antigenic novelty. Young adults would have been primed in infancy with other than H1N1 viruses (i.e. viruses circulating earlier than 1908), which may explain their unusual susceptibility to fatal outcome with the swine H1N1 virus.

Social factors. Wartime crowding, population dislocations, stress.

Environmental factors

Crowding and stress-inducing environmental factors. Difficult to separate from host factors, above.

Coincident or consequent bacterial epidemics. Bacterial pathogens may have enhanced the pathogenicity of primary influenza virus infections or infected as secondary invaders.

Box 1.2 What determinants of influenza virus pandemicity were operative in 1918?

through the production of protease enzymes recently shown to facilitate influenza virus multiplication.[26]

Will there be another 1918?

This is not a simple question, and it deserves a carefully considered, balanced and thoughtful answer. The direct and honest answer is that no one knows. However, this is not a very satisfactory response to a concerned public who have been informed repeatedly recently by otherwise responsible scientists that a pandemic (of some intensity) is 'inevitable'. The question raised usually implies two questions:

1   Will a virus as virulent as the agent of 1918 confront us again?
2   Can we control it if it does?

The correct answer to the first question is, 'It is possible', and to the second, 'Given the present state of our medical technology and competence (including vaccines, antivirals and antibiotics), yes, probably.' And to those who say 'another pandemic is inevitable', I point to the extinction of the dinosaurs, the conquest of smallpox and the proximity of asteroids.

Postscript

In writing this chapter, I have tried to provide a frame of reference and a focus for future historical as well as scientific investigations. During the 1998 conference, I was made aware of the extent of my ignorance of historical facts and analyses that would enlighten some of my speculation about such matters as viral virulence and transmissibility. Perhaps with these areas of scientific ignorance revealed, future historical research can address these questions with greater focus and specificity. For example, no precise figures on age-related morbidity in 1918 exist, in contrast to the reasonably reliable data on mortality for some countries. In order to understand the relative sparing of the elderly from the high mortality of the young adults, we must know whether fewer elderly were infected or fewer had severe disease. Regional historical and even anecdotal data can inform us on this point and in turn direct our scientific inquiries.

2 Genetic characterisation of the 1918 'Spanish' influenza virus

Jeffery K. Taubenberger

At the end of the First World War, in the northern autumn of 1918, an influenza pandemic of unprecedented virulence swept the globe, leaving up to 40 million dead in its wake, with unusually high mortality among young healthy adults. The virus responsible for this catastrophe was not isolated at the time, and perhaps the most lethal infectious agent of all time was seemingly lost for study. The search for the agent responsible for the pandemic began in earnest in 1918 and resulted 12 years later in the isolation of the first influenza virus in swine in 1930 and in humans in 1933. The following 70 years of study have shed much light on the biology of influenza viruses, but many unanswered questions remain. It is now possible to study the genetic features of the 1918 virus thanks to the incredible foresight of the US Army Medical Museum, the persistence of pathologist Johan V. Hultin, and advances in the molecular genetic analyses of fixed tissue specimens as applied by the Molecular Pathology Division at the Armed Forces Institute of Pathology in Washington, D.C.[1]

The study of the 1918 virus is not just one of historical curiosity. Since influenza viruses continually evolve by mechanisms of antigenic shift and drift, new influenza strains, as emerging pathogens, continue to threaten human populations. Pandemic influenza viruses have emerged twice since 1918, in 1957 and 1968. The risk of future influenza pandemics is thought to be high.[2] An understanding of the genetic make-up of the most virulent influenza strain in history may facilitate prediction and prevention of such future pandemics.

The 1918 influenza pandemic

The influenza pandemic of 1918 was exceptional in both breadth and depth. Unlike most subsequent influenza strains, which first appeared in Asia, the initial wave of the 1918 pandemic seemingly arose in the United States. The first wave of influenza in the northern spring and summer of 1918 was highly contagious but caused few deaths (Figure 2.1). The spring wave was also clearly global, with reports not only from the USA, but also

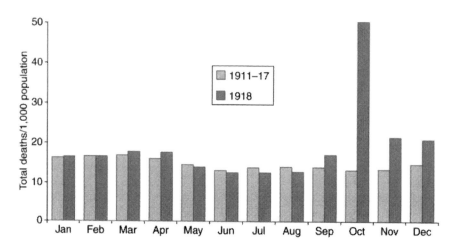

Figure 2.1 Death rates in the United States by month, 1911–17 and 1918.

Note
The spike in mortality in the autumn of 1918 is a result of the 1918 influenza pandemic.

Europe and Asia. In late August, a virulent form of the disease emerged and swept the globe in six months. The main wave of the global pandemic occurred between September and November of 1918, killing over 10,000 people per week in some US cities. Outbreaks of the disease swept not only North America and Europe, but also spread as far as the Alaskan wilderness and the most remote islands of the Pacific. Large proportions of the population became ill; 28 per cent of the US population is estimated to have been infected. The disease was also exceptionally severe, with mortality rates among the infected over 2.5 per cent, compared to less than 0.1 per cent in other influenza epidemics.[3] Incredibly, some isolated populations had mortality rates of over 70 per cent.[4]

Furthermore, in the 1918 pandemic most deaths occurred among young adults, a group that usually has a very low death rate from influenza. Influenza and pneumonia death rates for 15–34 year olds were more than twenty times higher in 1918 than in previous years, with 99 per cent of excess deaths among people under 65 years of age[5] (Figure 2.2). It has been estimated that the influenza epidemic of 1918 killed 675,000 Americans, including 43,000 servicemen mobilised for the First World War.[6] The impact was so profound as to depress average life expectancy in the USA by over 10 years[7] (Figure 2.3).

Indirect information about the virus

Analyses of antibody titres of 1918 flu survivors from the late 1930s and historical projection of phylogenetic analyses suggest that the 1918 strain

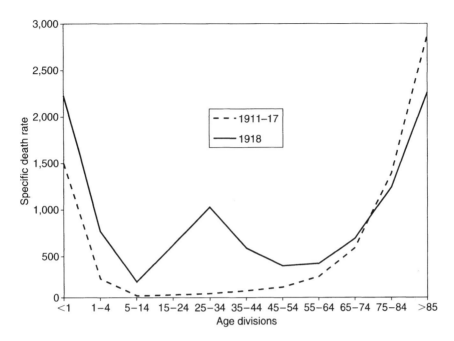

Figure 2.2 Influenza and pneumonia mortality by age, United States.

Note
Influenza and pneumonia specific mortality by age, including the pandemic year 1918 and
the average of the interpandemic years 1911–15, is shown. Specific death rate is per 100,000
of the population for each age division.

Key: 1918 pandemic (solid line), average of interpandemic years 1911–17 (dashed line).

Figure 2.3 Life expectancy in the United States, 1900–60, showing precipitous drop
in 1918 because of deaths due to the 'Spanish' flu.

was an H1N1-subtype influenza A virus,[8] probably closely related to what is now known as 'classic swine' influenza virus. This swine connection also relates directly to the 1918 flu where simultaneous outbreaks of influenza in humans and pigs were reported around the world during the second wave.[9] While historical accounts suggest that the 1918 flu spread from humans to pigs, the relationship of these two species in the development of the 1918 flu has not been resolved.

The avian association with the 1918 flu has also not been determined.[10] The natural reservoir for influenza virus is thought to be wild waterfowl.[11] Periodically, genetic material from avian strains emerges in strains infectious to humans. Since pigs can be infected with both avian and human strains, they have been postulated to be an intermediary in this process.[12] In 1979, an avian influenza A virus (without reassortment) entered the swine population in northern Europe, forming a stable viral lineage.[13] Influenza strains with recently acquired genetic material have been responsible for pandemic influenza outbreaks in 1957 and 1968.[14] Until recently, there was no evidence that a wholly avian influenza virus could directly infect humans. This barrier was dramatically broken in 1997 in Hong Kong when at least eighteen people were infected with an avian H5N1 influenza virus and six died of complications after infection.[15] The relationship of the 1918 influenza virus to swine and avian viral strains is one of the primary goals of this project. How influenza viruses move between species is extremely important for our understanding of the emergence of pandemic influenza strains.

Finding samples of the 1918 flu for study

In 1951, scientists from the University of Iowa exhumed bodies of victims of the 1918 flu that had been buried in permafrost in Teller Mission, an Inuit fishing village on the Seward Peninsula of Alaska.[16] This village, now called Brevig Mission, suffered extremely high mortality during the influenza pandemic in November 1918. Available records show that influenza spread through the village in about 5 days, killing seventy-two people, representing about 85 per cent of the adult population.[17] During the 1951 expedition, samples of lung, brain and other organs were taken for histologic analyses and viral culture. All attempts to culture live influenza virus from these specimens were unsuccessful. Molecular genetic analyses of the samples were impossible at that time (the structure of DNA was not determined until 1953!).

In 1995, my laboratory in Washington initiated a project to perform a genetic characterisation of the 1918 influenza virus using archival formalin-fixed, paraffin-embedded autopsy tissues of 1918 flu victims stored in the National Tissue Repository of the Armed Forces Institute of Pathology (AFIP) in Washington, DC (USA). A search of the archives revealed over seventy autopsy cases of US soldiers who had died of influenza pneumonia in the autumn of 1918. We used techniques to isolate RNA that had been optimised for fixed tissue specimens based on previous studies.[18]

In total, seventy-eight autopsy cases of victims of the lethal second wave of the 1918 pandemic were examined for this study. Seventy-four of these consisted of fixed tissues. The majority of these individuals had died of secondary bacterial pneumonia, the most common cause of death during the pandemic. Because many had had clinical courses longer than one week, it was extremely unlikely that any of the tissue samples from these cases would still retain influenza RNA. However, a subset of individuals had died within one week, with very unusual and characteristic lung pathology including massive pulmonary oedema or haemorrhage. These patients literally drowned in their own serum or blood, often in as little as 48 hours. While these pathologic changes have been seen in other influenza outbreaks (including the 1957 'Asian' flu), its prominence in 1918 is one of the cardinal features of the 'Spanish' flu. It was on this subset of patients that we concentrated.

In 1996 we found the first positive case, an autopsy lung sample from a soldier who had died on 26 September 1918 at Fort Jackson, South Carolina. He had presented with pneumonia and influenza symptoms, was admitted to the camp hospital, and expired 6 days later. At the autopsy it was noted that he had suffered a lethal bacterial pneumonia of his left lung, with only very early inflammatory changes in his right lung, a fact confirmed by re-examination of the microscopic slides in 1996. The changes in the right lung, acute focal bronchiolitis and alveolitis, are consistent with primary influenza viral pneumonia. Indeed, no influenza RNA was recovered from his left lung. The influenza RNA recoverable from the right lung was fragmented into pieces no longer than 150 bases in length. An initial genetic characterisation of the 1918 influenza from this sample was carried out, and the sequence of fragments of five influenza genes was determined.[19]

In order to confirm that the sequences derived from this case represented those of the lethal second wave of the 1918 flu, additional cases were sought. A second archival autopsy case was identified in 1997. This was also a soldier who had died on 26 September 1918, at Camp Upton, New York. He had also presented with pneumonia and had had a very rapid clinical course, with death in just 3 days after onset of symptoms. Microscopic examination of sections of his lung revealed massive acute pulmonary oedema. Influenza RNA fragments in this case were also no greater than 150 bases in length.[20]

Pathologist Johan V. Hultin submitted a third case to the Armed Forces Institute of Pathology in 1997. Dr Hultin was a team member of the 1951 University of Iowa project. After reading about our results with fixed tissue, he contacted us about obtaining new frozen lung biopsies of 1918 flu victims from the same mass grave sampled in 1951. He obtained permission of the Brevig Mission City Council and in August 1997 obtained *in situ* frozen lung biopsies of four victims of the 1918 flu. These samples were placed in fixatives for histologic analysis and RNA isolation. No attempt to culture virus was made. Lung tissue samples of one of these cases, an Inuit female nicknamed 'Lucy' by Dr Hultin, was positive for influenza RNA. Histologically, sections of her lung show evidence of massive pulmonary haemorrhage, consistent with a rapid clinical course. Unfortunately, influenza RNA fragments in this case are no longer than those obtained from the fixed cases.[21]

1918 influenza sequence results

The broad goal of this project is twofold: first, to discover where the 1918 influenza virus came from, and how it got into people, and second, whether there were any genetic features of the sequence that would give insight into the exceptional virulence of this strain.

The best available technique to analyse the relationships among influenza viruses is phylogeny, whereby hypothetical family trees are constructed by computer programs which take available sequence data and use them to make assumptions about the ancestral relationships between current or historical flu strains. Since influenza genes are encoded by eight discrete RNA segments that can move independently between strains by the process of reassortment, these evolutionary studies must be performed independently for each gene segment.

We compared the complete 1918 haemagglutinin sequence to those of numerous human, swine and avian sequences in phylogenetic studies. The 1918 haemagglutinin gene always grouped with the strains that infect humans and swine, never with the avian sequences. While it has sequence similarities with avian haemagglutinin genes, we feel that the most likely explanation is that the haemagglutinin gene was adapted for life in mammals prior to 1918. Whether that was in a human or a pig is still unclear. Since the historical record shows that the pandemic virus affected people (in the first wave) before swine (only noted in the second wave), we favour the hypothesis that the 1918 influenza virus moved from humans into swine, not *vice versa*. Sequence results show, however, that the 1918 sequence is very similar to the common viral ancestor of both human and swine H1 strains and that the human and classic swine H1N1 influenza strains up to the present are descendants of the 1918 virus.[22]

Little is known about how genetic features of influenza viruses affect virulence. Virulence of a particular influenza strain is complex and involves several features including host adaptation, transmissibility, tissue tropism and replication efficiency. The genetic basis for each of these features is not yet fully characterised, but is most likely polygenic in nature. There are, however, several identified mutations that do radically change the behaviour of a given flu strain. In the case of the 1918 virus, we have already screened for some of these mutations and found them not to be present.

The influenza gene sequences that have been generated from these three cases have been nearly identical. The complete coding sequence has been generated to date from the haemagglutinin and neuraminidase genes of the 1918 influenza virus.[23] Haemagglutinin (HA) and neuraminidase (NA) are found on the external surface of the virus and play a key role in binding and entry into target cells. They are also the principal targets of the humoral immune system during infection.

The complete coding sequence of the HA gene was generated from the South Carolina case and was confirmed using RNA from the New York and Alaska cases. Out of the 981 bases of the HA1 domain of the gene, only two nucleotide differences were noted between the cases. One base difference would not have changed the amino acid coded for at that site, and one (in the New York case) would change an amino acid as compared to the sequence of the South Carolina and Alaska cases. Interestingly, that change occurs at one of the critical amino acids involved in receptor binding. The overall receptor binding pattern for the 1918 haemagglutinin is most similar to those of classic swine influenza strains, and it is possible that the New York case specifically could bind both avian- and mammalian-type receptors, a property it would share with classic swine influenza viruses.[24] The complete coding sequence of the NA gene was generated from the Alaska case, and confirmed with the other cases. No sequence differences between the cases were noted.[25]

A model example of a genetic change in an influenza gene leading to increased virulence is the HA cleavage site mutation seen in some avian influenza strains.[26] For viral activation the haemagglutinin protein must be cleaved into two pieces by a protease supplied by the host. Some avian influenza strains can cause systemic disease in birds, instead of the normally benign and limited infection of the gastrointestinal tract. These mutant strains are often associated with near uniform mortality of infected birds. Such strains have been termed 'fowl plague virus'. This mutation has never been seen in H1 subtype haemagglutinins, but as it would have offered an appealing explanation of the 1918 flu's virulence, we examined this site in our initial analysis. However, the 1918 strain (as confirmed in all three cases) does not possess a mutation at this site.[27]

A second genetic change was recently proposed to account for the virulence of the 1918 flu.[28] In this model, a change of a single amino acid in neuraminidase may allow viruses a 'back door' approach to ubiquitous haemagglutinin cleavage and tissue pantropism by sequestering plasminogen. However, like the haemagglutinin cleavage site mutation, this change was also not observed in the 1918 neuraminidase sequence.[29]

Meanwhile, we have analysed partial sequences of all the remaining gene segments of the 1918 viral isolates and will soon determine their full-length sequences. We anticipate completing the sequences of both the Matrix and Non-Structural gene segments soon. Such information will enable us to conduct phylogenetic analyses of each segment, and will help elucidate the origin of the 1918 virus. Each of these genes has features that may play crucial roles in explaining the uniqueness of the 1918 influenza. Whether any particular genetic features of the virus can be related directly to its exceptional virulence is yet unclear, but genetic analysis is still likely to yield significant insight into the behaviour of this virus.

Even as the genetic structure of the Spanish flu virus is becoming fully known, however, other questions may never be answered due to the passage of 80 years. For instance, how may differences in immunity have affected mortality rates among different age-groups during the 1918 pandemic? Also, since no avian influenza strains are available from 1918, it remains unclear how much bird flu strains have changed in the last 80 years. Until such samples can be found, it will be impossible to determine which of the differences between the 1918 sequences and modern bird flu sequences are due to adaptations for humans and which are due to drift in avian sequences. Nonetheless, knowledge gained by studying this all-too-successful human pathogen can still be applied to understanding and perhaps to preventing, or at least predicting, the emergence of future influenza viruses with pandemic potential.

Acknowledgements

I would like to thank Ann H. Reid and Thomas G. Fanning for helpful discussions and fruitful collaboration. This work was partially supported by grants from the American Registry of Pathology, the Department of Veterans Affairs and by the intramural funds of the Armed Forces Institute of Pathology. The opinions or assertions contained herein are the private views of the author and are not to be construed as official or as reflecting the views of the Department of the Army or Department of Defense. This is a US government work; there are no restrictions on its use.

Part II

Contemporary medical and nursing perspectives

3 The plague that was not allowed to happen

German medicine and the influenza epidemic of 1918–19 in Baden[1]

Wilfried Witte

Given the pre-eminence of German medicine at the start of the twentieth century, it is intriguing to inquire into its response to the influenza epidemic of 1918–19, for this posed one of the most formidable challenges ever to the capacity of emerging biomedicine to counter disease, claiming, as it did, some 250,000 German lives in a matter of months. As this chapter will show, this was a challenge which found it seriously wanting, a situation which it has sought to reverse ever since then. The chapter will broach this complex topic by examining the initial response among doctors and medical scientists in one of Imperial Germany's most progressive states, the former Grand Duchy of Baden.

From the start, publication of information about the epidemic was restricted throughout war-enveloped Germany. Already in January 1918 the *Reich* had directed that statistics on infections were not to be discussed in public. The publication of local statistics of any kind on the population (births, marriages, deaths) was banned by the *Oberzensurstelle* (Supreme Board of Censorship) and the *Kriegspresseamt* (Board of Wartime Press) in Berlin.[2] Consequently, reliable statistical data on the influenza epidemic was not readily available, especially as this disease was not notifiable.

As a result, it was not until 29 May 1918 that the first headlines on the 'mysterious disease', seemingly originating from Spain, appeared. According to this news from the press agency Reuter, Spanish doctors had advised serious prophylactic regimens, as the situation was similiar to the one in 1889, the year a serious influenza epidemic had last occurred.[3] As soon as the infection crossed the German border, it was officially labelled 'influenza' and declared a minor disease. The first 'mass infections' were reported from Nuremberg in Franconia,[4] but the extent of the disease and the seriousness of the cases were not publicised.

When the more serious second wave of the epidemic struck in autumn 1918, the situation deteriorated and it reached threatening dimensions. This time the first reports were published on 21 September, the source being the *Progrès de Lyon*. A 'new mysterious disease' had been reported from all over Spain which, it was said, could easily turn into typhus.[5] According to the press, two days later Madrid officially called it 'influenza and fever epidemic'. The *Pforzheimer Anzeiger* insisted that Spain should close its border with France immediately to minimise risk of infection.[6] Again, the term 'Spanish flu' was readily adopted in Germany.

In the midst of this attempt to suppress news about the epidemic, how did German medicine respond to the question of the identity of this 'mysterious disease' at the end of the First World War and what did it recommend should be done?

Its answers, and the role of doctors and medical scientists in implementing them, will be the dominant subject in what follows. They will be examined at four levels: the national, the provincial (in this case the *Land* of Baden), the municipal (again with a focus on Baden) and at the level of individual medical scientists and practitioners (whose experience in Baden did not differ much from that of Germany in general).

In general, the *Reich*, with its ministries in Berlin, dominated the politics of the state of Baden. The *Reichsgesundheitsrat* (the National Council of Health), summoned by the *Reichsgesundheitsamt* (National Office of Health) for advice, met twice, on 10 July and on 16 October 1918. At the first meeting, Richard Pfeiffer, from Breslau, the eminent discoverer of what many contemporaries believed was the causative agent of influenza, *haemophilus influenzae*, affirmed that in the current case the disease was apparently influenza according to his bacteriological studies, though pneumonia did supervene sometimes, mostly in robust individuals. The Council consequently advised the 'rapid instruction' of the public through the daily papers and asked the states to transmit 'summarised' information to Berlin. Upon the request of Prinz Max von Baden, the new Chancellor of the *Reich*, the *Reichsgesundheitsrat* assembled again in October. Despite the gravity of the situation, the infection still was not made notifiable, nor was a majority found for the 'prohibition of gatherings', though schools were to be closed if necessary. The Council basically concentrated on instructing the population to wash their hands, gargle with salt water and rest in bed.[7]

What effect did these decisions have on Baden? Did the Grand Duchy comply with the line of policy pursued by Berlin, as it had done so often since the foundation of the *Reich* in 1871? It seems so.

In Baden, the *Landesgesundheitsrat* (State Council of Health) played the same role as the *Reichsgesundheitsrat* did for the *Reich*. This body had been constituted by state law in 1882. In 1918 several prominent physicians were counted as members of the council, among them Hermann Kossel and Ludolf Krehl from Heidelberg, and Martin Hahn and Oskar de la Camp from Freiburg.[8] Due to the war, the term of office of the *Landesgesundheitsrat*, constituted in 1911, had been prolonged until 1920.

How did this body react when it was faced with the influenza epidemic? It did nothing. The final report of Baden's Ministry of the Interior for the years 1913–24 merely stated that 'A meeting of the *Landesgesundheitsrat* did not take place. . . . No urgent matters were on the agenda.'[9] Clearly, ministerial bureaucracy intended to carry on without exposing its decisions to debate. As for the closure of schools, in order to put this on a legal basis, the Ministry of Culture declared on 15 October that the 1911 regulations to fight infectious diseases, in which influenza was not mentioned at all, would also apply to 'the situation of epidemic incidence of the so-called Spanish flu'.[10] Influenza was not made notifiable, however.

According to the *Amtliches Verkündigungsblatt* (Official Bulletin) issued in Baden's capital, Karlsruhe, on 13 November 1918, 'Special measures to combat the epidemic do not seem likely to be successful according to the general view of the medical profession.'[11] Denying the threat, or at least significantly downplaying it, seems to have been the official stance at national and state level in 1918.

However, was this true at the local level in the towns of Baden, where doctors and nursing staff directly confronted the epidemic? Bodies such as those mentioned above existed only at national and state level, but also at the local and municipal level (*Ortsgesundheitsrat*). These were constituted to advise the respective municipal or local councils. At Baden-Baden, for instance, a municipal committee for public healthcare (*Ausschuß für öffentliche Gesundheitspflege*) decided in mid-October to close the schools in the area until the beginning of November.[12] At Freiburg, members of the town council met with civilian and military doctors during the second half of October 1918. One of the members was Oskar de la Camp, professor of internal medicine and paediatrics at the university hospital. These meetings decided that the 'causative agent of the Spanish disease' did not coincide with that of 'influenza'. The former was attributed to a concurrent infection with streptococci as secondary germs. This committee gave qualified backing to gargling, and recommended that the closure of schools be continued and that the cinemas be 'ventilated' thoroughly.[13]

In Heidelberg, although many cases of infection were reported, the death toll remained low. Those who had been infected were urged to stay in bed and to avoid coughing in front of others. 'Effective preventive measures' simply did not exist, beyond the use of calcium chloride as a substance to aid bodily resistance.[14]

In Mannheim, whether theatres, cinemas or other 'places of entertainment' should be closed caused a major dispute. On 17 October 1918 the town council discussed the decision of the local council of health that not only schools, but places of entertainment should be closed as well. General agreement was reached that the depressed spirits of the population should not be lowered even more and it was decided to address an inquiry to the district office,[15] the very body that had announced the measure originally.[16] Apparently the town council appealed to the Ministry of the Interior at the same time. In response, *Ministerialdirektor* Karl Weingärtner sent a telegram to the district office on 19 October giving official orders to revoke this regulation. The repeal of the order[17] after only one day infuriated the *Gesellschaft der Aerzte* (Society of Physicians) at Mannheim, which declared:

> The plague has increased in extent and virulence to a great degree. The doctors are near exhaustion. The hospitals are overcrowded, the nursing staff tremendously overburdened. However, after a break of one single day the advertising boards invite the population to come together to all sorts of meetings or amusements, which is the best way to further spread the epidemic.[18]

Yet the town council would not change its stance,[19] but the protesting physicians finally convinced the district office to have the order reinstated in November.[20] This victory did not last long, however.[21]

In southern Baden a medical initiative was taken by the Catholic Church. There, due to the 'multiple infections', the archiepiscopal authorities began to organise training in nursing for the staff of *Caritas* (a Catholic welfare organisation). 'Young girls' so trained were to visit the patients at home in their own respective communities.[22] It can be assumed that this appeal was widely followed, for in September 1920 an anonymous physician complained in Baden's General Medical Council journal about overzealous 'Catholic nurses' exceeding their competence and being a nuisance to rural doctors.[23]

How did medical science in Germany and in Baden respond to the epidemic? Even before the outbreak of the influenza epidemic, there was confusion about the disease. The term 'pseudo-influenza' was generally used for an unspecified 'infection similar to influenza',[24] while Wilhelm Hildebrandt, a clinician from Freiburg serving in the wartime army, declared in 1919 that 'influenza had spread extensively at least since 1916'.[25] Once the epidemic itself struck in 1918, an intensive search for the causative organism began, and several articles appeared with the title: 'Influenza bacillus discovered'.[26] The Heidelberg hygienist, Hermann Kossel, maintained at a meeting of the *Naturhistorisch-medizinischer Verein zu Heidelberg* (Heidelberg Society for Natural History and Medicine) on 16 July 1918 that the test material contained streptococci, staphylococci and pneumococci,[27] a position which coincided with the findings of many of his colleagues.

The confusing nomenclature was deplored by Gustav von Bergmann, a clinician from Marburg, as early as 27 November 1918. To a meeting of the *Aerztlicher Verein zu Marburg* (the Marburg Physicians' Society) he pointed out that the infection had generally been called 'influenza' during the years of 1889–92, whereas in 1918 it was being called 'grippe'. It was a fact, however, he maintained, that the 'Spanish disease' and the 'grippe' were identical, and that the latter was identical to 'influenza'.[28] At a meeting of the same organisation on 18 December, Bergmann went even further and argued that the term 'influenza bacillus' could not be replaced by the term 'Pfeiffer's bacillus', as proof of the specific pathogenicity of Pfeiffer's bacillus had not been furnished.[29]

Richard Pfeiffer himself and his colleagues at Breslau were forced onto the defensive. Yet they continuously kept up their claim that the causative microbe of the 'Spanish flu' was Pfeiffer's influenza bacillus.[30] The head of the Robert-Koch Institute in Berlin, Fred Neufeld, also supported the thesis of this 'aetiological role of Pfeiffer's bacillus'.[31] But his was a diplomatic answer to the persistent question as to what really was the causative agent. Nobody was keen on overturning a theory that medical science had accepted since the late 1890s. As Otto Leichtenstern had put it in 1892, 'The leading discipline in the aetiology of acute infectious diseases, bacteriology, has solved – as we can see – the difficult problem of finding the specific causative agent (of influenza) after long and futile attempts.' He had looked forward when he had argued that, 'If the "Bacillus influenzae" that R. Pfeiffer discovered in 1892 proves to be the sole pathogen of influenza in the future, as we all expect it to be, then this discovery will be the most important triumph of our contemporary influenza period.'[32]

But this expectation was obviously disappointed by the events of 1918–19. Doubts were formulated by different medical scientists: for instance, in 1919 Bernhard Möllers declared:

> It is true that the Pfeiffer bacillus has been found in various cases of sputum and pus of those with flu and in different organs and tissue liquids of corpses and that it has been produced in pure culture. But these cases contradict other ones, where even trained observers could not find the Pfeiffer bacillus at all or only scarcely, although they worked exactly following the rules.

Möllers' ambivalent conclusion was that, 'Not to find the bacillus is not a proof that the bacillus is not the pathogen of the flu.'[33] Other physicians and specialists were not as tactful as Möllers. But nobody could then answer the basic question from their own research.

In 1921 the pathologist Carl Fahrig highlighted a further problem that the bacteriologists could not answer – whether a person who died from pneumonia had in fact been a case of influenza.[34] But he had to concede that even pathologists were unsure of the answer.

The belief that the often fatal complication of influenza was in fact a 'pest of the lungs' and not an 'inflammation of the lungs' was expressed more than once.[35] In general, the medical profession denied these assumptions, but some members declared their support for the idea, either because of pneumonia's rapid course,[36] or because the dead bodies sometimes turned black.[37]

The debate on why exactly the epidemic proved so lethal to 'the robust' was dominated by the Fischer–Grabisch controversy. The 26-year-old physician, Albert Wilhelm Fischer[38] from the University of Halle, argued that young adults demonstrated particularly violent reactions of the immune system and that the sudden lysis of the bacteria would swamp the body with toxic substances.[39] Alfons Grabisch, an assistant physician at the clinic for skin and venereal diseases at the University of Kiel, retorted that the young and strong had a deficient immune system because the infectious germs, which – as antigens – would have stimulated the production of antibodies, had not fully infected their bodies before.[40] Others pointed out that the number of pregnant women who died was extremely high. The most plausible explanation offered was their increased susceptibility to infections as a result of their changed condition.[41] But this immunological argument remained one among several in debates that ultimately produced no solutions.

What conclusion can be drawn from these numerous conflicting theoretical approaches? An evidently complex reaction was a paradox in terms of traditional bacteriology. 'Virus' became the crucial term. As van Helvoort has observed, this term did not possess the same meaning in 1918 as today. Its conception remained on the bacteriological level.[42] Initially, 'virus' had implied nothing but a 'poison', i.e. a toxic pathogen. The research on the 'virological' character of this 'poison' in 1918–19 was not a starting point for virology as a scientific discipline.[43] The first level of the discussion revolved around the question as to whether *haemophilus influenzae* was the specific causative organism. The thesis of *Mischinfektionen* (concurrent infections) dominated the second level. The lethal factor in the infection was unambiguous: pneumonia. Obviously, the pathogen reaction was for the most part toxic. 'Secondary germs', mostly streptococci, were held responsible for the toxicity. Epidemiological thinking at the third level was dominated by speculation about an 'invisible filterable virus',[44] the infectious agent which was accompanied by a secondary germ, a streptococcus for instance. Different terms for the imaginary discoveries circulated. The hygienist, Walter Kruse, from Leipzig, called the new pathogens 'aphanozoae'.[45] Heinrich Prell from Tübingen coined the term 'aenigmoplasma influenzae'.[46] The last level in the aetiological discussion within the German-speaking area was reached by Hermann Sahli, with his theory of a 'complex virus'. This clinician from Berne elaborated the following explanation: with concurrent infections, the different germs reacted symbiotically, infiltrating the human cells jointly, with Pfeiffer's bacillus being 'primus inter pares'.[47]

Many critics among the medical epidemiologists dismissed this whole bacteriological debate on aetiology and instead supported the 'Bergmann-dictum' ('the Spanish disease is influenza vera') and sought recourse in the pre-bacteriological, historical–geographical pathology of the sort August Hirsch had pursued. Even the terms '*Ziep*' and '*Pips*' reappeared.[48] This was a convenient way to resurrect traditional concepts.

Along with aetiology, the second priority in the theoretical discussion focused on phenomena of the central nervous system. Initially in 1918, the relatively low mortality rate still permitted influenza to be categorised as a mere 'fashionable disease'.[49] Of course, this is a traditional attitude in regard to the history of influenza, which simply encourages ignorance towards the epidemic, which is characterised as merely a 'psychological' problem, not a disease.[50] In autumn 1918 this attitude towards the flu could not be maintained any more. Many serious cases occurred with the nervous system being affected. Many epidemiologists pointed out that this phenomenon was a constitutive element in former influenza epidemics. Moreover, the question was raised whether flu could thus become a chronic disease. Having studied 'nervous phenomena' since the beginning of the century, Willy Hellpach, psychologist, physician and politician from Karlsruhe, forcefully suggested the term '*Nervengrippe*' at the beginning of 1919.[51] As a result, from the frequent occurrence of a specific 'sleepy sickness' following the flu, especially in 1920, 'encephalitis choreatica' or 'encephalitis lethargica' were mentioned more and more.[52] However, Constantin von Economo, a Viennese neurologist who had first described 'encephalitis lethargica' in 1917, always rejected the idea of equating influenza encephalitis with the disease he had discovered.[53]

Far removed from these theoretical debates, at the level of the individual medical practitioner, two principal approaches to the influenza epidemic can be distinguished, a conservative therapeutic approach, as against a more aggressive form of treatment. The latter was the approach adopted by doctors who wanted to apply a specific regimen. Numerous means were chosen to combat the toxic pathogen. Shortly before the war, Julius Morgenroth, a scientist from Berlin, and his colleagues had discovered the chemotherapeutic effect of certain quinine alcaloides on cocci.[54] Thereafter three quinine derivatives were employed against pneumonia and pyothorax, Optochin, Eukupin and Vuzin (i.e. Ethylhydrocupreine, Isoamylhydrocupreine and Isooctylhydrocupreine). All three of them were meant to be effective against streptococci and staphylococci. Optochin was introduced onto the market in 1913, Eucupin in 1916 and Vuzin in 1917.

Optochin, which was said to be a bactericide in regard to pneumococci, was generally known to cause blindness. The German army prohibited the drug in July 1917.[55] However, in 1918, in view of the large number of lethal pneumonia cases resulting from influenza, many doctors – according to their personal preferences – decided to use Optochin or Eukupin, with Vuzin becoming more commonly used in 1920.[56] Frequently these were combined with other drugs. Wide use was also made of serotherapeutics, with convalescent serum being very popular.[57] At Karlsruhe, Ernst Riese was one of the proponents of the use of *Antistreptokokkenserum Höchst* against streptococci,[58] but other, unspecified sera such as the diphtheria serum were used as well.[59] In toto, the aggressive therapy contained a strong experimental element. The principle of 'polypragmatism' was applied: try anything!

The more conservative therapeutic approach favoured by other doctors was in full conformity with the administrative policy of the prohibition of meetings. As the transmission of influenza resulted from droplet infection, a fact that was generally known, the population was urged not to cough at each other and, where possible, meetings of larger groups were restricted. Apart from these two preventive measures, doctors and nurses had recourse to symptomatic general treatment or to traditional home remedies. Digitalis, caffeine, camphor, strychnine and the like were prescribed to stimulate heart and circulation. Internal disinfection (numerous iodiferous and formalin drugs) was added to external disinfection. Furthermore, a great number of antipyretics (such as Antipyrin, Salipyrin and Pyramidon) were used. A number of completely different medications were generally given: some doctors tended to opt for compressions against suppurative foci,[60] others had absolute confidence in the stimulating effect of alcohol, be it 'old sherry'[61] or 'new wine',[62] while some even recommended beetroot,[63] triggering a 'rush for beetroots' in Pforzheim.[64] And, in order to counter 'polypragmatism', some doctors argued strongly against aggressive therapy. Among them was Ignaz Zadek, a Berlin physician. Zadek recommended one major therapy: if the trachea was affected, the patient should sit in an arm-chair or similar furniture – i.e. sitting vertically – because it was better not to sleep in bed so as to prevent pneumonia or empyema.[65]

However, 'light forms' of the disease did not need a doctor and merely required bedrest and a strengthening of the body's defences. A symptomatic and general approach was, however, unsuitable for serious pneumonia. According to the prevalent medical theory, 'bad cases' demanded a specific remedy, in which case physicians did not waste time by focusing their therapy on the *haemophilus influenzae*, but rather on the secondary germs.

Yet, as the leading German clinicians admitted in 1920, a regimen of specific drugs had proved ineffective as far as 'the most serious cases' were concerned.[66] Indeed, they were probably rather detrimental in their effects. In short: in case of serious complications, patients could either agree to general, unspecific treatment, or expose themselves to dubious experiments, or rather pin their hopes on fate.

Taken overall, the German medical response at all four levels – the national, the provincial, the municipal and the individual – was, in the midst of the war effort, largely able to do little more than oversee the epidemic. A national health policy did not yet exist beyond that of the activities of the medical police. The expression *Gesundheitspolitik* (health policy) was coined – at least for Germany – by Alfons Fischer, a physician and social hygienist at Karlsruhe.[67] His great influence in favour of a 'policy of social hygienics' in Weimar Germany, as it was propagated by Julius

Moses,[68] did not yet exist in 1918–19, at least in the test case of the influenza epidemic. Documentary evidence does not indicate whether the epidemic played a dominant role in shaping Fischer's thinking. Another social hygienist at Baden, Ernst Kürz, did reflect on the epidemic, however. In 1920 he suggested a fundamental reform of Baden's health system, calling for the employment of so-called *Distriktärzte* (district physicians) having civil service status and for the establishment of elected health councils at all levels.[69] By and large, however, such calls went unheeded. During the last year of the First World War, the subsequent German revolution and the beginning of the Weimar republic, the term 'flu' was quickly overwritten, mentioned at best only when a speaker did not turn up because he was sick.

Physicians were not keen on creating an 'influenza monument', for it would have symbolised their 'shame' about their helpless medical–scientific community, mostly dominated by bacteriological thinking. Nor, as far as public health politics were concerned, is there much to be reported. Like the medical profession, politicians certainly did not want to remember the epidemic, for there was nothing significant worth mentioning in this regard.

These attitudes contributed to the 'mentality of forgetting', as Crosby described it.[70] The majority of the medical profession, together with the politicians and government public health officials, hoped that oral evidence would not survive for very long in a literate society and wrote about the influenza epidemic only when medicine and politics could not cope with the situation. A public discussion was not desired, the public was to be quiet.

Ultimately, diseases are experienced individually. For a common perception of an epidemic, society needs an enduring image recalling the existence of the epidemic phcnomenon. Yet, as Walter Benjamin put it, a crucial element of progress is memory's capacity to leave behind the ruins of the past.[71] If, for instance, in its 'progress', medicine ignores an inglorious plague episode, it is perhaps possible that history will forget it. In large measure, this is what happened to the influenza epidemic in its immediate aftermath, and ever since.

4 'You can't do anything for influenza'

Doctors, nurses and the power of gender during the influenza pandemic in the United States

Nancy K. Bristow

In the autumn of 1918, student nurses at Fort Des Moines answered a call to service, joining the fight against epidemic influenza then raging in the American midwest. Recording the experiences of her classmates for the school yearbook, one student, Mabel Chilson, recalled the resolve with which she and her cohorts faced the dreaded disease. 'We wondered, "were we helpless or could we fight?" With eager determination we entered the ranks.'[1] Once at work, according to Chilson, the nurses 'soon became the happiest family, and when off duty we had jolly good times. The greatest comfort we possessed was the knowledge that each girl was doing her best and making good as a nurse.'[2] Though challenged by the epidemic, Chilson and her colleagues found in their work confirmation as women and as nurses.

As they enrolled in the struggle against the epidemic, these nurses responded to a desperate need. When the influenza epidemic had reached the United States a few months earlier, it had struck a nation whose store of both nurses and doctors had been significantly depleted as a result of the war effort.[3] Their forces drained by the needs of the war, healthcare professionals like Chilson now faced the most serious epidemic in the nation's history. Though influenza was a familiar yearly visitor, this manifestation was different from its predecessors in horrifying ways.[4] Striking with a pace previously unimaginable, in the autumn of 1918 influenza sometimes killed patients within hours and prostrated cities within days. Only weeks after its appearance, the epidemic had infected even the most isolated communities of the United States.[5] Spreading quickly, this virus was also shockingly lethal. By its end, the epidemic had claimed well over 500,000 victims in excess of influenza's usual toll.[6] Its victims, too, were unusual. Though influenza was sometimes deadly, it commonly struck hardest among the very young and the very old. This time, though, influenza attacked young adults, those usually best able to weather severe cases of influenza, with special virulence.[7] And finally, while deaths were traced to a range of causes, common symptoms were frequently frightening, including, for instance, discoloration of the extremities, laboured breathing, a bloody or sputum-ridden cough and a face shaded to blue or purple, the last a result of patients drowning in their own bodily fluids.[8]

In the context of this ghastly disease and its epidemic incarnation, Nurse Chilson's positive response to her experiences is noteworthy, made all the more so by the extent to which other nurses recorded similar reactions. Mabel Chilson's sense of satisfaction with nursing efforts during the epidemic was mirrored in the diaries, letters and more public published accounts of nurses throughout the United States. Though acknowledging the horror of the disease and the wretched state of its victims, nurses often recounted their experiences in the epidemic positively, emphasising the opportunity it held for meaningful ministration.

Doctors and nurses worked together closely during the epidemic, and yet most accounts by doctors reflected no similar sense of satisfaction. 'You can't do anything for influenza,' one medical man still conceded years later.[9] Ignorant of the disease's aetiology, uncertain of the best methods of treatment, and unable to halt the expanding epidemic, physicians more often expressed a sense of helplessness as individuals and of humility as members of a profession.

That doctors and nurses could react so differently to their shared work during the epidemic requires explanation. By 1918, healthcare in the United States was the province of two distinct professions – medicine and nursing – and each of these professions was defined, at least in part, by the presumed gender identity of its practitioners. The medical profession had become an almost exclusively male preserve, with nursing the acceptable alternative for women. As doctors and nurses responded to the epidemic in 1918 then, they did so in the context of a sex-segregated medical system in which gender shaped both the roles and the responsibilities of healthcare providers. Presenting doctors and nurses with vastly divergent standards by which to measure their achievements, it is this gendering of the healthcare professions that best explains the different reactions expressed by doctors and nurses to their experiences during the epidemic.

Medicine had not always been so clearly the province of men. In the early years of the American colonies, care of the ill was shared by men and women.[10] By the late eighteenth century, though, a growing number of physicians began to imagine themselves members of a more exclusive profession, basing this identity on formal education.[11] It was in this context that male practitioners of medicine moved to exclude women from the profession.[12] During the nineteenth century the struggle over professional identity persisted. 'Regular' physicians, those associated with the allopathic medicine that today dominates medical practice in the United States, faced enduring competition from a variety of directions – from Americans who continued to trust lay providers to adherents of competing forms of 'irregular' medicine that included practices ranging from diet therapy to hydropathy and homeopathy.[13] In this context, both men and women continued to play prominent roles in healthcare provision.[14] By 1918 though, the 'regulars' had consolidated their power in the medical profession and had established for themselves a position of prestige in American life. At the same time, they had succeeded in eliminating all but a few women from the practice of medicine.[15] As male practitioners developed a professional identity over the course of the nineteenth century, then this identity was increasingly associated with the doctor's masculinity.[16]

This change was accompanied by parallel developments in the field of nursing. In the closing years of the nineteenth century, nursing, like medicine, professionalised.[17] Yet nursing's emergence from a domestic responsibility to a paid profession did nothing to change its identification as a 'woman's job'.[18] The emergence of the nursing profession, however, did have significant implications for the place of women in medicine. As the historian Mary Walsh explains,

> The existence of nursing clearly reinforced the notion that only men should become doctors. If women were interested in medicine, the argument went, nursing was the natural vehicle by which they could realise their objectives. The result was a neat division of responsibilities: men would cure the patients through surgery and medicine; women would provide care and maintenance – the traditional female 'nurturing' role.[19]

By the time of the flu epidemic, these gendered notions of American healthcare were firmly established, and provided the standards by which Americans, both caregivers and laypeople alike, would judge the performance of doctors and nurses.

When the epidemic struck in 1918, Americans immediately expressed their faith in the power of modern medicine and its practitioners to protect them from serious harm. 'There seems to be no occasion for special alarm or panic about the matter', one newspaper editor explained in October 1918, 'for the disease is evidently one which the American medical profession is perfectly able to handle.'[20] As evidence of their confidence in the efficacy of modern medicine and the proficiency of its practitioners, Americans granted the medical profession significant power to determine what measures should be taken to combat the epidemic.[21]

Though public health boards and politicians sometimes downplayed the seriousness of the epidemic, physicians soon recognised the 'scourge' influenza represented, and the challenge its epidemic incarnation represented.[22] Facing an epidemic unprecedented in its power, physicians were forced to admit how little they understood about influenza. Throughout the epidemic, medical authorities ranging from the United States Surgeon General to those physicians publishing in the *Journal of the American*

Medical Association were forced to concede that the 'causative agent' for influenza remained a mystery.[23] Uncertain of the cause of the initial illness, doctors were similarly unable to explain the secondary infections that accompanied influenza and which were often responsible for patients' deaths.[24]

With no clear understanding of the aetiology of the disease, doctors found a cure elusive, though not for lack of effort on the part of American scientists.[25] Many doctors directed their hopes and their energies toward the development of a flu vaccine.[26] Not knowing the cause of the disease, however, scientists' search for a cure was bound to prove fruitless. By November 1918 the editors of the *Journal of the American Medical Association* were cautioning Americans against placing their faith in vaccines.[27] The United States Public Health Service soon agreed, warning Americans about the potential danger associated with the vaccines and acknowledging that no cure was yet available.[28]

Confounded by both the disease and the epidemic, doctors increasingly conceded their inability to affect either one. Noting the heated disagreements pitting doctor against doctor, one physician acknowledged the inadequacy of medical knowledge these disagreements reflected:

> It was freely confessed by all that we are at sea as to the proper methods of treatment, cure and prevention; that we do not know as yet how to prevent and control the spread of the disease, and that most of the methods employed in fighting it, though pronounced efficacious by some of their adherents, have been held of little value by others.[29]

Stating it more simply, as one doctor did, 'There was just nothing you could do.'[30]

Incapable of stopping either the disease or the epidemic, doctors often confessed that there was little they could really offer their patients. As one physician recalled, 'There wasn't much a doctor could do. The patient would be dead before he could get back to see him ... I guess the coffin makers were the ones who were busy at that time.' And further, 'The main thing of visiting every day was to find out who was dead and then bury them.'[31] Helpless before the disease, some physicians concluded that their medical efforts were pointless. 'Listening to the testimony of many health officers that their efforts to combat the disease seemed of no avail, no matter what they did', one doctor wrote in late 1918, 'One almost came to the conclusion that our struggle against the epidemic is futile.'[32] Some doctors even worried that their efforts to work with the sick might do more harm than good.[33] In this context, some doctors concluded, 'The best thing that the physician can do for the patient is to leave the patient alone.'[34]

For many this sense of powerlessness was completely unexpected.

Certain about the utility of germ theory, confident in their scientific methods and proud of recent successes in the field, many doctors had, by the early twentieth century, developed a belief in the ability of medicine to handle any scourge.[35] As one account explained shortly after the epidemic, 'The most astonishing thing about the pandemic was the complete mystery which surrounded it.... Science, which by patient and painstaking labor has done so much to drive other plagues to the point of extinction has thus far stood powerless before it.'[36] Influenza appeared to defy the gains made by science and the mastery over disease it had recently claimed.

Confronted with the reality that this epidemic was beyond their control, many physicians expressed a new sense of the limitations of their profession. One observer argued that 'existing medical knowledge has been at fault in the present epidemic', while another described 'the total bankruptcy of the present health administrations in the country'.[37] While some physicians continued to maintain the efficacy of their work during the epidemic, such reactions were rare.[38]

Far more common were expressions of horror, accompanied by disappointment and humility, reactions that sometimes reflected a meaningful change in an individual's personal or professional self-image. 'It is disappointing that the Epidemiologist was helpless before the great epidemic of influenza', one practitioner lamented. 'Such barriers as we tried to throw in the way of its spread were swept away as chaff before a mighty tempest.'[39] Disappointed in the performance of the profession, some practitioners chose to criticise medicine for its arrogance. One physician published a piece entitled 'A General Confession by the Public Health Authorities of a Continent', and in it quoted Victor C. Vaughan, a leading epidemiologist, who admitted, 'The saddest part of my life was when I witnessed the hundreds of deaths of soldiers in the army camps and did not know what to do. At that moment I decided never again to prate about the great achievements of medical science and to humbly admit our dense ignorance in this case.'[40] Having once maintained the heroic image of medicine, this leader in the field exchanged his former celebration for a cautious humility.

For some, including Vaughan, the reaction to the epidemic, and to medicine's failure to check either the disease or the epidemic, was quite personal, and promised to haunt them long after the tragedy of the epidemic had passed. Recalling images he knew he could never forget, Vaughan wrote in his memoirs:

> I see hundreds of young, stalwart men in the uniform of their country coming into the wards of the hospital in groups of ten or more. They are placed on the cots until every bed is full and yet others crowd in. The faces soon wear a bluish cast; a distressing cough brings up the blood stained sputum. In the morning the dead bodies are stacked

about the morgue like cord wood. This picture was painted on my memory cells ... in 1918, when the deadly influenza demonstrated the inferiority of human inventions in the destruction of human life.[41]

Others agreed that they would never forget the frightful sights of the epidemic, or their own inability to control it.[42] Mystified by the disease and unable to slow the epidemic or save their patients, doctors found mostly disappointment in the epidemic, and often recalled it as an exercise in horror and humility.

Working alongside doctors, nurses often shared in the sense of aversion as they witnessed the destruction caused by the epidemic, and agreed that these images were ones that would stay with them forever. As one nurse, Anna C. Jamme, recalled her first visit to a military flu ward, 'From the moment I left the train I saw that terrible look of horror in the face of everyone whom I met. . . . The wards were quiet with the stillness of death. . . . It was a spectacle never to be forgotten.'[43] While acknowledging just how dreadful the epidemic had been, Jamme's reaction to what she saw, and the impact it had on her understanding of her profession, were quite different from those expressed by many doctors. Describing nurses who 'stood to their tasks like brave soldiers' and detailing the appreciation her nurses received from commanding officers, Jamme articulated her admiration for the 'splendid work' of nurses during the epidemic.[44]

Others, too, shared this response. 'The happy memories of the epidemic are many', wrote Eunice H. Dyke. 'The list of treasured experiences', she concluded, 'is long.'[45] Though few were as effusive as Dyke, nurses' memories of the epidemic, at least those they recorded, were rarely as wholeheartedly negative as those of physicians. While most shared the doctors' sadness, and even revulsion, at the suffering and dying they witnessed, this dismay was often coupled with more positive associations with this period in their lives.

That nurses were able to remember their work during those months so much more positively reflects how differently from physicians they understood what they had accomplished during the epidemic, an understanding closely linked to their notions about nursing and about womanhood. Perhaps most significantly, nurses frequently felt they had been able to do a great deal of good during the scourge, providing meaningful service to their patients. Often the nurses' sense of accomplishment reflected a success as simple as providing basic comfort. Describing the work of a Red Cross nurse in the mountains of Virginia, one account detailed how important basic caregiving was, asking, 'Can you imagine what it meant to those people ... to have a capable, willing woman appear suddenly in their midst, and without any preliminaries set to work and make them comfortable – a veritable angel of mercy in a cap and apron.'[46] For nurses, simply to provide comfort was an accomplishment, and one worthy of angels.

Other accounts celebrated even greater accomplishments, suggesting that these simple acts played an important role in the patients' survival.[47] As Clara D. Noyes, Acting Director of the Red Cross Department of Nursing suggested, 'The work required of the Nursing Service was at this time stupendous.... The death total was enormous, over 400,000 in the United States. What it might have been without an organized Nursing Service would be impossible to state.'[48] Nurses did not suggest that they had cured influenza or stopped the epidemic; they did, however, feel that their ministrations had proven useful, and had contributed in a meaningful way to patients' well-being.

Their work during the epidemic, nurses seemed to suggest, had demonstrated both the importance and the quality of nursing in the United States, and so nurses left the epidemic with a heightened view of their profession. One nurse explained:

> I think we are apt to consider the wonderful work of our pioneer nurses, and feel that we in this commercial age are not developing in the profession, women of the same capabilities, of the same devotion to an ideal and with the same nursing spirit. If we have ever felt this our experiences of these last two years and particularly during the epidemic will renew our faith and give us courage to go on.[49]

Proud of their profession, nurses' personal reactions to the epidemic were often markedly positive. 'I am so glad to find that I can help', one volunteer nurse proclaimed.[50] Others, too, professed their happiness in being able to do the work of a nurse. Recounting the death of a volunteer nurse after only eight days, a Red Cross report emphasised the satisfaction the young woman had found in her work: 'In the last moments she stated she had obtained more joy from her work in the past eight [days] than she had in the twenty five years of her life.'[51] Overworked to a state of exhaustion and witnesses to terrible disease and death, nurses nevertheless embraced their experience in the epidemic. 'It was a most horrible and yet most beautiful experience', one woman explained.[52] Though deeply saddened, this nurse nevertheless also found beauty and nobility in her experiences during the epidemic.

As these accounts suggest, as healthcare providers thought about their experiences in the influenza epidemic, they held themselves accountable to gender-specific standards of professional performance. Men working as physicians measured themselves against the heroic masculine measures of medicine, expecting dominance, even mastery, over disease, and in the face of the epidemic experienced both personal and professional disappointment. In sharp contrast, women working as nurses measured themselves against the responsibilities of womanhood, demanding nurturance and support of their patients, and found themselves worthy, experiencing in their work, as a result, both personal and professional satisfaction.

Doctors' and nurses' interpretations of their gendered responsibilities, and their ability to fulfil those responsibilities, were reinforced by the reactions of the American public to their work during the epidemic. Though the epidemic ravaged the United States as it did the rest of the world in 1918 and 1919, citizens often lavished significant praise on both doctors and nurses for their efforts.[53] Much of this praise was gender-neutral, heralding heroic qualities shared by doctors and nurses alike. For instance, contemporaries commended the 'devotion to duty' exhibited by both doctors and nurses, and acknowledged the courage and nobility of those who endangered their own health as they cared for others.[54]

While both men and women were heroes, in many accounts the nature of their heroism, as described by their contemporaries, proved gender-specific.[55] Doctors, for instance, were often praised for the skill with which they fulfilled their responsibilities. Describing the contribution of doctors from Camp Crane in Pennsylvania, one account emphasised that these accomplished practitioners were male:

> The noble work accomplished by these officers not only checked the epidemic but saved thousands of lives.... Only by hard and skillful work were they able to save the large percentage of lives which they did. In all places where these men have been stationed the disease has been wonderfully checked.[56]

That the characteristic of expertise or skill was associated with doctors but not nurses was highlighted still more obviously in an editorial published during the epidemic in a small town newspaper in the Pacific Northwest. Describing an epidemic 'becoming worse instead of better', the newspaper noted the shared devotion of doctors and nurses. When the time came to herald the skill of practitioners, though, only doctors warranted this praise: 'The doctors and nurses are working overtime', it explained, 'and to the physicians too much credit cannot be given for the able manner in which they are combating the situation.'[57]

Though contemporaries rarely applauded nurses for their skill or their expertise, they were nevertheless ready to compliment the women in white for care imbued with feminine qualities. While both doctors and nurses were celebrated for dedication to their work, when shown by nurses this commitment was understood to be distinctly selfless in its quality.[58] As an article in the *Literary Digest* described this selflessness, 'In the fight against influenza ... devoted women have served in the front ranks and many of them, uninspired by the interest and honor that helped the dough-boy act the hero, have gone down to death, if not unwept, at least unsung.'[59] Understood to be driven not by a desire for glory but by a dedication to service, women were commended for their quiet commitment to duty.[60]

In caring for others, nurses were understood to be acting in distinctly feminine ways, and accounts often used familiar female imagery to describe their work, referring to nurses as 'ministering angels' or referencing the motherly quality of their care.[61] Emphasising the particularly feminine qualities of these women's work, a tribute to nurses at a military hospital explained, 'The hospital was started in the early days without nurses, but now includes this necessary and helpful and pleasant part of hospital life – the white gowned sister of mercy, who bring[s] not only healing and practical assistance to the sick, but an indefinable spirit of cheer that only womanhood can give.'[62]

In their expressions of praise for the work of doctors and nurses, commentators acknowledged different standards, gendered standards, by which these groups should be measured. When criticism came, it often reflected these same gendered notions. Having accepted medicine's claims to cultural authority, and having come to understand that authority as masculine in content, Americans expected doctors to live up to masculine standards of success, standards that called for complete mastery over disease. As physicians proved unable to control the epidemic, some Americans began to voice criticisms of the medical profession, criticisms that emphasised the failure of physicians to fulfil their masculine roles as skilful practitioners. In the pages of the *New York Times*, a pair of editorials in October 1918 clearly articulated these sentiments. The first, entitled rather boldly, 'Science has failed to guard us', opened with an attack on both science and its practitioners. 'When the history of this influenza epidemic comes to be written', it argued, 'it will not reflect much glory on medical science, or, to be more explicit and to recognize the great truth that responsibility is always personal, on the doctors in whom medical science is embodied.'[63] This editorial did not suggest that doctors had not cared about their work, or even that they had proven entirely incapable. Even so, the writer did not hesitate to reiterate his criticism that physicians had failed the American people.[64] A week later the same newspaper returned to this topic, noting what it viewed as the arrogance of a profession that had for too long trumpeted only its successes.[65]

The loss of public confidence in physicians' expertise soon led to a willingness to question their authority and to challenge their advice.[66] From the beginning some Americans had defied the cultural authority of allopathic medicine, suggesting that influenza and its epidemic incarnation needed to be understood from an entirely different perspective based not in science but in religion. For these opponents, medical treatments were meaningless because they attacked only symptoms, not causes, of the national emergency. For instance, Christian Scientists, who rejected both the 'materialistic therapeutics' of allopathic medicine and the theories of disease on which they were based, found in the epidemic's virulence, and traditional medicine's inability to control it, clear support for their position.[67] One soldier, aware of the losses from influenza among his fellow troops, wrote home to his mother and, acknowledging his own belief in 'the power of mind over matter', claimed, 'If every one could have the same faith in the Father-Mother God everything would be ... different I am thinking.'[68] For this Christian Scientist, a cure for influenza was available to all who would understand it appropriately. Other Americans shared with Christian Scientists the notion that religion, not medicine, offered the best guide to comprehending the epidemic, yet posed a rather different religious interpretation. Seeing in the epidemic the wrath of a God angry with a sinful world, for instance, the popular evangelist Billy Sunday proposed the use of public prayer to beat the epidemic.[69]

Still others worked outside organised religion, yet brought their own folk interpretations to bear on the epidemic. One American penned a letter to the Public Health Service suggesting that the service encourage the wearing of a red ribbon around the chest, because 'the Flu is the Devil and Devil don't work with Red'.[70] In New Orleans tradition led many locals to turn to voodoo, buying charms, 'anything from a white chicken's feather to an ace of diamonds for the left shoe', or the performance of an incantation, 'repeated three times a day when rubbing vinegar over the face and palms: "Sour, sour, vinegar – Keep the sickness off'n me."'[71]

If resorting to voodoo was an apparently dramatic divergence from the practices of allopathic medicine and from reliance on the authority and expertise of physicians, it was only an extreme example of the far more common tendency of Americans to fall back on folk remedies as the epidemic advanced. Throughout the country even Americans who subscribed to the basic belief in a scientific approach to health and disease turned to folk 'cures'.[72] One 'lover of our Boys' in Michigan recommended powdered lobelia, sprinkled on chests readied with olive oil for 'fine results'.[73] In South Chicago a Mrs Ann Olds Woodson offered 'the old woman's (octigenarian's [sic]) remedy' that involved two or three large, ripe red peppers, stewed at a boil for an hour or two with the windows and doors secured.[74] In Louisiana the superintendent of a Methodist hospital recommended a quilt made of wormwood, sandwiched between layers of flannel and dipped in hot vinegar placed on the chest of flu sufferers.[75] Other folk remedies ranged from the inhalation of smoke 'from wood or wet or damp straw or hay' to the burning of 'Coal Tar' to 'destroy *any germs*', from the consumption of pine pitch to asafoetida necklaces, from onion plasters to an onion diet, from abstinence from whisky to heavy doses of the same medicament.[76]

The number and range of alternative therapies posited by Americans during the epidemic suggest, perhaps, the desperation many people experienced as the nation struggled against a disease raging out of control. It also demonstrated some Americans' ready willingness to reject physicians and their allopathic medical training. If some Americans, such as Christian Scientists, dismissed altogether the power of medicine in curing disease, others accepted the intellectual framework of medicine – at least the notion that humans might intervene to fight disease and encourage good health – but rejected the hegemony of trained physicians. Advocates of folk medicine were one example of this challenge.

Private citizens intent on selling 'cures' to make a profit out of the epidemic were another example. Dr Kilmer's Swamp-Root promised to heal kidneys damaged by a bout of influenza, while Dr True's Elixir purported to 'ward off Grippe', and Dr Allen's Number Seven claimed to have met with 'universal success' in 52 years of preventing 'fever, influenza and pneumonia', even when taken by patients suffering from colds.[77] Demonstrating these companies' attempt to share the mantle of medical authority, many of the products bore the name of a doctor or offered the 'scientific' evidence of their efficacy as part of the sales pitch.

Attempting to establish their value through an association with allopaths and their methods, the patent medicine producers had little chance of displacing the physicians' authority. Other rivals offered a more comprehensive challenge in the form of alternative systems of medicine that shared the scientific method while discounting the pre-eminence of allopathy. Perhaps most notable was the threat seemingly posed by 'irregular' practitioners, members of those medical sects that had competed with the allopaths for dominance in American medicine. During the epidemic chiropractors, for instance, maintained that their treatments could protect Americans from the dangers of influenza. Determined to be taken seriously, one chiropractor, Julius C. Leve, made clear both his own scientific pedigree and that of his field: 'As a graduate Chiropractic of the Palmer School of Chiropractic, the leading and best equipped school of its kind in America, and with some years of practical experience, I can safely say: Were Chiropractic adjustments given these boys, many lives would have been saved and many diseases aborted in a short time.'[78] Accepting the masculine definition of medicine – that it had as its purpose the prevention and cure of disease – chiropractors challenged the allopaths' success in fulfilling that responsibility, and offered themselves and their theories of medicine as an alternative.

Determined to retain their cultural authority, many physicians continued to present themselves as experts, and described their abilities in opposition to the superstitions of the past.[79] In the midst of the epidemic, though, such claims rang hollow for many others, physicians and laypersons alike. Claims to expertise did little to counter the reality of a disease and an epidemic freely terrorising the nation. For many doctors the epidemic would always remain the low point in their professional lives, an historical moment in which they were forced to abandon the pride in their profession for an unwelcome humility caused by haunting memories of patients lost. And though the public would almost universally herald the devotion shown by physicians during the epidemic, their willingness to return to earlier folk remedies or to experiment with patent medicines and alternative therapies suggested a growing loss of confidence in the ability of allopathic medicine to fulfil its masculine claims.

That nurses escaped the damage to their personal and professional identities, and found in the epidemic instead a meaningful opportunity for service that only enhanced their confidence as women and as nurses, suggests how complete was the gendering of healthcare roles by the early twentieth century. Doctors, having established an almost exclusively male profession, had also embraced a set of standards for the profession that required them to exhibit what they understood to be the masculine qualities of skill and expertise, qualities demonstrated only when patients got well and diseases were cured. Nurses, on the other hand, relegated to a female profession, operated under a different set of what they viewed as female standards, expecting themselves to demonstrate qualities of self-lessness and compassion as they nurtured and cared for, rather than cured, their patients.

The epidemic did nothing to alter these gendered understandings of the healthcare professions and their practitioners. Ironically, in the aftermath of the epidemic, physicians persisted in defining their profession's responsibilities in masculine terms, and even used their failure during the epidemic as a justification for additional research monies to ensure that next time medicine would be ready to play its established role in mastering disease.[80] Though the epidemic was a medical catastrophe unmatched in its time, it did not have the power to alter established beliefs about men and women, or about their roles in American healthcare.

This limitation on the epidemic's cultural influence may provide a partial solution to one of the puzzles that has long interested historians of the epidemic in the United States. In the years following the epidemic, though Americans privately recalled its horrors, few memorialised the epidemic publicly.[81] Historians, most notably Alfred Crosby, have offered a variety of explanations for this silence, noting, for instance, the relative familiarity of epidemics in 1918, the peculiarities of the disease and the epidemic that allowed Americans to forget, the distractions of a war that overshadowed the epidemic in many Americans' minds, and the purposeful desire of many Americans in the aftermath to forget the horrors of both the war and the epidemic.[82] The story of doctors and nurses may offer an additional element to our understanding of this mystery. Neither gender norms, nor Americans' perceptions of the role of medicine and nursing, were changed by the epidemic. Though the epidemic was a monumental, even catastrophic, event, it simply did not affect how Americans viewed their world.[83]

Part III

Official responses to the pandemic

5 Japan and New Zealand in the 1918 influenza pandemic

Comparative perspectives on official responses and crisis management[1]

Geoffrey W. Rice

Introduction

Japan and New Zealand are both archipelagos on the Pacific rim, both volcanic in geology and both prone to earthquakes. Their topography is strikingly similar in some regions, and both countries normally get a lot of rain in the west. Yet the similarities stop there: the populations and cultures of these two island-states were and are very different. New Zealand in 1918 had a little over 1 million people, including about 50,000 Maori, the indigenous Polynesian inhabitants. The European population was predominantly British, Scots and Irish, scattered along the coasts or thinly inland. There were only four cities, small by European or North American standards; regional centres and market towns were very small even by British standards. Yet it was a well-educated, well-fed and materially advanced population; a colonial fragment of the most advanced European or 'western' societies of the time.[2] Japan, by contrast, was an ancient and complex culture, with a very different set of values and world-view. It had been isolated from the rest of the world for centuries, and opened to Western influences only from the mid-nineteenth century. Japan's rulers had quickly adopted Western science and technology, including medical science, and expanded its industrial and manufacturing capacity at an astonishing rate. Japan's army was modelled on that of Germany, as were its medical schools; its navy was modelled on Britain's Royal Navy, just as its railway network had been built mostly by British companies. Japan had beaten a major power in the Russo-Japanese War of 1904. Yet the bulk of its 57 million people in 1918 were still rice-growing peasants, even though its towns and cities were growing fast.[3]

Despite gross contrasts in the size and distribution of their populations, Japan and New Zealand had broadly similar experience of the 1918 influenza pandemic. The virus entered through major seaports, and was spread rapidly by well-developed railway and steamer services. The chronology of onset conforms to central-place theory in both countries, with larger towns and cities affected first, and smaller centres and country districts following later. Despite being in different hemispheres, Japan and New Zealand experienced their most severe phase of the 1918 flu in tandem, with peaks of mortality in November and a steep decline in deaths during December. Overall morbidity rates were fairly similar, estimated at 40 per cent in New Zealand and 33 per cent in Japan, but some of New Zealand's worst-affected localities had morbidity rates between 60 and 90 per cent. Japan suffered another wave of flu mortality in 1919, but New Zealand had no significant return of the deadly 'Spanish flu'. Most strikingly, Japan and New Zealand emerged from the pandemic with low death rates by world standards, 4.5 per 1,000 for Japan, 5.8 for New Zealand's European population. However, the death rate for New Zealand's indigenous Maori population was about seven times that of its European population.[4] Japan's death rate remains the lowest of all known Asian death rates in the 1918 pandemic, and the reasons for this are not obvious. We still do not know very much about China or Korea in the 1918 pandemic, which would provide the closest comparisons with Japan in terms of cultural values.

Responses to initial warnings

Both Japan and New Zealand had ample warning during September of the severe second wave of the 1918 influenza pandemic from cable services and overseas newspaper reports of alarming death tolls in France, Germany and North America. October brought yet more appalling news from London, Western Europe and South Africa. Australia imposed a strict maritime quarantine from 18 October 1918, but New Zealand did not.[5] Japan closed some ports to foreign vessels in October, but then relaxed the ban when it was obvious that a large-scale epidemic was already established. Health inspectors went to some lengths in Japan to establish how the influenza had arrived, and the culprit they finally identified was the *Hozan-maru* from Siberia, which had docked at Urashio.[6] But Japan's railway network made the port of entry irrelevant; the infection was spread very rapidly to all the major cities, and then spread outwards into country districts, like overlapping ripples in a pond. The same pattern of diffusion is evident in New Zealand, with Auckland as the main port of entry and the railways spreading it throughout the rest of the country. Returning troopships in October were the likely culprits, rather than the passenger liner *Niagara*, which most people blamed at the time.[7] In both Japan and New Zealand, health authorities were initially slow to respond to the potential threat; but once the epidemic broke out, they reacted quickly to organise and deal with it. In both countries, the rapidity with which the severe wave of the flu developed caught everyone by surprise; what seemed a 'normal' flu suddenly paralysed whole communities and began to kill people in astonishing and unprecedented numbers.

Resources

New Zealanders in 1918 would have regarded themselves as well provided with medical resources in the shape of hospitals, doctors and nurses, on paper at least. As part of the British Empire, the medical profession was organised as a branch of the British Medical Association, and the sole medical school at Otago University prided itself on keeping standards equivalent to those at Edinburgh. New Zealand had 985 medical practitioners on its register in 1918, or one for about every thousand of population.[8] But when the influenza pandemic reached New Zealand, nearly a third of these doctors were overseas, serving in the New Zealand Medical Corps or the British Army. There were 692 in the country, including retired doctors, and many of them came down with the flu – fourteen died. Nurses were also in short supply – more than a quarter had volunteered for overseas service, leaving 1,675 in the public hospitals, of whom thirty-seven died in the epidemic. New Zealand had sixty-five public hospitals in 1918, together with six mental hospitals, six state maternity hospitals, five TB sanatoria and four infectious disease hospitals. In addition there were over 250 private hospitals, mostly very small maternity homes. There were 4,000 beds available in the public hospitals and during the 1918 flu they recorded 7,399 admissions; but many thousands more patients were cared for in temporary influenza hospitals.[9]

Japan, by contrast, in 1918 had only 1,237 registered hospitals, 50,853 registered doctors and 33,534 nurses for a population of 57 million. As late as 1920, only two-fifths of these doctors were graduates of Imperial medical schools or Western-style colleges.[10] With a ratio of one doctor per 1,120 of the population, it is obvious that very few Japanese flu sufferers ever saw a doctor, or the inside of a hospital, or enjoyed the benefits of Western-based medicine. Most Japanese patients were nursed at home – there was simply nowhere else for them to go.

Central agencies

New Zealand's Department of Public Health in 1918 was the newest and smallest of its government departments. Established in 1900, it had grown rapidly, in parallel with the expansion of New Zealand's hospital system before the First World War. By 1918 it could boast (on paper) a national staff of 160; but this included part-time port health officers. Each large town had a District Health Officer and a staff of health inspectors, but head office staff before the war totalled just twelve. By 1918 it was down to eight: the Chief Health Officer, his deputy, two sanitary inspectors, three clerks and an office boy.[11] As we shall see, this tiny government department was simply overwhelmed by the 1918 crisis.

Japan's equivalent of the New Zealand Health Department in 1918 was the Central Sanitary Bureau of the Ministry of the Home Office. This is the name which appears on its annual reports, but some sources refer to it as the Bureau of Public Hygiene, or (misleadingly) as the Health Ministry. It appears to have been as small and rudimentary in 1918 as its New Zealand counterpart. Japan's official report on the flu epidemic disarmingly admits that nobody in the bureau could recall what had been done in the previous influenza epidemic of 1890.[12] So much for institutional memory! As in New Zealand, officials had no precedents or established procedures, and had to improvise as the epidemic worsened. Five inspectors were sent out to 'assess the degree of tragedy' in six prefectures in late October 1918, but the Bureau had to borrow three more inspectors from the Home Office to get reports from four more prefectures. (Japan was divided into forty-six prefectures, excluding Okinawa.) Port officials and quarantine stations were sent copies of overseas reports of alarming influenza mortality, and were simply asked to prevent the infection from entering Japan. The official notification of severe influenza on 23 October 1918 consisted mostly of these overseas reports, which it summed up in these words: 'The misery is appalling.' The notice urged all in authority to 'attend to the health of our nation' and to take suitable steps to prevent the spread of influenza, but gave no details of such measures. Directives were issued over the next few weeks giving more specific advice about treatment, but the Central Sanitary Bureau essentially left the local authorities to work out the details for themselves.[13]

Crisis management

New Zealand's Minister of Public Health in 1918, George Warren Russell, later told the Epidemic Commission that at one point the Health Department's Head Office was reduced to himself, Miss Maclean (assistant Inspector of Hospitals) and a cadet – 'with the whole country in flames'.[14] Both the Chief Health Officer and his deputy were on secondment to the Defence Department, and Dr T.H.A. Valintine (the Chief Health Officer) was overseas. Key health officers like Dr Joseph Frengley and Dr R.H. Makgill were quickly released by the army and came to Wellington to lend a hand, but Russell remained in charge, which was unusual for the political head of a government department. His style was autocratic and abrupt, so he managed to offend many civic leaders by blaming the epidemic on their failure to clean up the slums they had neglected in their towns. Yet Russell made sensible decisions under pressure and gave New Zealand decisive leadership at a time of crisis. Schools, theatres, cinemas and billiard halls were closed to prevent the spread of infection, but not hotels – it took a public outcry to force Russell to close the hotels as well. To avoid public panic, he ordered newspaper editors to suppress all mortality statistics; yet this had the opposite effect, and rumour magnified losses from tens to hundreds and even thousands of deaths.[15]

Russell's most important policy decision was to harness local resources

IN CASE OF ACCIDENTS.
The Citizens' Committee to the Rescue.

Figure 5.1 Cartoon satirizing anti-influenza measures.

Source: *New Zealand Observer*, 16 November 1918. Reproduced here with permission of Auckland City Libraries, New Zealand.

under local control. In a telegram sent to all civic leaders of boroughs and town boards on 12 November, he set out in clear concise language a scheme of local organisation to deal with the epidemic. The usual pattern of response was that the mayor would call a citizens' meeting to set up a relief committee, which usually included a spokesman for the local doctors, and representatives of the Red Cross and St John Ambulance

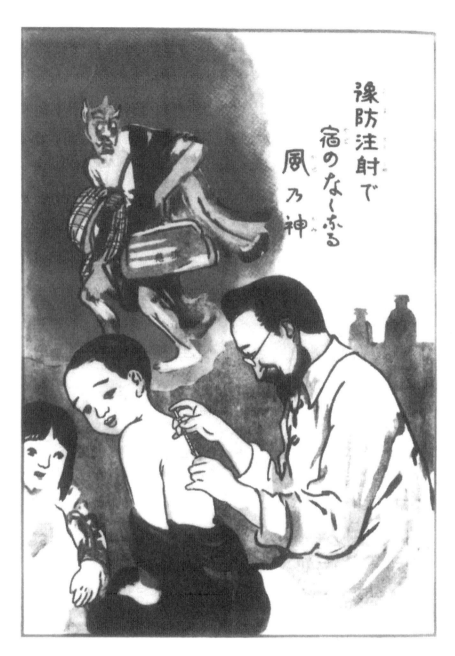

Figure 5.2 'By means of inoculation, the God of the Flu has nowhere to stay.' Japanese illustration of inoculation of children.

Source: *Ryūkosei Kanbō* [The Influenza Epidemic], Tokyo, Central Sanitary Bureau, 1922. Reproduced here with permission of the National Diet Library, Japan.

Figure 5.3 'Don't cough without covering your mouth. Flu is passed on like this!'

Source: *Ryūkosei Kanbō* [The Influenza Epidemic], Tokyo, Central Sanitary Bureau, 1922. Reproduced here with permission of the National Diet Library, Japan.

Associations. The town would be divided into blocks, with one doctor or nurse assigned to each block, to avoid overlapping and waste of time. (The system originated in Auckland, on the advice of Lieutenant-Colonel E. Jennings, a veteran of the South African War of 1899–1902, who had seen the block system used there in a diphtheria epidemic.) An appeal for volunteers and nurses would be made in the newspapers. New Zealand had a highly literate population in 1918 and every town of any size had its own newspaper. Large public notices were printed giving nursing instructions, or the location and telephone numbers of block depots where cases could be reported and medicines collected, but posters were not widely used in New Zealand, as nearly everyone had access to a daily newspaper. Once the blocks were defined, volunteers began door-to-door inspections, referring more serious cases to a doctor, or arranging a motor ambulance to remove the worst cases to the hospital. These two new technologies, telephones and the motor car, made it much easier for New Zealand to cope with the 1918 flu than it had with the 1890 flu epidemic.

What helped New Zealand most of all to cope with the 1918 flu was the fact that the country was on a war footing; the army provided equipment and personnel at short notice for many places in need, and the strong network of voluntary patriotic societies developed during the war quickly turned their energies to epidemic relief work. This was what enabled so many communities to organise so quickly. It might have been a very different story if the epidemic had struck in peacetime.

Japan had no equivalent of New Zealand's autocratic Minister of Public Health in 1918. We do not even know the names of the health bureaucrats, or the author of the official report on the epidemic. (It was probably Fujikawa-Yu.) Japan's official management of the 1918 flu crisis took place at the Prefectural level, where the police played a key role in informing the public of measures for prevention and treatment of influenza. The police were also responsible for gathering statistics of morbidity and death. As in New Zealand, the printed word was the main means of communication with the general public, but newspapers in Japan in 1918 were few in number and small in circulation; most people could not read their archaic Chinese characters. Posters and leaflets were mass-produced in 'simple characters' and distributed through the primary schools, advising complete bed-rest and plenty of fluids for flu sufferers. As in New Zealand, children in Japan seemed largely immune to the severe wave of the 1918 flu. Prefectural authorities went to great lengths to put up posters in public places such as cinemas, bath houses, post offices, railway stations and ferry terminals. In Osaka, the health authorities simply ordered the railway companies to put a poster in every single railway carriage, as well as putting up over 100 billboards around the city. In some places, officials used the intermissions during films and plays to give talks and distribute leaflets. In Saitama prefecture, the air base at Tokorozawa arranged an air-drop of leaflets in remote districts. In Fukui prefecture, officials commandeered motor cars to visit remote villages. The prevailing theme in posters and leaflets was 'self-help'. But there was no thought of closing cinemas, schools or theatres. In Tokyo, one police official remarked that authorities in Korea had banned all public gatherings, even for worship, and he sighed, 'But we can't do this in Japan.' One wonders why. Here at least is a clear contrast with official crisis management in New Zealand.[16]

Apart from the block system of household patrols, another distinctive feature of official responses to the 1918 influenza in New Zealand was the use of temporary hospitals or influenza wards set up in school or church halls. The rationale was that a doctor and a few nurses could thus keep an eye on a dozen or twenty cases at once, rather than exhaust themselves by travelling to see them in their homes. In the main centres, the first temporary hospitals were really overflow wards for the public hospitals, but in smaller towns lacking a hospital of their own, the temporary hospital was a key element in controlling the epidemic. Japan appears to have made little or no use of such temporary influenza hospitals.

Preventive measures and treatment

Japan's three main officially-sanctioned preventive measures against the 1918 flu were gauze masks, gargling and injections. Police were ordered to wear masks in twelve prefectures, and masks were made compulsory for all members of the armed forces during the epidemic. In many prefectures, schoolgirls were set to work mass-producing gauze masks, which were then distributed by the Red Cross, women's patriotic groups and the young men's associations, right down to village level. In some towns, people were not allowed on public transport or allowed to enter a theatre or cinema without a mask. Even to this day in Japan, it is common to see people on the street or on a subway train wearing a mask; it usually means they have a cold and do not wish to spread infection. This common practice probably originated in the 1918 pandemic.

Gargling was recommended by all the prefectural officers, and the Pharmaceutical Association was asked to prepare a standard solution which was distributed to all households. In some places, public gargling facilities were set up in local schools, offices and factories. Again, the effectiveness of this practice is uncertain, but it gave people something to do and helped keep public morale high.

The third official preventive measure which characterised the Japanese response to the 1918 flu was inoculation. Most of the Japanese medical articles published in English relating to influenza in the years 1919–22 were reports on inoculation. The Kitasato Institute in Tokyo marketed a variety of vaccines for use against typhoid, cholera and TB. Their influenza vaccine was adopted by the Health Service as its main weapon in the fight against the flu, and was mass-produced early in November 1918. Tokyo city set up thirty-three inoculation stations. Doctors who had been running a smallpox vaccination programme were transferred to the influenza campaign. Volunteers from the Tokyo Doctors' Medical Association gave free injections at night to the poor and the *burakumin* (outcasts). In Kanagawa the prefectural office claimed to have inoculated almost the entire population. Most of these vaccines were mixtures of attenuated pneumococci, streptococci and Pfeiffer's bacilli. Some doctors claimed remarkable results and, while useless against the influenza virus, they may have had some effect on the secondary pneumonic infections which were the real killers in 1918.[17]

Apart from advice to avoid crowds and keep windows open, the main officially-sanctioned preventive measure against the flu in New Zealand was the inhalation of an atomised spray of 2 per cent zinc sulphate solution. This method had been used in the military camps with some success during outbreaks of influenza and other respiratory ailments in 1916 and 1917, and was first used for the flu in Auckland in late October 1918. There were only a few sprayers in the country, of course, so the government ordered mass-production of a simple device by the railway workshops in the four main centres, and their distribution to country towns and block committees in the cities. As the only officially recommended preventive, people flocked to use the inhalation sprayers in great numbers, creating crowds and long queues at first, when there were only a few devices operating. There is a strong likelihood that this crowding together of anxious people did more to spread infection in the early stages than to prevent it.

Another officially recommended prevention reflecting uncertainty about the aetiology of influenza was disinfection of premises and clearing away of 'germ-producing rubbish'. Borough councils launched great clean-up campaigns, burning rubbish and spraying footpaths with disinfectant. Manufacturers of Jeyes Fluid, Pynetha, Brittol and Chloromenthene must have made huge profits that year. When supplies ran out, some smaller towns used sheep-dip to spray the streets – a characteristically New Zealand response!

One treatment first used in Auckland and then widely copied throughout New Zealand was the 'standard influenza remedy', produced in bulk by the hospitals and distributed through chemists and block depots. It was basically a strong expectorant cough medicine, containing alcohol, quinine and hydrochlorate of strychnine. Whatever it did for pneumonia, it was certainly a popular palliative. Over 30,000 bottles were distributed in Auckland alone, and one member of the Citizens' Committee remarked, 'It's amazing the quantity they get through'. No wonder – the pubs were shut!

Official urgings to use inhalation chambers and cough medicines probably reinforced the prevailing underestimation of the seriousness of influenza in New Zealand. Many people tended to regard it as they would a cold – something to be shrugged off as quickly as possible. Working men, acutely conscious that their families depended on their wages, got up too soon and struggled back to work, suffering relapses which could prove fatal in 1918. Newspaper cartoonists referred to 'fighting the flu' and likened it to a wartime campaign, so people got the idea that they should struggle and strive against it, rather than go to bed. Here is a strong contrast with Japan, where the official advice was to go to bed and stay there until you got better.[18]

Unofficial responses

It is all very well to set up block committees and temporary hospitals as official measures in crisis management, but the outcome for patients depends crucially on what is done by the staff in such places. There was enormous variation in the treatments used by doctors and in hospitals in both countries. Overall assessment of epidemic management has to take account of treatments both available and actually used. The most interesting contrasts between Japan and New Zealand in the 1918 pandemic emerge at the local level, indeed at the household level, and reflect major cultural differences, especially in the unofficial remedies adopted by ordinary people.

Whereas popular remedies in New Zealand were almost entirely futile, ranging from alcohol and tobacco to garlic and camphor bags (even sugar cubes soaked in kerosene), in Japan most households had access to herbal remedies that were effective in controlling the high fever associated with pneumonia, which was the real killer in the 1918 flu.[19] Traditional *kanpo* medicine has enjoyed a considerable revival in Japan in recent years; in 1918 it was still the mainstream of medical self-help, and cheap enough for all but the poorest households to keep a boxful of remedies. The standard charge for a boxful of *kanpo* bags in 1918 was 10 *sen*, or half the price of a bottle of cough mixture from a chemist. The system of deferred payment meant that it was easy for salesmen to persuade housewives to accept a box, so that most households would have had *kanpo* remedies on hand when the pandemic hit. The most commonly-used remedy for fever was *kakkonto*, a mixture of dried ephidrine, peony and ginger root. This is still widely used in Japan to ease headache, joint pain, nasal congestion and fever. Complete bed rest, *kanpo* remedies and plenty of green tea (which contains vitamin C) would have assisted Japanese flu sufferers far more effectively than the unofficial remedies used in New Zealand.

Ethnic minorities

Almost nothing is known about Japan's official policy towards its indigenous people, the Ainu, during the 1918 influenza epidemic; indeed, there may not have been one. Their care was probably left to local volunteers, as was that of such marginal groups as the homeless poor and *burakumin* (outcasts). In contrast, New Zealand's official responses to the epidemic showed considerable concern for its indigenous Maori population, or at least concern to prevent the spread of infection from Maori settlements to centres of European population. The Health Department printed thousands of pamphlets in Maori in early November, giving advice on the care of influenza patients, but their distribution was slow and erratic. Most Maori settlements were caught unawares by the severe wave of the epidemic, and death tolls were high in places where nearly every adult was stricken. Maori belief in *makutu* (magic) may explain the 'fatalism' observed by relief workers, where flu sufferers 'just turned their faces to the wall and died'. Not all Maori settlements had access to a *tohunga* (a priestly expert in spiritual and medicinal matters), but some of their remedies for fever were positively dangerous for pneumonia sufferers, such as being sent to sit in a sacred stream or pool. One official response, pursued with some vigour, was to prosecute *tohunga* for ritual treatments which Pakeha authorities regarded as little more than faith-healing.

Still mostly rural in 1918, and found mostly in the North Island, the Maori population (about 51,000) was much more susceptible to influenza than New Zealand's European population, largely because of lower standards of housing, nutrition and sanitation. Many smaller rural settlements were poverty-stricken from loss of land, and had few resources to cope with a crisis such as the 1918 flu.

Hospital board policies on the admission of Maori flu sufferers varied from place to place, some admitting all flu patients regardless of race while others set up temporary Maori flu hospitals. Only a few North Island towns refused to allow Maori into town, and such bans were short-lived, but travel restrictions were placed on Maori (as in the 1913 smallpox epidemic), which seriously disrupted the central Maori funeral ritual, the *tangi*. The Minister of Health instructed district health officers as early as 7 November that *tangi* and all such Maori gatherings were prohibited for the duration of the epidemic. Many Maori flu victims were buried beside the temporary hospital where they died and, as a result, some schoolyards, as well as churchyards, became *tapu* (sacred) and remain so to this day.

Official assistance to the Maori population included sending supplies of medicine and blankets to the worst-affected areas, and directing doctors and nurses to assist as the epidemic eased in towns and cities. Several Maori temporary hospitals were equipped by the army, and organised by army medical personnel. The Minister for Native Affairs, Dr Maui Pomare, led the relief effort after recovering from flu himself, and toured central North Island settlements – his car was described as a 'miniature pharmacy' on wheels. He also helped to organise a system of inspection to co-ordinate local relief efforts in Maori districts, but by the time this became effective, the worst of the epidemic was over. Official statistics grossly underestimated Maori mortality in the 1918 flu, partly because many deaths were registered late or not at all. Reports by police and relief groups paint a grim picture in some remote settlements, but overall the Maori death toll was about 2,160 or 4.2 per cent of the Maori population. Despite this loss, the population recovered quickly, and has continued to grow to the present day.[20]

Conclusion

Though we are forced to generalise, we must remember that country-by-country comparisons are very generalised indeed, and that national death rates conceal a host of extreme local variations. Japan and New Zealand, with such contrasting cultures and populations and medical services, such different official and unofficial responses to the crisis, nevertheless emerge with fairly similar national death rates, and similar national morbidity estimates. Perhaps that is the key: that both countries were more fully exposed by their advanced transport systems to the mild earlier wave of the 1918 pandemic, thus gaining a higher level of immunity to the deadly second wave, than peoples as unfortunate as those in South Africa or India, or Polynesia, which suffered the world's worst known death-rates in 1918.

6 Coping with the influenza pandemic

The Bombay experience[1]

Mridula Ramanna

Introduction

The British policy towards epidemics which repeatedly appeared in nineteenth-century India, was one of cautious intervention.[2] By the first decade of the twentieth century, there was limited acceptance of Western medicine and public health measures, and this was due to the presence of Western-educated Indian doctors in hospitals and dispensaries, most of which had been established with Indian initiative and funding. At the same time, Indian medicine and indigenous practitioners continued to be popular, because they were time-tested and less expensive.

This chapter examines the responses, both official and non-official, to the influenza pandemic of 1918–19, termed 'a national calamity' by the Sanitary Commissioner, Government of India.[3] Studies have shown that the death tolls from this epidemic was 17 to 18 million in the Indian sub-continent, more than all the military casualties sustained in the First World War.[4] The sickness first came to the city of Bombay in June 1918, and appeared in the United Provinces and the Punjab in July and August. The second outbreak, which occurred in September, was virulent in the Western, Central and Northern provinces of India. The British Government of India could barely cope and admitted the inadequacy of its medical organisation.[5] There was speculation about the causes and uncertainty regarding the treatment to be prescribed. Besides, medical practitioners were depleted in number, since many were away on war service. In such circumstances what efforts were made to combat the onslaught of the epidemic?

While government reports, in typical officialese, referred to the 'whole-hearted endeavours' of provincial administrations in providing relief, they also paid tribute to the non-official support. The Preliminary Report of the Government of India even declared loftily, 'Never before, perhaps, in the history of India, have the educated and more fortunately placed members of the community, come forward in such large numbers to help their poorer brethren in time of distress.'[6]

The focus in this chapter is on Bombay Presidency, based on an examination of the statements and actions of the public health officers in the cities and the reports of charity organisations. It shows how co-operation between the health officials and voluntary associations saved lives. In response to the appeal by the former, the latter raised funds, distributed medicines, set up temporary hospitals, and propagated the vaccine when it was made available. However, relief was not extended to the villages, because there was neither the infrastructure nor the resources. To most Indians in rural areas, who were left untended, the epidemic was seen as one more in the continual stream of epidemics that took more Indian lives than British. Yet a study such as this can be useful to an understanding of the way societies respond to epidemics of deadly diseases. The archival sources consulted include reports prepared by the Governments of India and Bombay, those filed by Health Officers, accounts left by voluntary agencies and private medical practitioners, and newspaper reportage.

The June 1918 outbreak

The incidence of an unusually widespread epidemic seems to have been first noted in the city of Bombay on 10 June 1918, when seven police sepoys, one of whom was working in the docks, were admitted to hospital, suffering from a non-malarial fever. The Health Officer, J.A. Turner, traced the day-to-day progress of the disease. Between the 15th, when workers of Messrs. W. & A. Graham & Co., a shipping firm, were affected, and the 20th, employees of the dockyard, the Bombay Port Trust, the Hong Kong and Shanghai Banking Corporation, the telegraph, the mint and the Rachel Sassoon Mills were struck down. Mortality began to increase suddenly from the 19th and, within 3 days, mass absenteeism was noted in offices and banks. Turner observed that Bombay, in June, was like a 'huge incubator, with suitable media, already prepared for the insemination of germs of disease', an overcrowded city with a large working-class population, living in conditions 'which lend themselves to the rapid spread of disease'.[7] From a daily mortality of ninety-two on 21 June, the figures rose to 230 on 3 July. The *Times of India* reported, 'Nearly every house in Bombay has some of its inmates down with fever and every office is bewailing the absence of clerks.'[8]

It is significant that, from the outset, differences of opinion regarding the source of the epidemic appeared within the colonial establishment. While Turner held that the crew of a ship which had docked had brought the fever to Bombay at the end of May, the Government of India claimed that the crew had contracted the fever in Bombay. This had been the characteristic response of the authorities, to attribute any epidemic that they could not control to India and what was invariably termed the 'insanitary condition' of Indians. Thus the Sanitary Commissioner, Bombay, Lieutenant-Colonel Hutchinson, believed that influenza was endemic to

India. It was also contended that there were cases in jails outside Bombay Presidency in 1917 and a local epidemic in Salsette in April 1918. Turner, on the other hand, pointed out that he had anticipated the disease as early as 1915, since Bombay was a port of arrival and dispatch for troops. Charges were traded between Turner and the Health Officer of the Bombay Port about the latter's failure to report cases. The vigilant local press commented on this negligence, the *Bombay Chronicle* contending that the city and the whole of India had paid 'dearly' for this neglect, while the *Times of India* castigated the failure of the Health Department, despite the *lakhs* (hundreds of thousands) of rupees spent on it.[9] Concern was also expressed in the Municipal Corporation over the suppression of information about the disease among personnel on military vessels.[10] On 20 June a hospital ship arrived in Karachi, and the majority of the patients developed influenza within 48 hours. Both in Bombay and in Karachi, it is unclear where the infection was contracted but, as Mills has observed, it is likely that the epidemic was introduced from outside.[11]

The June outbreak lasted 4 weeks, took 1,600 lives, and, in the words of Turner, 'at least a million working days, an incalculable amount of discomfort, expense and inconvenience'.[12] It was found that the epidemic was confined to those working indoors. The sickness rate in offices and mills was 25 per cent for Europeans, 33 per cent for Indians and 50 per cent for children. Turner observed that unlike cholera, smallpox and plague, where the causative agents were known and their spread could be controlled, influenza came 'like a thief in the night, its onset rapid, and insidious'.[13] In the rest of the Presidency, the infection was widespread in June and July, but as the case mortality was low, a marked rise over mean mortality was not found.[14]

The second epidemic

The second wave, which began in September 1918, was believed to have started in the Deccan and then travelled to the coast. It first appeared in the towns and soon spread to the rural areas. The authorities found it difficult to compile statistics, since influenza was not among the main heads under which mortality was recorded, and the reporting agency was 'for the most part ignorant of medicine and some [of those reporting] are hardly literate'.[15] It was found to be especially fatal among those between the ages of ten and forty, the most 'vigorous of the population'. Deaths of women were found to be more numerous than men; for every 1,000 living between the ages of twenty and forty, sixty-two men and seventy-nine women died.[16] Mortality was estimated at 1,086,758 for the months of June to December 1918, taking the excess of total mortality over the mean of the previous 5 years, the peak being reached in October. In certain areas of the Presidency, particularly Sind, effects on the mortality curve were apparent even in January 1919. Village officers, not being conversant with the symptoms, returned all deaths under the general head of 'fevers'.[17] Even in cities, part of the mortality went under 'respiratory diseases'.

Comparatively lighter mortality was observed in the coastal towns, ascribed to the diurnal variations in atmospheric temperature and less overcrowding.[18] Bombay City was an exception and showed a rise in mortality from 219 deaths on 16 September to 768 on 6 October. Between 10 September and 10 November, mortality exceeded the normal by 14,678. In the total mortality of 20,258, there were 10,506 men and 9,752 women.[19] Mills has noted an average 50 per cent increase in still births during the peak influenza mortality months of September and October.[20] The failure of the south-west monsoon in 1918 and the resultant crop failure had already severely affected the Presidency. Consequently, Bombay City had had to cope with a large influx of migrants from districts affected by 'scarcity and dearness of food'.[21] In Ahmedabad, 3,527 deaths occurred, of whom 1,934 were women, and 1,593 were men, the higher death rate of the former being ascribed to the habit of confining themselves to ill-ventilated and congested dwellings. It was also observed that women, being engaged in housework, did not take to bed immediately. Though the standard of living of mill workers in this city was higher than that of labourers, the equally high incidence among them was ascribed to their working conditions. The Health Officer of Ahmedabad found high mortality among the low castes, who were both 'poor and under privileged'.[22]

Governmental response

Apart from collecting statistics, how did the Bombay Government respond? The Sanitary Commissioner, Bombay, maintained that influenza was one of those diseases which had little respect for public health laws and little could be done to prevent its spread. He recommended prompt isolation of the infected, opening up of ill-ventilated dwellings, encouraging people to sleep in the open and disinfecting the clothing of influenza patients. He held that Indians, like people elsewhere, had overwhelming confidence in the efficacy of drugs, but the real need was for nursing and nourishment.[23] The Surgeon-General, R.W.S. Lyons, in his instructions, recommended gargling, with diluted potassium permanganate and aspirin, and warned against the use of quinine as a prophylactic or a curative. Announcements in the *Times of India* provided guidelines to employers and householders, namely gargling with permanganate of potash, fresh air and immediate medical attention when fever appeared.[24] For those who developed pneumonia, hospitalisation was advised.[25] Lyons reported that all hospitals and dispensaries had expanded their accommodation and suitable, well-ventilated school rooms had been used. Of a total number of 233,346 indoor and outdoor patients at hospitals and dispensaries, 220,000 were recorded under the head of 'influenza'; the rest were either treated by private practitioners or not at all.[26] Not only was the number of doctors depleted because of the war, but all of them were concentrated in the towns, while some of them were also incapacitated by influenza.

While the Surgeon-General claimed that district officers had done all in their power to combat the epidemic and had saved many lives, the local press did not seem to think so. The *Bombay Chronicle* observed that officials had remained in the hills during the emergency, while *Young India* pointed out that the Government, which at other times claimed to be the *maa baap* (mother and father) of the people, now chose 'to throw them on the hands of providence'. The *Gujarati* wanted to know what highly paid Government experts were doing to help people in their distress. The contention was that the wide social gulf that existed between the people at large and high government officials prevented the latter from realising the sufferings of the former. The *Praja Mitra and Parsi* observed that the public would naturally turn towards the Government, which should take people into its confidence. The press offered suggestions too; thus the latter newspaper wanted shops selling grains to be set up, while the *Akhbar-e Islam* recommended that Government should construct huts in the open for the poor, and provide a better water supply.[27] The scarcity of food grains was another contentious issue and only in October did the Government stop the export of wheat. The other factor was ignorance of the nature of the disease. A letter writer, in the *Times of India*, who signed as 'A Seeker after Facts' wanted a conference of medical men to debate the nature of the fever.[28] Another letter criticised the inaction and referred to the large sums spent by the municipality, including the high salary paid to the Health Officer who, it was stated, could not even correctly diagnose the fever.[29] The *Sunday Chronicle* commented that everything had been left to the municipality and local philanthropic institutions, the paralysing atmosphere in the Bombay Secretariat having kept the '*maa baap* of the people in a state of coma'. The *Jam-e-Jamshed* commented on the apathy of the Government and declared that the arrangements were insufficient for the vast population of Bombay.[30]

Purushotamdas Thakurdas and S.B. Upasani raised the issue of the funding of relief measures in the Bombay Legislative Council. The Government, in its reply, maintained that it had limited funds available.[31] Confusion and inconsistency seem to have marked the response of the authorities throughout the Presidency. Thus, when the District Magistrate of Bijapur wanted to release sick prisoners from the jail which was short staffed, the Government would have none of it.[32] The Karachi Municipality closed all cinemas and theatres for three months, leading to protests by the owners to the Bombay Government against this arbitrary injustice when in the city of Bombay thirteen cinemas and eleven theatres remained open.[33] Sandra Tomkins has referred to similar protests by cinema operators in England, even as overcrowding in trains and trams continued.[34]

Another aspect of the Government's response was its efforts to enquire into the epidemiology of influenza, which appeared to resemble the less severe epidemic of 1891. The weight of evidence at the time seemed to point to Pfeiffer's influenza bacillus as being the cause. When the second wave appeared in September 1918, with its attendant high mortality, investigations were begun at the Bombay Bacteriological Laboratory, established under W.M. Haffkine in 1896, and at the Central Research Institute, Kasauli, founded in 1900. However, difficulties in the detection and isolation of the bacillus were experienced. The efforts of Indian researchers, Drs Soparkar and Gore of the Bombay Laboratory, were particularly noteworthy. They worked independently and produced nutrient media which gave results similar to those in use in Europe.[35] Valuable work was also carried out in Karachi. Though the relationship between Pfeiffer's bacillus and influenza had not been definitively established, it was felt that there was enough evidence to justify a vaccine. Information was sought from South Africa regarding the constitution of the vaccine used there, which was then prepared at Kasauli and issued for the use of the military.[36] Later the formula adopted by the War Office conference of bacteriologists was cabled to India, and vaccine was prepared on these lines at Kasauli.[37] This was issued for preventive purposes only. Meanwhile, Lieutenant-Colonel Liston, Director of the Bombay Laboratory, had prepared a vaccine, consisting only of influenza 'bacilli' (250 million), which was issued for use in selected communities. Finally, in December, at an informal conference of bacteriologists held in Delhi, the constitution of the vaccine was decided upon. It had the following constituents: 500 million influenza and 100 million *pneumococcus* 'bacilli' for the first dose, and double this for the second dose.[38] It was prepared at both the above-mentioned laboratories and at the King Institute of Preventive Medicine, established in Madras in 1903. The vaccine was distributed free of charge.[39]

Voluntary effort in Bombay

Despite these steps, the inadequacy of governmental resources to provide immediate relief was apparent, and the Sanitary Commissioner admitted as much. Turner appealed to the public of Bombay City, observing that the ignorance and superstition of the people, their different social surroundings and modes of life made it difficult for the authorities to check the spread of disease. He pointed out that in Western countries, people would take heed of warnings and recognise the need for action, while here, in India, it was difficult to get people to listen to any advice contrary to their way of thinking.[40] The public response was immediate, and there was co-operation between the authorities and the public in providing relief. Accommodation for serious patients was made available in the Government-run Jamsetjee Jejeebhoy, Goculdas Tejpal and Infectious

Diseases hospitals, and at a military camp in the suburb of Dadar. The Bombay Municipal Corporation formed a medical sub-committee including Rahimtulla Currimbhoy, president of the Corporation as chairman, and Dr Kavasji Dadachanji, president of the Bombay Medical Union, Sir Cowasji Jehangir, and Dr M.C. Javle as members.[41] They were instrumental in gaining the assistance of the voluntary associations. They visited dispensaries and brought to the attention of the Controller of Prices the need to reduce the high prices of medicines. Letters were sent to 'large employers of labour' suggesting the steps to be taken, while mill managers were summoned to discuss preventive measures to be adopted in mills. Posters were put up in English, Marathi and Gujarati, advising the people to call in medical help or go to hospitals. Arrangements were made for the distribution of milk and 'pneumonia jackets'.[42] By way of affording additional facilities for the poor in the disposal of their dead, burning- and burial-fees were suspended at the municipal cemetery. The military authorities provided orderlies and ambulances for the removal of patients to hospital. Private medical practitioners advocated sanitary education of the public, since they felt that nothing could be expected of the municipality, and 'their salvation lay in their own hands'.[43]

Among the non-governmental organisations, the Hindu Medical Association took the lead. Under the guidance of a committee of doctors, volunteers made house visits and directed those who had no one to nurse them to hospitals. Two wards in the Maratha Hospital were set aside for influenza patients, supervised by Dr Abraham S. Erulkar, and a small hospital was opened in the Jain hostels, attended by Drs G.V. Deshmukh and D.D. Sathaye. The patients were mainly poor mill workers 'who were ill fed and lived in badly ventilated dark rooms with smoky atmosphere full of coal and dust'.[44] Initially, the people seem to have been uncommunicative and had to be persuaded to avail themselves of treatment. 4,195 out-patients were treated at various centres maintained by the Association.

The other body which responded to Turner's appeal was the Social Service League. Founded in 1911 by social reformers, N.M. Joshi, N.G. Chandavarkar, Dr B.K. Bhatavadekar, B.N. Motivala and G.K. Parekh, the League had among its aims the provision of medical relief and the promotion of sanitation and hygiene. It had conducted anti-tuberculosis campaigns, and provided training in first aid. Now, the League set up the Influenza Relief Committee comprising industrialists, judges and doctors, and a fund of Rs. (Rupees) 52,148 was collected.[45] Funds came from the trustees of the N.M. Wadia Charities, and from individuals, ranging from Rs. 500 donated by Parbhuram Popatram who was a well-known Ayurvedic practitioner, to small sums given by anonymous donors. Twenty centres in different parts of the city were opened to distribute a stock medical mixture, milk and clothing, which eventually reached 17,684 persons. While arrangements were made for the temporary boarding and lodging of patients discharged from hospitals, a special corps arranged for the cremation of the dead. The work of the League was particularly lauded by the *Times of India*.[46]

Temporary hospitals for castes and communities were set up. The Jains were the first to open a hospital at Girgaum. The Lohanas opened a facility at Mazagaon, Marwaris at Kalbadevi, Bohras at Null Bazar, Pathare Prabhus at Chowpatty,[47] while the Parsis were provided with beds at the Parsi Fever Hospital and the Bomanji Petit General Hospital at Cumballa Hill, a ward of twenty beds also being set apart for Parsi patients at the Arthur Road Hospital. A group of Parsi volunteers formed the Parsi Emergency Corps, which included a *batakiwalla* (town crier) who made announcements about dispensaries, and arranged for an ambulance, while a division of nurse volunteers from the St John's Ambulance Brigade Overseas, representing various communities, ensured that rules regarding river pollution were not violated.[48]

Twenty-five organisations provided 200 volunteers. These were provided by community and caste associations of the Dawoodi Bohras, the Ismaili Khojas, who had done exemplary work during the plague epidemic of 1896, the Cutchhi Lohanas and the Bhatias, the Pathare Prabhu Social Samaj, the Kitte Bhandari Aikyawardhak Mandali, the Kshatriya Bhandari Dnyati Samaj and the Gaud Saraswat Brahmin Mitra Mandal; professional associations like the Kamgar Hitwardhak Sabha and the St George's Nursing Association; youth organisations like the Radiant Club, the Students' Brotherhood, the Students' Social Union, the Young Men's Hindu Association, the Young Men's Mahomedan Association, the Young Men's Khoja Association, the Presidency Students' Federation, and professors and students of Wilson College; political groups like the Home Rule League; and miscellaneous bodies like the Temperance Association, the Bombay Humanitarian League, the Matunga Residents' Association and the Swajan Hitachintaka Samaj, the Telugu Free Library and the Church Missionary Society.[49] The volunteers included twelve doctors, two of whom were women, and senior students of the Grant Medical College. The Western India Turf Club lent their premises as an office, while the Japanese and Shanghai Piece Goods Association operated two relief stations. Blankets provided by textile mills, cologne waters and tubes of menthol given by Messrs Gobhai & Company and fuel for cemeteries from Hindus were acknowledged.[50] Most of these efforts benefited the poor. Measures for the reduction of infant mortality continued after the epidemic had abated, with the aid of the Bombay Sanitary Association and the Lady Willingdon Scheme.[51] This organisation, which was concerned with the diffusion of knowledge of sanitation, ran a library, a museum and held lectures on hygiene for women. This wide cross-section of volunteers and donors reflected the cosmopolitan character of the city.

The *Hindusthan* rightly observed that the principal burden had fallen on the philanthropic sections of the public.[52] Turner, for his part, paid credit to all these organisations and also acknowledged the support of officials like the Vaccination Superintendent, the Deputy Health Officers, the sanitary and conservancy staff, who had been relieved of their regular duties, and the personnel of the registration branch, birth *karkuns* (clerks), disinfecting staff and death *ramoshis* (recorders).[53]

Other cities of the Presidency

Relief was organised in the other cities on similar lines. In Poona, H.N. Apte, the president of the Municipality, supervised the opening of a temporary hospital.[54] Under the leadership of Vithal Ramji Shinde, the Depressed Classes Mission provided relief, assisted by the Arogya Mandal and the Poona Volunteer Corps.[55] At Sholapur, a few doctors and citizens supplied free medicines. The Municipal Commissioner of Surat established two travelling dispensaries and an infectious diseases ward at the local civil hospital, while volunteers visited houses and distributed medicines, including a 'medicated mixture' prepared by Dr Gajjar and supplied free to the Municipality.[56] The Parsi Orphanage, Jain Hospital and Mitra Mandal did relief work in this city.[57] In Karachi, aid came through a fund, collected at the initiative of Jamsetji N.R. Mehta, and twelve mobile dispensaries and bands of volunteers. Led by Dr Haji Gulam Husein Kassim, a municipal councillor, doctors provided free medical treatment. Information regarding rest, nourishment and preventive measures were disseminated through the press and the distribution of leaflets both in English and the vernaculars.[58] The Citizens' Influenza Committee, assisted by the Salvation Army, took up the task in Hyderabad.[59]

In Ahmedabad, the Gujarat Sabha, an association concerned with social and political reform since 1884, set up the Influenza Relief Committee, and a hospital with 125 beds was opened in a building donated by Seth Jamnabahi Baghubhai, a local businessman. The St John's Ambulance Division transported patients to the hospital, while the Salvation Army provided the nurses, and medical students of Byramjee Jejeebhoy Medical College and schoolteachers volunteered their services for house-to-house visits. As in Bombay, funds came from mills like the Ahmedabad Advance Mills; mill owners like Ambalal Sarabhai; and associations, including the Panch Kuva Mahajan, a body of cloth traders, Maskaty Mahajan, a group of cloth merchants, and the Yarn Merchants Mahajan. Twenty-four dispensaries were established and some 3,000 patients were given relief. As elsewhere, the epidemic was particularly virulent in the crowded localities, like Dariapur, where Dr Tankariwalla rendered sterling service. Lady Chinubhai, who belonged to the family of Ranchodlal Chotalal, the pioneer of public health in Ahmedabad, and Pestonshaw Vakil lent their motor cars for work in the neighbouring villages. The Gujarat Sabha also provided funds to the Salvation Army to reach villages on the outskirts of Ahmedabad, and in the districts of Kaira and Panch Mahals. The District Local Board met the expenses of travel, boarding and lodging of the medical students who worked in these villages and supplied them with thermometers and stethoscopes.[60]

In contrast to other cities, the Municipality of Ahmedabad seems to have been obstructionist to relief efforts, refusing the use of one of its school buildings as a hospital. In fact this indifference to the suffering of the people and the 'chronic insanitary condition of the city' were the subject of six editorials in *Praja Bandhu*. The paper pointed out that, while the burden of taxation had been going up, municipal expenditure had been on the high salaries of the Municipal Commissioner, the Engineer and the Health Officer. 'We do not know what would have been the condition of the suffering poor, if the Gujarat Sabha had not come to their rescue.'[61] Subsequently, the *Praja Bandhu* started a fund to aid the efforts of the Sabha. The weekly also drew attention to the need to close all cinemas and theatres.[62]

Influenza raged in the Sabarmati Ashram, Ahmedabad, where Mahatma Gandhi, Charles Andrews and Shankarlal Parikh were all affected. Gandhi may have initially had his views about treatment of his own case, for the *Praja Bandhu* commented that many differed from Gandhi on his ideas, but 'Mr. Gandhi's life does not belong to him – it belongs to India'.[63] He seems to have accepted the prescription of rest and a liquid diet during convalescence, and had this advice to give to others, 'Even after we feel that we have recovered, we must continue to take complete rest in bed and have only easily digestible liquid food. So early as on the third day after the fever has subsided many persons resume their work and their usual diet. The result is a relapse and quite often a fatal relapse.'[64]

Conclusion

This focus on Bombay Presidency has shown that, though the state response was inadequate, there was collaborative effort between the Government and the public in providing relief in the cities. The same was the case in other regions of India. The epidemic struck India at a time when it was least prepared for it. Medical personnel were depleted in numbers and those who remained in civilian duties were also stricken by influenza. There had been a total failure of the monsoon practically throughout the country and, consequently, food scarcity was another aggravating factor: staple food grains were available at 'famine prices' and the shortage of fodder had enormously reduced the quantity of milk available.[65] Hardly any part of the country escaped the epidemic, as the *Social Service Quarterly* pointed out, whether it was the hill tops of Simla, or the few healthy sanitary quarters of modern cities, like Bombay, or the slums of Ahmedabad, or isolated villages.[66] The Surgeon-General conceded that mortality would have been reduced had it been possible to provide immediate medical aid and suitable nourishment to those attacked.[67] The

British admitted that, though everything that could have been done with the resources available was done, yet 'the vast majority of sufferers were without skilled attention'.[68] The absolute lack of any public health organisation in rural areas and the total helplessness of the rural population in the face of the calamity are evident. At the same time, the authorities contended that, with a population so uneducated and with a relatively low standard of living, 'the control of the epidemic was outside the scope of human endeavour'.[69] E. Selby Phipson, special assistant to Turner, averred that, if any hope of understanding the activity of influenza 'is remote in England, it is utopian in Bombay' where the 'public health conscience is limited'.[70]

Notwithstanding this comment, there was remarkable public involvement, as has been shown above. While the well-to-do escaped lightly, the suffering of the poor would have been more acute if not for the co-operation between the social organisations and the local authorities. Turner paid tribute to the voluntary effort in Bombay City thus: 'Such was the whole-hearted devotion and co-operation of all the workers in organising and carrying out the various measures of relief that there is probably no house in the City or unit of population that has not had a chance of relief.'[71] The Western-educated medical fraternity rose to the occasion, but was as uncertain of treatment as their British counterparts. The *Indian Medical Gazette*, which received many letters to the editor recommending a variety of remedies, namely belladona, laudanum, camphor, creosote and a mixture of iodine and chloroform, remarked on the faith of Indian doctors in drugs.[72] Despite the warning by Surgeon Lyons against its use, there was hoarding and an enormous price rise of quinine in Ahmedabad.[73] This points to a failure in the dissemination of information. In Bombay, Indian doctors met at least five times during the crisis, to discuss strategy, but as Dr Sathaye pointed out, while medical literature was enriched with contributions from everywhere, the absence of Indian contributors was due to the want of facilities for independent research.[74]

Both non-official and official agencies made recommendations of measures to be adopted in the event of a future outbreak. Voluntary organisations, in their reports, suggested not only the establishment of more dispensaries and hospitals, but also making them 'attractive to all classes', the opening of more medical colleges and training of nurses, and urged the extension of medical facilities to rural areas. Private medical practitioners recommended 'drastic' sanitary measures for purifying air and water, and long-term measures like mass education, the 'amelioration of economic conditions' and more facilities for research by independent practitioners.[75] The Government of India issued a memorandum on influenza in 1919, which also recommended the education of the public, with instructions such as 'keep fit, avoid infection, [follow] healthy living', and suggested the closure of schools, colleges and cinemas, the wearing of face masks and the use of disinfecting sprays and gargles. Further, it advised that 'maritime' governments should make pneumonia a notifiable disease under the Indian Ports Act.[76] The Bombay Provincial Government was permitted by the Government of India to exercise powers under the Epidemic Diseases Act, 1897, to formulate the necessary rules to prevent a future outbreak of influenza.[77] As the Sanitary Commissioner of Bombay had noted in 1918, when the history of the epidemic would be written, 'the divergence in mortality between the nursed and un-nursed' would become apparent. The training of nurses was in its infancy and, outside the city of Bombay, there was no nucleus of trained nurses to provide relief, hence the training of Indian nurses for district work was recommended.[78]

Another significant response was the advocacy of Indian medicine, both by the press and the voluntary agencies, to remedy the lack of infrastructure. The *Deccan Ryot* observed that the 'doctor', as the practitioner of Western medicine was known, depended on a supply of medicines from Europe or America, making him both expensive and unreliable in times of emergency. On the other hand, Indian medicine was cheap and could be dispensed by schoolmasters, postmasters and village officers, who could be trained as apothecaries.[79] The *Kesari* suggested that villages could be served by itinerant doctors, who could be *vaids*, dispensing indigenous medicine. However, as the paper pointed out, the provincial governments were opposed to *hakims* and *vaids*, as was apparent from the Government's reply to questions raised in the Imperial Legislative Council.[80] The *Praja Mitra and Parsi* referred to attempts made to put down the indigenous system through the operation of the Bombay Medical Act, and speculated as to what could be the condition of the large mass of the people, when even the small section dependent upon practitioners of Western medicine had felt the dearth of adequate medical relief.[81] It would seem that *Ayurvedic* and *Unani* medicines were used in the treatment of patients in the community hospitals and dispensaries.[82] Yet, the colonial medical establishment was convinced that the pandemic had shown the universal demand for Western medicine, and that the people were beginning to realise that there was 'only one system of medicine'.[83] Thus, while the men on the spot like Turner seemed to be aware of the value of collaboration with the public for coping with the epidemic, the attitude of the Government of India was to continue to subscribe to the long-held view that it had all the answers.

The other strong Indian sentiment expressed was in keeping with the political temper of the time, when the national movement was passing under the charismatic and dynamic leadership of Mahatma Gandhi. The press warned the Government that it was not enough to call the epidemic 'a world scourge and then sit with folded hands'. A war had to be waged against the enemies of the public, namely plague, malaria and influenza.[84] In an editorial entitled 'Public Health', written in the aftermath of the Jallianwala Bagh incident, *Young India* asked whether the Government realised the startling psychological effects of the epidemic. The feeling on the streets of Bombay was that, to a Government which allowed sixty *lakhs* of people to die of influenza 'like rats without succour', it would not matter if a few died by shooting.[85] This anguish was an expression of the contemporary mood of the country.

Part IV
The demographic impact

7 Spanish influenza in China, 1918–20

A preliminary probe

Wataru Iijima

Historians of Europe, Africa, America and India have paid attention to epidemics of disease because of their impact on population trends, social change and colonial relationships. By contrast, little attention has been given to epidemics and the epidemiological transition in China, although recently studies have been produced on epidemics of bubonic plague and Asiatic cholera.[1] Epidemics of disease occurred frequently in different parts of China from the nineteenth century to the mid-twentieth century, resulting in relatively high mortality. Given the large population in China, these localised epidemic outbreaks had little influence on overall population trends, yet control of epidemic disease and the establishment of a public health system have been crucial in creating a system of modern government for China.[2]

The purpose of this chapter is to examine the outbreak of the Spanish influenza pandemic in modern China towards the end of the First World War. There were few reliable central government statistics in modern China before the 1930s, and no reliable demographic sources for an analysis of the impact of the Spanish influenza. The Ch'ing Dynasty government had started to collect vital data in some large cities in the 1900s, for example in Peking and Tientsin, but this data was limited to persons who lived in the centre of those cities. After the 1911 Revolution the collection of even these statistics was discontinued. During the next two decades constant civil war meant the central government did not control the whole of China. After 1928 the new Nationalist Government endeavoured to establish a public health system and collect vital data from all over China, but statistical data was limited to many large cities and some rural districts in the 1930s. Because of the lack of basic statistical sources, many scholars of Chinese history have not researched epidemics and modern China's epidemiological transition.

It is clear that in demographic terms the Spanish influenza pandemic must rate as one of the most serious in the history of epidemics. The pandemic certainly affected China from 1918 to 1920 as I examine later, but it is a subject largely ignored by scholars except for the brief references provided by Patterson and Pyle.[3] In their studies they conclude that China was seriously hit by influenza in 1918; but it is by no means sure how seriously. In this chapter, I examine the impact of Spanish influenza in China using the records of the Chinese Maritime Customs (CMC) in the treaty ports, which records information on epidemics, including influenza.[4] At this time the CMC operated the only quarantine system in China, directed by a foreign inspector of Chinese maritime customs, foreign consuls and the Chinese director of maritime customs, so it was in a good position to monitor epidemics in areas subject to its authority. Consequently, in this chapter two series of reports by the CMC are analysed, the *Decennial Reports* and the *Returns of Trade and Trade Reports*. However, as the CMC records are limited, the study is extended by looking at data from neighbouring areas: at the British colony of Hong Kong, and also at Taiwan and the Kuang-tun Leased Territory, both of which were then under Japanese colonial rule. I will also discuss the case of Japan, where the influenza pandemic occurred between 1918 and 1920, in order to compare the situation there with that of China.[5]

Influenza in China

Before discussing the extent of the pandemic in modern China, it is necessary to raise the issue of how it reached there and the type of influenza virus involved. Where the virus originated was a controversial issue at the time. For example, one American scientist stated that Spanish influenza in Europe had its origin in China, having been brought from the east by the many Chinese labourers employed by the British and French on the Western Front during the First World War.[6] However, Dr Wu Lien-teh, the most eminent Chinese scientist of his day, and director of the Manchurian Plague Prevention Bureau, disagreed. He concluded that the type of influenza virus in China was the same as that in Europe and that the influenza in China had spread east from Europe.[7] Scientists in the Shanghai International Settlement also researched the virus type and concluded that it was the same virus as in Europe and had reached China from there.[8] Patterson and Pyle share this belief.[9]

The CMC reports have special value for an analysis of epidemic disease for several reasons. First, the fifty or so treaty ports were fairly widespread, although mainly large cities on the coast and on the large rivers. Second, the CMC reports, compared to those of the Christian missions, were more methodically kept. And finally they stand out because of the lack of other official data. Thus we can see from *The Decennial Reports* for 1912–21 and *The Returns of Trade and Trade Reports* for 1918, 1919 and 1920, that sixteen treaty ports had cases of Spanish influenza from 1918 to 1920; outbreaks are not recorded in any of the other treaty ports. *The Returns of Trade and Trade Reports* for 1920 stated that influenza occurred in only one treaty port, Hankow.

From the description in these reports, the occurrence of influenza in the treaty ports (see Table 7.1) can be divided as follows:

a   'great epidemic', 'raging', 'outbreak', 'many victims', 'serious', 'a great number of people', which were used to describe Hankow, Chinwangtao (Tangshan, Shanhaikwan),[10] Chungking, Ichang, Wenchow, Kiungchow;
b   'not severe (serious)', 'mild', 'several deaths', used to describe Shanghai, Amoy, Wuchow, Tengyueh;
c   fact of occurrence was recorded for Newchang, Lungkow, Soochow.

The China Year Book summarised the situation of 1919 as follows: the Spanish influenza first spread to the northern Chinese cities of Harbin, Peking, and Tientsin from Russia, then a few months later it spread to the southern coastal cities of Shanghai and Hong Kong.[11] This seems to confirm that there was a wave of Spanish influenza in 1919.

On Hankow, a large treaty port and commercial centre in the middle Yangtze River, the *Decennial Reports* said that the city had seen a 'great influenza pandemic'.[12] The *North-China Herald* (*NCH*), the most prominent English-language newspaper printed in Shanghai, carried frequent reports on the incidence of influenza in certain Chinese cities. For example, Wuchang, the city neighbouring Hankow, suffered a serious outbreak in 1918.[13] By 1920 the *Returns of Trade and Trade Reports* stated that the outbreak of influenza in the city that year was a 'milder type than in the previous year'. As these reports do not contain mortality figures from influenza, it is difficult to assess the extent to which the disease touched these treaty ports. But it is also clear that Spanish influenza occurred in some major cities, in some cases the outbreaks being serious. Unfortunately, the paucity of the data does not allow any detailed analysis of the extent of morbidity or mortality.

Information is equally patchy about the situation in other districts. In Liu Tin, the market town of Kwangtung province, more than 100 people died of influenza in 3 weeks during December 1918.[14] There were also many deaths in the villages near Weihaiwei, the main port of Shantung province, the same month.[15] In north Honan province, a large number of fatal cases were also reported,[16] while in Taikuhsien, the commercial centre of Shansi province, the victims numbered literally thousands of people; deaths of young children were also reported in some districts.[17] In the case of Kweilin, a large city of Kwangsi province, fatal cases were frequent, with Spanish influenza affecting not only the city itself, but also the entire surrounding areas.[18] In the case of Shaohsing, a large city and market town of Chekiang province, bad water, poor food and failure to isolate sick cases probably increased the number of deaths. A conservative estimate for the city placed the death toll at 1,000. The influenza attacked people of all ages, but cases of fatal pneumonia were mostly found among older people.[19]

Table 7.1 Spanish influenza in China, 1918–20

Treaty port	Decennial Reports, 1912–21	1918	1919	1920
Harbin			Not very severe	
Hunchun		A brief visitation		
Newchwang	Occurrence			
Chinwangtao	Raging		Many victims	
Lungkow	Occurrence			
Chungking	Broke out			
Ichang	Serious		Confined to the crew of a foreign gunboat	
Hankow	The great epidemic	Epidemic torment	Occurrence	
Shanghai	Not serious	Occurrence		
Soochow	Occurrence			
Hangchow		A number of deaths	Occurrence	
Wenchow	Many victims			
Amoy	Several deaths	A number of deaths		
Wuchow	Very mild			
Kiungchow	Outbreak			
Tengyueh	Not of a very severe type	Mild form		Milder type than in the previous year

Sources: China. The Maritime Customs, *Decennial Reports, 1912–1920;* China. The Maritime Customs, *Returns of Trade and Trade Returns, 1918, 1919, 1920.*

As one of the largest trading ports in China as well as of East Asia, Shanghai was very vulnerable to disease being brought in from outside the country. Shanghai was divided into three districts, the Shanghai International Settlement, the French Concession and the Chinese city. Shanghai had over 2 million people in these three districts in 1918, mostly Chinese. About 24,000 foreigners and about 780,000 Chinese lived in the Shanghai International Settlement.[20] Between June and September 1918, there were 266 deaths from influenza among the Chinese and 6 among foreigners in the Shanghai International Settlement. Of course, these statistics are limited to that area of the city under the control of the health section of the Shanghai International Settlement; the actual death toll from Spanish influenza in Shanghai was much higher than this figure indicates. It is possible that Spanish influenza occurred among the Chinese poor, particularly labourers who worked in the port. However, the *NCH* also reported that compared to other countries, China had not suffered very badly from influenza and that Shanghai largely escaped a severe outbreak.[21]

The Department of Public Health in the Shanghai International Settlement, alerted to the threat of the influenza pandemic, took preventive measures. For example, on the tramway arrangements were made to wash and disinfect every car each night, while they were sprinkled with disinfectant and brushed out after every journey.[22] It is difficult to confirm whether the outbreak in Shanghai was less serious than it might have been because of the preventive measures taken, or for other reasons. However, reports in the *NCH* echoed the information contained in the CMC reports, that Shanghai did not experience a severe outbreak of influenza. *Shen-pao,* the largest Chinese newspaper printed in Shanghai, also reported the deaths of Chinese people from Spanish influenza in May and October of 1918, and a further thirty deaths from the infection in February of 1919. These reports confirm the occurrence of Spanish influenza in 1918 to 1919, but also indicate that the outbreak was not severe.[23] Both English- and Chinese-language newspapers reported serious cases of Spanish influenza in cities and villages all over China, but in general the English-language press was more interested in this than were Chinese newspapers.

So, it can be concluded, on the basis of admittedly limited evidence, that the Spanish influenza pandemic did spread to China and that there were high levels of morbidity and frequent reports of deaths in some Chinese cities. However, there is as yet insufficient evidence to argue that the whole of China was affected severely. In their study of Western medicine in China, published a decade and a half after the influenza pandemic, Wong and Wu did not give much space to Spanish influenza in China.[24] This failure to describe the extent of the influenza pandemic is in common with much other contemporary Chinese medical writing, but it must be borne in mind that by the 1930s the Spanish flu pandemics had already slipped from official note in most parts of the world.

The situation in Hong Kong, Taiwan, southern Manchuria and Japan

From the above analysis, we can say with a reasonable degree of certainty that Spanish influenza did occur in China between 1918 and 1920, and that it was the same virus that struck the rest of the world. As to the extent of the pandemic in China, there is a serious need for further investigation. In the absence of detailed Chinese records, a start can be made by exploring the situation in three adjoining territories not under Chinese rule, Hong Kong, Taiwan and southern Manchuria, using British and Japanese colonial records. Table 7.2 shows the mortality figures from Spanish influenza in Hong Kong from 1918 to 1920, with 1,396 deaths attributed to it over the 3 years, a rate of ±0.25 per 100 of the population. However, it must be remembered that these figures included only deaths which occurred in the Colony's hospitals. At that time Hong Kong was divided into seven districts. Many Chinese labourers lived in Victoria, the Peak on Hong Kong Island and in the southern area of the Kowloon Peninsula, and would not have been taken to hospital.[25] Although there were outbreaks of Spanish influenza, mainly among the Chinese communities, the annual administrative reports by the Hong Kong government paid little attention to these.[26] The data collected by the Hong Kong government was based on the number of deaths in hospitals; it is clear that the colonial government under-recorded the total number of deaths from the Spanish flu.

In Japanese-ruled Taiwan it is very clear that Spanish influenza in 1918 to 1920 was far more severe, with deaths from the infection totalling 25,394 in 1918 (a rate of 0.69 per 100) and just under that in 1920.[27] Native Taiwanese appear to have been appreciably more vulnerable than Japanese residents there (see Table 7.3). The number of deaths from Spanish influenza in 1918–20 was the same as the number of deaths from malaria, the biggest killer on the island at that time,[28] so it is clear that the influenza outbreak in Taiwan then was pandemic and had a huge impact on society.

Japan had invested heavily in healthcare institutions in its colony of

Table 7.2 The number of deaths from influenza in Hong Kong, 1918–20

	1918	1919	1920
British and foreign community – civil	14	23	27
Chinese community – Victoria and Peak	231	182	186
Harbour	24	43	47
Kowloon	129	193	276
Saukiwan	6	1	5
Aberdeen	0	7	1
Stanley	1	0	0
Total	405	449	542

Source: R.L. Jarman (ed.), *Hong Kong Annual Administration Reports, 1918, 1919, 1920.*

Table 7.3 Deaths from influenza in the towns and districts of Taiwan, 1916–25

	T'ai-pei		Hsin-chu		T'ai-chung		T'ai-nan		K'ao-shun		T'ai-tung		Hua-lien		Total	
	T	J	T	J	T	J	T	J	T	J	T	J	T	J	T	J
1916	77	0	37	0	6	0	170	0	77	0	0	0	0	0	367	0
1917	71	0	24	1	5	1	108	1	51	0	0	0	0	0	259	3
1918	646	78	336	8	345	8	3,371	51	1,137	26	121	12	139	30	6,095	213
1919	79	26	65	2	42	11	186	26	78	1	22	1	9	1	481	68
1920	1,362	218	1,556	38	2,098	102	2,855	114	1,157	26	6	5	24	10	9,058	513
1921	46	10	16	0	127	1	52	4	43	5	1	0	0	0	285	20
1922	68	7	28	0	70	1	291	7	122	15	3	0	0	0	582	30
1923	70	16	14	0	10	0	96	2	54	3	0	0	0	0	244	21
1924	64	6	50	2	73	0	87	5	54	2	0	1	0	0	328	16
1925	58	4	12	0	42	0	80	2	67	5	0	0	6	0	265	11

Source: The Japanese Colonial Government in Taiwan, *Population Trends in Taiwan*, 1916–25.

Note

T = Taiwanese, J = Japanese

southern Manchuria. The initial wave of the flu pandemic arrived in the region in the spring and summer of 1918 brought by migrant labourers from northern China. In both the Japanese and Chinese communities women appear to have been more likely to die from the virus than men. The Japanese population in southern Manchuria, mainly in the urban area of Dalian, was not affected by influenza until early in the winter of 1919. Although levels of morbidity posed a serious crisis for the Japanese health authorities, nevertheless the mortality rate from the pandemic appears to have been relatively low when compared to Japan. A recent study suggests that the mortality rate was 0.32 per 100, that is under 3,000 deaths out of a population of *c.*800,000.[29]

It might also be helpful here to look briefly at the situation in Japan. Three waves of influenza occurred in Japan from August 1918 to July 1921. In general, the pandemic occurred first in large cities and then spread to other rural districts.[30] According to Japanese government statistics, 23.8 million people were infected by Spanish influenza and about 220,238 died over these 3 years, a mortality rate of *c.*0.45 per 100.[31]

Thus, the Spanish influenza mortality rate in 1918 in the three territories adjoining China (Hong Kong, southern Manchuria and Taiwan), and also Japan ranged from 0.25 per 100 of the population (Hong Kong) to 0.69 per 100 of the population (Taiwan) (see Table 7.4) However, care should be taken in assessing the degree of accuracy and the comprehensiveness of these statistics. The data from Taiwan and southern Manchuria are more accurate than those for Hong Kong. Hong Kong's statistics were based only on the number of deaths that occurred in hospitals. By contrast, the data for Taiwan and Kuang-tun were based on research by health authorities with the help of police. In general, the coverage and accuracy of the statistics under Japanese colonial rule were better than those in the British, French and Dutch colonies in Asia. Thus, the outbreak of Spanish influenza is better recorded in Japan, southern Manchuria and Taiwan than in Hong Kong. The close relations and constant movement of people and goods between Japan and her island colony probably were responsible for the more extensive spread of influenza in Taiwan.

Table 7.4 Influenza in Japan, Taiwan and Hong Kong, 1918–20

	Population (million)	Deaths by influenza in 1918–20	Death ratio over 3 years
Japan	54.7	220,238	0.40
Southern Manchuria	0.8	2,560 (1918 only)	0.32 (1918 only)
Taiwan	3.76	16,428	0.44
Hong Kong	0.56	1,396	0.25

Sources: Japan: The Japan Statistical Association, *Historical Statistics of Japan*, Vol. 5, 1988. Taiwan: The Japanese Colonial Government in Taiwan, *Population Trends in Taiwan*, 1918–20. Hong Kong: R.L. Jarman (ed.), *Hong Kong Annual Administration Reports, 1918, 1919, 1920*.

It is clear that Spanish influenza occurred in varying degrees of virulence in Taiwan, Hong Kong, southern Manchuria, Japan and in the major cities of the Chinese littoral. However, how extensive was the outbreak in the rest of China? Patterson and Pyle in their study 'The 1918 Influenza Pandemic' tried to estimate the number of deaths by Spanish influenza in China as a whole. They argued that between 4.0 and 9.5 million people died in China, but this total was based purely on the assumption that the death rate there was 1.0–2.25 per cent in 1918, because China was a poor country similar to Indonesia and India where the mortality rate was of that order.[32] Clearly their study was not based on any local Chinese statistical data.

If, however, we were to extrapolate from the mortality rates in Hong Kong and Kuang-tun which, for all their deficiencies, were based on local statistical data for two mainland districts, then a far lower estimate of Spanish flu deaths emerges for China. Instead of Patterson and Pyle's 4 to 9.5 million, a projection from Hong Kong's rate of 0.25 per cent and Kuang-tun's 0.32 per cent of the population produces a death toll of between 1 million and 1.28 million people. The fragility of such figures cannot be overemphasised, however, especially as they stand in sharp contrast to the tolls in neighbouring Taiwan and Japan, based as they are on the far higher mortality rates of 0.69 per cent and 0.45 per cent respectively.

If one were to try and sustain the figure of 1 to 1.28 million Spanish flu deaths in China suggested above, a crucial question would have to be resolved: why did the Spanish influenza pandemic strike China less seriously than either Taiwan or Japan? The most obvious answer to this would lie in the extensive human traffic to, from and within Taiwan and Japan, which rapidly spread the pandemic far and wide in those territories. Compared to this, the movement of people within inland China, with its poorly developed transport system, was far less speedy and comprehensive. This might explain too why the Spanish flu, at least according to the *China Year Book* and Wong and Wu, did not have a major impact beyond some port cities.

Conclusion

Very tentatively, therefore, and bearing in mind that an absence of evidence does not necessarily mean evidence of absence, it might be provisionally proposed that, between 1918 and 1920, the Spanish flu did hit China's eastern ports and cities, some quite severely, but that it did not explode from there into the interior, as elsewhere in Asia, largely because of limited population mobility. Very obviously, as Patterson and Pyle pointed out 10 years ago, a host of local studies are urgently needed to test the validity of this hypothesis.

8   Flu downunder

A demographic and geographic analysis of the 1919 epidemic in Sydney, Australia

Kevin McCracken and Peter Curson

In mid 1918 Australian quarantine officials became aware of an influenza epidemic emerging in Europe. As the year unfolded, they watched as the epidemic developed into pandemic proportions and cut a swathe through Europe, the Americas, Africa, Asia and, ultimately, neighbouring New Zealand. Concerns about the pandemic's potential threat to Australia steadily rose as the disease's illness and death toll became known and struck closer and closer to Australian shores. To try and shield the country from the threat, quarantine procedures were introduced at all Australian ports in October 1918, and for a while public health authorities believed that Australia might be spared the pandemic's ravages. These hopes were not to be realised, however, and by the end of 1919 more than 12,000 Australians had lost their lives in the epidemic, and many hundreds of thousands more had suffered an attack of the disease.[1]

While the epidemic left a heavy mark on hundreds of communities across Australia, the place to most feel its brunt was Sydney, the country's largest metropolitan centre. During the course of the outbreak an estimated 36–37 per cent of the metropolis' population went down with the flu, and about 3,500 persons died from it.[2] This chapter examines the epidemic, the most intense health crisis the city has ever experienced, from the viewpoints of demography and geography, charting its uneven course through the metropolis' various population sub-groups and areas.

Origins?

The exact origins of the epidemic in Australia are unknown. The first cases were recorded in Melbourne in early January, the disease almost certainly having been introduced by one of the overseas vessels quarantined there. No direct evidence, however, was ever found linking any infected ship and cases on shore. This lack of any traceable connection in fact saw Dr J.H.L. Cumpston, Commonwealth Director of Quarantine, argue in June 1919 that the maritime quarantine defence had provided Australia with 'absolute immunity' and that 'There is ... much evidence ... that the present epidemic form of influenza is the product of a slow evolution of an influenza already established in Australia in July and August, 1918 [rather than due] ... to the introduction of fresh sources of infection from outside.'[3]

Cumpston stands virtually alone on this view. Despite the absence of a clear ship-to-shore connection, the general opinion is that the 1919 epidemic was a new type of influenza, introduced to Australia by an overseas vessel. This was certainly the belief of New South Wales health authorities. There had been an above-average prevalence of influenza across Australia during spring 1918 (the outbreak underlying Cumpston's theory) and a possible link was considered in the official report to the State government published a few months after the epidemic. Dr W.G. Armstrong, the Deputy-Director of Public Health, however, concluded that:

> The theory which appears to best fit in with all the circumstances ... is that two separate infections reached Australia; one of low virulence in August, 1918, and the second of highly intensified virulence which actually reached Australia in January, 1919, and would have reached us in October, 1918, had it not been for the operation of the quarantine cordon.[4]

Subsequent writers have favoured this view. Writing two decades later, Burnet and Clark rejected any linkage between the two outbreaks on the basis of the very different age incidence of mortality in the 1919 epidemic.[5] More recent writers have also questioned Cumpston's absolute faith in the quarantine protection system. McQueen, for example, draws attention to the fact that Cumpston himself complained of medical officers on some troop ships falsifying records in order to avoid extended quarantine.[6] Virtually all signs thus point to the infection having been introduced to Australia by an overseas vessel in early January 1919. But though rumours abounded, the precise point of entry remains uncertain.

Sydney, 1919

Before the analysis of the outbreak, a brief profile of Sydney in 1919 will be sketched to give readers a picture of the stage on which the epidemic played out its act. As officially defined at the time, metropolitan Sydney comprised forty-two local authority areas – the central City of Sydney, plus forty suburban municipalities and one shire. In total the metropolis embraced an area of approximately 480 square kilometres, extending in a broad belt from Manly and Ku-ring-gai in the north to the shores of Botany Bay and the Georges River in the south. To the east it was bordered by the Pacific Ocean, to the west by the municipalities of Homebush, Strathfield and Enfield. The Government Statistician's estimate of the mean population living within this area in 1919 was 810,700 persons.[7]

By 1919 Sydney's population was in the midst of a significant demographic and epidemiologic transition. Mortality and fertility had been falling for over 30 years, infectious diseases were gradually being brought under control and the degenerative killers like heart disease, stroke and cancer were assuming more importance. The pace of mortality decline had been especially rapid since the turn of the century. Back in 1900 the metropolis' crude death rate had been 12.4 per 1,000 population and the infant mortality rate 115 per 1,000 live births. Less than two decades later in 1918 the two rates had been respectively brought down to 9.4 and 60.[8]

At the same time, increasing suburbanisation was beginning to transform the spatial and social life of many of Sydney's inhabitants. The electric tramway and the rail system had encouraged suburban expansion to north of the harbour, as well as south and west of the City of Sydney. In most cases residential development clustered around the tram and rail stations or along the coast. Despite this, about a third of Sydney's population continued to live within 5 kilometres of the central business district, and the city centre still accounted for well over half of all metropolitan employment, as well as the majority of all retail, wholesale and entertainment facilities.

The social geography of Sydney had also become more vivid over the preceding two decades, with clear lines being drawn between the emerging middle-class public transport suburbs and the inner city where many of the poor continued to live, often in timeworn tenements, as opposed to the detached cottages of the suburbs. Directly to the south of the city centre lay a group of working-class industrial suburbs, notorious for their noxious living and working conditions. Finally, to the immediate north and east of the city centre were located a group of more advantaged ocean- and harbour-side suburbs, extending from North Sydney and Mosman, north of the harbour, through Vaucluse and Woollahra to Waverley and Randwick on the southside.

The temporal path of the epidemic

It was in this Sydney on Saturday 25 January 1919 that residents woke up to read in their morning newspapers that a suspected case of influenza was under observation in one of the city's suburbs. On the following Monday morning it was reported that the case, plus two other suspicious ones, was at Randwick Military Hospital and was 'highly infectious influenza, (but) probably not pneumonic'.[9] This hope was quickly put to rest the next morning, however, with headlines announcing 'Influenza in Sydney; Four cases identified' (see Figure 8.1).[10]

The initial suspect (and subsequently first positively diagnosed case) was revealed to the public to be a soldier who had arrived in Sydney from Melbourne (where pneumonic influenza was suspected, but not officially declared) on Tuesday 21 January. It transpired that the soldier had stayed

INFLUENZA IN SYDNEY

———•———

FOUR CASES IDENTIFIED

———

STATE AUTHORITIES TAKE DRASTIC PRECAUTIONS

———

Pneumonic-influenza has appeared in Sydney.

Four cases have been definitely identified, and between 17 and 19 suspicious cases have been reported. They are all in the Randwick Military Hospital.'

The whole of the State's anti-epidemic organisation has been brought into operation. The Federal authorities have declared the State an infected area, and have imposed drastic restrictions on all communication with other States.

All theatres and other public places of entertainment will be closed as from to-day.

The schools will not reopen to-day.

Figure 8.1 The arrival of 'Spanish' flu in Sydney, January 1919.

Source: *The Sydney Morning Herald*, 28 January 1919. Reproduced here with permission of *The Sydney Morning Herald*.

with relatives in the city for 48 hours before being admitted to Randwick Military Hospital on the Thursday. The soldier's condition apparently was very infectious and the flu reportedly spread very quickly to other soldiers and several medical personnel within the isolation ward at the hospital. Over the next few days several other soldier arrivals from Melbourne were admitted to the hospital, so that by late afternoon on Tuesday 28 January there were twelve definitely identified cases plus several other suspicious ones at the Randwick compound. On that date, two non-military cases were also confirmed within the city, both, like the soldiers, having recently been in Melbourne. In sum, during the week ending 1 February, twenty-three cases were positively diagnosed, all of whom had either been infected in Melbourne or had been directly infected by recent arrivals from the southern city. Within a few days into February, however, victims with no direct Melbourne connections came to light and the general community outbreak began.

Over the following 5 weeks the *Sydney Morning Herald* reported a small daily stream of new cases and the occasional death, in the slow build-up style typical of most epidemics. A week-and-a-half into March, however, the tempo of the outbreak lifted (Figure 8.2). For a few days tallies of new cases rose into the twenty to thirty range, before lifting again to an even higher level over the last 2 weeks of the month. Deaths rose in tandem, from the odd daily fatality or two in mid March, to double figures and then up again into the low twenties per day by the end of the month.

At this point the tempo abruptly went up another notch, developing what in retrospect proved to be the epidemic's first wave. During the week ending 5 April, 765 new cases were admitted to hospital and 188 deaths occurred. The following 2 weeks in turn saw 1,025 and 1,002 new hospital admissions and 293 and 290 deaths. These 2 weeks subsequently proved to have been the peak of the wave, figures for the following 2 weeks falling respectively to 876 and 767 hospital admissions and 194 and 132 deaths.

To the relief of authorities and the public-at-large fresh cases and

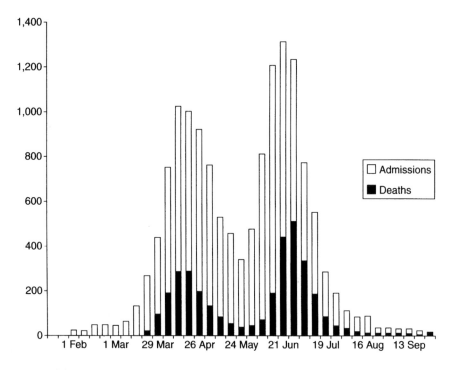

Figure 8.2 Hospital admissions and deaths from influenza, Sydney, 1919.

deaths continued to wane, and from early May daily hospital admissions fell well below three figures, giving rise to hopes that the epidemic would peter out. The last few days of that month, however, brought signs of a recrudescence that, within the space of a very short time, confirmed itself as an even more powerful second epidemic wave. Daily cases admitted to hospital surged to levels above those of the April wave and swamped the capacity of the hospital and medical system. Mortality statistics similarly started to rebound and quickly rose well past the toll at the peak of the first wave. The second half of June was devastating, over a thousand people dying, more than 2,500 being hospitalised (many more would have been if bed capacity had been greater) and thousands upon thousands of others being laid up bedridden in their homes. At the height of this period it was reported that:

> In some suburbs the disease has visited almost every house in every street – in fact whole families have been ill at once; that is the case at the present moment; and so highly infectious is the disease that those who have been called in to nurse the patients have themselves become infected within a few hours of the time of entering upon their duties. In the flats of Darlinghurst, Randwick, Cremorne, Kirribilli, and North Sydney few of the occupants have escaped the disease, which has swept through from floor to floor with amazing rapidity, rendering old and young hors de combat. Every large business house in the city, every public institution and utility, has had to carry on with greatly depleted staffs. . . .[11]

Fortunately, however, July brought respite. On Monday 30 June, the *Sydney Morning Herald* informed readers of signs of 'slight improvement', noting the weekend's 276 hospital admissions were substantially down on the 396 reported for the preceding weekend. The next day the paper carried a report that health authorities were optimistic that the height of virulence had been passed. The following weeks fortunately saw this assessment proved correct, new cases admitted to hospital falling away from daily tallies of one hundred plus to figures in the twenties and thirties by the end of the month.

Concerns about another recrudescence were expressed alongside conjecture about whether immunity levels in the population might have been built up sufficiently to protect against a third wave. No third wave was to occur, however, and by early August new hospital admissions had dropped to a trickle. Daily deaths from the flu reached single figures on 24 July and then dribbled away over August to the odd one or two per day, before virtually disappearing. Over the last 3 months of the year there were only fifteen deaths registered under influenza, just a fraction of the regular daily toll of a few months earlier. The flu had returned to its normal role as a very minor player on the city's epidemiological scene.

Explaining the waxing and waning

Why the epidemic carved this temporal path remains unknown. Part of the explanation presumably lies in the realm of virology and perhaps antigenic transformation of the infective agent. Influenza viruses are notoriously unstable and extremely expansionist, and thus it is possible that the virus of the first wave reassorted itself into a more virulent organism in the second wave, more frequently progressing to severe viral and secondary bacterial pneumonic complications.

Probably some of the preventive measures introduced (and removed) by the authorities also played a role. When the disease was first diagnosed in late January, a variety of restrictions and other preventive measures was quickly enacted by the State Cabinet: all theatres and public places of entertainment were closed; compulsory wearing of masks on trains, trams and ferries and in public streets, places and buildings; closure of schools, public telephones and liquor bars; additional inoculating depots to be opened; prohibition of race meetings and church services; removal of patients to hospital; strict quarantine of contacts (see Figure 8.3). As mid February arrived and no signs of an epidemic explosion seemed to be emerging, modifications relaxing some of the restrictions were introduced. Then, at the end of the month, all restrictions regarding public gatherings were abolished and compulsory masking in the open air (except inside public conveyances such as trams, trains and ferry boats) suspended. Provisons for removal of patients to hospital, quarantining contacts and inoculation were retained, however.

As has been described above, the epidemic started to pick up pace from a week-and-a-half or so into March. Whether the lifting of the regulations played any part in this can only remain conjecture. The increased mixing made permissible by their revocation is a plausible linkage, but the upsurge might equally well have occurred anyway. Whatever the case, masking regulations and tight restrictions on public gatherings were reimposed in late March–early April, along with a fresh inoculation campaign. Again, what impact these measures had can never be conclusively proven one way or the other. As is known, new cases and deaths increased to peak in mid April and then fell away over the last part of the month. Time-wise this supports a link, in the words of the Deputy Director-General of Public Health (Dr W.G. Armstrong) 'the improvement [occurring] at about the time it might have been expected' after the imposition of the measures.[12] The restrictions on public assembly would certainly have reduced the degree of population mixing and, accordingly, the risk of infection. However, how big an impact this had is uncertain. Breadwinners still had to go to work, householders still had to go out to buy supplies. Likewise, inoculation probably gave some protection, but just how much is unknown.[13]

In mid May, after several weeks of further decline in new cases and

To the People of New South Wales

A danger greater than war faces the State of New South Wales and threatens the lives of all. Each day the progress of the battle is published in the Press. Watch out for it. Follow the advice given and the fight can be won.

Already the efforts made by the Government have had the effect of keeping the New South Wales figures down. But everybody is not yet working, so from TO-DAY on the Government insists that the many shall not be placed in danger for the few and that

EVERYONE SHALL WEAR A MASK

Those who are not doing so are not showing their independence—they are only showing their indifference for the lives of others—for the lives of the women and the helpless little children who cannot help themselves.

CABINET DECISIONS:

At a special meeting of the Cabinet, held yesterday, the following recommendations of the Consultative Council (Medical Section) were adopted:—

1. Long-Distance Trains.—No need to restrict railway travel in New South Wales as yet, although it may be necessary to do so at any moment.
2. Hotel Bars, Restaurants, Tea Houses.—Not to be closed at the present time, but the 250 cubic feet regulation to apply to them.
3. Retail Shops.—Space regulation to apply; also prohibition of Bargain and Clearing sales, and a recommendation that orders be telephoned.
4. Church Services.—Prohibition of both indoor and outdoor services.
5. Auction Rooms.—Prohibition of all sales in rooms.
6. Libraries.—Reading rooms to be closed down.
7. Billiard Rooms.—To be closed.
8. Race Meetings.—Prohibited.
9. Theatres, Music Halls, Indoor Public Entertainments.—Prohibited.
10. Beaches.—No restrictions to be placed upon the free uses of the beaches on the ground that the risk of infection is likely to be more than counterbalanced by the benefits that will ensue.
11. Open Air Meetings in the Domain and Other Places.—Prohibited.
12. Churches and Schools Outside the County of Cumberland.—Not to be closed. Local authorities not to act on own initiative, but to be asked to refer to Public Health Department in every instance.

GENERAL RECOMMENDATION.

That, as far as possible, the people be encouraged during the course of the epidemic to take all possible advantage of fresh air as a means of increasing the natural resistance to infection, and of lessening the risk of infection, and also to avoid crowds.

W. A. HOLMAN, Premier.

Figure 8.3 Proclamation of N.S.W. Government regulations to control the epidemic.

Source: *The Sydney Morning Herald*, 3 February 1919. Reproduced here with permission of *The Sydney Morning Herald*.

deaths, the Government once again lifted all restrictions, following recommendations from its medical advisory body, the Consultative Medical Committee. Within a fortnight of the change both new cases and death toll reversed their decline and the city went into the second wave of the epidemic. To what extent the revoking of the restrictions played a part in this is another unknown. If the virus had changed genetic character, a major second wave was probably virtually inevitable. However, it seems (with the benefit of hindsight!) that this wave was perhaps given an easier run than might have been the case if the restrictions had been kept in place. This time around, there was no major reimposition of restrictions, just advice to the public – to submit to inoculation and re-inoculation and to avoid big assemblies of people. The State Premier warned that tough regulations would be gazetted if it was felt necessary, but no major ones ever were and the epidemic went on to ultimately play itself out as shown in Figure 8.2.

Might weather, perhaps, also have played a part in the ups and downs of the epidemic? Daily, weekly and seasonal weather conditions are known to be linked to a variety of human health problems,[14] amongst them influenza with its well-documented winter seasonality. The possible role of weather in shaping the epidemic's rhythm has been investigated in a number of case studies, but little convincing evidence has been uncovered.

Amongst Sydney's health authorities there was certainly the view that weather was not an irrelevant factor. For example, the *Sydney Morning Herald* of 13 March carried a statement by the Minister of Public Health (Mr J.D. Fitzgerald) that:

> A review of the situation by medical officers of the Health Department showed that the position [of the pandemic] might be affected by the onset of cold, changeable weather, and a proportion of severe and fatal cases among the infected may increase.

Later, looking back after the epidemic, the Deputy Director-General of Public Health (Dr W.G. Armstrong) drew a definite weather connection with the second wave, writing in the official report of the outbreak that:

> The weather during the course of the second wave was very unfavourable, and was marked by a succession of strong and cold westerly winds of the type that is usually accompanied by the occurrence of many cases of pneumonia when they prevail in Sydney in the winter months.[15]

Examination of weather records of the time, however, does not back up Armstrong's argument to the degree one might expect from his words. With the move into winter, temperatures certainly dropped in June 1919 (the heart of the second wave), but by Sydney standards it was not a markedly cold June. The mean shade temperature for the month indeed was 3°F higher than the 61-year average for the metropolis. A day-by-day analysis reveals there were occasions where a drop in temperature tallied with increased cases, but no consistency can be discerned. Analyses of lagging case and death figures a few days behind weather conditions are similarly inconclusive.

The most striking weather feature during the epidemic months did not in fact involve temperature, but rather rainfall, namely exceptionally heavy rain during May. Rain fell on 25 days of the month, dropping a total of 23 inches on the city, over four times the normal May total and producing the wettest May in the Weather Bureau's 79 years of records. This period, as discussed earlier and shown in Figure 8.2, corresponded with the tailing away of the first wave of the epidemic. Whether there was any connection can obviously never be proven. New cases and deaths had started falling before the start of the 'big wet', but perhaps the lengthy spell of wet conditions accentuated the decline through discouraging people from getting out and circulating as much as they might otherwise have done, thus reducing the mixing of infectives and the healthy. In June the metropolis returned to dry weather, rain only falling on 5 days and the city getting less than half its normal rainfall. Along with the fine weather, the month saw the city go into the second wave of the epidemic. Did this better weather possibly contribute to the new wave through encouraging more population circulation?

Counting the costs – the overall death toll

The mortality toll of the epidemic can be seen in two contrasting lights. From a strictly biological perspective it was a mild killer. As noted in the introduction to this chapter, an estimated 36–37 per cent of the city's residents (i.e. approximately 300,000 persons) were laid low with the flu during the epidemic, of whom about 3,500 died. Thus, from a case fatality point of view, the death rate was only about 1.2 per 100 persons attacked. By comparison, a bubonic plague outbreak in the city two decades earlier had had a case fatality rate of 34 per cent. In simple probability terms therefore, Sydneysiders had a high chance of getting the flu, but a very low likelihood of dying from it.

On the other hand, the very high incidence of the infection made the epidemic a major mortality crisis. Discounting the normal annual toll from influenza (i.e. 100–150 deaths), the epidemic took off about 3,350 persons to early graves and lifted the metropolis' crude death rate by about 4.1 per 1,000 population (See Table 8.1). Over 2,000 marital unions were ruptured by the death of a partner and for several thousand children it saw the loss of a mother or father. For the victims, assuming a life expectancy of 60 years, the epidemic stole in the order of 85,000 years of potential life.

Table 8.1 Population size and mortality, Sydney, 1918–20

	1918	1919	1920
Estimated mean population	785,000	810,700	884,790
Total deaths	7,862	11,907	9,429
Influenza deaths	134	3,484	118
Crude death rate (per 1,000 population)	10.02	14.69	10.66
Crude influenza death rate (per 1,000 population)	0.17	4.30	0.13

Sources: *NSW Statistical Register*, 1918–19, 1919–20 and 1920–21.

Varying risks – mortality differentials

How evenly was this mortality burden shared around? During the height of the epidemic's second wave tramway employees requested increased pay and other concessions because of the special risks they saw themselves exposed to 'in coming in such close contact with the travelling public'.[16] The Railway Commissioners, however, rejected the claim, stating 'all sections of the community are liable to attack, and in approximately the same degree'.[17]

On their first grounds the Commissioners were correct. The epidemic could and did attack all elements of the population. Newspaper obituaries and general reporting of the epidemic starkly showed this. The second assertion by the Commissioners was less valid. The epidemic did not make a perfectly even-handed sweep through the city. Males were more likely to die of the disease than females, people in their mid-twenties to late-thirties suffered the highest mortality, some occupational groups were hit harder than others, and death rates varied substantially between different parts of the metropolis.

Although there is not as much information available on morbidity, there were clearly also substantial variations in attack rates. For example, Dr Armstrong reported that a large post-epidemic survey of work establishments found attack rates ranged from 24.6 per cent for government department employees, to 43 per cent for shop and merchant office staff, to 44 per cent for factory workers, to 54 per cent for bank and insurance office employees.[18] The government department percentage patently masks considerable variation within that sector. For instance, in mid June the press reported 5,000 railway and tramway employees were officially off duty sick with the flu, 4,000 of these being from the metropolitan area. On the basis of 1921 Census figures this was around 42 per cent of the metropolis' total railway and tramway workforce. To that figure have to be added the (unknown) numbers who fell ill at other stages of the epidemic.

Age and sex mortality patterns

Almost certainly the most commented upon demographic characteristic of the 1918–19 pandemic has been its distinctive mortality age selectivity. Whereas 'normal' outbreaks of influenza tend to impact especially heavily on the elderly,[19] research from a wide range of countries has shown the pandemic's mortality toll by contrast to have been highest in the years of young to middle adulthood, or what might be termed the prime years of life. No really satisfactory explanations of this atypical patterning have ever been produced.

Examination of the official statistics of the epidemic shows Sydney's experience to have broadly conformed to this pattern, but with some local idiosyncrasies also showing up. On a straight age basis the epidemic hit the 25–39 years age-span with most force. Collectively this age-group accounted for 27.0 per cent of the metropolis' population, but suffered almost twice that proportion (48.7 per cent) of the registered deaths. All age groups below that span experienced less than their pro rata share of fatalities (i.e. 44.9 per cent of the population, 18.1 per cent of the deaths). Above that span the patterning was mixed, persons aged in their forties and their mid-sixties and beyond having around 25–30 per cent higher death rates than population numbers would have predicted, while those in their fifties and early sixties suffered roughly in proportion to their population strength.

While the particularly fatal focus on persons in the prime of life characterised the epidemic from beginning to end, interestingly it was most especially pronounced during the first wave (March–May). During that onslaught fully 53.5 per cent of all deaths came from the ranks of the metropolis' 25–39-year-olds. Through the second wave (June–July) persons in that age-range were again the most severely buffeted, but not quite to the same savage extent as earlier, this time contributing 45.6 per cent of fatalities. This lower percentage principally reflected increased deaths in the 50+ age group. In the first wave this group (16.0 per cent of the population) had escaped relatively lightly (12.9 per cent of deaths), but during the second surge they felt the epidemic's hand more heavily (21.0 per cent of deaths).

When the age patterning in turn is looked at separately for males and females, more complexities are found (Figure 8.4). First, this disaggregation shows that, while the heavy toll in the 25–39 years age-span was felt by both sexes, it was more pronounced in the male population. For females, excess mortality was, in fact, nearly as great amongst the elderly (65+) as it was amongst the 25–39 years cohort. Amongst elderly males the 'young-old' (65–74 years) escaped with slightly below expected mortality. However, the 'old-old' (75+) males' death rate was significantly elevated.

Overall the epidemic took a substantially heavier mortality toll of males than females, the crude death rates for the two sexes for the year being

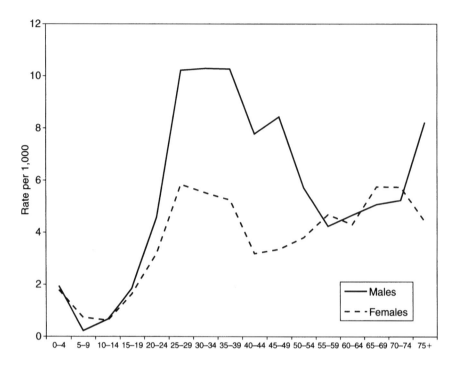

Figure 8.4 Age-specific death rates from influenza, Sydney, 1919.

respectively 5.3 and 3.3 per 1,000 population. As Figure 8.4 indicates, this male disadvantage was largely the product of mortality in the 25–49 years age range, rates for the two sexes below and above that range (with the exception of the 'old-old') being fairly comparable. For some reason the sex differential was most marked in the first wave (March–May) of the epidemic. During that stage male mortality as a whole was more than twice the female rate, with the differential weighted even more heavily against males in the 25–49 years age-span mentioned above. During the second wave male mortality was still higher than that of females, but the relative difference between the aggregate male:female rates narrowed to the order of around 1.3:1.

Why these age and sex differences occurred is impossible to explain with certainty. No age–sex based tabulations of influenza morbidity (attacks) are available and so nothing can be said as to whether mortality rates reflected attack rates, or whether some segments of the population, once getting the flu, were more vulnerable and likely to succumb to it. One might expect, for example, that the elderly would fit this latter pattern but, as shown above, death rates were not consistently significantly elevated within the older population. Statistics for influenza victims whose death certificates also mentioned other long-standing conditions certainly show some were probably in a vulnerable state of health when influenza struck.[20] For example, sixty-eight of those who died had organic diseases of the heart, while thirty-three had tuberculosis. Another 143 were classified as having 'ill-defined heart failure', some instances of which would have been prompted by the pneumonic-influenzal attack, but other cases of which probably represented undiagnosed chronic heart trouble. No age data, however, exists on these victims. Also, these instances of co-morbidity are not enough to explain the observed mortality differentials.

Conceivably, the higher mortality of males may have reflected some greater biological susceptibility on their part to the particular viral strain responsible for the epidemic, but at 80+ years' distance from the event that can only remain conjecture. It is interesting to note though, that the disproportionately higher male mortality of 1919 is not evident in the death statistics of the two surrounding (i.e. 'ordinary' influenza) years. In 1918 non-pneumonic influenza claimed thirty-four males and fifty-seven females in the metropolis, while in 1920 the male and female figures were balanced at fifty-nine deaths each.

Rather than biology, differential socio-behavioural risk factors relating to mobility and mixing within the metropolis probably explain most of the age- and sex-patterning. In this regard workforce participation was probably particularly relevant, through exposing large numbers of workers to elevated risks of infection on public transport to and from work and in their workplace environments – leading to the observed heavy death toll across the working ages. Extending this argument, the higher workforce participation rates of males (67.7 per cent of the population) over females (22 per cent of the population) in turn was a likely key factor behind the substantially heavier mortality of men. Male-dominated practices such as drinking in hotel bars (even though restrictions were placed on how long patrons could stay in hotels) and attending crowded sporting events were other likely sources of increased risk of infection. To re-emphasise though, these hypotheses are just that. No definite connections can be proven.

Socio-economic differences in mortality

Despite considerable searching, a feature of much previous research on the pandemic has been, with the exception of the distinctive age-pattern, the relative lack of patterning exhibited by the outbreak. For example, in the introduction to his wide-ranging edited volume on the urban impact of the pandemic in the Western world, Van Hartesveldt writes that, aside from the age oddity, 'few other patterns emerged with . . . clarity, for the flu paid little regard to wealth, climate, or other factors'.[21]

In the case of Sydney too, wealth offered no absolute protection from the outbreak. No echelon of society or the workforce escaped the flu's call. Victims ranged from medical practitioners, architects and barristers through to undertakers and bootmakers, to scavengers and labourers. Within this eclectic toll, however, there was a degree of social gradient to the epidemic, lower-status groups tending to suffer more than their higher-ranking fellow residents.

Some evidence for this can be directly gleaned from data published on the occupations (and ages) of males who died from influenza during 1919.[22] Unfortunately this data relates to the State as a whole, rather than just the metropolis. Nonetheless, by matching these records with occupational tabulations from the 1921 Census it is possible to get an idea of socio-economic differentials in the mortality toll – and reasonably confidently assume that these State-level patterns at least broadly applied within the metropolis. Death rates derived from matching these two data sets are presented in Table 8.2 and show the inverse social gradient claimed above.[23]

The actual mechanisms by which occupational mortality differentials emerge are always difficult to disentangle. In some cases direct on-the-job risk factors are involved. In other cases the differentials rather reflect more general life style and socio-economic status factors. Certainly some jobs would have brought their workers into especially close contact with the public and therefore, inevitably, with infected individuals. As noted earlier, the tramways employees believed their jobs exposed them to special risks of this nature, a claim that the Table 8.2 (and sick leave) figures suggest, despite the Railway Commissioners' denial, had some

Table 8.2 Death rates from influenza per 1,000 males aged 15+, by occupational group, New South Wales, 1919

Occupational group	*Rate per 1,000*
Professional	4.3
Commercial	4.8
Domestic	6.0
Industrial	6.2
– Labourer	12.0+
Transport and communication	6.5
– Railways and tramways	5.9
– Roads	6.4
– Seas, rivers, harbours	7.8
– Postal and telegraph services	5.5
Primary producers	2.4
All occupations	4.8

Sources: Deaths by occupations data: *NSW Statistical Register 1919–20*.
Occupations of males data: *Census of the Commonwealth of Australia, 1921. Part X. New South Wales – Population of Local Government Areas*.

Note
The rates are based on the assumption that the *Statistical Register* and *Census* allocations of individuals to occupational groups were identical. The open-ended value for labourers is due to the census tabulations burying labourers within the 'undefined industrial' class.

merit. The large number of deaths among road carters, carriers and draymen probably also had some foundation in their widespread travelling and mixing with the public. A similar hypothesis seems plausible for many of the fifty hotel workers who lost their lives during the epidemic. Workplaces that involved large assemblies of workers in close proximity to one another (e.g. the Post Office) were likely similarly risky.[24]

Besides the direct workplace determinants of elevated mortality risk, the socio-economic consequences of occupational position were presumably also important, through influencing housing quality, dietary standards and general standards of well-being. For many Sydney workers on low incomes, life in crowded, sub-standard housing was the norm, conditions especially conducive to the transmission of a droplet-spread infection such as influenza.[25] No data on the subject exists, but variations in dietary standards in turn would probably have meant differing levels of overall physical health between groups and hence of abilities to survive attacks of the flu. For the moment the question of socio-economic patterning will be left here. The subject, however, is returned to in the latter part of the next section on the geography of the epidemic.

The geographical patterning of the epidemic

As outlined earlier in the chapter, the first positively diagnosed case of pneumonic influenza in Sydney was a soldier who arrived in the city by train from Melbourne on Tuesday 21 January. The soldier stayed with relatives in the inner city area of Paddington for 2 days before being admitted to hospital. Whether he infected persons in that suburb in his 2-day stay there can obviously never be proved, but it would certainly seem a reasonable possibility as he was definitely highly infectious immediately afterwards, when persons in contact with him in hospital promptly went down with the infection. It was also reported in the newspapers that the soldier's brother at Paddington had developed a slight rise in temperature on the following Saturday morning. No follow-up reports of the brother's condition, however, were published. Whether the soldier from Melbourne was the source or not, the suburb was soon producing its own cases, *Sydney Morning Herald* reports on 3, 4, 10, 12 and 18 February detailing confirmed cases admitted to hospital from the area.

Several similar plausible models of infected arrivals from Melbourne seeding local areas within Sydney can be sketched. Another soldier, for example, stayed with people in Darlinghurst and Mascot before being admitted to hospital, and several Darlinghurst cases appeared soon after. The close geographic proximity of Paddington and Darlinghurst (i.e. adjoining suburbs) also makes some linkage between the early outbreaks in these two areas a possibility. Two other late January arrivals from Melbourne respectively spent time in Enmore (with relatives) and central Sydney (at a hotel) before hospitalisation. A number of other confirmed cases who had recently come from Melbourne are also known to have spent time in the community before their illness led them to being hospitalised, but details of where they actually stayed within the metropolis are unavailable.

A 'mystery' case may also have played a role. In a 28 January item on the first soldier case, the *Sydney Morning Herald* reported that the soldier:

> ... had travelled in the train with a civilian resident in Sydney, who had been spending a holiday in Melbourne. The civilian had been sick all the way, suffering from a bad headache and feverishness.

This civilian was also referred to in the Department of Public Health's official report of the epidemic, but no trace was ever found of the person. Whether this passenger had the flu and perhaps infected his fellow traveller before disappearing into Sydney to infect others can thus only ever remain a matter for conjecture.

Early on, cases were concentrated in the inner city, but fairly quickly spread out beyond this core. For example, by 20 February, 4 weeks after the first case, the epidemic had reached out to more distant areas such as Willoughby, Ryde, Hunter's Hill, Burwood, Enfield and Canterbury, and in fact even further afield to several extra metropolitan districts (e.g. Auburn, Bankstown, Lidcombe and Hornsby). The Canterbury municipality (10–11 kilometres from the city centre) for some reason was particularly hit, between 7 and 27 February producing twenty-one reported (hospitalised) cases, the most from any area outside the central city. All of these areas were on the city's rail or, in the case of Hunter's Hill, ferry network, and this, in conjunction with the large central city concentration of jobs, meant diffusion of the outbreak through the metropolis was both easy and virtually inevitable.

It is not possible to trace the evolving geographical spread and intensification of the epidemic beyond about 3 weeks into March. Up until that point the metropolitan newspapers gave details of the number of new cases coming from particular areas. The burgeoning number of cases, however, saw that reporting briefly drop down to just giving the names of areas that cases came from (the numbers from each area no longer being given), and then locational details of cases being dropped altogether. Data on the total number of cases of pneumonic influenza notified in the metropolis was subsequently published in the annual report of the Medical Officer of Health, but in the text accompanying the tabulated data the Officer himself stated that 'the number of attacks officially notified was no criterion, either as to the extent or distribution locally of the disease'.[26] As noted earlier, close to 300,000 persons were estimated to have been attacked. Official notifications of pneumonic influenza, however, only totalled 9,817.

The first fatality from the epidemic occurred on 10 February at the

Coast Hospital, this unfortunate distinction falling to a railway worker of the inner city suburb of Waterloo who had been admitted to the hospital the day before.[27] The remainder of February saw nine further deaths, from scattered locations across the metropolis. A small number were also reported from fringe suburbs beyond the metropolitan boundary proper. This pattern continued for the first 3 weeks of March. As the epidemic picked up tempo, however, an inner city focused mortality began to take shape. Data limitations do not allow a week by week spatio-temporal charting of the death toll,[28] but the uneven geographic pattern ultimately cut across the city by the outbreak is clearly shown in Figure 8.5. As depicted on the map, a contiguous group of thirteen inner city local government areas formed the spatial core of the epidemic, all registering age–sex standardised mortality ratios (SMRs)[29] from the flu above the metropolitan norm. These local authority areas were home to 40.7 per cent of the metropolis' population, but suffered 53.5 per cent of the epidemic's deaths. Outside this inner core five other areas suffered above average mortality: Eastwood, Homebush, Hunter's Hill, Botany and Hurstville. All other areas escaped with below average mortality, the least hit localities being the north of the harbour and Parramatta River local government areas of Ryde, Lane Cove, Ku-ring-gai, Willoughby and Manly, plus the eastern suburbs municipality of Vaucluse.

Overall, male and female SMRs traced similar geographies. As noted earlier, male death rates during the epidemic were substantially higher than female ones, but in relative terms they tended to follow similar patterns, areas in which males were heavily or lightly hit generally exhibiting a similar level for females ($r = 0.801$). In a few areas though, the two sexes fared quite differently. For instance, in Leichhardt females suffered significantly above average mortality while their male counterparts were hit with below average force. In Mascot, on the other hand, the reverse occurred, females escaping with significantly lower than average losses while the males of the area were hit quite seriously. Another 'aberrant' case was Redfern, where again the female SMR was substantially more elevated than the male ratio would have predicted. No obvious explanations for these cases can be found in their resident population or area characteristics.

These patterns of respectively high and low mortality suggest linkages with the demographic, social and economic topography of the metropolis briefly profiled earlier in the chapter – and also appear to fit, at least partially, epidemiologically plausible models of differential epidemic mortality. To test these apparent associations and models more formally, correlation and regression analyses were conducted between the influenza SMRs and selected 1921 Census-based independent variables measuring aspects of population density/crowding, population mixing and socio-economic status. Brief comments on these variables follow.

In seeking to explain the geographical patterning of a highly infectious

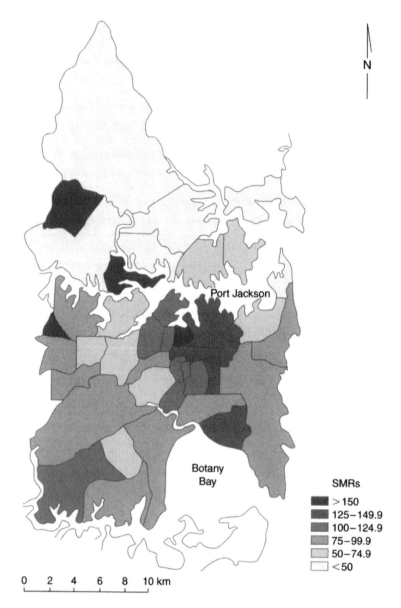

Figure 8.5 Age–sex standardised influenza mortality ratios, Sydney, 1919.

disease such as influenza, the variable that probably most immediately comes to mind is population density, since conditions of population crowding facilitate the disease's droplet mode of infective spread. Crowding is obviously possible in a number of contexts – the residential environment, travelling to work, in the workplace and in social situations. For the analysis here though, suitable disaggregated data by area only existed for density dimensions of the residential environment.[30] In one sense this is working over already ploughed land, the Government Statistician's 1920 report of the epidemic having stated that 'the highest death rates were in areas where population was most congested'.[31] However, the report did not pursue exactly how strong the density factor was.

Population mixing was seen as another likely factor involved. To some extent the idea of mixing is subsumed within that of high population densities/crowding. Another side of mixing though is the circulatory one, that is the degree to which people moved around the city and the extent to which therefore they were likely to cross paths with infected individuals. In the absence of direct data on movement patterns within the metropolis, participation in the paid workforce was used as a surrogate indicator of mixing, in the sense that the going out to work that paid employment generally involved would have brought the workers concerned into contact with other people.

The final set of postulated explanatory variables were a number of socio-economic indicators covering housing, labour force status and occupational class. Like population mixing, aspects of socio-economic status are inherent in the population density/crowding variables, lower socio-economic class often meaning consignment to small, crowded housing quarters. That is clearly not the only way, however, that socio-economic status might conceivably have affected the level of mortality. In general, higher socio-economic class presumably translated into higher material standards of living (e.g. housing quality, nutritional level) that in turn translated into better health status than enjoyed by the city's poorer classes. While the flu killed many previously perfectly healthy individuals, it is likely that overall the better the person's prior level of health, the better his or her chance was of warding off or surviving an attack. It also seems reasonable to presume that present-day research findings, showing lower socio-economic class people to be disadvantaged in such areas as health knowledge and health-seeking behaviour, probably also applied 80+ years ago.

The simple correlations (r) between these variables and the influenza SMRs are given in Table 8.3. With an analytical framework of forty-two areas and a probability level of <0.05, all coefficients of ±0.30 or more rate as statistically significant. As can be seen, in all instances where this is the case, the coefficients are in the direction hypothesised in the discussion above. None of the variables, however, registered anything stronger than a moderate relationship with the epidemic's varying areal death toll.

On a comparative basis the results show mortality to have followed the city's socio-economic status contours more closely than the lines of the other predictor variables considered. The association between death rates and population densities, as measured by persons per room, was next strongest, but somewhat lower than the Government Statistician's

Table 8.3 Correlations (*r*) between 1919 standardised influenza mortality ratios and selected 1921 Census demographic and socio-economic indicators, Metropolitan Sydney

Constructs/Variables	r
Population density/crowding	
Persons per square kilometre	0.25
Occupied dwellings per square kilometre	0.23
Average number of persons per occupied private dwelling	0.47
Average number of persons per room (occupied private dwellings)	0.53
Population mixing	
Male population – per cent breadwinners	0.02
Female population – per cent breadwinners	0.01
Total population – per cent breadwinners	0.20
Socio-economic status	
Male breadwinners – per cent in professional occupations	−0.60
Male breadwinners – per cent in manufacturing occupations	0.39
Male breadwinners – per cent employers	−0.60
Male breadwinners – per cent unemployed	0.51
Occupied private dwellings – average weekly rent	−0.57
Occupied private dwellings – per cent owner occupied	−0.46

qualitative comments perhaps might have seemed to imply.[32] No significant metropolitan-wide association was found with gross population density (i.e. persons per square kilometre). There was clearly some relationship in the older established, more fully developed areas, but the failure of the gross measure to portray the 'real' densities in the built-up parts of a number of high SMR areas with large non-residential expanses of land (e.g. Eastwood, Botany and Hurstville) brought the total metropolitan correlation value down. No sign of co-variation with mortality meanwhile was shown by any of the population mixing variables. This result more probably reflects inadequate operationalisation of the mixing construct than faulty logic in the hypothesised relationship.

Multiple regression and correlation analysis were then used to explore how well the chosen predictor variables might in combination 'explain' the areal patterning of mortality. By forcing all the variables listed in Table 8.3 into a regression model, the level of statistical explanation can be lifted quite substantially, but this is more a statistical artefact than any genuine increase in understanding. Many of the variables are highly inter-correlated and make no significant independent contribution to statistical explanation.

No great success either was found through more selective models. Basically, once a 'successful' socio-economic variable (e.g. per cent of male breadwinners in professional occupations or per cent of males unemployed) was entered into a model, little significant gain was made by adding the persons per dwelling or persons per room density measures, or any of the other chosen indicators. In various runs of these models no significant multiple correlation of better than around 40 per cent was achieved.

Conclusion

The 1919 influenza epidemic ranks as the greatest health and social disaster in Sydney's history, killing around 3,500 residents of the metropolis in the space of a few months, laying low several hundred thousand others with attacks of varying severity, and causing widespread social and economic disruption. The epidemic hit Sydney in two distinctive waves separated by about a month, the second wave being much more powerful than the first. No satisfactory explanation, however, has yet been advanced to explain this temporal pattern. Possibly it had something to do with genetic transformation of the virus, possibly something to do with the various preventive measures introduced (and removed) by government authorities. Perhaps Sydney's weather conditions also played a role through influencing human behaviour.

Like all epidemics, the influenza outbreak had a differential impact on the metropolis' population. As elsewhere, young adults suffered the highest mortality, with males in particular being affected. While the epidemic affected all social groups in the city, it would appear that the working class and blue-collar workers experienced the heaviest death rates. Geographically, the epidemic also had a differential impact on Sydney, with the inner city area suffering the greatest mortality. Correlation and regression analyses using socio-economic status and population density (persons per room) predictor variables 'explained' around 40 per cent of the spatial variation in death rates. How much of the remaining mortality variation was patterned, or was simply epidemic randomness, awaits further research.

9 The overshadowed killer

Influenza in Britain in 1918–19

N.P.A.S. Johnson

1918 was not a good year to be a young adult in Britain. Long years of war had killed and maimed tens, if not hundreds, of thousands of your peers and now something as apparently innocuous as flu was to come to claim more. Now, what *The Times* called the 'great plague of influenza'[1] came to blight thousands more lives through illness and death, claiming more than 225,000 deaths throughout England, Scotland and Wales in little less than a year. Many of these deaths were of young adults – of the 141,989 civilian deaths recorded as being due to influenza in England and Wales some 45 per cent were of people aged 15–35.[2] The influenza pandemic of 1918–19 is considered to have killed some 40 to 100 million people world-wide and infected half the world's population, a billion people.[3] Just before this the 4 years of the First World War had an estimated death toll of 10 million.

In many instances the case fatality rates in epidemic and pandemic influenza are no greater than in 'normal' years, around 2 to 3 per cent. However, in 1918 morbidity was so much greater that the resulting mortality was tremendous. Some countries and some peoples suffered dreadfully. Western Samoa experienced one of the highest death rates as it lost 22 per cent of its population (30 per cent of the adult males, 22 per cent of the adult female population and 10 per cent of children).[4] In some isolated cases, e.g. Canadian Inuit, even higher fatality rates are found, with up to 100 per cent of some communities felled.[5]

The pandemic struck the world in three waves. The first was in the northern summer of 1918, the second in the northern autumn and winter of 1918, and the third early in 1919. It was the second wave that really killed. For example, in England and Wales some 64 per cent of deaths came in the second wave; 10 per cent in the first and 26 per cent in the last. This pattern of three waves was repeated virtually everywhere.

Britain's experience of this pandemic exhibits many similarities with how it struck elsewhere. This was a pandemic in the truest sense, a global epidemic, in which the universalities, the common features such as the timing, the three waves, the age distribution of mortality, the generally low case fatality rate and the pneumonic complications, with the 'heliotrope cyanosis' that turned the faces of so many of those who died blue and purple, are so striking and so pervasive that they almost become banal while also rendering trivial local variations. It is these universal character- istics that allow us to recognise that this was a singular pandemic of influenza, particularly the age distribution of mortality and the severity of so many cases, particularly the blue-purple cyanosis.

Britain has a long acquaintance with influenza. The Registrar-General (RG) has been recording influenza mortality since 1837. Currently, between 3,000 and 4,000 people die each year in Britain as a result of influenza and influenza-related causes. In the winter of 1989–90 an estimated 29,000 Britons died during an influenza epidemic.

Never before in the influenza record was there to be such an upturn as was seen in 1918 (Figure 9.1). Apart from the war, 1918 was a relatively healthy year in England and Wales, until the flu-ridden final quarter. The influenza pandemic transformed it into the first year, since national records began, in which the number of deaths exceeded the number of births.[6]

Mortality

The British experience of the pandemic appears to match that of much of the rest of the world, as reported in the literature. The pandemic was visited upon the British in the three waves, bringing massive morbidity

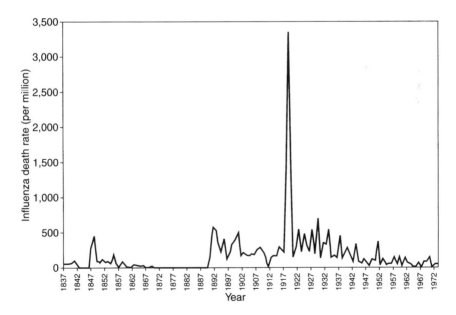

Figure 9.1 Long-term influenza mortality in England and Wales.

Source: Data taken from the *Annual Report of the Registrar-General* for period 1837–1973.

and attendant excessive mortality, disrupting normal life and carrying away many, especially young adults. This wave pattern is readily apparent when influenza mortality is plotted (Figure 9.2).

The RG maintained that during the 46 weeks of the pandemic in England and Wales some 151,446 people had died, of whom 140,989 were civilians. The annualised[7] civilian death rate for influenza in England and Wales was then 4.774 per thousand.[8] In Edinburgh the RG for Scotland stated that 17,575 Scots had died, at a rate of 4.3 per thousand.[9] However, these were deaths allocated to influenza only.

One of the most difficult areas for those working on past outbreaks of disease is that of data. What data there is tends to be patchy and of questionable reliability. How much confidence can we have in the data and its validity? This has long been a concern with medical or vital statistics. For example, Mooney quotes from the *49th Annual Report of the Registrar-General (ARRG)* that 'It is useless ... to shut our eyes to the imperfections of our records. To be without trustworthy means of comparison is doubtlessly an evil, but to ignore the difficulties and deal with the records as thoroughly reliable would be still worse, for it is far better to be without statistics at all than to be misled by false ones.'[10] Notwithstanding such pessimism, is it not better to use what data we have while recognising its limitations?

The nature of influenza has long given rise to problems of misdiagnosis and under-reporting of influenza deaths. However, it has been recorded as a cause of death in England and Wales from the latter half of 1837,

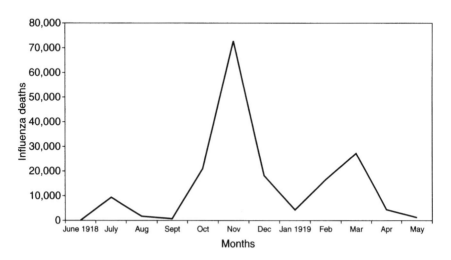

Figure 9.2 Influenza deaths in England, Scotland and Wales.

Sources: Registrar-General, *Report on the mortality from influenza in England and Wales* and Registrar-General for Scotland, *Report on the Mortality from Influenza in Scotland during the Epidemic of 1918–19: A Supplement to the Annual Reports of the Registrar-General for Scotland*, Edinburgh, HMSO, 1919.

since the start of registration. The recording of influenza has not been subject to the changes of definition and methods of recording that have punctuated the recording of many diseases as the International Classification of Diseases has grown inexorably.

The English RG's report did, however, recognise that there was likely to have been an under-estimation of influenza mortality:

> It is well known that during influenza epidemics the mortality attributed to the disease does not represent the whole of that caused by it. The entries under other headings, especially those of respiratory disease, are always found to increase during an epidemic, and ... it is still necessary to make allowance for these increases in mortality, allocated to other causes but really attributable to influenza, in endeavouring to measure the loss of life.[11]

Consequently, the RG devised three methods for estimating the total mortality attributable to the pandemic.[12] These were devised to calculate all the 'excess' deaths that could be claimed to have been caused by the pandemic but were not recorded as influenza deaths. The first method, the specific cause method, involved comparing the deaths for each quarter of the pandemic against deaths in the previous 5 years (1913–17) for specific causes of death. Several causes of death were examined for 'excess' deaths based on annualised death rates and these deaths then re-allocated as influenza-caused deaths. The causes included were pneumonia (all forms); bronchitis; 'organic heart disease'; and pulmonary tuberculosis (phthisis). The excess mortality was then added to the recorded influenza deaths to reach an estimate of total pandemic mortality.

The second method employed, the 'other' causes method, compared the healthiness of 1918 to the average for the previous 5 years for the 'other causes' (not influenza and not those causes listed above) and then assumed that, in the absence of influenza, the total mortality would have been in the same ratio as between these causes in 1918 and in the previous 5 years. The 'excess' mortality could then be regarded as influenza-related. From this method 1918 was shown to have 86.89 per cent of the mortality of the average for the previous 5 years for those 'other causes' (94.2 per cent in Scotland), making it a relatively healthy year. Taking the average mortality from all causes over the previous 5 years and taking the percentage of this, it was possible to calculate the 'expected' mortality. Removing this figure from the recorded mortality meant the remainder could again be claimed to be the excess influenza mortality and added to the recorded figure to obtain another estimate of total pandemic mortality.

The third method of estimation was the '1918 improvement' method. This was based on the assumption that mortality would have been similar to that found in the first and second quarters of 1918. In England and

Wales total mortality for the first quarter of 1918 was 86.5 per cent of that for the 1913–17 average, while in the second quarter of 1918 it was 89.6 per cent, an average of 88.0 per cent. In Scotland the figures were 81.3 per cent and 87.4 per cent respectively, an average of 84.4 per cent. From here expected mortality was calculated and compared with actual mortality. Again the excess could be claimed as influenza-related.

For England and Wales 151,446 deaths were recorded as being due to influenza, with 140,989 of these being civilian deaths. Using the various estimation methods, with their different comparison periods, the RG calculated total influenza mortality for the pandemic as shown in Table 9.1.

This estimate was rounded. 'In view of the uncertainties of the estimation,' the RG argued, 'the round figure of 200,000 deaths attributable to the epidemic ... may be accepted.'[13] The calculated civilian mortality figure actually agreed rather well with the simple increase in mortality between each quarter of the pandemic and that of the corresponding quarter one year earlier, as shown in Table 9.2.

The allocated figure of 140,989 gave an annualised civilian death rate due to influenza of 4.774 per thousand. An adjusted tally of 185,000 civilian deaths raised this to 6.264 per thousand for England and Wales.

The Registrar-General for Scotland stated that the official, registered mortality for the pandemic was 17,575, giving an annual death rate of 4.3 per thousand population. This figure included 'not only those deaths of which influenza was the sole named cause, but also those deaths of which influenza was one of two or more named causes, the latter being far more numerous'.[14] Thus the official figures are based only on those deaths recorded with influenza as a cause of death. The RG claimed that total mortality was probably of the order of 22,000.[15]

Applying the English RG's excess methods calculations to the

Table 9.1 Recalculated influenza deaths (England and Wales)

Population	Total
Female	~100,000
Civilian male	~84,000
Non-civilian male	~14,000
Total deaths	~198,000

Table 9.2 Simple increase in mortality (England and Wales)

Earlier quarter	Mortality	Pandemic period	Mortality	Increase
Q3 1917	94,591	Q3 1918	114,218	19,627
Q4 1917	112,741	Q4 1918	241,218	128,477
Q1 1918	138,005	Q1 1919	191,922	53,867
Total increase				184,311

Table 9.3 Recalculated influenza deaths (Scotland)

Method	Estimated total pandemic mortality
Specific causes	33,143
'Other' causes	27,650
1918 improvement	33,771

Scottish data leads to an upward revision of the mortality figures, given in Table 9.3.

These figures indicate that the recorded influenza mortality of 17,575 is a marked understatement of the total mortality associated with the pandemic. The higher recalculations of total mortality are near to doubling that figure. The revised estimates of mortality give annualised death rates of 6.8 to 8.3 per 1,000. Consequently, the total mortality for the 1918–19 influenza pandemic in Britain would appear to be of the order of 225,000 rather than the recorded 169,021.

Causes

The RG selected five specific causes to include in the recalculation of influenza mortality. Were these selections justified? Was it necessary to include all of these causes? One way to investigate this is by assessing the relative importance of each of these causes to total mortality and by examining the age–sex structure of the mortality caused by these specific causes. The relative importance of each specific cause of death can be demonstrated by collecting the number of deaths from these causes and total deaths for males and females in England and Wales for each year in the period 1911–19, as published in the *ARRG*, and calculating what proportion of total mortality was caused by the specific causes. 1911 saw changes in reporting areas and the disease definitions used, thus data prior to that is less comparable.

The relative importance of the five specific causes for female mortality in England and Wales is shown in Figure 9.3. These trends indicate how important each disease was through this period while, to some extent, removing the problem of changing populations and population structure. The female population figures are considered more reliable than those for males which were disrupted by the war. The trends for males exhibited the same patterns as shown here for females. It was apparent that both influenza and pneumonia showed a marked increase in relative importance in 1918 and that both bronchitis and organic heart disease displayed an increase in relative importance in 1919. However, phthisis seemed to actually decrease during 1918–19. Were those who would 'normally' have died of tuberculosis being claimed by influenza or were their deaths attributed to influenza?

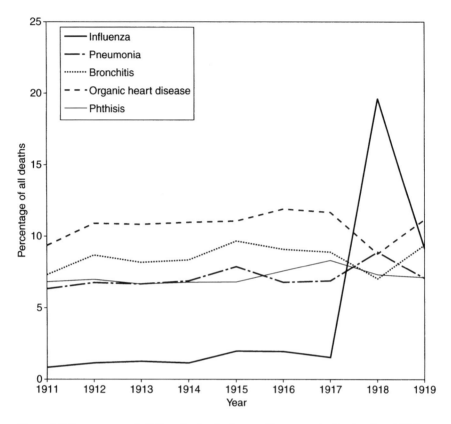

Figure 9.3 Percentage of all female deaths by specific causes in England and Wales.

Examining the age–sex distributions for each cause could reveal changes in the nature of the mortality brought by the disease. This was done by collating and averaging deaths for each cause in age-groups for the periods 1911–17 and 1918–19 for females and males. From this it was apparent that influenza mortality rose steeply, particularly in young adults. Bronchitis displayed similar patterns of mortality in both periods, as did phthisis, with only some increases in female mortality at certain ages, notably young adults. Pneumonia claimed more lives at all age-groups among both men and women, whereas organic heart disease actually showed a decrease during the pandemic period. Again, were those who may have died of this cause dying of influenza or were their deaths attributed to influenza? From these two examinations of the causes it seems that deaths attributed to bronchitis and organic heart disease may not have been particularly influenced by the pandemic. A link between phthisis deaths and the influenza seems more problematic, while pneumonia deaths appear to have risen in concert with the pandemic, as expected.

One cause that was not investigated by the RG was encephalitis lethargica. It was only much later that the connection between influenza and encephalitis lethargica was acknowledged.[16] In England and Wales encephalitis lethargica was only recorded as a separate cause of death in the period 1920–30, and 1921–30 in Scotland. Total recorded encephalitis lethargica deaths for this period were 10,673 in England and Wales and 1,203 in Scotland. Thus another 11–12,000 deaths could possibly be added to the tally of the pandemic mortality.

Age and sex mortality

The single most notable feature of this pandemic was the age distribution of mortality. Influenza mainly claims the older and younger segments of the population. This was not the case in 1918–19. Young adults bore the brunt of mortality in this pandemic. Throughout the literature this pattern of mortality is regarded as the single most extraordinary (but characteristic) feature of this influenza. It was a feature that was widely recognised at the time. Figures 9.4 and 9.5 show the age distribution of mortality in England and Wales, and Scotland respectively.

The basic statistics from the RG's report led the Ministry of Health to conclude 'the mortality in England and Wales, as a whole, attributable directly or indirectly, to influenza, is without any precedent in magnitude ... the toll taken at the young adult ages of life is without *any* know [sic] West European or North American precedent.'[17] The Ministry report also noted that there had been an increase in influenza deaths 'at 15–35 years of age, from 8 to 10 per cent to 45 per cent' of the total mortality caused by influenza.[18]

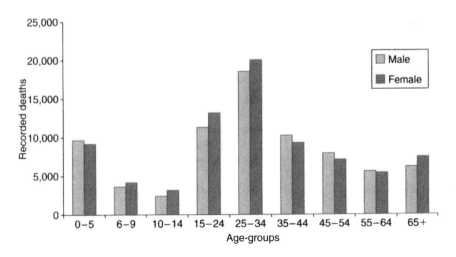

Figure 9.4 Age distribution of influenza mortality in England and Wales, 1918–19.

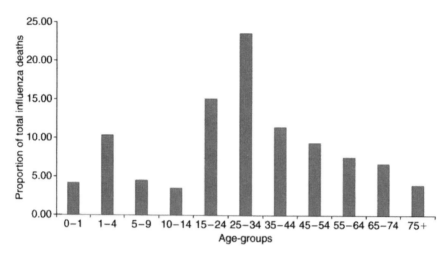

Figure 9.5 Age distribution of influenza mortality in Scotland, 1918–19.

In Scotland the Registrar-General recorded that the 'most conspicuous feature of this distribution is the great frequency of death at the younger adult ages, 20 to 40 . . . This distribution differs markedly both from those of previous influenza epidemics and also from the distribution commonly found from all causes of death.'[19] Indeed, the RG's report went on to note that 'fully 50 per cent. [of the mortality occurred] between ages 15 and 44'.[20]

This age distribution of mortality is consistent through the three waves of the pandemic in Britain. It first appeared in the first wave of the pandemic, but was absent from the influenza mortality for 1920. It is this pattern of influenza mortality by age that can be used to determine the length of the pandemic and to confirm that it came in three waves to Britain, and that there was no fourth wave as is suggested for some countries.

Various explanations for this age-differentiation of mortality have been proposed, but no single one has been widely accepted. Explanations such as malnutrition or reduced immunity due to wartime conditions fail to address the fact that this pattern was found in belligerent and non-belligerent nations alike. There is as yet no convincing explanation for the universality of this pattern, and thus the tendency is to regard the virus strain as peculiarly lethal to young adults. In many cases the sheer vitality of the victim was seen as contributing to death – the fittest and healthiest seemed the most likely to suffer the heliotrope cyanosis with its almost invariably terminal outcome. One suggestion is that, as their immune systems swung into excessive action, they were effectively drowned![21] Apparently as the second wave declined in morbidity, young adult mortality actually increased.[22]

While it was the young adults who suffered the greatest mortality above all others, there is little reporting of any significant variation in mortality by sex. Again, this is more or less consistent throughout the pandemic the world over. Different locations may show a slight differentiation between the sexes, but these are not significant or consistent. In England and Wales slightly more female deaths were recorded than male. This was also the case in Scotland, where 52.2 per cent of recorded influenza deaths were of women. The overall influenza death rate was 432 per 100,000, with the female rate being slightly higher at 437 per 100,000 and the male rate as 426 per 100,000. However, the Registrar-General discounted this variation as being significant when writing that the

> small observed difference between the male and female death-rates should not be accepted as a reliable indication of influenza having been in fact more fatal in the female population than in the male, for these rates depend on estimated populations, and at present time these estimations are not very reliable, their reliability being reduced by the long period which has now elapsed since the taking of the last census and also by the effect of war conditions on the population being unascertained ... the two distributions are very similar.[23]

However, this rather masks what may be an important component of the female mortality – the deaths of pregnant women. Influenza mortality levels can be considerably higher among pregnant women, often associated with abortion, miscarriage and/or stillbirth.[24] For example, in Scotland some 266 deaths from 'diseases and accidents of pregnancy and child-birth in association with influenza' were recorded.[25] These constituted 2.9 per cent of the total recorded female influenza deaths and 'equal a death-rate of 13 per 100,000 of the female population'.[26] However, this rate relates to the entire female population, not that of the 'population at risk', the pregnant female population. It does not allow us to determine if influenza had a notably deleterious effect on pregnant women or if they perished in much the same proportion as the rest of the population.

Demographic impact

An event of such magnitude with high levels of mortality must have great demographic consequences. These can include changes in patterns of nuptiality and fertility, the effective loss of life years for a community or nation, and the number of children orphaned. Some researchers have started to examine the dimensions of these impacts.[27] However, in Britain and a number of other countries, it is extremely difficult if not impossible to separate out the demographic effects of the pandemic from those of the First World War. This is largely due to the fact that both events impacted so heavily on the same segments of the population, the young adults. Examining the basic demographic statistics actually reveals little of the pandemic. Figure 9.6 illustrates the crude death rate (CDR), crude birth rate (CBR) and infant mortality rate (IMR) for England and Wales for the first 30 years of the twentieth century. It is readily apparent that while the CDR jumped sharply in 1918, from 14.4 per 1,000 in 1917 to 17.3 per 1,000, before dropping to 13.7 in 1919, the CBR and IMR are less affected by the pandemic. The CBR that had been in sharp decline throughout the war and had the lowest recorded levels to that time, stabilised in 1918 before a slight rise in 1919 preceded a marked increase in 1920. It is perhaps plausible that the pandemic may have diminished or delayed this increase. Infant mortality had been trending downwards for some time, with only a minor reversal of this trend during 1918. Again, this may be attributable in part to the influenza.

The deaths of more than 2,500 pregnant women from flu have already been noted. Obviously then at least 2,500 births were foregone in Britain. It is impossible to quantify the additional deaths of pregnant women not recorded as such, but it is likely that they would not be insignificant. It was those pregnancies terminated by abortion, miscarriage or death that were recorded, and even they are an understatement. This leaves another issue still untouched. What about those pregnancies that never happened, the averted births due to the deaths of women who may have borne children? Using fertility rates and the numbers of female deaths by age, it is possible to make an estimate of these averted births.[28] From these it appears that in the vicinity of 5,000 births were averted due to the deaths of the potential mothers from influenza during the pandemic.

Egalitarian flu?

One possible explanation for variation in influenza mortality may lie in socio-economic status. Perhaps in those areas where people were more prosperous and healthier they were better able to cope with the pandemic. They may not have avoided the disease and morbidity may have been relatively uniform, but ill-health is (and was) not just a matter of exposure. The existing state of health, state of housing and access to healthcare could be significant. The RG's report examined the putative link between influenza mortality and both general health standards and wealth (indicated by the average death rate for 1911–14 and the proportion of indoor domestic servants in 1911 respectively) in London's Metropolitan Boroughs. These showed little or no relationship with influenza mortality, and the RG concluded that the 'mortality of the late epidemic fell almost alike on the sanitarily just and on the unjust'.[29] A similar study by the Ministry of Health found little association between existing death rates and the pandemic.[30]

Another dimension investigated and found to show little association was overcrowding, including measurements of number of persons per dwelling, persons per room and other aspects of 'bad housing'.[31] Crowd-

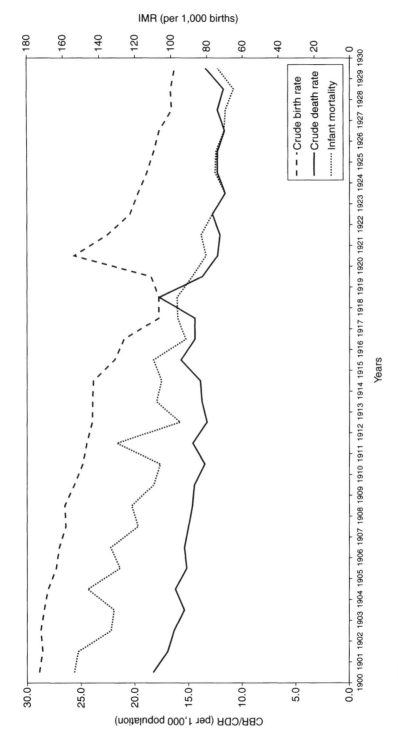

Figure 9.6 Vital statistics, England and Wales, 1900–30.

ing may not have been an issue as the virus was so virulent, so infectious that the 'necessary exposures and contacts of *all* persons living under urban conditions are sufficiently numerous to provide opportunities of transfer so effective that any increase above the average is relatively a factor of negligible order'. Such findings led Tomkins to contend that 'the epidemic was remarkably democratic in its victims'.[32] A recent examination of 1911 and 1921 occupation data and possible relationships with influenza mortality suggested that while influenza mortality was spread across the entire community, there may have been an element of class differential in this mortality, but there was not a particularly strong association.[33] The RG's decennial supplement claimed that influenza mortality varies 'definitely, though not greatly, with social class'.[34]

Morbidity

Mortality data have their limitations. However, they are at least collected and collated systematically. This is not the case for morbidity data. Influenza morbidity data are rarely collected and are generally of little value. Influenza is often self-diagnosed and self-treated and only a small proportion of cases ever comes into contact with the medical profession, and even then diagnosis is not certain. That is true now just as much as it was in 1918. The available but limited morbidity data does not allow us to make particularly strong statistical statements about case fatality and the like, but may afford some insight into the pandemic and an understanding of levels of social disruption that it brought.

Estimates of morbidity and case fatality rates vary, where they are given, but generally suggest that Britain's experience was much like that described elsewhere. Frazer noted that the 'number of actual cases ... is not known; but it would appear that the case mortality rate amongst the civilian population was low, being not more than 1 to 3 per 1,000'.[35]

Contemporary reports and official inquiries give an indication of morbidity. However, it is advisable to treat these with caution, as Van Hartesveldt[36] counsels when discussing the Manchester Medical Officer of Health, James Niven's block surveys that suggested morbidity of approximately 25 per cent.[37] Sources such as newspaper reports also give an indication of morbidity levels. For example, one story from *The Times* during the spring wave of the pandemic reported that a textile house of 400 workers 'had 80 on the sick list on Saturday, and yesterday ... another 20 had to give up'. The same report noted that in Newcastle some mines had absentee rates as high as 70 per cent.[38] Within a week Wigan coalfields were reporting one-third of the workforce absent due to influenza.[39] Similar morbidity among prisoners of war at a Hampshire camp was also reported on 23 July.[40]

With the arrival of autumn and the second wave, newspaper stories on the influenza became more common. From these it is possible to track the increasing toll the disease was taking. Through this period numerous reports detail the numbers of police and fire personnel ill, and dead, in addition to reports on government workers, London Omnibus Company staff, telephonists, teachers and postal workers. The reported morbidity is often only given as the number of absentees, but sometimes as a percentage. The rates range from 25 to 50 per cent. The figures for London's Metropolitan Police Force and the London Fire Brigade also give an indication of case fatality rates. Apparently some 96 Metropolitan Police died in October and November 1918. The 35 deaths in October had been from a reported 1,448 reported cases. That figure is likely to be an under-estimation, but represents a 2.4 per cent case fatality rate. If this rate is held constant, then the 96 deaths in those 2 months suggest a minimum of 4,000 cases in that one police force alone. Nine London Fire Brigade members also died in that period, from a reported 126 cases, giving a case fatality rate of 7.1 per cent. This would appear to be rather high and suggests a significant under-reporting of cases.[41] Certainly influenza was widespread. In Reading an insurance agent reported visiting 49 houses and 'found that in 46 the residents were affected'.[42] These contemporary reports not only give an indication of morbidity and case fatality rates but also of the impact the pandemic had on British society.

Ubiquitous flu

Origins and points of entry

The consensus view has been that the pandemic strain of the virus probably originated in the midwest of the United States before being transported to France with and by the American forces. In France it became widespread among the warring armies, at the same time being disseminated around the globe, facilitated by the movement of so many people due to the needs and repercussions of war.[43] However, recent research has suggested that the virus may have been present in the British military at home and in France sometime earlier.[44] This is not to say the British military or Britain or France were the source of the virus, as the virus may well have been present prior to these observations. However, it re-opens the debate on the actual origins of the virus strain. Notwithstanding this debate over the ultimate source of the virus strain, it is certainly true that major outbreaks occurred among the armies in France and among US troops in transit and at home early in 1918. Undoubtedly some of the first Britons to suffer from the 'new' influenza were those in the armed forces.

It is difficult to confirm the early pattern of introduction and spread in Britain as the number of cases was presumably quite small and attracted little attention. Deaths occurring at this time may well not have been recorded as influenza deaths and it would have only been when deaths started increasing that attention was drawn to the disease. The RG retrospectively dated the start of the pandemic in England and Wales to the week ending 29 June 1918, but certainly cases were being reported prior to that week which saw a sharp increase in influenza mortality. However, the actual start of the pandemic in England and Wales could possibly be dated at about 19 May 1918. That week saw 511 deaths attributed to influenza, whereas the previous week had recorded 79 influenza deaths. Prior to that date, influenza deaths at ages over 55 exceeded those under 55. From 19 May to 15 June deaths were about equal above and below 55; from the week ending 22 June, the younger ages showed more deaths. But it was the week ending 29 June 1918, with its marked increase in influenza deaths, most of which came in the younger age groups, that can be said to be the start of the pandemic proper in Britain.

Thus, sometime in 1918 influenza was brought back into Britain, probably by troops travelling through the ports and probably through many ports more or less simultaneously.[45] Glasgow, Portsmouth, Southampton and Liverpool were all suggested as likely ports of entry as they apparently reported influenza cases (and deaths) earlier than many other centres. *The Times* later reported that cases of influenza had occurred in the Navy's Grand Fleet at Scapa Flow and at Rosyth in April and suggested that Glasgow was 'the seat of the first outbreak among the civil population – and that occurred in May, 1918'.[46]

Hierarchies and contagion

In what little has been written on the pandemic in Britain there is little consideration of the spread of the pandemic. Apparently the first and third waves hit hardest in the north and in larger urban areas, except London, whereas the second wave was more concentrated in the south. Overall, however, mortality was fairly similar in all parts of the country. There appear to be two components to the diffusion of influenza. First, a hierarchical component, followed by a contagious one. Recent research elsewhere indicates that the location in the social and political hierarchy, and not just geographic location may be more important.[47] In Britain the disease seems to have been brought into the country via a number of ports, then moved to the larger urban centres before percolating down the urban hierarchy, being dispersed across the country by the transport networks to cities, towns and villages where contagious diffusion, the person-to-person transmission, spread it at the local level. There is support for this view in the contemporary literature. For example, a December 1918 report in *The Times* stated that 'the ports were first involved ... Next the disease reached London, to which no doubt it was brought by travellers in the through trains. From London it radiated again, visiting Birmingham, Nottingham, and other centres. It is still raging at full fury in the smaller country districts which have now become involved.'[48] This pattern of some ports first, London next and then descending down the urban hierarchy can be seen in Figure 9.7, showing the epidemic curves

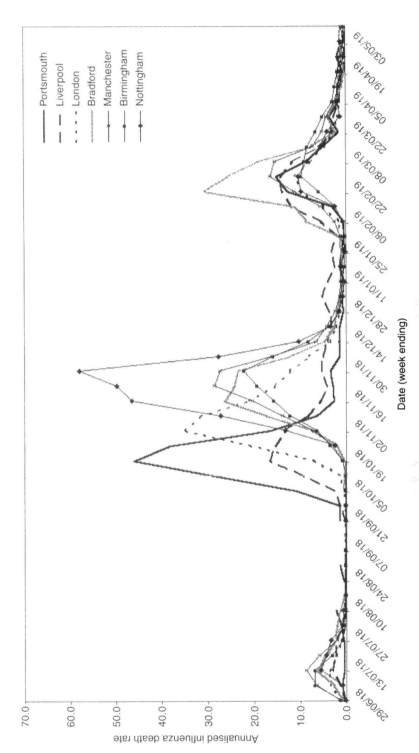

Figure 9.7 Influenza mortality in selected cities in England, 1918–19.

for a number of cities. In this graph it is clear that some ports, here represented by Portsmouth and Liverpool, peaked earlier than London, with smaller and more distant centres showing the later peaks (examples included here are Birmingham, Bradford, Manchester and Nottingham).

The RG's report supported the hierarchical hypothesis by stating that 'It is not that the towns suffered excessively, for the rates for all classes of area throughout the whole epidemic were much the same, but the towns suffered first, and during the first wave of the epidemic they suffered considerably more than the rural towns.'[49] Pandemic influenza reached into every corner of the world with little exception. It was not to spare any part of the British Isles, even reaching the Western Isles eventually. Eigg, for example, was hard-hit when the disease reached there in March 1919.[50]

The RG for England and Wales determined that, based on elevated influenza mortality, the pandemic had tormented and killed for 46 weeks in both countries, from the week ending 29 June 1918 through to 10 May 1919. The mortality was spread across the nation. The RG concluded that the 'more populous centres suffered very slightly more ... but the incidence upon town and country was very nearly equal. The northern parts of the country ... suffered decidedly more, on the whole, than the southern.'[51] Indeed, the Midlands suffered as much as the north, and in the south it was the south-west and East Anglia that escaped the worst of the pandemic. This pattern generally supports recent work that suggests that urban areas, coastal areas and areas well served by mass communication and transport links suffered higher mortality than rural, inland and isolated areas.[52]

Transport networks and the military

Global shipping networks, commercial trading and passenger craft, and soldiers returning home took the disease all around the world. From ports and landing places the local transport networks, particularly the railways, carried the virus from large cities to the smallest, remotest settlements.[53] The movement of military forces and labour undoubtedly contributed to the rapid spread of the disease. Thus, while the war may not have caused the pandemic, it may well have facilitated it. William Hamer, London County Council's Medical Officer of Health (MOH), certainly thought so when he wrote, 'It is difficult to say how far the epidemics of the last twelve months were influenced by the special conditions arising out of the war, but increased traffic, closer aggregation of persons, and the movements of population, both civil and military, no doubt contributed in assisting spread of the disease.'[54] The full extent of the role of the military in facilitating the disease, particularly in Britain, is still to be determined. However, it is apparent that the transport networks, moving both the civilian and military populations, played a major role in determining the spread of the disease.

The crowded trains were recognised as being a problem. The MOH for Essex, Dr Thresh, attributed 'the spread of the disease along the lines of railway from London to Southend, Epping, Waltham, Colchester and Cambridge to overcrowding in railway carriages, and says that while this continues it is useless to ask people not to attend churches, cinemas, and meetings where they do not get half so much crowded together as on the railway'.[55]

Disruptions

Undoubtedly influenza severely disrupted commercial activities and social life; the levels of morbidity, the lack of staff in businesses, the impairment of services, the sheer number of bodies could not be ignored. However, it was an impact that seems to have been soon forgotten. The first wave seems to have had little noted impact. The second wave certainly had an impact with its massive mortality. When the third wave came, public awareness and concern were great, as is evident from the increased coverage of influenza in both the newspapers and the medical journals, and in the increased advertising of flu remedies, along with increased pharmacy sales.[56] Perhaps it is the fact that mortality in the third wave did not reach the peaks of the second that contributed to the disappearance of influenza from the collective memory.

Britons may have become used to the strain of life in a nation at war, but the influenza was to bring great disruption to transport and communications, the emergency services and most other aspects of life. Bus and train services were curtailed, schools, hospitals, chemists, post offices, bakeries and laundries were short-staffed, police and fire services stretched, undertakers unable to make enough coffins and prepare enough graves to bury all the bodies properly. Some undertakers had to decline orders, while in some areas the cemeteries were opened up for longer hours to allow for more interments. In many locations local authority or military personnel were brought in to help. The Postmaster-General was driven to asking people to only make necessary phone calls as the services had been 'interfered with' as many operators had failed to take their places.[57] Tomkins noted that 'Particular concern was voiced over the impact of absenteeism on war-related industries such as mining and munitions, but all services, employers and institutions were affected.'[58]

So great was the disruption that even the politicians noticed. Despite the fact that the pandemic was not mentioned in parliament until the end of October 1918 (Westminster was one of the last London boroughs to show an increase in influenza mortality), it did actually curtail their activities occasionally. In Sunderland the influenza prevalence led to the candidates' decision to abandon 'house-to-house canvassing during the election campaign and not to convey electors in carriages on the polling day'.[59] Even events such as the Lord Mayor's Procession in London were affected. The government 'regretfully' withdrew an invitation to the 'Governments of France, Belgium, Japan, Greece, China' as the epidemic 'rendered it unwise to receive contingents' of troops and consequently the only foreign troops that would take part would be those from the United States of America, Portugal, Italy and Serbia that were already in Britain.[60]

The social impact of the influenza outbreak brought economic consequences. It was reported that whereas 'previously the number of paupers in "receipt of relief" fell to a minimum at the end of October before rising slowly through the winter, 1918 saw an increase in paupers numbers in October before falling back in December'.[61] Another economic impact was that on the insurance companies. The Prudential's exposure to influenza claims was noted in the City pages where the reporters speculated as to whether the annual reports of the life assurance companies would set out influenza-related losses as they had done with war-related claims. In January 1919 it was reported that 'In eight weeks the Prudential is known to have paid as much as £620,000 in claims attributed to influenza, which compared with £279,000 paid on account of direct war losses in the same time, the latter amount itself being the largest paid during any similar period of the war.'[62] The Prudential's annual meeting revealed that in fact, between 2 November and the end of the year, some £650,000 had been paid out 'in the industrial Branch alone in consequence of the epidemic'.[63]

Official action

While the influenza was killing thousands (and costing the insurance industry enormous sums), what were the various levels of British government doing? Not very much it would seem. The response of government, and the medical establishment, has been characterised by Tomkins as a 'failure of expertise'.[64] The leading public health body in Britain in 1918 was the Local Government Board (LGB). It was to take quite a low profile in the pandemic, issuing the occasional 'Memorandum'[65] with advice on how to avoid and treat influenza, distributing a film about influenza prevention, and generally leaving the local authorities and their MOHs to take what action they saw as appropriate. Other actions eventually taken at the national level included the regulation of quinine, a slight relaxation of alcohol controls (for medicinal purposes of course), a refusal to increase the meat ration and the eventual release of some doctors from military service to resume civil practice and help in the battle against flu.[66]

Eyler depicts 1918–20 as a significant time in that longer period of great change in British public health.[67] It was a period of change from small government towards a more welfare-conscious state. There were also other changes in Britain and its place in the world, changes in the conception of disease, changes as medicine established itself as 'scientific' and 'professional', and changes in the government structures concerning health and disease as the Ministry of Health came to replace the LGB. Indeed, some used the passivity of the LGB to enhance their calls for a Ministry of Health. But whereas the pandemic led to the creation of new public health organisations elsewhere,[68] the ministry was already an idea whose time had come. Moves towards changes in British public health had already been under way for some time. Landmarks such as the Public Health Acts of 1875 and 1890, the 1906 Education (Provision of Meals) Act, and the 1911 National Health Insurance Act had already been achieved. As Berridge notes, 'social reform in the health sphere has clear Victorian antecedents'.[69] However, *The Times'* medical correspondent was certainly keen on an active Ministry and argued the case on a number of occasions, as did a number of letter writers.[70] Lees has argued the First World War delayed reform of the British medical and welfare policy as it 'distracted politicians and reformers alike',[71] so possibly the pandemic aided in the revitalisation of this process.

While the LGB was criticised for its passivity and for the delay in its actions, it was not actually criticised for the nature of those actions. It acted wholly in keeping with the nature and beliefs of the medical establishment. It also justified its inactivity and failure to take more proactive measures, such as quarantine, by arguing that they would not work anyway and that in a country at war, they were not possible or practicable. Sir Arthur Newsholme (Medical Officer at the LGB) publicly admitted, when opening the Royal Society of Medicine's 'Discussion on Influenza' in November 1918, to delaying the distribution of the first *Memorandum on Influenza* as he considered the nation's 'major duty is to "carry on" ... it was necessary to "carry on", and the relentless needs of warfare justified incurring this risk of spreading infection and the associated creation of a more virulent type of disease or mixed diseases'.[72]

So, in the national and military interest it was 'business as usual' – an attitude encouraged by the press and the medical establishment. Any action, any treatment then was left to the local authorities which had primary responsibility for public health through their MOHs. With no centralised or co-ordinating body, this led to a very mixed range of responses, with some MOHs effectively denying there was any such epidemic, whereas others provided as much assistance as they could. Tomkins, in examining the responses of the London boroughs, recognised various levels of response. This ranged from little or no response, to those which acted on the LGB's recommendations and passed on information to those boroughs that focused on 'dealing with the effects of the epidemic',[73] including home nursing, domestic help, hospital and burial services.[74]

Quarantine and closures

With a disease that is so freely transmitted as influenza, quarantine is rarely likely to be successful. However, this did not stop attempts at quarantining from being attempted at national and local levels. The only national quarantines to have any significant success were those imposed in American Samoa and Australia, and in Australia it was breached eventually. Local quarantine included, in some cases, the prohibition and closure of cinemas, theatres, music halls, churches and Sunday schools. Much of this generated local controversies, particularly the closure of churches.

The decision as to whether or not to close schools was also often a controversial one. And in Britain central government left the decision to the local authorities. Closures became widespread, with the major exception of London, where closure only happened if staff absenteeism made it impossible to keep the school open.[75] The controversy over school closure usually revolved around the question of whether the children were better off at school or not and where they would be if not in school.

In Britain closure of places of public entertainment and restrictions on gatherings of people were largely left to the local authorities. The notable exception to this was cinemas. Here the LGB published regulations that limited the duration of performances and prescribed ventilation practices that had to be followed. These absurd measures were more a reflection of the 'anti-vice concerns regarding the perceived immorality of cinemas rather than sound public health'.[76] They are also an indication of the medical establishment's deep loathing of the 'kinema', a dislike driven by class tensions as much as anything, as recently revealed by Chris Lawrence.[77] Naturally the cinema operators resented being singled out and even mounted demonstrations and legal challenges. This sense of injustice was probably heightened as some authorities more or less ignored the regulations, while others enforced them rigorously. It is interesting to note that other forms and locations of entertainment and recreation, such as public houses, were largely absent from these debates.

Britain's medical profession and the flu

The medical profession was unsure what it was battling – a bacillus or a 'filter-passing' virus, and could not agree on how to combat the disease. Consequently, a vast array of remedies was suggested and argued about, with alcohol being both the most popular and the most controversial. Others, often graphically promoted in advertisements, included the influenza-preventing properties of Lifebouy soap, Oxo, incandescent gas burners, aspirin, quinine, opium, ammonia, camphor, eucalyptus, iodine, salicylate of soda, blood serum, permanganate of potash, mercury perchloride, colloidal silver, creosote, turpentine, snuff, cinnamon, salt water, smoking, beef tea, cocoa and disinfectant. The medical profession, still dazzled by the discoveries of the bacteriological age, tried to find a vaccine for an as yet unseen enemy. Remedies, treatments and vaccines were debated at length in the pages of *The Times*, at meetings such as the Royal Society of Medicine's 'Discussion on Influenza' in November 1918, or that of the Royal Institute of Public Health in February 1919. One doctor or authority would advocate one action, only to be contradicted by another. Issues such as nasal douching and masks were hotly discussed, but none so much as alcohol. Tomkins suggests this indicates a secure profession.[78] Could it not also be interpreted as being the response of a profession that did not know what to do, but was not short on opinion, a secure and arrogant profession but one lacking the knowledge to cope?

For many years Newsholme of the LGB, in his writings on public health, 'wrestled' with the themes of a rising, individualistic and moralistic health care that promoted the power of doctors, with an attendant rejection of environmentalism and an extension of the commodification of healthcare. Kearns illustrated this in examining Newsholme's writings on tuberculosis, then proceeded to demonstrate how public health at this time was 'conceived of in terms of the needs of National Efficiency; the need for a population ready for imperial combat. We might define social diseases at this time as those complaints resulting from personal failings and which reduce national efficiency.'[79] Thus, influenza as a social disease can be linked to sanitation. Certainly the connection between the pandemic, sanitation, national efficiency and the 'fitness' of the population was being discussed.[80]

Sanitation was certainly regarded as critical – much of the LGB's advice was about sanitation; many of the newspaper reports, particularly *The Times*' medical correspondent's comments, focus on sanitation – either for the individual or in demands for a new Ministry of Health. Personal cleanliness and morality were especially invoked when it came to the regulation of the cinemas, over and above that for public gatherings. This was rather undermined then when the RG concluded that the 'mortality of the late epidemic fell almost alike on the sanitarily just and on the unjust'.[81]

Failure?

What contributed to what has been seen as the failure of British medicine? The quest for professional status, the belief in the power of 'scientific' medicine prevailing over preventive means and a rejection of state intervention are all seen as factors. However, while Tomkins, for one, considered the medical profession to have failed, she also argues that Britain, and particularly the LGB, had a sound infrastructure of hospitals and volunteers and was also well versed in dealing with epidemic disease.[82] This last position was certainly one that was attacked in the press during and after the epidemic. Rather, it was felt that the medical profession, particularly in teaching, had somewhat neglected infectious disease and accorded it lesser importance than surgery and chronic conditions.[83]

The British medical profession was still in the process of establishing itself professionally and scientifically. During the nineteenth century British medicine had consolidated itself as a profession, demarcating divisions of labour, regulating membership and differentiating between the acceptable orthodox and criminalising the unorthodox, while also undergoing something of a separation into scientific medicine and public health. This separation and the dominance of scientific medicine go some way in explaining the reaction (and inaction) of the British medical authorities and profession, that Tomkins has typified as a 'failure of expertise'.[84] They had faith in their ability to find the scientific solution – identify the causative organism and then the problem would be solved. Once the cause was identified, the belief was that the creation of a vaccine would be but a simple step. Now, at the start of the twenty-first century, we are still searching for that long-term preventive. The virus' propensity for change may well work against this ever happening.

The pandemic placed the medical profession under great strain. Within the healthcare system at the time, the view was one of desperation, extreme fatigue and unpreparedness. The superintendent of one London hospital wrote in his notebook that 'We could hardly have been worse placed for dealing with an epidemic' before going on to describe how staff changes, staff shortages and having to deal with cases from other hospitals lead to such a difficult battle with the pandemic that the 'labour and distress of that time especially was terrific. Indeed it hardly bears thinking about. Not only was there a great increase in cases, many critically ill with influenzal pneumonia but the staff also began to go down like ninepins.' This situation escalated until he 'collapsed completely in December ... and returned in the middle of February'.[85]

Overshadowed or overlooked?

The vagaries of human memory and the pandemic have interested a number of scholars, notably Crosby.[86] Why is it that so many Western nations have little collective recollection of this massive pandemic? In Britain, the records relating to the release of military medical practitioners for civilian practice is one of the few aspects of the pandemic that is apparent in the British archives. Compared with the archival records on the pandemic in other nations, the British archives seem very scant. Whereas in many nations the imprint of the influenza can be found across the whole gamut of government activities, in Britain it is far more difficult to find traces of the epidemic. This paucity of material may reflect the lack of attention paid to (domestic) influenza by the newspapers and the medical press of the time. Their interest seemed to be restricted to the foreign (largely 'Imperial') reports before being awakened by the high mortality of the second wave, an interest that seems to have found only surprise at the relative mildness of the third wave of the pandemic. This lack of interest seems to have been even more prevalent among the medical and governmental ranks.

The first wave had been quite mild with low case fatality rates. Perhaps that led to complacency, and then the mildness of the third wave revived this complacency – it was *only* influenza. This was not an epidemic that struck a nation oblivious to its existence. Newspapers had certainly covered the 'story' of the influenza – this was not something that crept up on the British – either in the first wave in the spring or in the deadly second wave. The scale of the second wave was certainly known to Britons, especially the impact it had already had in the Empire, particularly South Africa. Perhaps it reveals an Imperialist and racist view – 'they' were struck by the pandemic because 'they' are backward, inherently weak and they do not have the sophisticated and advanced medical care 'we' have. Certainly at the time of the second wave its scale was appreciated. *The Times* commented that 'Never since the Black Death has such a plague swept over the face of the world; never, perhaps, has a plague been more stoically accepted.'[87] As Newsholme had counselled, it was necessary to 'carry on'!

Overshadowed by the war, the influenza pandemic was quickly disregarded then and has largely been overlooked ever since. There are only three major works on the British experience of the pandemic; two contemporary official reports, by the Registrar-General and the Ministry of Health, both produced in 1920[88] and, more recently, the work of Sandra Tomkins.[89] The British experience is briefly touched upon in a number of simple overview works on the pandemic[90] and there is the occasional local work.[91] It could be argued that the two official reports were regarded as the definitive works on the pandemic and consequently there was no need to re-examine the pandemic in Britain.

This was a true epidemic, the British experience of a disease that came in three waves killing more than 225,000 Britons, and yet one which had little long-term resonance. It was, in many ways, an unregarded killer, but not one totally devoid of its lighter moments. Marylebone Police Court heard a rather novel defence proposed when two men, Sidney H. Birkbeck and Frank A. Dyton, were remanded on a charge of attempting to steal a 'commercial motor car'. Dyton's mother presented a doctor's certificate suggesting his behaviour was due to the after effects of influenza! As *The Times* reported, 'The magistrate remarked that it seemed rather a serious development of the disease.'[92]

10 Death in winter

Spanish flu in the Canadian subarctic

D. Ann Herring and Lisa Sattenspiel

The Spanish flu struck the Keewatin District of the central Canadian sub-arctic in early winter and hopscotched through the region, decimating some communities while leaving others unaffected. Mathematical models of the spread of the epidemic in three Cree fur trade communities (Norway House, Oxford House, God's Lake) show that social organisation effects, such as population size and contact rate, were far more significant in determining the toll taken by the epidemic than mobility patterns, such as the rate of travel between communities. Because the Spanish flu struck in winter when people were dispersed on the land in small family hunting groups, the effects of the epidemic were markedly different from what would have been the case had it struck in summer when families aggregated in large numbers around fur trade posts. Mortality during the 1918 flu tended to be channelled into a relatively small number of families, rather than more broadly among the population in general. This research points to the need to scrutinise specific ecologies and social contexts to understand better the ways in which the global phenomenon of the 1918 influenza pandemic played out in a variety of different ways at the local level. It also emphasises the importance of drilling down from regional and national mortality rates to focus on variation in death tolls within and between communities.

The arrival of the Spanish flu in Canada, as was the case for many former and current British colonies, was intimately linked to the return of troops who had fought for Great Britain during the First World War. As demobilised soldiers headed home, first by troopship from Europe to Canada's east coast, then by train westward across the country, influenza travelled with them, its tentacles reaching into smaller communities along trade and transportation routes. Although there is some question about exactly when Spanish flu reached Canada, the first civilian outbreak was reported in Victoriaville, Quebec on 8 September 1918.[1] It took a mere month for the deadly epidemic to traverse the nation from coast to coast.[2] By the end of the winter of 1918–19, it is estimated that one in six people in Canada had contracted the virus, with some 30,000 to 50,000 succumbing to it.[3]

In this chapter we take a close look at Spanish flu in one small part of northern Canada and at the factors that contributed both to the spread of the epidemic in the region and to the death toll exacted by it. We begin with a description of the arrival of the third wave of the epidemic in Winnipeg, the capital of the Province of Manitoba, then follow its progress northward to the Hudson's Bay Company (HBC) fur trade region known as the Keewatin District. We then focus on three Cree First Nations communities and examine the epidemic's impact on them, with special consideration paid to the influence of travel patterns and patterns of contact within and between these settlements. From this analysis, we suggest that the local expression of the 1918 influenza pandemic was heavily influenced by specific features of the local ecology and, most especially, by the nature of social organisation that characterised northern life in winter.

Flu reaches the Province of Manitoba

Spanish flu reached Winnipeg, the capital of Manitoba and the largest city in the HBC's Keewatin District, on 30 September 1918. Sick soldiers travelling west on a troop train brought the virus with them to Winnipeg; within 4 days of being taken off the train, two of the soldiers had died, along with a local railway worker, the first civilian casualty in the city.[4] Although there was initial optimism that the epidemic would be less fierce than was reported for the eastern part of the nation, conditions deteriorated quickly.

On 12 October 1918, the *Manitoba Free Press* published on its front page a proclamation from the Manitoba Provincial Board of Health ordering that 'All schools, churches, theatres, dance halls, and other public places in Winnipeg and suburbs will be closed for an indefinite period at midnight tonight as a precautionary measure against the spreading epidemic of Spanish "flu", of which 12 new cases were reported in the city yesterday.'[5] (The ban remained in place for 6 weeks until late November.)[6] Despite this and other public health actions aimed at staunching its flow, influenza raced through Winnipeg and on into outlying areas. By 31 October, 2,162 cases had been reported throughout the city. Homes reporting cases were placarded and quarantined. There was a shortage of nursing help and calls for volunteers – no nursing experience required – went out to the populace.[7]

News of the epidemic's devastation spread as quickly as the disease itself. Many small towns in the prairie provinces of Manitoba, Saskatchewan and Alberta made futile attempts to protect themselves by instituting a complete quarantine.[8] No one was allowed to leave town and many businesses were ordered to close temporarily. Spanish flu nevertheless continued its inexorable spread further west and into the Canadian north, with The Pas reporting its first suspected case on 25 October.[9] It sped across the Keewatin landscape, most probably reaching Norway House on 4 December 1918 with a dog team carrying the mail packet from Cross Lake, where the epidemic was already raging.[10]

The Canadian north

Although many places were fortunate to escape the epidemic altogether,[11] when Spanish flu struck small northern communities where people lived off the land, it hit hard. Most people relied on foods gathered and hunted from the bush, with basic supplements such as flour, tea and sugar traded for furs at Hudson's Bay Company stores. Families out on winter traplines with few provisions were in a particularly precarious position, far away from help and extra HBC supplies. When influenza arrived in their midst, there was little in the way of stored food, and daily life collapsed when almost everyone contracted influenza. Whole families lay prostrate without anyone to feed them or maintain fires in the dead of winter:[12]

> My first recollection is being on a hammock like swing and seeing beds all around the room and one woman reaching down inside her blouse in front and bringing out her small purse and giving it to my Dad. This was during the Spanish Flue [sic] Epidemic. My Dad was the only one that was not sick and was pretty well alone for a number of days making the rounds to different houses to see that they had enough wood inside to keep the fires going and to take any bodies that were in the house.... They said if the sick that died had stayed in the house where it was warm [sic]. They went out too soon and got cold and had a relapse.[13]

In their struggle to replenish diminishing supplies of food and fuel for their families, many of the ill perished after developing the deadly secondary complication of pneumonia.[14] Tuberculosis was rife among Aboriginal people in the Keewatin District at the time,[15] an underlying condition that easily could have contributed to pneumonia among many Spanish flu victims.

The Reverend Henry Gordon's description of the Grenfell Mission at Cartwright, Labrador, is particularly poignant and characterises the devastation influenza wrought in northern locales:

> It has struck the place like a cyclone, two days after the Mail boat had left. After dinner I went on a tour of inspection among the houses, and was simply appalled at what I found. Whole houses lay inanimate all over their kitchen floors, unable to even feed themselves or look after the fire.... I think there were just four persons in the place who were sound.... A feeling of intense resentment at the callousness of the authorities, who sent us the disease by the Mail-boat, and then left

us to sink or swim, filled one's heart almost to the exclusion of all else. The helplessness of the poor people was what struck to the heart.... It was very upsetting, people crying, children dying everywhere.[16]

It was often impossible to bury the dead in the frozen earth of a northern winter. Sometimes bodies were wrapped in sheets and placed on rooftops, out of the reach of hungry dogs. These ghostly shrouds lay exposed until they could be buried when the ground softened in spring.[17] At Norway House, where the HBC kept draught animals for hauling, bodies were collected and stacked like cordwood until they could be buried:

> Of course that time they say that an ox carried people when they were dead. They were picked up by an ox and they brought him here, there were a little cabin here at that time, see, and they put the bodies in there. There were so many people, you know, they can't bury them all and after that, when they all gathered and they were buried in a box. They just threw the bodies in a box, I don't know how many in that box. And they had big cranes you know and they put those bodies together and there's a lot of people and children.... There was an awful, they have an awful time, difficult time, to gather all the people and to bury them. Though some of these people were kept in the cabin until after, they didn't have much lumber to use for coffins, and they just buried them like that in a bag.[18]

The study communities

Norway House (see Figure 10.1) is one of the communities that form the basis of this study: the others are God's Lake and Oxford House. All three are former HBC fur trade posts located in the Canadian Shield, an ancient mass of crystalline rock that surrounds Hudson Bay, and extends from Labrador in the east to the Mackenzie basin in the west. Although the fur trade was in steep decline by the turn of the twentieth century, many of the HBC posts in Canada's interior were still operating. In fact, most of the Aboriginal people in the northeast were engaged in the fur trade economy or in fishing, though more southerly areas were increasingly being drawn into a cash economy based on other natural resources, such as lumbering and mining.

The HBC divided Canada into districts as a means of better managing the various fur operations across its vast business empire. The three communities under scrutiny – Norway House, Oxford House and God's Lake – are located in the Keewatin District. Norway House was the largest ($n = 746$)[19] and most important of the three fur trade posts in our study. Located at the southern end of the Nelson River trade axis, the main route between York Factory on the coast of Hudson Bay and the rich fur-bearing land of the interior, Norway House rose to prominence during

Figure 10.1 Interior of a Hudson's Bay Company Store, believed to be
        Norway House, *c*.1907–10.

Source: George Burnham Boucher Photograph Collection, Provincial Archives of Manitoba,
Hudson's Bay Company Archives 1985/33/10 (N5824). Reproduced here with permission of
Hudson's Bay Company Archives, Provincial Archives of Manitoba.

the mid-nineteenth century to become the key provisioning centre for the
northern trade network.[20] Described by Hallowell as 'the crossroads of a
continent',[21] it was the administrative, storage and trans-shipment centre
for the Keewatin District. Oxford House, on the other hand, was far less
central to HBC operations by the time of the 1918 epidemic, but nevertheless was in direct contact with Norway House. Situated along the once
heavily-used Hayes River route that connected Norway House to York
Factory, its strategic importance had diminished as the orientation of the
fur trade shifted south in the late nineteenth century. With a resident
population of 322, it was less than half the size of Norway House. God's
Lake, the smallest ($n = 299$) and most peripheral of the three HBC posts,
was connected to the other two via less central routes.

In view of its central role in HBC trade operations, perhaps it is not
surprising that Norway House was affected by the 1918–19 pandemic.[22]
Estimated Spanish flu mortality rates derived from Anglican Church
parish registers for the Jack River Mission at Norway House suggest that

some 183 deaths per 1,000 population occurred during the epidemic.[23] This represents an astounding sevenfold increase in deaths relative to the two decades on either side of it. It is almost inconceivable that approximately one-fifth of the adult population over the age of twenty perished during the epidemic.[24] Nathaniel Queskekapow, a 72-year-old Cree elder, not yet born when influenza struck Norway House, nevertheless knew about many aspects of the epidemic:

> After the war was over, that war was over, then came the flu. That's where it came from. So it was very strong on the south side and the people were just, somebody was walking over there and somebody dropped, just like a shot. Even the children, they, about 10-year old, they just fell down and died. Like that. They don't, you don't bother anybody, just fall right down.[25]

The actions of local leaders helped stem the spread of the epidemic. Quarantine efforts reduced considerably, but did not completely curtail, movement in and out of Norway House when the epidemic engulfed it in December 1918 and January 1919.[26] In any event, the reduction in the extent of contact may have helped to weaken the chain of infection such that its satellite posts, including Oxford House and God's Lake, were unaffected by the epidemic.[27] On the other hand, influenza failed to reach other satellite posts in the Keewatin, such as Poplar River, where there was no quarantine.[28] At the provincial level, moreover, there were notable differences in the reported death toll among Indian Agencies in Manitoba,[29] as was the case between provinces. Estimated mortality rates range from a low of less than 10 per 1,000 in the Province of Quebec to a high of 60 per 1,000 in the Provinces of Alberta and Manitoba.[30] The general estimate that 3 per cent of Aboriginal people in Canada died during the 1918 epidemic evidently is misleading,[31] masking significant variation in the way the epidemic played out at provincial, regional and local levels.

This diversity in the local expression of the pandemic, even among communities with close economic, geographic and cultural links, led us to begin to explore the factors that may have left some vulnerable to the 1918 flu while keeping others apparently protected from it.[32] In this chapter, we examine two features of contact and their potential effects on the impact of the epidemic in the Keewatin District: travel patterns that allowed the 1918 flu to spread from place to place, and, within communities, contact that influenced the spread of infection from person to person once the epidemic arrived.

Contact and spread of the 1918 pandemic

There is no doubt that the nature and extent of contact was crucial for the spread of the 1918 influenza pandemic, which involved the worldwide transmission of a new virus in a relatively short period of time. This rapid movement through time and space, typical of influenza epidemics throughout history, is the outcome of contact between an infected person from one community and one or more susceptible persons from another. This contact takes place when at least one person travels to the place where contact occurs. Because influenza has a short, 2-day incubation period, studies of the diffusion of the 1918 epidemic require detailed information about the structure of daily life and the activities that led people to travel from one place to another, creating the opportunity for infection to spread through contact. Once the influenza virus reached a new community, however, another set of local factors came into play, namely demographic features, such as the size and age composition of the community, as well as the nature and extent of social circumstances that enhanced or diminished the likelihood of healthy individuals coming into contact with an infected person.

Some of our previous research, which has taken the form of simulation experiments on the potential for the epidemic to spread from place to place, has made use of the fact that Norway House, Oxford House and God's Lake differed in size, travel patterns and importance to trade in the region. In fact, a major goal of the simulations has been to explore the relative influence on death tolls of the extent and patterns of contact between communities (travel) and within communities (social organisation). Our analyses to date show that travel patterns had a substantial impact on when influenza epidemics reached different communities and how long they lasted in a given community. The simulations also reveal that once influenza spread to a community, social organisation features, such as the size of the local population and the rate of contact between people, determined the number of people who actually contracted the disease. In other words, while travel patterns affected the timing of the epidemic and where it spread, it was the structure of everyday life and the amount of contact between people – elements of social organisation – that actually affected the death toll.[33] Surprisingly little attention has been paid to the organisation of daily living and how this may have shaped the impact of the 1918 outbreak.

The epidemiological importance of social organisation to the outcome of the 1918 influenza epidemic is particularly compelling within the cultural context of the fur trade in the Canadian north. At the time of the Spanish flu epidemic, most people still derived the bulk, if not all, of their income from managing and harvesting fur-bearing animals, and from trans-shipping mail and goods from post to post. The size and composition of these fur trade communities, moreover, shifted dramatically during the annual cycle, in response to seasonal changes in climate, resource availability, modes of travel and subsistence activities.

The extent, means and speed of travel, for instance, changed quite markedly with the seasons. From spring to autumn when waterways were free of ice ('break-up'), canoes and boats carried trippers,[34] goods and pathogens from place to place by river. A spring journey downstream from Norway House to Oxford House was relatively short, taking about 3 days; the same journey upstream in autumn took 7 days, twice as long as in the spring.[35] When waterways were frozen in winter ('freeze-up'), people travelled overland by dog team and snowshoe, taking 6 days to complete the journey between the two posts.[36] Certainly the potential for spread of a disease like influenza, with its 2-day incubation period, would be quite different in this region, depending on the season.

The nature and extent of contact within communities also varied with the seasons. In winter – the time of the 1918 outbreak – family trapping groups were scattered in the hinterland, often far away from HBC posts. The fundamental unit of organisation on winter traplines was two or more married couples with their children.[37] The exigencies of the heavy labour involved in the fur trade, which entailed managing a variety of animal species spread over broad tracts of land and processing large amounts of fur, required a complex sexual division of labour, as well as the co-operation of several nuclear families. Most often, trapping groups consisted of families related through the male line: a father and one or more sons, or several brothers. The size of the group depended on the composition of the families working the traplines. If an area proved to be resource-poor, the group might split up and join other related families where the hunting was better.[38] The wide dispersal of family trapping groups on the landscape in winter is illustrated by the fact that some traplines were as far as 300 miles away from the HBC post at Norway House, as well as its supplies of flour, tea and chopped wood.[39] Some families lived in the vicinity of the post year-round and derived most of their income from HBC wage labour, rather than from fur trapping *per se.*

In summer, family groups congregated in large numbers in the vicinity of the HBC posts.[40] This striking modification in the opportunity for and extent of social contact during the annual cycle led us to wonder whether the impact of the Spanish flu could have been shaped by the fact that it struck the central subarctic in winter, when social contact occurred primarily *within* families, rather than in summer, when social contact was extensive *between* families.

Defining travel patterns

Because influenza circulates with the speed of available transport, it was necessary to describe and quantify travel patterns during different periods of the annual cycle. HBC post journals provide a source of information on daily travel and inform our understanding of mobility between the three communities around the time of the 1918 epidemic.[41] The HBC post journals were intended to be daily diaries of fur trade business activities at each post.[42] As such, they mention arrivals and departures to the post of individuals, most of whom were trappers or trippers engaged in the fur trade. In some instances, there is sufficient nominative detail to allow the researcher to track the movements of specific individuals from post to post.

To develop general profiles of movement for each of the three communities, the daily entries in the HBC post journals were sifted for references to arrivals and departures at the respective posts from October 1918 through to December 1920.[43] With the aid of several student research assistants,[44] information on dates, travellers, places of origin and destination, mode of travel and reason for travel were noted, then entered into a data base for each location. The entries were checked for errors, cross-referenced to small-scale maps of the region for that period,[45] then concatenated into monthly estimates of travel. These, in turn, were combined into seasonal travel estimates.[46] The mobility data extracted through this process are best viewed as rough approximations, but we are confident nonetheless that they represent general patterns of movement in the region, consistent with other published accounts.[47]

The seasonal travel estimates derived for the period surrounding the 1918 pandemic show that the majority of traffic between HBC posts occurred in summer when movement was facilitated by open water.[48] This is illustrated by Figure 10.2 which summarises, by season, the visits recorded in the Norway House Post Journal from the autumn of 1918 to 1920. Almost one-half of the recorded visits to the post occurred during the summer months (June to August), while the other three seasons contributed almost equally to the balance of travel for the year. Viewed on a month-by-month basis, it is evident that the vast majority of travel occurred during break-up (May to November) compared to freeze-up (December to April) (see Figure 10.3). Harsh winter weather and dispersed family groups tended to reduce contact with the post to a small number of trappers and mail couriers.

The means of travel, and number of individuals travelling, changed with the seasons. Boat and canoe travel predominated during the summer (June to August) and accounted for most of the visits in which it was possible to discern the means by which people arrived at the post. Boats and canoes were sufficiently large to carry many people. Although it is impossible to determine from the HBC post journals exactly how many people arrived in each boat, it is clear that this was a form of mass transit that could bring whole families to the post. In contrast, the instances of winter travel recorded in the Norway House post journals primarily involved dog teams freighting mail from post to post and men coming into the post from family traplines for supplies.

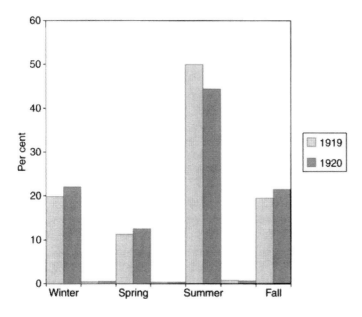

Figure 10.2 Proportion of travel by season, Norway House, 1919 and 1920.

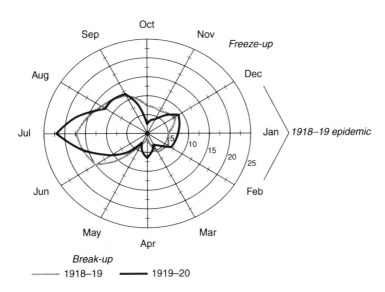

Figure 10.3 Per cent travel by month (each ring is 5 per cent), Norway House, 1918–19, light line and 1919–20, dark line.

Simulating influenza epidemics

Once the travel database had been created and organised by season, it was possible to estimate parameters necessary for computer simulations of the course of influenza epidemics in the three study communities. The simulations were based on a model system of ordinary differential equations that follows the progress of the influenza epidemic in individuals within the three communities (NH, OH and GL), allowing people to travel between locations and carry the influenza virus with them.[49]

Because travel was much less frequent in winter than in summer, winter simulations show substantial delays in the number of days it took for the number of influenza cases to peak. This can be seen quite clearly in Figure 10.4, which compares the simulated epidemic waves in summer and winter for God's Lake and Oxford House. The length of the delay proved to be affected markedly by the location of the initial case of influenza, with the longest delays in the epidemic peak for any particular location occurring when that community was not the locale of the initial case. Delays in the onset of the epidemic at Oxford House, for instance, are much longer when the initial case occurs in a person who was neither a resident of Oxford House nor visiting the community (delays range

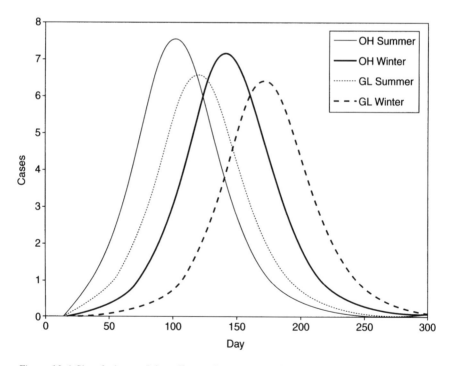

Figure 10.4 Simulations of the effects of summer and winter travel rates on peaking of cases of influenza at Oxford House and God's Lake.

from 30–38 days) than when the initial case was associated with the community (delays range from 1 to 5 days).

Interestingly, even though lower rates of travel typical of winter slowed down the progress of the simulated epidemics, they did not lead to significant changes in the number of influenza cases during the outbreaks. This confirms observations from a previous study, namely, that at least for communities like these where overall rates of travel are relatively low, changes in rates and patterns of mobility strongly affect the timing of epidemics, but only minimally affect the number of influenza cases within the community.[50] From these results, we infer that winter travel patterns had little to do with the variation in Spanish flu mortality rates among communities in this region.

The effects of social organisation were built into our influenza model by varying the within-community contact rates. It is evident from the results of these simulations that the severity of the outbreaks was strongly influenced by the degree of social contact within communities. Quite simply, higher rates of within-community contact led to more severe epidemics. Two situations are represented in Figure 10.5. In one, the contact rate at Norway House was set as twice the rate of the other two communities; in the other, all contact rates were equal (and set at the previous rate for Norway House). Because the rate for Norway House

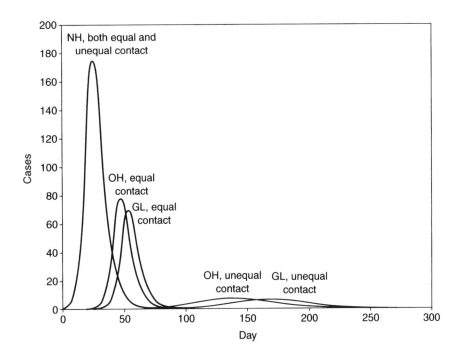

Figure 10.5 Simulations of equal and unequal within-community contact rates.

remained the same, there was no change in the epidemic peak there. On the other hand, increasing the contact rates for Oxford House and God's Lake affected both the timing of the epidemic (leading to earlier outbreaks) and the peak numbers of cases (resulting in much more severe epidemics).

Relating this back to what we know about social organisation in fur trapping communities, the simulations suggest that summer outbreaks, when larger groups of people coalesced in close contact in the vicinity of the HBC post, would probably result in a higher overall incidence of the disease than in winter, when families were sparsely dispersed on the land. During winter, moreover, individual families were forced to spend longer periods of time in intimate contact as they managed their traplines, separate from other families. Consequently, if Spanish flu entered a family group, theoretically, all or nearly all would become infected because the risk of a susceptible family member coming into contact with an infected relative was high, given the small size of the family groups. Marked heterogeneity in the impact of the epidemic on families during a winter outbreak would also be expected, with many escaping the epidemic altogether and others facing near or total annihilation. In a summer epidemic, the cases would be spread among many families, reducing between-family heterogeneity compared to a winter outbreak, but the severity of the epidemic within the community as a whole should be greater simply because of the higher rate of contact between all its members.

Norway House

To test these predictions from the simulation experiments, we turned to information on mortality at Norway House in 1918. Specifically, we wanted to investigate the family distribution of deaths from Spanish flu. Our model predicted that deaths should not be randomly and widely distributed between families, but that there should be marked differences in the effects of the epidemic on family groups. We consulted Treaty Annuity Pay Lists (TAPL) for Norway House to address this question. The TAPL documents are rough censuses compiled annually by Government of Canada Treaty Party officials who visited each reserve during the summer to pay $5 to registered Indians. This was one of the terms under which land had been ceded by First Nations to the Canadian Government in a series of treaties that began to be enacted in 1876. At each location, a treaty official recorded the number of male and female adults and children paid per family, and entered the information on an accounting sheet beside the name of the head of the family. Only the head of the family was actually named, so it is not possible to do nominative family reconstitution from this source. The Treaty Annuity Pay Lists also list the number of births, deaths and migrations per family during the previous year. While there is no doubt that under-enumeration and errors occur in these records, they nevertheless offer a reasonably good approximation of the family distribution of vital events from one year to the next.

To examine the family distribution of mortality at Norway House during the Spanish flu epidemic, Treaty Annuity Pay Lists for the Band for 1918 and 1919 were compared. This comparison yielded 107 recorded deaths among 237 nuclear family units between July 1918 and July 1919. Although there is no means of determining which of these deaths were attributable to the epidemic, this level of mortality is far in excess of the roughly 15 to 25 deaths listed annually for the early twentieth century and can be considered a proxy estimate of the epidemic's toll.

Examination of the distribution of deaths among these 237 family units (Table 10.1) shows that the majority, some 70 per cent ($n = 167$) of the families listed in the TAPLs, reported no deaths during the course of 1918–19. In fact, partitioning the 107 deaths by nuclear family initially yielded a Poisson-like distribution, but when the observed values were fitted to the Poisson distribution, it became clear that mortality was anything but random (LRX^2 = 17.3, df = 2, p <0.05). Significantly fewer families than expected experienced only one death, and more families than expected either had no deaths, or two or more deaths.

Closer scrutiny of the seventy families with recorded deaths in 1918–19 further illustrates the very focused nature of the ravages of the Spanish flu (Table 10.2). Almost one-quarter of all deaths ($n = 25$) clustered within seven nuclear families. The Salmon, Moose, Fisher and Muskrat families[51] were completely wiped out, while the two Robin families and the Marten family came close to extinction. Some 56 per cent of the deaths that year were found within 10 per cent of the surnames listed in the Treaty Annuity List, signifying the localisation of the epidemic's impact on families related through the male line. Evidently, the high mortality rate at Norway House between July 1918 and July 1919 was linked to the devastation of particular families, not the community as a whole.

Table 10.1 Distribution of deaths at Norway House by nuclear family, July 1918 to July 1919

No. of deaths	No. of families observed	No. of families expected	Deviation
0	167	150.60	16.40
1	44	68.28	−24.28
2	19	15.48	3.52
3+	7	2.63	4.37

Likelihood ratio Chi square = 17.3, df = 2, p <0.05

Table 10.2 Norway House families with three to five deaths, July 1918 to July 1919

Family*	Alive 1918	Died 1918–19	Survived
Salmon	3	3	none
Robin	4	3	1 child
Robin	5	3	mother and child
Marten	4	3	father
Moose	4	4	none
Fisher	4	4	none
Muskrat	5	5	none
Total	29	24	4

Note
* pseudonyms

Emily Day, a Norway House elder born in 1909, recalled in 1992 the heart-breaking story of her own family's experience of the 1918 epidemic. Everyone in her household fell ill, save her. Her mother died and the other members in the household perished one by one. Only Emily and a baby survived. Other families suffered similar calamitous fates:

> There were children in Cross Lake they say that, they well, they were sucking, you know, their mothers, and the mother died and also the old people ... so those people, those babies that were found sucking their mother while the mother died, they were kept. Still today, they are still living. I know there are three people in Cross Lake, their last name was North, those three men they were babies at that time and they were brought up by another person who was called North, so they become North. That's how we become different names, because the different families that we have been raised by. So that's that. And the babies that were left, the other mother would feed these people, feed these babies in their breasts, along with their children.[52]

Discussion and inferences

Much of the research on the 1918 influenza pandemic examines illness and death at the national, regional or urban scales of analysis. This is not surprising, given that available statistics, rough though they may be, tend to have been collected for these higher order levels of aggregation. Less attention has been paid to the ways that families, households and towns were disrupted and even destroyed by the epidemic.[53] Yet, the Norway House study makes it clear that, while mortality rates from epidemics are useful approximations of *community* devastation, they tell nothing of the social disruption to individual *families* because of illness or death, nor of the depletion of specific lineages.[54] Some families at Norway House continued to thrive and raise children to maturity, while others in their midst lost all or nearly everyone to the 1918 flu. This is what people remember; this is what has meaning for them, not the crude mortality rates that we students of the pandemic continue to generate.

Why has there been so little attention to the family context of mortality? To a great extent, this reflects the difficulty and time-consuming process of data gathering and record linkage that is necessary to develop a detailed, micro-social picture of the effects on specific families of the H1N1 virus. Difficulties aside, a local history approach reveals how variable the devastation from the 1918 epidemic was at Norway House. It is doubtful that this is unique either to this community, or the Keewatin District, or to Canada and beyond; rather, it is very likely that communities elsewhere in the world showed similar variation in the toll taken among families by the Spanish flu.

It is also clear that circumstances, specific to the times and peculiarities of place, mediated the effects of the 1918 influenza pandemic. In fur-trapping economies like those of the Keewatin District, social organisation was fluid in response to the seasonal availability of resources. Our analysis of simulations and the family distribution of deaths during the 1918 flu at Norway House suggest that the pattern of mortality was heavily influenced by the nature of winter social organisation; namely, small extended family groups, sparsely settled on the land, in occasional contact with the Hudson's Bay Company post. This created an epidemiological landscape of risk within which families, on average, were relatively protected from the flu. On the other hand, any family unlucky enough to be exposed to the virus – probably through contact with the HBC post at Norway House – was likely to be hit excessively hard by it.[55]

Perhaps the ability of particular families to survive the epidemic was also tied to the adequacy of food supplies and, hence, to differences in the productivity of the land base managed by family groups. This would have determined how much exertion was required for family members to forage for food and to gather wood while already debilitated by illness. After all, survival from this particular flu epidemic depended on the extent to which a steady supply of food and water could be maintained, as well as the ability to keep fires going in the middle of a subarctic winter.

Is this situation unique to the Canadian north? We think not. Many regions of the world are characterised by dramatic seasonal changes in climate, such as distinct wet and dry seasons in the tropics, that are, in turn, associated with behavioural and social changes that would influence the transmission of disease. The Norway House study points to the need for carefully considering how local ecologies and social contexts may have canalised the effects of the global phenomenon of the 1918 influenza pandemic, creating diversity in the experience of the disease and variable death tolls. In the case of Norway House, it would appear that the fur-trapping economy, timing of the outbreak in winter, and tendency for sporadic travel from traplines to the post, and between posts, contributed to the funnelling of influenza mortality into some families and not others.

11 Spanish influenza seen from Spain

Beatriz Echeverri

Spanish influenza had nothing 'Spanish' about it. The name refers to the reputed origin of the pandemic of 1918–19 and is totally unjustified. There is no evidence whatsoever that the influenza virus of 1918 spread from Spain to the rest of the world. On the contrary, the first signs of the epidemic were registered in an army camp in the United States during the month of March of 1918. The infection travelled to France with the American Expeditionary Force, where the first cases were accounted for in April.[1] It was 2 months after the epidemic explosion in America that the famous 'Spanish Lady' hit the Iberian Peninsula.

Despite this, it was as late as 29 June 1918 that the senior official in the Spanish Health Department, Dr Martin Salazar, reported to the Royal Academy of Medicine of Madrid, that he had no information about a pandemic of influenza in the rest of Europe. Hence, some local observers deduced that the name of Spanish influenza was justified.[2] This leads us to the only possible explanation for the misnomer. Information about the epidemic was censored in the countries involved in the war. For that reason, and because the war merited much more attention than what was then regarded as a mild epidemic, news of the first wave was scarcely publicised if at all in many European countries.[3] In non-belligerent Spain, on the contrary, the epidemic was fully reviewed in the press from the appearance of the first wave.[4] Newspapers in Madrid, during the months of May and June, reported the closing down of theatres and the suspension of telegraph and postal service due to the flu. The King, the Prime Minister and part of the cabinet were reported stricken with 'the soldier of Naples', as the flu was called, because it was as catchy as the song in an operetta then currently being performed.

By the time the second wave hit the country, the majority of the medical observers denied the Spanish origin of the pandemic. Yet it does seem that Spanish press coverage of the epidemic, even during the second wave, was more extensive than in most of Europe. The reports on the 'ravages' caused by the pandemic in Spanish newspapers seemed 'excessive' to the eminent Dr Marañón, compared with coverage in France, where the only reports in the press were scientific opinions and official statements.[5]

At the turn of the century, Spain had the highest death rate in Europe, only surpassed by that of the Russian Empire. There is a wealth of contemporary medical testimonies of the terrible living conditions in the Spanish cities.[6] During the latter part of the nineteenth century, a timid industrialisation process had begun that led, slowly and at times waveringly, towards a demographic transition. As can be observed in Figure 11.1 and Table 11.1, during the first two decades of the new century, crude birth and death rates were falling. This path of progress was interrupted in 1918 by the pandemic of influenza, when the crude death rate rose almost 50 per cent above the rate of the previous year. It was not until 1921 that this falling trend was reversed. The reduction was again arrested temporarily during the years of the Civil War (1936–9).

During the First World War Spain experienced unexpected economic prosperity due to its neutrality. This new-found affluence favoured only a few. The growth of foreign commerce helped to fuel the most rapid price inflation since the beginning of the century. The working classes were especially affected, in particular the two-thirds of the population involved in agriculture. Many rural workers migrated from the countryside to the towns and also to France. This movement of people undoubtedly helped to spread influenza. The First World War was thus a time of penury and social discontent, distress which was further aggravated by the pandemic, but not always in ways which would be expected.

The evolution of the pandemic

The evolution of the pandemic in Spain during the three waves can be followed from the monthly provincial mortality records which provide cause of death.[7] To avoid possible distortions, only deaths attributed to

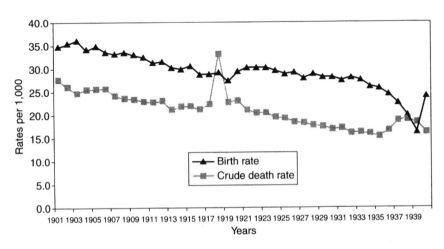

Figure 11.1 Crude death and birth rates, Spain, 1901–40.

Table 11.1 Crude death and birth rates, Spain, 1901–40 per 1,000

	Crude birth rate	Crude death rate
1901	34.8	27.7
1902	35.4	25.9
1903	36.2	24.8
1904	34.1	25.5
1905	34.9	25.6
1906	33.6	25.8
1907	33.2	24.2
1908	33.6	23.5
1909	33.0	23.6
1910	32.6	22.9
1911	31.4	22.8
1912	31.6	23.1
1913	30.4	21.0
1914	29.8	22.0
1915	30.7	21.9
1916	28.9	21.3
1917	28.9	22.3
1918	29.2	33.2
1919	27.7	22.8
1920	29.3	23.2
1921	30.3	21.2
1922	30.3	20.4
1923	30.3	20.5
1924	29.6	19.5
1925	28.9	19.4
1926	29.4	18.6
1927	27.9	18.4
1928	29.0	17.9
1929	28.1	17.5
1930	28.2	16.8
1931	27.4	17.2
1932	28.0	16.2
1933	27.6	16.3
1934	26.2	15.9
1935	25.7	15.6
1936	24.7	16.6
1937	22.5	18.8
1938	20.0	19.1
1939	16.4	18.4
1940	24.3	16.5

Source: J. Nadal, *La Población Española*, Barcelona, 1986.

influenza are taken into account in this part of the analysis. A study of the morbidity records would have been desirable also, but the information that is available is fragmentary and unreliable. Influenza was not a notifiable disease and when, during the second wave, it became obligatory, medical and health workers were so overwhelmed by the number of cases that the records are seriously impaired.

Figure 11.2 Epidemic diffusion of influenza through the railways in Spain.

In Figure 11.2, an effort is made to trace the diffusion of the infection during the first wave. Observers at that time pointed out that the pandemic entered the country through France.[8] The comings and goings of thousands of workers from Portugal and Spain, as temporary labour to replace enlisted workers in France, carried the virus across frontiers. During the first 3 months of 1918, 24,090 Spanish workers entered France and 9,012 returned, a pattern that continued until the end of the war.[9] The main points of exit by railway were the frontier towns of Bayonne, in the Basque region, and Perpignan, in the Pyrenees. At Medina del Campo, then a major railway junction, passengers converged on their way to the northern plateau, westwards to Portugal or to Madrid, in the centre of Spain. The provinces of Madrid, Cuenca, Toledo and Salamanca were the first to register an increase in mortality from influenza and other respiratory diseases in May. As a rule, the infection appeared first in towns that were joined by the railway or in those towns that had close commercial relations with each other.[10]

The city of Madrid seems to have been a major diffusion point for the infection. The epidemic coincided with St Isidro, the feast in honour of its patron saint, particularly famous for its bullfights, which attracted a large number of visitors from outside the capital. As shown in Figure 11.2,

Madrid was the centre from which most of the railway lines radiated out to the rest of the country, especially to the southern provinces of Extremadura and Andalusia. It is not surprising then, that some observers related the beginning of the epidemic with the arrival of travellers from the capital.[11] In northern Spain, migrant workers crossing the Pyrenees, via Perpignan, transported the infection to the eastern coast. By June the epidemic had reached to most of the country. It was pointed out that the first outbreaks occurred in urban centres from where the infection spread with extraordinary swiftness. This was especially true in the southern portion of the peninsula, an area with a number of fairly large cities. The press and medical observers also constantly referred to military personnel as important agents of the spread of the infection.[12] On frequent occasions, the first cases of influenza occurred among civilians when soldiers had been sent home to convalesce.

A cursory glance at Table 11.2 is sufficient to confirm that, during the first epidemic wave, there was little cause for alarm. As would be expected in any influenza epidemic, a slight increase in the national crude death rates during the months of June, July and August occurred. However, mortality from influenza in June rose 250 per cent above the average rate of the first few months of the year. An increase in mortality rates from influenza was observed in all but a few of the Spanish provinces. Figure 11.3 shows how the first wave had a greater impact on provinces situated in the centre and the south of the country, where the highest specific mortality rates for influenza ranged from 0.34 to 0.65 per thousand.

The first signs of the second deadly wave appeared in late August. The provinces of Tarragona, Castellon and Murcia, on the eastern coast, registered a rise in the number of deaths from influenza during that month. Was this more virulent infection also introduced from France, as most contemporaries thought?[13] The rise of mortality in the eastern coastal region could be a clue in favour of that premise. This was the region from which the largest number of workers, impoverished by the economic crisis, migrated to Provence and the Rhone valley during the war years.[14] There was therefore a constant movement of men and women across the frontier who could easily have reintroduced the infection. On the other hand, did the infection continue to smoulder among the population until the virus mutated into its new more lethal strain? The path of the first

Table 11.2 Crude death rates and cause-specific mortality rates for influenza in Spain per 1,000, 1918

	Jan	Feb	Mar	April	May	June	July	Aug	Sept	Oct	Nov	Dec
CDR	1.84	1.80	2.09	1.80	1.70	2.14	2.16	2.12	2.55	7.84	4.61	2.40
CSMR	0.04	0.04	0.03	0.05	0.04	0.14	0.08	4.68	37.60	381.34	194.21	48.80

Source: *Boletín Estadín Estadístico Demográfico-Sanitario.*

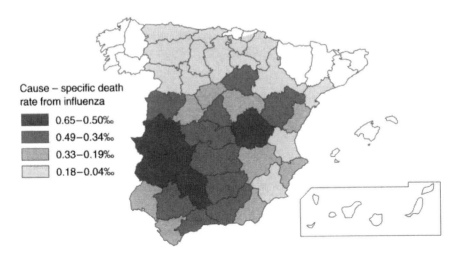

Cause – specific death
rate from influenza

■ 0.65–0.50‰
▦ 0.49–0.34‰
▨ 0.33–0.19‰
□ 0.18–0.04‰

Figure 11.3 First epidemic wave in Spain.

Source: Originally appeared in *La Gripe Española: La pandemia de 1913–19* by Beatriz Echeverri Dávila, Colección Monografías 132, CIS, 1993.

wave is easy to follow from the Mid-West in North America to most of
Western Europe in a matter of 3 months. Yet, the second wave, as far as we
know, seems to have exploded simultaneously during the last week of
August in Brest, Freetown and Boston and, as the evident rise in mortality
shows, in the eastern coast of Spain. We also know that places as far apart
as New Zealand and Great Britain, Bombay and Bogota, New York and
Seattle, registered the highest mortality from influenza during the week
that ended 26 October.[15] The chronological simultaneity of the second
epidemic explosion seems to reinforce the hypothesis that the virus
mutated on site, regaining its capacity to produce a pandemic, this time of
unimagined consequences.

Whether homebred or imported – or both – the virus on this occasion
was spread in much the same way as during the first wave. Movement of
people due to the war was again an important factor.[16] During the first
days of September, because of the flu, several travellers coming from
France were put under quarantine in Irun, the Spanish frontier town in
the Basque country.[17] Reports on 12 October tell of 900 workers returning
from France, fifteen of whom had to be put under quarantine.[18] The army
also played a significant part in the diffusion of the infection throughout
the country. September was the month when soldiers were recruited.
These young men either carried the infection with them or fell prey to it
on arrival at the army camps. To make things worse, the army sent many
sick recruits back home, thus spreading the infection to isolated rural
communities that had been left untouched by the first wave.[19] Some

recruits died on the way home.[20] In retrospect, however, considering the unhealthy living conditions of military quarters and the particular risks to young adult males, the death rate from influenza among military personnel appears to have been no higher than among civilians.[21] This may have been due, in part, to the fact that the camps had been heavily hit during the first wave, possibly ensuring a certain degree of immunity. However, one should bear in mind that soldiers who died at home were not included in army records, thus perhaps keeping the number of military deaths recorded artificially low.

Harvest festivals and feasts in honour of patron saints were celebrated in hundreds of towns and villages during the early autumn and served as potent diffusers of the virus. There are abundant reports in newspapers that attribute the explosion of the epidemic in many towns to the celebration of these feasts. Dr Garcia Duran, the chief health inspector of Valladolid, for example, traced the beginning of the epidemic in his province to the feast of St Antolín, celebrated in Medina del Campo in the first week of September. In particular, he lamented the case of the town of Olmedo: 'In the midst of an epidemic, with a seriously ill person in most of the houses, with many families in mourning because of deaths already occurred . . . and by a majority of votes, the villagers agreed not to suspend the bullfight!'[22] A few days later it was Dr Duran's turn to make a decision. The city of Valladolid was about to celebrate its festivities, and though the pandemic was ravaging through most of the province, he agreed with the provincial health council to delay the official declaration of an epidemic until late September because of the economic interests involved in a week of activities that included animal and local product fairs and bullfights.[23]

Panic set in as the death toll started to rise. At the sight of the extreme gravity of many of the cases, doctors were filled with apprehension. There was also confusion in the medical profession at the nature of the outbreak, although the majority of the cases could be easily identified as influenza. There was talk among the medical professionals of Pappatacci fever, pneumonic plague or dengue. To calm all rumours and gather information about the evolution of the epidemic in neighbouring France, a commission, headed by Dr Marañón, was sent there.[24]

The medical profession fought against the infection with all the means they had to hand. In severe cases, doctors applied intravenous injections of colloidal solutions of silver and platinum. Bleeding was still popular in Spain and was extensively used during the pandemic. As a somewhat sceptical doctor wrote: 'Although this resource did not relieve or cure anyone, it brought comfort to the patient and the family.'[25] Pneumococcal and streptococcal vaccines and antitoxins were utilised with uneven results. A renowned medical doctor and senator, Dr Mestre, publicised the use of diphtheria antitoxin as the best therapy against the flu. This resulted in a great demand for the antitoxin and a heated dispute as to its efficacy, not only among the medical profession, but also in the Senate.[26] Once more it was Dr Marañón and his commission who settled the controversy by affirming that the use of diphtheria antitoxin to combat influenza was unheard of in other countries. They recommended instead the use of other more specific antitoxins against the secondary complications caused by the pandemic.[27]

There was a severe shortage of doctors, especially in the rural areas, so much so that medical students were frequently sent from Madrid to help in remote villages. Although the medical profession during the epidemic lacked the means to save the lives of many people who were seriously ill, they could at least give out the simple instructions for the care of the sick. Frequently the flu victim lay in a room without ventilation, surrounded by family and friends, with alcoholic liquors, such as brandy or *cazalla*, as their sole nourishment. Various purgatives, garlic and lemons, were also promoted as sure cures for flu.

Medical and health workers often had to fight against the sanitary ignorance of the people and, on occasions, to battle against religious beliefs and the Catholic hierarchy. Churches remained open throughout the epidemic and many religious ceremonies and processions were celebrated *pro temporae pestilentiae*, providing a magnificent occasion for the further spread of the virus. In the first days of October, for example, the Bishop of Zamora, concerned 'because the reigning evil is due to our sins and ingratitude', organised a week-long series of religious acts in honour of the Virgin Mary.[28] Although the sanitary officials protested and tried to prevent people crowding into churches, it was to no avail. At the end, the Bishop congratulated himself on the large attendance 'as one of the most significant victories Catholicism has obtained'. Zamora was the capital that registered the highest mortality during the epidemic. But although some religious authorities can be accused of unjustified ignorance during the epidemic, it must not be forgotten that among the thousands of anonymous heroes and heroines who put their lives in danger so that the sick could have care and assistance, there were many nuns and priests.

One of the first steps taken by the health authorities was the establishment of sanitary cordons at all railway stations. Passengers were made to disembark, examined and those who showed symptoms of the flu were put in quarantine. Those allowed to proceed with their journeys were generously sprayed with foul-smelling disinfectants. Passengers on route to Portugal were, on various occasions, treated in a rather off-hand way. At the railway junction of Medina del Campo, under the watchful eye of the Guardia Civil, they were detained in carriages for 7 or 8 hours, until they could be hitched up to another train. The Portuguese and French borders were closed on several occasions in a desperate attempt to detain an enemy that was already inside the country. These xenophobic measures were useless for, as a Portuguese senior sanitary official pointed out, the only nation that could rightly call the pandemic 'Spanish' was Portugal, as they had received the infection from their neighbour.[29]

Just as ineffectual were most of the sanitary measures that were imposed. As Dr Martín Salazar, the senior sanitary official in Spain at that
time, admitted in a pessimistic report to the Royal Academy of Medicine
when the first wave was coming to an end, the control of an infection like
influenza was almost impossible. All the actions that had been taken to
impede its expansion were highly unsuccessful because a great number of
ambulant sick were spreading the infection. He pointed out that one of
the worst problems was that most of the population was terribly ignorant
about the forms of infection. Finally he denounced the lack of means, of
medical personnel and of laboratories, and lamented that the only health
organisation that existed was a bureaucratic mess, smothered by paper-
work.[30] In fact, this account anticipated the situation during the second
wave, when the reaction of the sanitary institutions was retarded, insufficient and, in many instances, negligent.

Sanitary cordons established at seaports were generally more successful.
Passengers travelling by sea were less numerous than those travelling by
land, and so they all could be put under quarantine, thus helping prevent
the spread of infection on land. That was the reason why influenza mortality rates during 1918 and 1919 in the Canary Islands were scarcely noticeable. Moreover, it was reported that the belated appearance of the second
wave in the port of Cadiz was due to the enforced sanitary cordon.[31]

The spread of the disease could not be stopped; the battle, since the
beginning of the second wave, was against death. According to official
registers, during the month of September influenza caused 7,856 deaths;
this was approximately the same number of deaths attributed to influenza
each year during the first two decades of the century. The number was
certainly appalling, more so if we consider that many deaths from influenza were not registered as such. But the worst was yet to come. During
October, when the epidemic reached its peak, the crude mortality rate
rose more than 300 per cent above its median monthly rate. There were
79,484 deaths attributed to influenza that month, which accounted for 52
per cent of the total deaths during the three waves. By December the pandemic had practically disappeared.

The whole country, except the Canary Islands, showed high cause-
specific death rates from influenza during this second wave. As shown in
Figure 11.4, death rates oscillated between 0.50 to 14.0 per thousand. This
time the infection had devastating effects on the north and east of the
peninsula. The hardest hit provinces were Burgos and Zamora in the
north, and, exceptionally, Almeria in the south.

The time of arrival of the third epidemic invasion is hard to place
because it overlapped the second wave. It spread slowly through the
country between January and June of 1919. The number of deaths officially registered as caused by influenza during the third wave was 21,094.
From an epidemiological point of view, this wave was less explosive than
the two that preceded it. Observers agreed that clinically it manifested the

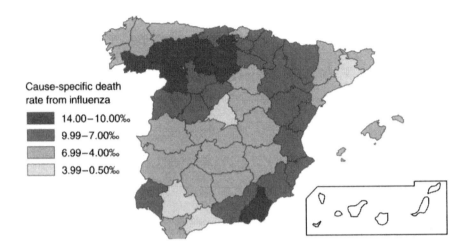

Figure 11.4 Second epidemic wave in Spain.

Source: Originally appeared in *La Gripe Española: La pandemia de 1913–19* by Beatriz Echeverri Dávila, Colección Monografías 132, CIS, 1993.

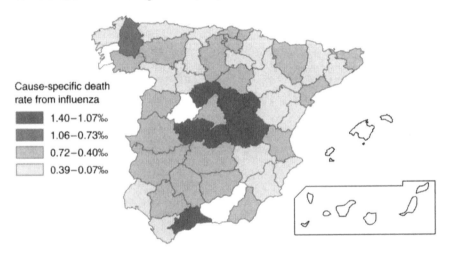

Figure 11.5 Third epidemic wave in Spain.

Source: Originally appeared in *La Gripe Española: La pandemia de 1913–19* by Beatriz Echeverri Dávila, Colección Monografías 132, CIS, 1993.

same severe characteristics of the second wave. But mortality was lower, its maximum rates ranging from 1.07 to 1.40 per thousand, probably due to the absence of eligible hosts (see Figure 11.5). In 1920, 17,841 deaths were attributed to influenza in what could be considered, though not taken into account in this chapter, as a fourth wave of the epidemic. This time, infants of less than one year were the principal victims as they were the only part of the population that lacked immunity against Spanish influenza.[32]

Mortality during the epidemic

Officially, 165,024 persons died from influenza in Spain during the three epidemic waves, in the period May 1918 to June 1919. Death from almost all causes increased during 1918, compared to death rates in the non-epidemic years. It can be assumed that the influenza virus, directly or indirectly, caused this excess mortality. Nevertheless, as we are aiming at a conservative estimate, only deaths by causes clearly associated with an epidemic of these characteristics have been computed. Excess mortality by those causes is shown in Table 11.3. The most important increases were registered in diseases affecting the respiratory system, probably due to differences in criteria when the diagnosis was made. Influenza also produced substantial increases in mortality among the chronically ill (chronic bronchitis, tuberculosis and heart diseases), parturient women (puerperal septicaemia), the aged (senility), and the very young (diarrhoea and congenital weakness). In the absence of any other known cause, we must assume that the increase of deaths attributed to 'other diseases' was also due to the epidemic. The sum is a total of 257,082 deaths, which means that 12 per thousand of the population of Spain died because of the epidemic. The large number of deaths is impressive and can be compared to other recent demographic tragedies – the 237,000 victims of the cholera epidemic of 1853–5, and the 345,000 deaths caused during the Spanish Civil War between 1936–9.[33]

In Spain, as in the rest of the world, the pandemic of 1918–19 caused an unusual mortality pattern among different age groups. Death rates in other pandemics of influenza (e.g. in 1957 and in 1968–9) were highest among infants (0–1 years) and the older population (aged over 60), but in 1918 the largest number of deaths occurred among young adults (20–40 years). The death rates from influenza, distributed by age groups and sex in Spain during 1917 and 1918, are shown in Table 11.4 and Figure 11.6. The discrepancy, between mortality in a non-epidemic year such as 1917 and 1918, is striking. In 1917 deaths from influenza concentrated, as expected, in the two most vulnerable age groups, while in 1918 young adults, aged 25 to 39, recorded the highest rates. Mortality was also very high among the age groups that immediately preceded and followed these (20–24 and 40–44). The second age group that was most affected by the pandemic was infants under one year. It must be recalled that infant mortality in Spain was still very high in the first decades of the century. Overall, infant mortality rates in 1918 rose only 20 per cent over those registered in 1917.

At the beginning of the century, the mortality sex ratio in Spain was

Table 11.3 Epidemic excess mortality (1918 over 1913–17) classified by cause during 1913–17 and 1918

Causes	Mortality 1913–17	Mortality 1918	Excess mortality	Increase %
Respiratory diseases	27,292	51,330	24,038	88
Pneumonia	13,254	19,714	6,460	48
Acute bronchitis	23,012	32,311	9,198	40
Chronic bronchitis	10,878	14,318	3,440	32
Pneumonic TB	25,822	34,046	8,460	32
Heart disease	35,496	42,277	6,781	19
Diarrhoea * and enteritis*	44,794	55,591	10,797	24
Congenital weakness	16,270	19,172	2,902	18
Puerperal septicaemia**	3,165	3,917	752	24
Other diseases	86,879	100,016	13,137	15
Senility	21,374	25,467	4,093	19
Total	308,236	398,159	90,058	33

Source: Movimiento Natural de Población (1920).

Notes
* Relates only to infants under 2 years of age.
** Includes other puerperal deaths.

Table 11.4 Cause-specific mortality from influenza in 1917 and 1918, by age and sex, per 100,000

Age	Sex	1917	1918
0–1	M	85	1,095
	F	66	885
1–4	M	39	907
	F	35	975
5–9	M	10	344
	F	11	427
10–14	M	5	264
	F	4	364
15–19	M	12	602
	F	11	612
20–24	M	16	750
	F	12	929
25–29	M	12	1,172
	F	13	1,158
30–34	M	15	1,178
	F	14	1,073
35–39	M	27	1,006
	F	12	787
40–44	M	28	734
	F	20	605
45–49	M	36	602
	F	26	462
50–54	M	38	484
	F	35	468
55–59	M	67	475
	F	55	433
60+	M	174	662
	F	181	747

Source: Movimiento Natural de la Población (1920).

104:100. However, during 1918, it fell to 99:100, indicating that more women than men died during that year. Let us first consider age and sex differences for deaths from all causes in a non-epidemic year, compared with those in 1918, as shown in Table 11.5. In 1917 there were still slightly higher death rates for women in age groups between 15–34 years, which can be attributed to childbirth deaths. This can be considered normal in a country then in the process of an epidemiological transition. But in 1918 this disadvantage extended to girls aged 5–14. The change must be attributed to the epidemic for, as shown in Figure 11.6, more women than men, between the ages of 1–24 years, died from influenza. The biggest difference is among the 10–14 age group where female mortality was 40 per cent higher than male mortality. From 25–60 years, however, the tendency shifted and more males died from influenza.

There are few records that permit adequate differentiation of mortality according to sex during the pandemic of 1918–19, especially since most of

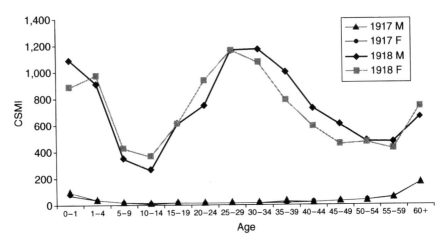

Figure 11.6 Cause-specific mortality from influenza in Spain, by age and sex, 1917 and 1918, per 100,000.

Table 11.5 Mortality rates per age and sex for all causes, 1917–18, per 1,000

Ages	1917		1918	
	Male	*Female*	*Male*	*Female*
0	230.1	192.8	275.4	231.9
1–4	41.3	38.8	61.1	59.1
5–9	6.7	6.8	11.7	13.2
10–14	3.4	3.4	6.8	8.8
15–19	5.3	5.5	13.6	13.8
20–24	7.2	7.0	17.7	18.8
25–29	7.2	7.6	22.9	23.3
30–34	7.4	8.0	23.8	23.7
35–39	8.7	8.7	22.6	20.4
40–44	10.8	9.5	21.0	18.2
45–49	14.0	10.0	22.6	16.7
50–59	22.4	16.4	29.1	22.9
60+	83.1	77.3	91.6	89.1

Source: Movimiento de la Población (1920).

the countries that collected reliable statistics had a large proportion of men between 18–45 years away at war. However, house surveys carried out in the United States, immediately after the pandemic, are an interesting source of information on this aspect.[34] Among the surveyed communities, case fatality rates for influenza were consistently higher among women below the age of 15 and over the age of 60. Between the ages of 15–60, male fatality rates were higher than those of the opposite sex. The difference was greatest among those aged 20–40. It appears that in the United States too, women were more vulnerable to death by influenza during childhood and early adolescence than men.

There seems to be no evidence, however, of excess female mortality during the more recent pandemics of 1957–8 and 1968–9 which might indicate a higher vulnerability of females to influenza, except in periods of high risk such as childbearing. It is of course possible that this was another unique characteristic of the 1918 virus. Another possibility is that the difference observed was due to the persistence of residual cultural behaviours in societies that were undergoing social and economic modernisation. It can be suggested that, in the presence of a crisis like the pandemic, girls, then habitually more neglected and less well nourished than boys, had to carry the added load of caring for the sick. They were therefore more exposed to the virus and less prepared to fight its assault. A more detailed examination of age–sex differentials in mortality during those first decades of the twentieth century in Spain is necessary.

Factors that contributed to regional mortality variations

In Spain, as elsewhere, there were marked regional disparities in the impact of the pandemic. While the epidemiological characteristics of the pandemic of 1918 allow us to assert that all humanity was defenceless against that particular virus, the question is, why was death so unequally distributed? The establishment of very successful sanitary controls or geo-graphical isolation can explain very few of the differences observed. On the other hand, poverty, with its usual concomitants of malnutrition, an unhealthy environment and disease, is a very important risk factor during any epidemic. In addition, at a time when there was still no effective therapy against the complications of influenza, the difference between life and death could depend, to a large extent, on such simple factors as the care and feeding of the ill. In 1918, even in relatively developed countries, institutions responsible for such simple tasks were overwhelmed, if not paralysed, by the enormous number of the ill and dying. Obviously, the situation was much more critical in communities that lived in conditions of extreme poverty and with very rudimentary health care institutions.

Beyond this, differences in mortality are harder to explain. Case fatality rates canvassed in house-to-house surveys by the US Health Service after the pandemic showed variations ranging from 3.0 per cent to 0.8 per cent among communities.[35] In Spain, at a local level, there were differences in the death toll among city districts, which can be attributed to economic inequalities.[36] At a provincial level, where mortality rates from influenza varied from 0.50 to 14.0 per 1,000 during the second wave, poverty, as a risk factor, does not seem to have been the main influence. Contrary to what would have been expected, regions of secular high death rates and poor sanitary and economic conditions, such as Extremadura and

Andalusia, had lower influenza death rates during the epidemic than more developed areas such as the Basque country or Catalonia.

Immunity acquired by a previous contact with the virus, whether by infection or vaccination, is the best defence against influenza. However, our knowledge of the mechanisms of immunity conferred by an infection of influenza is limited, because of the complex mutations the virus experiences. Experimental studies made among animals and human groups indicate that immunity conferred by an infection of influenza can last from 6 months to 20 years.[37] The opinion of many specialists in 1918 was that an attack conferred immunity against the following wave.[38] However, as eminent a virologist as Sir Macfarlane Burnet questioned the existence of acquired immunity against the influenza virus of 1918.[39]

Nevertheless, a glance at the maps of the three epidemic waves in Spain suggests that immunity against the influenza virus, acquired during the first wave, is one of the factors that best explains regional differences in mortality. Thus, we see that the spring wave, the most benign of the three, had a bigger impact on the provinces situated in the centre and south of the peninsula where influenza mortality rates ranged from 0.34 to 0.65 per thousand. The second, more lethal wave affected the northern and eastern portion of the country with greater force, with death rates of up to 14.0 per thousand. This could indicate that the populations of the centre and south of the peninsula had acquired a degree of resistance against the virus. As for the third wave, though it seems to have been as lethal as its predecessor, it acted like the smouldering embers of a great fire, which flared up to attack those members of a weakened population that still lacked immunity.

The importance of some of the factors that intervened in the different outcomes of the epidemic can, up to a point, be measured or evaluated by simple correlation coefficients. The first hypothesis to be confirmed is that those provinces that suffered an important epidemic invasion during the first wave, acquired, to a certain degree, immunological defences against the second, more virulent, wave. Owing to the absence of morbidity data, the statistical analysis was carried out using the death rates from influenza in the fifty Spanish provinces during the first wave and those from the second/third wave.[40] The resulting coefficient, $r = -0.354$, although not very high, confirms the negative association between the two variables. A second correlation was carried out between the same indexes but only among the thirty-seven provinces with death rates from influenza above the national average in either the first or the second/third wave. In this way, an attempt has been made to avoid other factors that could intervene in some provinces that had relatively low death rates during all the epidemic. The resulting coefficient is more significant, $r = -0.653$, and seems to confirm the existence of an acquired immunity.

As has been pointed out before, poverty and its attendant conditions are important factors in the outcome of any epidemic of infectious disease. It was consequently important to evaluate the influence of the economic and sanitary status of the provinces on the differences in death rates. Due to the absence of reliable specific indicators of economic development for all provinces during the first decades of the century in Spain, indirect indicators of social and economic status were used.[41] The first one is the infant mortality rate for each province between 1914 and 1917. This rate is considered by specialists to be linked directly to the sanitary conditions of the region and indirectly to its level of development. The result, r = 0.517, confirms the existence of a positive association. The second index used is bodily height. Generally accepted as a good indicator of the nutritional status, and of the disease environment during childhood, it can be assumed that the average height of a population is linked with both its economic and sanitary conditions, although other influences cannot be excluded.[42] The outcome, r = −0.318, less significant than the former, nevertheless seems to confirm that poverty was an aggravating factor during the pandemic.

In view of the unusual death distribution by age that this pandemic caused, it was anticipated that provinces with a greater proportion of young adults would show higher death rates. Therefore, the percentage of young adults aged between 19–39 years in each province was evaluated. However, the coefficient, r = −0.556, is negative – a result contrary to the hypothesis mentioned above.

Population density has a great influence on the incidence of such an extremely infectious disease as influenza. A strong positive association would be expected between pandemic mortality in the Spanish provinces and their degree of urbanisation. The index of urbanisation used was the percentage of the population living in cities of 10,000 inhabitants or more. Again the result is significant, r = −0.668, but the opposite sign of what was expected. A cogent explanation for this contradictory result is that the immunity factor has intervened in the last two correlation coefficients, even though an effort has been made to eliminate its effects. It must be remembered that, according to observers at the time, the impact of the first wave was more pronounced in the cities than in the rural areas, and cities, because of immigration, had a higher percentage of young adults.

Some demographic consequences

The most obvious impact of the pandemic of 1918–19 was the extraordinary number of deaths it caused. It interrupted the declining pattern in mortality in Spain for a period of 3 years. Yet from a demographer's point of view, its consequences went beyond that. The weddings that were not celebrated and the children that were never conceived must also be taken into account. At the beginning of the century, in Spain, there was a relative consistency in the annual cycle of marriage rates. Autumn was harvesting time and also the moment when many young couples married. It is not surprising, then, that a slight decrease in marriages occurred during 1918. But a year later, widowers were picking up the pieces and finding a new spouse. Although not all related to the effects of the epidemic, there was a strong increase in marriages during the next 5 years, especially among widowers, proof of human resilience.

In Table 11.1 it can be seen that the pandemic appeared to have no effect on the birth rate in 1918; on the contrary, there was a slight increase. The reason lies in the seasonality of conceptions and births at that time. Invariably, the highest peak in birth rates was in January and February, followed by a minor increase during the autumn. Obviously, the children born in 1918 were conceived before the appearance of the epidemic in May. But if the epidemic had no consequences on the number of births in 1918, it did have an important negative effect on the number of conceptions during that year. In consequence, the birth rate in 1919 diminished significantly. However, during the following years, until 1923, birth rates recovered, following the increase in marriage rates.

The epidemic was so lethal that, in 1918, it caused the biggest annual deficit in natural increase (−4.0 per cent) of the last two centuries. It surpassed even the deficit of 1885, the year of the last cholera epidemic (−1.7 per cent) and that of 1939, the worst year of the Spanish Civil War (−2.0 per cent). It is true that in the space of a few years, the population recovered, but the children born around the years of the pandemic belong to a diminished generation. They were born to parents who also belonged to 'short' cohorts, punished by the cholera epidemic of 1885 and the Cuban-American War of 1898. Furthermore, it seems that children born in the years preceding the pandemic or during the pandemic had higher probabilities of death during their first 15 years of life than others, due to the sequels of the infection.[43] This was precisely the unfortunate generation that was, in turn, ravaged by the Spanish Civil War.

12 A holocaust in a holocaust

The Great War and the 1918 Spanish influenza epidemic in France[1]

Patrick Zylberman

According to a French military doctor who had served on the Western Front: 'The Great War had not experienced epidemics, a unique fact in the history of warfare.'[2] To people at the time this came as a surprise. But the menace did not come from where it was expected. Typhoid, smallpox, meningitis, dysentery and even tetanus (but not malaria) were all nearly eradicated in the French armed forces. Furthermore, no cholera cases occurred in the army between 1914 and 1919, and only eight cases of typhus. This stands in stark contrast to the devastation caused by typhus on the Russian and Serbian fronts.[3] This prophylactic discipline in the French armed forces contrasted starkly with the negligence of civilian public health. Epidemics harried the civilian population, fatalities rising from 0.04 per thousand of the population in 1913 to 0.14 in 1918. Soldiers in the barracks at the rear, a group in large part similar to civilians in relation to epidemics, were just another testimony to that contrast. In a military doctor's words:

> Ordinary, peacetime epidemic diseases (measles, scarlet fever, mumps, diphtheria) just barely reached troops on the front. The latter were usually considerably less infected than soldiers in the rear [were].[4]

What impact did wartime conditions have on civilian health? Definite answers have been attempted to this question even though it involves a host of overlapping and interacting factors.[5] Some scholars have claimed that the 'Spanish' flu was a *sui generis* event rather than the outcome of wartime conditions. But even if the war itself did not bring about influenza, does that mean that fatalities due to the flu cannot be seen also as an additional outcome of hardship suffered at the end of the war? I will argue that unequal distribution of material resources on the home and battle fronts affected the population's ability to survive associated bacterial infections which were the immediate cause of the largest number of deaths. Let us look more closely at this question while bearing in mind that the often very unreliable statistics about local or regional case studies might well qualify some of the conclusions drawn here.

Civilian and military fatalities

From boot camps in the Middle West, the influenza epidemic reached
France in April–May 1918 at Camp no. 4 near Bordeaux, the chief dis-
embarkation port for the American Expeditionary Force (AEF).[6] Following this first 'spring' attack, a much more brutal 'autumnal' onslaught
occurred in August at Brest, where US soldiers were then landing. The
French called this new assault the 'Swiss' wave, because many French
victims were prisoners-of-war returned to France through Switzerland.[7]
The reasons for this epidemic's unprecedented virulence have never been
explained. The high case-fatality and excess death rates for young adults
caused this second wave to take a toll never matched by subsequent epidemics. A third and less deadly wave hit during the winter of 1918–19.
With a rate of 3.9 deaths per 1,000 (according to a recent rough estimate),
France suffered less than other belligerents. The epidemic killed about
2.3 million people in Europe, the continent's general mortality rate (4.8
per 1,000) being five times as much as during the 1889–90 'Russian' flu
pandemic. Certainly, as physicians remarked, the flu was as deadly as the
war.[8]

Influenza reached the Western Front in April 1918, first among the
IVth Army (Château-Thierry, Soissons), then the IIIrd (Montdidier).
Sweeping over the combat zone, it killed 7,401 men out of 139,850 cases
between May and October. Alarmed, the Military Health Service asked in
May to be notified by telegraph of further outbreaks. By late June 1918,
chest complications, first of all bronchopneumonia, which sometimes
ended in mauve or heliotrope cyanosis, accounted for from 30 to 40
per cent of deaths.[9] After morbidity rates had reached 75 per cent in
May–June, during the German offensive, a remission followed for the next
2 months. Then, just as the autumn counter-offensive was launched, a new
outbreak of the epidemic occurred. In September, 25,000 men in the
French armed forces (and over 37,000 in the AEF) were laid low with the
flu. In Champagne, from 26 September to 5 October, the flu killed 30 soldiers a day; as many as 1,600 daily evacuees (i.e. one-third of the disabled
brought back from the battle line) had the flu. During 10 days in October
1918, 36,000 French troops fell ill, and 2,400 of them died. Soldiers who
had previously been gassed seemed to be particularly vulnerable, and
many died. Ambulances were 'flooded with the sick', and the number of
corpses outstripped the possibilities for burial. 'The disease attacked
almost entire battalions in a day', according to Hans Zinsser. Ministry of
War statistics from 1 May 1918 to 30 April 1919 record 408,180 cases (126
per 1,000) and 30,382 fatalities (9.3 per 1,000) in the French army. The
disease first swept through the AEF in the last week of September, then
appeared among French troops (12–20 October) and, lastly, the British
forces (from 27 October to 2 November). Shifted from one post to
another, poorly fed, crowded in trains and barracks, soldiers in the rear or

in training were more susceptible to the virus than troops at the front. The mortality rates in the French army were 17.7 per 1,000 for soldiers in the rear and 6.3 for soldiers at the front, with morbidity rates at 228 and 100 per 1,000 respectively. The epidemic swept from the rear up to the front line.[10]

In the civilian population, overall mortality, having increased rather moderately between 1913 and 1917, shot up from 20 to 25.1 per 1,000 in 1918 because of influenza. This rate had not been reached since the Italian (1859) and Franco-Prussian (1870–1) Wars. In the areas of France that had not been invaded, the flu increased the death rate by 40 per cent. The epidemic abated in 1919, even though mortality stayed high because of the still strong incidence of associated respiratory diseases, especially bronchopneumonia. In the spring of 1920, the epidemic came to an end, but not before more civilians had died. The official civilian death rate was three times lower than that for the military, but this comparison may be misleading. The usually quoted figure of 137,200 civilian victims (1918–20) is a conservative estimate, as those who fell ill often did not consult doctors, or the symptoms were not properly diagnosed.[11] Nor should it be forgotten that, although many people died of the flu, many died of other, associated epidemics, in particular pneumonia. For instance, in Toulon during that period, pleuropneumonia and pneumo-coccaemia were fatal in 10 per cent of the cases.[12] Physicians were urged to report flu cases, but did so 'very incompletely', according to Paul Faivre. Wartime censorship of statistics about the epidemic also reduces confidence in official sources. A more realistic estimate might be Patterson and Pyle's suggested figure of 240,000 civilian and military deaths during the deadliest wave in the autumn of 1918 (Britain officially recorded 225,000 deaths, and Prussia 223,000).[13]

Everyone agreed that death took a heavier toll among persons from 20 to 40 years old. This 'Apollinaire's syndrome' (referring to the poet Guillaume Apollinaire, who died of flu in November 1918, aged 38, and characterising the fulminant forms of the disease attacking young and healthy people) applied in France as elsewhere. Troops, young mothers, nurses, schoolchildren – many who died were healthy, robust people, although other factors may have been at work here, the older cohorts possibly having greater immunity since they had survived the epidemic of 1889–92. As the novelist, Roger Martin du Gard, wrote in his diary, 'Women and children around me are dying from flu within three days.' In the navy, Paul Strauss (senator from Seine Department) said, 'The flu felled young Navy recruits much more than older servicemen.' Relatively speaking, nursing infants and persons over the age of 50 were spared, at least during the autumn of 1918. 'Spanish' influenza thus differed from the flu epidemics of 1889–90, 1892, 1936 and 1957, all of which took a higher proportion of victims among the elderly.[14]

The epidemic struck Paris in the summer of 1918. Forty-eight flu deaths occurred in July and forty-five in August, compared with two during the same period in the preceding years. It peaked between mid-October and mid-November, then abated during December and January 1919, before reappearing from 9 February to 1 March. According to the Prefecture of Seine, from 30 June 1918 to 26 April 1919, it killed 10,281 people in the capital, accounting for 18.5 per cent of the total Parisian death rate. The capital's death rate during the whole epidemic was 2.9 per 1,000, admittedly a cautious estimate (Pottevin suggested a flu death rate of 3.5 per 1,000). In the city's vital statistics, flu victims as a category were confined to those registered as such by the *médecins-inspecteurs de l'état civil*. As a consequence, deaths caused by associated respiratory diseases were not counted as flu victims, even though bronchopneumonia was on the rise, and the incidence of pneumonia trebled during the autumn.[15]

The epidemic swept across the whole country. In Marseille, where the City Council did nothing, it caused terrible losses, yet the same occurred in Lyons where the municipality had taken quite energetic measures. Overall mortality per thousand in Lyons, from May 1918 to April 1919, was up 8.7 above the 1913 rate, i.e. 4,860 additional deaths, 20 to 40 per cent of which should probably be set down to influenza.[16] Clearly this holocaust in a holocaust, the 'Spanish' flu, needs to be more closely examined. At the time people were confused and afraid; there was much suffering. Influenza also took a toll in the armed forces, but it felled civilians with the same severity in France as in the Dutch East Indies or New Zealand, both thousands of miles away from the battlefield.[17]

A battle postponed

In 1910, the French army had one veterinary officer for 264 horses, but one doctor for 421 soldiers! In February 1914, by its own admission, it lacked 700 doctors.[18] Nonetheless, a dramatic change came about with the outbreak of war. On 2 August 1914, out of approximately 22,000 physicians, 18,000 were mobilised – that is 80 per cent of the profession. On 11 November 1918, the Military Health Service had more than 21,000 doctors for 4.3 million men; nearly 11,000 served on the front line (out of whom 85 per cent were from the reserves), and 10,000 were serving in the rear (98 per cent from the reserves) The resultant 1:203 ratio compares with 1:376 in the British army, which had approximately as many men in service.[19]

By late 1915, doctors were scarcer among the civil population than among the French armed forces. In Lille, hospitals used male army nurses as replacements for recent medical graduates to make up for all the doctors who had been conscripted. By 1916, certain areas were almost entirely deprived of medical services. In the Chamber of Deputies, Jean-Marie Guiraud, deputy for the Tarn Department, mentioned a town with

7,000 inhabitants which had not had a doctor for a month. Among the ninety practitioners in Le Havre before the war, only eighteen were still there in 1917, providing care for the 135,000 inhabitants, a ratio of 1:7,500. By comparison, the German and British civilian ratios stood at 1:5,777 and 1:2,344 respectively. The Department of Gard, a mining area, had one doctor for 10,000 inhabitants in March 1918. In October 1918, the Department of Loire was deprived both of medicine and doctors, like many other communes throughout the country. Even in Paris, police-run emergency services had to be instituted to try and make up for the lack of doctors.[20]

Nurses, hospital beds and ambulances were in equally short supply for the civilian population. With a high proportion of the country's doctors and nurses having been conscripted, the number available to tend sick civilians was seriously depleted. In Normandy, for instance, the usually quite efficient civilian health services ground to a standstill for want of vehicles and medical personnel. Most had been commandeered by the army. In Bordeaux, burials, the water-supply and rubbish collection were disrupted for lack of labour and horses (which had been requisitioned), and this added to the difficulties of coping with the epidemic.[21]

Hospital wards were filled with sick soldiers and could hardly be used for civilians. To cope with the steep increase in admissions, the public hospital system issued an order on 25 September 1918 to free beds. This resulted in only a quarter of the beds needed and so the sick could not be isolated. By mid-October, so many people suffering from the flu were asking to be admitted to hospital that access to beds had to be restricted. Patients were already packed into wards, with camp beds set up in order to expand capacity (by 40 per cent). The situation did not get any better before the first week of November, when the number of the sick started to decrease. At the height of the epidemic, hospitals fell short of everything: beds, personnel, ambulances and drugs.[22]

The state of mind of doctors was also an important factor. Few doctors had a practical approach for dealing with the flu; fear of ridicule and embarrassment often restrained them from using masks. Above all, officials were anxious not to alarm people (see Figure 12.1). The Ministry of the Interior, the Public Health Council in the Department of Seine, and the Académie de Médecine ordered the closure of theatres, cinemas, churches and markets, but to little avail, since prefects failed to enforce such measures for fear of annoying the public. Research never moved beyond an elementary stage. At the Académie des Sciences, in the autumn of 1918, Émile Roux's attempt to encourage reports from doctors and bacteriologists was not very successful.[23]

Would civilian mortality have been lower if medical personnel had been more available to civilians? It seems unlikely, though one must be careful of overstating how far this might have been so. In Great Britain, where health services were more extensive, better organised and less

PRÉFECTURE DU DÉPARTEMENT DE MEURTHE-ET-MOSELLE

CONTRE LA GRIPPE

PRÉCAUTIONS A PRENDRE

Des cas de grippe assez nombreux se sont produits, ces temps derniers, dans notre région, certains d'une gravité assez grande pour que le public soit invité à prendre quelques précautions en vue de se prémunir contre la maladie.

Il convient de remarquer tout d'abord qu'il s'agit en réalité de la grippe habituelle, l'influenza des années précédentes, se présentant toutefois avec quelques caractères particuliers et pouvant prendre facilement une forme sérieuse.

L'origine en est la contagion et surtout la contagion directe, le contact le plus souvent immédiat avec un malade.

Les malades doivent être aussitôt que possible isolés dans une chambre où ne doit pénétrer que la personne qui les soigne et qui doit s'astreindre à prendre elle-même les précautions indiquées.

L'isolement doit être pratiqué dès les premiers signes de maladie : courbatures, rhume de cerveau, fièvre.

Il y a lieu de tenir les malades au chaud et d'appeler un Médecin pour peu que les symptômes soient prononcés.

Les personnes qui se trouveront en contact avec les malades devront prendre des précautions spéciales, qui peuvent d'i reste être appliquées avec fruit par tous.

Au premier rang, se trouve l'hygiène soignée de la bouche et du nez, par lavages et gargarismes antiseptiques pratiqués deux fois par jour.

Les personnes ayant des contacts fréquents avec des malades, surtout dans les cas graves, devront s'obturer les narines avec des floches lâches d'ouate et se couvrir la bouche avec un petit tampon fait d'une mince feuille d'ouate entourée de gaze.

Elles devront également se laver les mains et la figure au savon après tout contact avec le malade.

Il est instamment conseillé de ne pas visiter les grippés, de se préserver des refroidissements brusques, d'user de boissons chaudes ou mieux, additionnées d'un peu d'alcool, de s'alimenter convenablement en buvant, si possible, du vin, enfin de fuir les agglomérations où les contacts sont trop répétés.

Docteur MACÉ.

Professeur à la Faculté de Médecine,
Directeur des Services d'Hygiène,
Vice-Président du Conseil d'Hygiène.

Nancy, IMP GER-LEVRAULT, imprimeurs de la Préfecture — 94,147-18

Figure 12.1 Precautionary measures against influenza advised in Nancy, France. (Courtesy Archives municipales, Nancy.)

depleted by the war, the epidemic claimed almost as many lives in a smaller population.[24]

Who fell victim to the flu?

We often read that the flu pandemic was rather 'democratic' since, although it affected age-groups differently, the effects did not differ so much across the socio-economic groups.[24] But influenza did not spread evenly among the two sexes. In the departments that had not been invaded, flu mortality in the 15–44 age range was higher among males than females. This, it has been argued, was a result of conscription, the male civilian population being made up to a large extent of those men whom the military had deemed medically unfit. Except for neutral countries, like Spain, which apparently registered a slight excess in female mortality during the autumn of 1918, excess male deaths were reputed to be a universal characteristic of the pandemic.[25] But in departments closer to the front the mortality patterns appear to have been somewhat different. There the differential between male and female flu deaths was small or even reversed. Indeed, historians and demographers have deemed it one of the main factors in the fall of women's average life expectancy during the war.

Before the war, women had been gaining an advantage in lifespan over men. In 1914, the average age of death for women was 53 years and 5 months compared to 48 years and 7 months for men. But a countervailing trend during the war had narrowed this gap considerably by 1918, down to 49 years and 7 months and 49 years respectively. After the war, the gap started widening again: in 1919 it stood at 54 years 3 months for women as compared with 50 years 10 months for men. Although no conclusive evidence may be brought to support this fully, other facts favouring this hypothesis of the flu epidemic as crucial in lowering women's life expectancy are supplied by the 1921 census. By 1921, the female population of 20–34-year-olds in the erstwhile frontline department of Meurthe-et-Moselle, for instance, had decreased 10 per cent since 1911.[26]

Similarly in war-engulfed Paris, in 1918 the incidence of flu was the same for both sexes, but the mortality was higher in women than in men (see Table 12.1). To be sure, the population patterns of wartime Paris were distorted by successive drafts of men aged 20–40, Allied soldiers on leave, refugees and demobilisation, and this makes it very difficult to accurately calculate comparative gender mortality. Any conclusion must therefore be very tentative. However, the death toll does seem to have been higher among young and adolescent females, in sharp contrast to previous influenza epidemics in which more men than women aged under 60 had died. (See Table 12.1, in which 'deaths from flu' means deaths due to 'cause No. 10 influenza', as defined by the *médecins-inspecteurs de l'état civil*.)

Table 12.1 Uncorrected death rates from flu per 1,000 population (1911) in Paris, according to age and sex, 30 June 1918–26 April 1919

Ages	Male death rates	Female death rates
0–1	3.14	2.82
1–9	1.34	1.65
10–19	1.79	2.79
20–39	2.20	4.90
40–59	2.62	2.48
60+	4.34	3.49

Source: Préfecture de la seine, *Epidémie de grippe*, p. 41.

Excess female mortality until the eve of the Second World War has been said to be closely linked to infectious diseases. According to a Spanish medical mission visiting France in the autumn of 1918, pregnant women were probably more 'sensitive' to infection when their condition made them less able to ward off influenza and its lethal consequences. Recent calculations of data from 1914 and 1918 have proven the relative vulnerability of women in the 20–25 year age-group. Statisticians did not notice any increase in the number of stillbirths in 85 departments, yet accounts at the time frequently mentioned stillbirths among women working in armaments factories near Paris; and endogenous mortality actually increased from 1918 to 1920. Moreover, girls born in 1918, 1919 and 1920 were more prone to illness and accidents throughout their lives as if, in the words of demographers, the Spanish flu left a durable signature on them.[27]

However, many other segments of the population were just as sensitive. Military training camps bringing together young conscripts from many towns, villages and hamlets under crowded conditions were tailor-made for spreading germs. Not only was morbidity higher in training battalions, but chest complications were also more frequent. Resistance to infection among recruits from rural areas was probably rather weak, owing to geographical isolation, the low socio-economic status of many people, and restricted access to health care.[28] Most arguments for the so-called 'democratic' theory of the epidemic try to prove that, in selected districts, the mortality rate and distribution of wealth do not correlate. Jacques Bertillon argued this in his study of the 'Russian' flu of 1889–90 in Paris. An entirely different picture emerges if we look at what happened in Nancy in the autumn of 1918. This front-line city had a lower death rate (approximately 2.5 per thousand) than Paris. The epidemic hit the very centre of the city, in the quarters of Saint-Sébastien and Sainte-Anne, which were islands of poverty and high mortality. In contrast with Paris, flu mortality in Nancy coincided with the geography of the general death rate. In other words, mortality and socio-economic status overlapped; the epidemic obviously attacked the poorer classes and neighbourhoods more aggressively.[29]

It is true that, in line with what Bertillon said of the 'Russian' flu, statisticians did not discover any link between the 'Spanish' flu's toll and the overall death rate in the various neighbourhoods in Paris, and they were surprised to find that the later epidemic had even struck the wealthy seventh *arrondissement* harder than the relatively poor and densely populated thirteenth. How could it be that the rich, not the poor, bore the brunt of the 'Spanish' flu? To explain this, statisticians concluded that a significant proportion of the population in the most affluent neighbourhoods of Paris were the lower middle classes, or even the poor. It was not the average overall population density that really counted; what mattered was the percentage of the population living in overcrowded housing. Military doctors were used to pointing out this factor; the more confined living quarters are, the more that people have contact, then the easier it is for an air-borne disease to spread. Why did the wealthy École Militaire, Auteuil, Porte Dauphine, Champs-Élysées and La Muette neighbourhoods have the highest flu mortality rates even though they all had low overall population densities? Because many of the capital's most poorly housed people, servants, maids and service-providers to the wealthy, lived there. The high death rate in these neighbourhoods owed much to the category of women aged between 20 and 30 years, most of whom were single and lived in cramped, wretched rooms on the top of densely populated floors of bourgeois buildings. As the overall statistics of the Prefecture of Paris were only broken down by *arrondissements*, the overcrowding of the servants' lodgings was masked. A large number of flu victims lived in places where there was not enough room to turn around (e.g. concierges or cooks), or worked in tiny, insalubrious work-shops meeting the needs of the better-off (e.g. craftsmen, cobblers, printers, tailors, cabinet-makers, jewellers, goldsmiths, dressmakers or laundresses). Women performed many of these jobs, a fact which makes sense of their already mentioned 'sensitivity' to the epidemic. In fact, one-quarter of all women who died of the flu in Paris were maids. The virus might well have behaved 'democratically', but the society it attacked was hardly egalitarian. The flu epidemic's impact on women might thus provide some clue to the effect of the 'Spanish' flu on the mainly civilian population.[30]

Blaming the war?

Without the war, would 'Spanish' influenza have caused so many casualties? Contemporary writers chiefly blamed the war for the tragic shift from a rather harmless illness to a devastating scourge. But how can we blame the war in the case of non-belligerents? Neutral Copenhagen and Stockholm were struck like Paris and Berlin. Present-day scholars consider the use of the expanded and more intensively utilised transportation network occasioned by the war, rather than the war itself, to be the real culprit. By mustering an enormous number of men on the front or in the rear, by crowding trains with soldiers going on leave, by moving and displacing people, the war broke down defences against contagion. The transport infrastructure helped to 'virally equalise' all categories, civilian and military, and all geographical areas.[31]

Epidemiological approaches must take into account complex forms of contingency. Combat by itself is not what ought to be considered, but instead a whole set of factors attendant on total warfare (the transportation of infected soldiers, inadequate medical services, re-allocated medical and nursing resources and personnel, a restricted food supply and overcrowding), all of them reacting in different ways to increase the stress and weakening defences against influenza. And not to be forgotten is the response of the authorities to the epidemic. Reacting to unforeseeable events as they happened and placing the successful conduct of the war above all else, they responded by switching resources from civilian health services and concentrating efforts on the armed forces. Even so, the 'Spanish' flu affected army tactics as well. Coming as the last military offensives were being launched, it decimated the ranks, made it hard to bring in reinforcements and disorganised logistics, in particular transportation.[32]

As previously pointed out, in the uninvaded areas, the pattern of mobilisation meant that male mortality exceeded female mortality, because the male population had been denuded of its healthier members. In the front-line areas, on the other hand, female mortality usually exceeded male mortality, this reflecting aspects of female disadvantage which had been aggravated by the special circumstances of war. Thus, national figures show that, during the war and especially during the epidemic, women may have temporarily lost their advantage over men with regard to the average age of death they had won very recently. As Hart has argued, social, cultural and economic 'forces might be conceived of as once-off historical events which set off demographic disturbances in some societies but not in others'. A link (more indirect than direct) between the flu and social conditions might have come into play along with the virus. Among these social conditions were wartime restrictions on housing, an exhausting day's work (in the Department of Seine, women formed about a third of the labour force in weapons factories in 1918), the poor quality of medical inspections conducted in the war industries, and women's lower wages. In addition, malnutrition and poverty existed in those neighbourhoods on the outskirts of cities, where prices were even higher due to the war; from the first year of the war, in these communes the meals served in free restaurants for mothers with children had tripled.[33] In other words, Paris' distinctive socio-geographical features, possibly repeated in a handful of front-line cities where those providing services to the rich were a not insignificant proportion of the population, lay behind a severe, albeit temporary, throwback – a return, under the appalling circumstances of the last months of the war, of all these specific risks linked to a bygone excess female mortality that had, in reality, been greatly reduced since the last quarter of the nineteenth century.

13 Long-term effects of the 1918 'Spanish' influenza epidemic on sex differentials of mortality in the USA

Exploratory findings from historical data

Andrew Noymer and Michel Garenne

How did the 1918 'Spanish' influenza epidemic affect sex differentials of mortality in the USA? For a first-order assessment of the demographic impact of the epidemic, the best place to look is at one of the most basic mortality statistics, the expectation of life at birth, $e(0)$. Figure 13.1 shows female and male life expectancy for the United States, 1900–95.

The influenza epidemic of 1918 left an unmistakable signature on the levels of $e(0)$ for men and women, with both sexes losing about 12 years of period life expectancy, a dramatic shift. Those losses were regained in 1919, however, so the overall effect was a downward 'blip', one year wide,

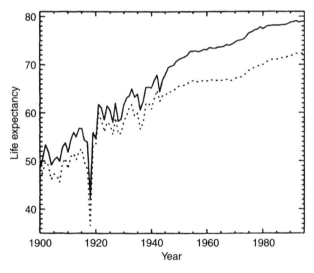

Figure 13.1 Expectation of life ($e(0)$, in years) in relation to date, for males (dotted) and females (solid), United States, 1900–95.

Sources: US Bureau of the Census 1975, Table B107–115; and Anderson, Kochanek and Murphy, 1997, Table 5.

in the mortality statistics. But what of *differential* mortality between males and females? Such a comparison is not evident from Figure 13.1 – while it is clear that females enjoy a consistent advantage over males in terms of life expectancy, it is less obvious how well males and females fared when compared to each other.

There are two main ways to compare two quantities: ratio and difference. Taking the ratio of male $e(0)$ to female $e(0)$ (or female/male) would give the *relative* longevity of males versus females (or females versus males). Subtracting male $e(0)$ from female $e(0)$ gives the *differential* longevity, i.e. females' advantage over males in terms of years lived. Sheps points out how rate differences can be more useful than rate ratio.[1] Mortality differences are always the same as survivor differences, whereas mortality ratios and survival ratios are different except in certain special cases, leading to a dilemma as to whether we should count the living or the dead.[2] The exploratory methods that will be used in this chapter are well suited to dealing with rate differences, so we shall concentrate on rate differences when we make comparisons between the sexes. We are interested in females' advantage over males in absolute terms (i.e. years of life lived), not in relative terms (i.e. $e(0)$ (males) as a percentage of $e(0)$ (females)).

Figure 13.2 presents such data. In spite of the fact that the levels of $e(0)$

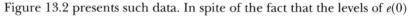
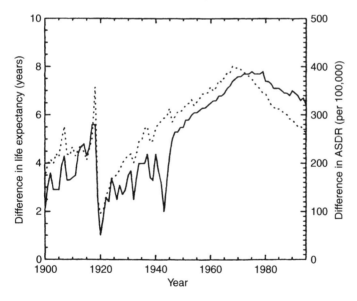

Figure 13.2 Females' advantage over males in expectation of life (solid, e(0), in years) and in age-standardised death rate (dotted, ASDR, per 100,000), United States, 1900–95.

Sources: Computed from data in Figure 1, and US Department of Health, Education, and Welfare (1956, No. 1, Table 1; and 1973, Table C); Grove and Hetzel, 1968, Table 62; National Center for Health Statistics, 1996, Tables 1–3; and Anderson, Kochanek and Murphy, 1997, Table 1.

for males and females rebounded in 1919 (Figure 13.1), the difference between males and females seems to have been affected by the influenza epidemic. After the 1918 epidemic, women lost much of their advantage over men in $e(0)$. By 1920, $e(0)$ for women was just one year longer than for men, and unlike the $e(0)$ curves, the difference curve did not return to trend rapidly. Women did not regain their pre-1918 advantage over men until the early 1950s. This result is not what one might expect given that the curves for either sex alone rebounded after 1918, nor is it readily obvious from Figure 13.1. A review of the mortality literature to date reveals no previous comment on this, even though it is a major feature of the trends in sex differences in mortality.[3]

Our immediate interest in this chapter is the relationship between the 1918 'Spanish' influenza epidemic and the sustained loss in women's advantage over men in terms of $e(0)$. We follow a line of exploratory data analysis, where successive graphs are used to demonstrate relations among variables.[4] Before taking on the main question, it is worth briefly taking a more general overview of Figures 13.1 and 13.2. Both male and female $e(0)$ rebounded from the losses due to the flu epidemic (Figure 13.1). Males rebounded more, however, and thus reduced much of their disadvantage in $e(0)$ compared to females. So, the striking drop in females' advantage observed in Figure 13.2 has to do with a male rebound that was not matched by females, rather than a drop in absolute levels of $e(0)$ for females. There are two other major features of Figure 13.2 that are worth noting, in spite of the fact that they are not directly related to the effects of the 1918 flu epidemic. In 1941–3, females again lost some of their advantage over males, though not nearly as much as after the 1918 flu epidemic (Figure 13.2). Unlike the 1918 event, however, beginning in 1944 and continuing to 1975, females regained the 1941–3 loss, and went on to extend their advantage to 7.8 years, its maximum to date in recorded vital statistics of the USA.[5] The other salient feature of Figure 13.2 is the slow decline, beginning in 1980, of women's advantage over men in terms of $e(0)$, a trend which has continued until 1995.

The 1941–3 event results from males gaining more than females during this period (Figure 13.1); one could speculate that the newly-discovered antibiotics aided males more than females, though such an explanation would not anticipate women's sudden recovery, starting in 1944. (A return to trend after a perturbation is, in fact, more usual in demographic statistics; it is the 1918 change, not the later one, that is different in this respect.) In the 1970s, both women and men continued to gain in $e(0)$, but after 1979 males gained more than females. This may be explainable either as the delayed impact of increasing tobacco use by women, or simply that it is harder to continue gaining in $e(0)$ once the high levels near 80 have been attained (or as a combination of both factors).

However, here we shall limit our detailed exploration to the most striking feature of Figure 13.2, the tremendous drop in the difference between female and male $e(0)$, and the role played by the 1918 influenza epidemic in this event. We aim to explain the tremendous drop in females' advantage over males in terms of $e(0)$, as well as why the trend took so long to rebound. To perform this analysis, cause-specific data are needed.

Cause-specific death rates

The life table is one of the most common ways demographers tabulate mortality, and it is from the life table that life expectancy, $e(0)$, is calculated. Multi-cause life tables are not available for every year for the USA; Preston, Keyfitz and Schoen published multiple-decrement life tables for the USA, but only for census years (1900, 1910, . . ., and for one additional year, 1964) which unfortunately is not frequent enough to permit the sort of analysis required.[6] However, age-standardised death rates for multiple causes are available for every year, and the age-standardised death rate (ASDR) is a summary rate that is comparable to the expectation of life. Both $e(0)$ and the ASDR are immune to changes in the age-structure of the population, and are therefore appropriate for the analysis of mortality patterns over time.[7] We have analysed cause-specific age-standardised death rates from the document 'Death rates by age, race, and sex, United States, 1900–1953: selected causes', published in 1956 as part of the series *Vital Statistics – Special Reports* by the US Department of Health, Education, and Welfare. This is the most comprehensive compendium of early twentieth-century death rates for the USA.[8] The dotted curve in Figure 13.2 presents male minus female age-standardised death rates for all causes for the USA, 1900–95.

Although both $e(0)$ and the ASDR are neutral with respect to changes in the age-structure of the population being studied, they use different ways to achieve this, which explains the differences between the two curves in Figure 13.2. The expectation of life at birth, $e(0)$, for a given year is the expected number of years lived by a hypothetical child born in that year, assuming the observed age-specific death rates for that year remain unchanged in the future (i.e. as the hypothetical child ages). It is neutral with respect to changes in population age-structure because the only factors that affect the age-structure of the hypothetical population used to calculate $e(0)$ are the observed age-specific death rates themselves. The age-standardised death rate (ASDR), on the other hand, measures what the crude death date *would* be, *if* the population structure was equal to some fixed reference population (in this case the 'US Standard Population' of the National Center for Health Statistics, which is based on 1940 data). The ASDR is calculated by applying the observed age-specific death rates to the standard population.

There are four major differences between the solid ($e(0)$) and dotted (ASDR) curves in Figure 13.2. The first difference is that in the period 1900–18, the difference between males and females was more stable in

ASDR than in $e(0)$. Second, females regained their pre-flu advantage more quickly in terms of ASDR than in terms of $e(0)$. Third, the temporary decline in females' advantage in $e(0)$ from 1941 to 1943 is not visible in the ASDR curve, which may indicate that an age-specific mortality change was responsible for the effect observed in the $e(0)$ curve.[9] Fourth, females attained their maximum advantage over men in 1968 in terms of ASDR, which was 7 years before the first of two peaks with respect to $e(0)$. Fortunately, the major feature that is of interest to us is the same in both curves. After the 1918 epidemic, females lost much of their mortality advantage over males, and this loss of advantage did not rebound when the overall mortality rates for females and males returned to trend in the years following. In terms of ASDR, males' excess over females declined by approximately 140 per 100,000, and did not return to pre-epidemic levels until the early 1930s. Therefore, in spite of the differences between the two mortality measures (i.e. the solid and dotted curves in Figure 13.2), it is clear that they are comparable enough for us to proceed with the analysis in terms of standardised death rates as opposed to $e(0)$.[10]

Death rates are additive, i.e. the ASDR curve for all causes in Figure 13.2 is the sum of all the cause-specific ASDR curves. The ASDR curve (male minus female) for all causes combined is disaggregated into its component parts in Figure 13.3. This plot is too crowded to discern exactly what is going on, but it is a start. We can see that one of the curves that contributes much to the total difference curve is the one labelled 'violence' (open triangles in Figure 13.3). The four causes which make up the 'violence' category are: motor vehicle accidents, other accidents, suicide and homicide. It is hardly surprising that men have higher mortality rates of 'other accidents' (these are primarily work-related), motor vehicle accidents, homicide and suicide.[11] We can state *a priori* that influenza's effects on the sex difference of mortality pertains to natural causes of death, not to violent causes such as accidents or homicide. Therefore, it is best to remove 'violence' from Figure 13.3.

In addition, we are interested in the *indirect* (i.e. long-term) effects of the influenza epidemic rather than its direct effects. The curve for influenza and pneumonia (except pneumonia of newborn) is the thin solid line in Figure 13.3, and it shows a major spike in 1918. That is, the epidemic not only raised influenza death rates, but the epidemic affected men more than women. In non-epidemic years, the sex differential in the cause-specific ASDR for flu and pneumonia was more or less stable; in the epidemic year, males had a great excess over females.

Figure 13.4 is a refined version of Figure 13.3 – violent deaths, as well as influenza and pneumonia, have been removed. We also leave out cancer and diabetes, both of which are important causes of death, but neither shows any change around 1918 in Figure 13.3. Cancer deaths contributed somewhat to the recovery of females' mortality advantage, as the male

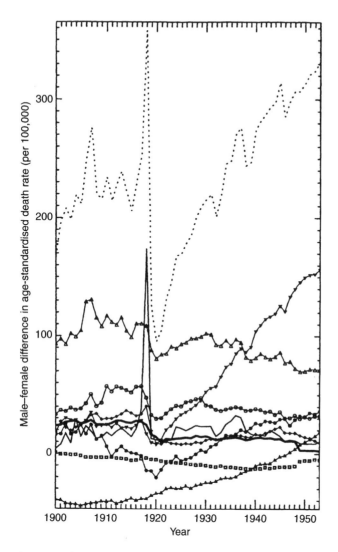

Figure 13.3 Male minus female ASDR, all causes and selected causes, United States, 1900–53.

Source: US Department of Health, Education, and Welfare, 1956.

Notes
Symbols, reading from top to bottom along the left axis: dotted line, all causes; open triangles, violence; open circles, other causes (residual); thick solid line, chronic nephritis; diamonds, tuberculosis, all forms; filled triangles/pointing down, heart disease; filled circles, unclassified; thin solid line, influenza and pneumonia (note 1918); open squares, diabetes; filled triangles/pointing up, cancer.

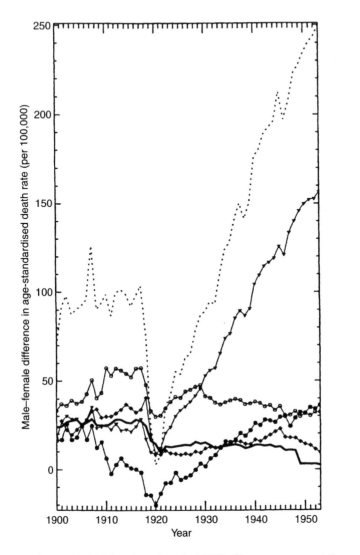

Figure 13.4 Male minus female ASDR, all causes except violence,
influenza and pneumonia; and selected causes, United
States, 1900–53.

Source: US Department of Health, Education, and Welfare, 1956.

Notes
Symbols, reading from top to bottom along the left axis: dotted line, all causes (excluding violence and influenza/pneumonia); open circles, other causes (residual); thick
solid line, chronic nephritis; diamonds, tuberculosis, all forms; filled triangles/pointing
down, heart disease; filled circles, unclassified.

minus female cancer-specific ASDR rose considerably throughout this period. The situation becomes more lucid in Figure 13.4. Causes labelled 'other' fell considerably in 1918; these causes fall into four sub-groups: 'chronic conditions', 'other infectious diseases', 'acute conditions' and 'childhood infectious diseases'. We now consider the roles of each of these groups of diseases.

The four 'childhood infectious diseases' are: acute poliomyelitis, measles, diphtheria and pertussis (whooping cough). Polio death rates experienced a brief but dramatic rise in the male–female differential in 1916, an epidemic year when males were more affected than females (the 1916 polio epidemic was the most severe one in the 1900–53 data set and, therefore, the most severe of the twentieth century). In 1918, measles experienced a rise in the sex differential of its cause-specific ASDR, but as with polio, an epidemic seems to be involved. The worst measles epidemic in the 1900–53 data set was one year earlier in 1917, and in 1918 the measles-specific ASDRs for males and females were both still above the long-term trend. With measles, the rise in the sex differential in ASDR was great in relative terms (to 1.8 per 100,000 in 1918 from levels below 0.5 per 100,000 for most years), but measles contributed little to the overall 1918 male–female differential in ASDR of 358 per 100,000. Interestingly, pertussis is more deadly for females than males, but exhibits a long-term trend towards more equal treatment of girls and boys. Pertussis' greater deadliness for females was especially true in 1918, when the ASDR for pertussis for either sex was at its highest rate in the 1900–53 data set. Diphtheria experienced some minor fluctuations, but does not exhibit very much differential mortality by sex, not even in the minor epidemic of 1921. It is clear that, even when disaggregated by cause, changes in the childhood infectious diseases did not greatly affect the overall trend in differential mortality by sex.

The causes that make up 'chronic conditions' are: cirrhosis, gastritis, ulcers of the stomach and duodenum, other cardiovascular and renal disease, general arteriosclerosis and hypertension (the latter two were recorded separately from other cardiovascular diseases only after 1930). There is not one clear pattern that emerges from examination of these diseases. Gastritis exhibits a highly uneven but unmistakable decline in male excess during the century, levelling off very close to zero (below 1 per 100,000) after the late 1940s.[12] This is, in fact, a big decline in relative terms, since at the beginning of the century, the male–female differences in the cause-specific ASDR for gastritis were about 8 per 100,000. The period of steepest decline in the sex differential for gastritis started in 1918. Notable declines in the sex differential of 'other cardiovascular/ renal conditions' and in cirrhosis started in the early 1910s, too early to have any relation to the 1918 influenza epidemic. These declines also serve as a caveat that coincidence should not be ruled out, for example in the case of gastritis. The late nineteenth and early twentieth century was a time of great hygiene improvements and gains in $e(0)$, and this brought changes in the patterns of disease.

The other patterns of the 'chronic conditions' are unremarkable with respect to changes that could be related to the influenza epidemic. The sex differential for cirrhosis plateaued for many years in the 1920s and then began a modest rise. For the other cardiovascular/renal conditions, the fall in the sex differential began after 1912 and reached a nadir in 1921 before climbing again. Lastly, the cause 'ulcers of stomach and duo-denum' showed a steady increase of male–female cause-specific ASDR during the period of interest (with a slight decline beginning in the 1940s).[13] If any of the changes among chronic conditions are related to the 1918 flu epidemic, then gastritis is the most likely candidate.

The 'other infectious diseases' are: syphilis, typhoid fever, meningococcal infections, rheumatic fever and dysentery. Male–female differences for cause-specific ASDRs were essentially zero for rheumatic fever, and the same holds true for dysentery, except for the period 1900–10, when women experienced a very small excess in dysentery-specific ASDRs. Meningococcal infections experienced small rises in the sex differential of the ASDR during epidemic years (i.e. intermittent epidemics of meningococcal disease). Typhoid fever shows a male excess in ASDR, declining throughout the century, with the difference effectively zero by the 1940s. Syphilis, not sur-prisingly, shows the highest sex differential of these causes. There is a small decline in the male excess death rate for syphilis, in 1919, which is explain-able in terms of competing risks. The 1918 flu epidemic, uncharacteristi-cally for influenza, affected adults rather than children and the elderly. Given that adults are the population at risk of death due to syphilis, and given the huge male excess mortality due to flu, some males who died of flu would have died of syphilis if they had not succumbed to the flu first, and so there is a small (and temporary) downturn in the male excess ASDR for syphilis just after the flu epidemic. On the whole, the category 'other infec-tious diseases' was unaffected by the flu epidemic, the only change of inter-est being a relatively small effect, attributable to competing risks.

Two causes comprise 'acute conditions': acute nephritis and stroke. Sex differentials for acute nephritis were both negligible and constant. Stroke, on the other hand, shows some dramatic changes in the years 1917–25.[14] Male ASDRs for stroke fell during those years and female rates were steady, with the result being a reversal in the sign of the difference curve. This is noteworthy because drops in the difference in ASDR, but not a reversal in sign, were observed for other causes (though the relative close-ness of male and female ASDRs for stroke obviously made a reversal pos-sible if the rate for one sex changed). Unlike the other observed changes, which took place in the same year as the flu epidemic (i.e. 1918), or were delayed by a year, the change in stroke started in 1917. This does not totally rule out a connection with the flu, however. Consider the subset of the influenza data which cover the years 1900 to 1930, inclusive, but excluding 1918 (obviously an outlier). In 1917, males' cause-specific ASDR for influenza was 193.4 per 100,000, 28.74 above the quadratic trend for males for the subset we are considering. Females' cause-specific ASDR in 1917 was 155.7, or 10.15 above the quadratic trend for females. The standard deviation of the residuals between the observed values and the quadratic trend (where again 1918 has been excluded) is 26.70 and 26.15 for females and males, respectively. Thus, males were 1.1 standard deviations above trend in 1917, while females were only 0.37 standard deviations above trend. While this is not causal proof, it provides circumstantial evidence that 1917 was not just an above-average flu year, but also that there was a bigger male excess as well. Stroke may be added to the list of diseases possibly affected by the flu epidemic.[15]

Aside from the causes labelled 'other' in Figure 13.4, four other curves merit attention: chronic nephritis, heart disease, tuberculosis (all forms) and unclassified. The sex difference in the cause-specific ASDR for chronic nephritis fell considerably in 1919, due to a drop in male rates. The same is true of heart disease, which experienced declines in the ASDR difference curve from 1918 to 1920, before males' ASDRs for heart disease began to exceed women's by greater and greater amounts. With 'tuberculosis, all forms', the sex differential in ASDRs declined in 1919 (Figure 13.4), and there is a very interesting pattern behind this, shown in Figure 13.5. Both

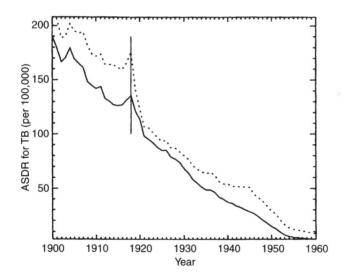

Figure 13.5 Male (dotted) and female (solid) ASDR versus date, for tuberculosis, all forms, United States, 1900–60.

Source: US Department of Health, Education, and Welfare, 1956, and Grove and Hetzel, Vital Statistics Rates in the United States.

Note
The vertical line indicates the year 1918.

male and female ASDRs for tuberculosis peaked in 1918, males more so than females. Following 1918, both males and females experienced a drop in tuberculosis ASDRs, males more steeply than females (Figure 13.5). This finding will be discussed in greater detail below.

'Unclassified' (in Figure 13.4) is a residual cause; the ASDR for all causes minus the sum of the cause-specific ASDRs equals 'unclassified'. The sex differential of unclassified causes does decline in 1918, but it also declines, somewhat less dramatically, in every year since 1913 (aided, in part, by the introduction of syphilis as a registered cause of death in 1910), so it is difficult to assert that the decline in 1918 is related to the influenza epidemic. From this exploratory analysis, five causes attracted our attention: chronic nephritis; tuberculosis, all forms; heart disease; gastritis; and stroke. The relative importance of those five causes in the overall decline of male minus female ASDR will be analysed in the following section.

Quantifying the decline in the mortality sex differentials

Figure 13.6 shows the dramatic declines in the sex differential of cause-specific ASDRs for the five causes identified above as possibly related to the 1918 influenza epidemic. Between 1917 and 1921, the smoothed trend of the ASDR for all causes (excluding violence and influenza and pneumonia) fell from 92 per 100,000 to 25 per 100,000; the fall of 65 per 100,000 is, essentially, what needs to be accounted for. The 'difference' value in the top of each panel of Figure 13.6 indicates the magnitude of the decline between 1917 and 1921 of the smoothed curve for that panel, allowing an accounting of the overall decline.[16] The male excess ASDR for tuberculosis, all forms, fell by 24.9 per 100,000, or 37 per cent of the total; this is more than for any other cause. The sex differential for chronic nephritis fell by 14.1 per 100,000, or 21 per cent of the total. Heart disease accounts for a decline of 8.9 per 100,000 between 1917 and 1921, or 13 per cent of the total. Stroke accounted for 11 per cent of the total decline in the difference between the sexes, with an absolute decline of 7.1 per 100,000. Confirming the doubts about the importance of gastritis, it accounted for only 4 per cent of the total decline; 2.9 per 100,000 in absolute terms. Together, these five causes make up 86 per cent of the observed decline in male excess ASDR between 1917 and 1921.[17] The remaining 14 per cent of the decline is due to the causes which have declining sex differentials, but which show no signs of being related to the 'Spanish' influenza epidemic.

Figure 13.6 also provides some insight into why the sex differential in ASDR did not return to the *status quo ante* until the 1930s. While the difference curves for stroke and heart disease returned to their pre-1918 levels by *c.*1926, those for chronic nephritis, tuberculosis and gastritis remained low much longer (Figures 13.4 and 13.6). Indeed, most of the

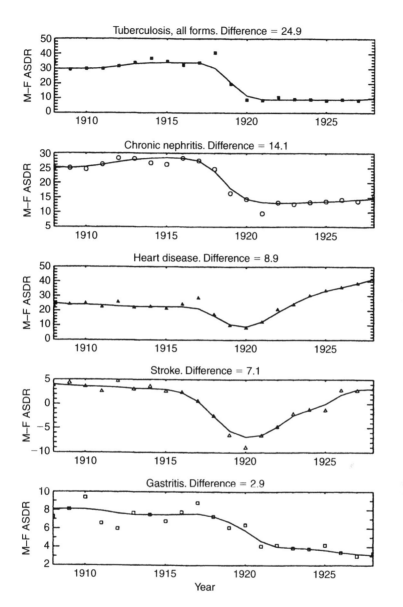

Figure 13.6 Male minus female ASDR, five causes (from top: tuberculosis, all forms; chronic nephritis; heart disease; stroke; and gastritis), United States, 1908–28.

Source: Data from previous figures.

Notes
Yearly points and 3RSSH, twice smoothed trend lines (cf. J.W. Tukey, *Exploratory Data Analysis,* Reading, MA, Addison-Wesley, 1977, regarding the smoothing technique). The 'difference' value in the right side of each panel is the difference in the smoothed curve between 1917 and 1921.

rebound in the sex differential in ASDR seems to be attributable to heart disease and cancer (Figure 13.4).

Discussion

Having quantified the relative importance of various diseases in the observed decline of the differential of male–female ASDR between 1917 and 1921, it now remains to offer some explanation of the putative causal role of influenza. As was already stressed, the techniques used here are exploratory and do not by themselves provide causal proof.[18] Common sense dictates that there were too many cause-specific changes just after 1918 for them not to have been related to each other or, more importantly, to some exogenous shock; the most obvious candidate for the latter is the 'Spanish' influenza. Indeed, because the pattern observed in Figure 13.2 is a difference of two series of vital rates, the probability of observing a similar trend if the male and female vital rates were each subject only to random fluctuations is effectively zero. Nevertheless, correlation does not prove causation, so it is worth probing possible biological and social mechanisms that could explain these extraordinary findings.

The role of tuberculosis is clearly a key one; TB accounts for 37 per cent of the observed decline in the sex differential in ASDR for all causes (excluding violence and influenza and pneumonia) between 1917 and 1921. Figure 13.5 provides some insight as to why the sex differential of TB mortality declined so much after 1918.[19] The natural history of tuberculosis infection includes a latent stage in some patients, when the bacillus has infected its host without causing acute symptoms. In developing countries today, up to 30 per cent of adults are infected with *Mycobacterium tuberculosis* (in the latent state), and clearly the situation was not drastically different when TB was one of the leading causes of death in the USA. The presence of this latent state provides a possible biological link between influenza, tuberculosis and the observed changes in mortality.

In Figure 13.5 we see that there was an increase in TB death rates in 1918 for both sexes, but more so for men. (Although the TB co-epidemic peaked in 1918 along with influenza, the ASDRs for tuberculosis were also above trend a year earlier in 1917, which is difficult to interpret, but as was already discussed, 1917 was also an unusual year for influenza, especially for males – the ASDR for influenza and pneumonia for males was higher in 1917 than in any year since 1907; this in spite of a declining trend since 1907.) This could be due to either an increase in tuberculosis transmission and hence an increase in new cases, or an increase in reactivation of latent cases (or a combination of both). It is possible that latent tuberculosis cases exposed to the 1918 strain of influenza virus were particularly likely to reactivate. This is plausible because it is known that a stress on the immune system can cause reactivation of latent TB. In other words, among latent TB cases exposed to the 'Spanish' influenza strain, the presence of reactivating TB infection may have exacerbated the influenza-related pneumonia. The reason the effect is stronger in men than in women would, ostensibly, be the same reason that the 1918 influenza was so much more lethal in men than women; that is, some poorly-understood mechanism.[20] It is also possible that there were more available male latents. The data does not refute this hypothesis, but we still need to explain the subsequent decline in male excess ASDR for tuberculosis.

The male–female mortality differential for TB declined after 1918 because male ASDRs for TB fell faster than female ASDRs (Figure 13.5). Tuberculosis is the most important single reason for the decline in females' overall mortality advantage shown in Figure 13.2. The most likely explanation for the greater drop for males' ASDRs for tuberculosis in the years following 1918 is that in the epidemic year itself, males experienced a higher ASDR for TB. During a transition period from high to low levels of tuberculosis prevalence (such as the early twentieth century), the level of tuberculosis mortality depends on both the level of current transmission and on the size of the pool of latents in the population (if we assume, except for 1918, that the rate with which latent cases become active is fixed). Given that males had a larger relative peak in 1918 for TB ASDRs, the size of the male pool of latent cases would have been relatively smaller than the female pool (compared to the previous trend), with the result that males' ASDRs would decline faster than females in the post-epidemic years. Such an explanation agrees well with the observed trends, and even if the male excess of TB deaths in 1918 is not sufficient to explain the magnitude of the post-1918 fall in male TB death rates, the possible increased susceptibility of latent TB cases to death from influenza would explain how the male pool of latent cases could become so diminished, especially since males were so much more affected by influenza in 1918 (Figure 13.3). Interestingly, this would have been a 'two-way street', whereby a relatively larger pool of tubercular latents increased males' ASDR for influenza in 1918, and this, in turn, decreased male ASDRs for TB in subsequent years.[21]

This is, in effect, an example of selection, which is noteworthy because selection effects have received much less attention in studies of the epidemiological transition than have other effects such as the changing relative importance of chronic versus infectious diseases, even though the magnitude of the selection effects observed here argues against neglecting selection effects. That an epidemic of one disease should have major and long-term effects on the demography of another disease, by killing off a sub-population which is more susceptible to both diseases, is perhaps not surprising, but it is rare to see much discussion of this in the demographic literature.[22] Due to this selection, then, the influenza epidemic's greater severity for men meant that the surviving cohorts of men were able to profit in terms of a lowering of tuberculosis rates that was much faster than women.

Interestingly, the other two infectious diseases shown in Figure 13.6, chronic nephritis[23] and gastritis, also show a diminution of male disadvantage that was long-lasting. Like tuberculosis, selective effects could be at work. The deadliest year (in terms of ASDRs) for chronic nephritis for both sexes in the 1900–60 data set was 1917. This, combined with the 1918 male excess mortality from influenza, could have been responsible for the greater diminution of male rates of chronic nephritis in the years following 1918. There was no strong co-epidemic of gastritis in 1918, but its mortality sex differential fell after 1918, and a similar selection effect may be responsible. It is also worth noting that non-respiratory infections of *M. tuberculosis* can cause both nephritis and gastritis, so it is possible that the TB connection holds for these two causes as well.

With stroke and heart disease, we see a different pattern. Men lowered their disadvantage for several years after 1918 for these causes, but then the sex differential returned to the *status quo ante* (Figure 13.6). It is known that heart disease patients have an elevated risk of dying from influenza, so the connection in and of itself is not remarkable. Heart disease and stroke are diseases of relatively older ages, which may explain why the effects were shorter-lived. It is known that the 'Spanish' flu had an unusual age pattern of mortality, in that young adults – not the elderly – were affected; the pool of heart disease-susceptible citizens would have been subject to a less strong selection effect. It makes intuitive sense that the infectious diseases, where transmission and a pool of infected cases are important, should have been affected for longer than heart disease and stroke, where new cases are recruited by ageing of cohorts rather than by infection. Further investigation is still needed, however, to scrutinise age-specific rates for the various causes. For example, the ages of excess male mortality in 1918 for influenza and TB should, according to our hypothesis of selection, predict the age-specific patterns of male reductions in mortality after 1918 (after cohort ageing has been taken into account).

The coincidence of the First World War and the outbreak of influenza is unfortunate, because it confuses our analysis. In Europe, the war itself had such strong selecting effects that the effects of influenza are much harder to see.[24] The USA is an ideal population in this respect, but the American participation in the war does make one wary to rule out anything. Could the observed effects be due to the concentration of young men (e.g. in Army barracks, before departure for Europe) and the implications that had on transmissible pathogens such as *M. tuberculosis*, rather than purely an influenza–tuberculosis nexus? Given the magnitude of the effects seen in Figure 13.2, a military explanation seems less compelling than that set out above, but the war reminds us that the populations we study are subject to more forces than just those of which our hypotheses take account.

Conclusion

This chapter has shown that a one-year epidemic can have long-lasting effects on a population. The 1918 'Spanish' influenza epidemic had a strong sex-specific selection effect which changed the sex differential of mortality (as measured by the expectation of life at birth, $e(0)$, or by the age-standardised death rate) for 15 years. Tuberculosis, chronic nephritis, heart disease, stroke and gastritis all witnessed lower male excess mortality in the years following 1918.

The effects can be explained by a selective effect of the influenza epidemic, whereby the huge male excess of deaths in the 1918 epidemic reduced male death rates in subsequent years, because more susceptible males were selected in 1918. The effect is proposed to be particularly strong for tuberculosis, since a pool of latent cases is a characteristic of the demography/epidemiology of TB. When considering the two-sex epidemiological transition in the United States, selection due to the 1918 influenza epidemic must be considered as a major component of observed changes. The explanations proposed here are somewhat speculative, but future work, particularly an examination of age-specific rates, will be able to test our hypotheses.

Part V

Long-term consequences and memories

14 'A fierce hunger'

Tracing impacts of the 1918–19 influenza epidemic in southwest Tanzania[1]

James G. Ellison

Hunger fell a long time ago, when we were very young. It was a serious hunger. There came a disease, syphilis. Lake Nyasa and even the mountains shook, although our houses did not fall. And there came a darkness. ... We were very young.[2]

They say that when the war of 1914 started there came a plague of small-pox. And this was followed by a hunger. The hunger then fell differently in different areas. The lateness of the rains was followed by hunger. It then came to fall on the whole country.[3]

In parts of Africa the influenza pandemic had dramatic long-term impacts, although people may not speak of the disease explicitly in oral histories. In southwest Tanzania, the pandemic claimed perhaps 10 per cent of the population and resulted in the worst famine recalled in oral histories. People associate the famine with the First World War, waged in the region from skirmishes at the German East Africa/Nyasaland border in 1914 to the final pillages before the German surrender in November 1918. As the opening quotations show, people also associate the famine with illness. That people name different illnesses, and not influenza, could lead to the interpretation that illness was incidental to the famine and sub-sequent developments. However, it was the peculiarity of the influenza of 1918–19 (high young adult morbidity and mortality rates) and its timing – both in the rhythmed yearly cycle (the planting season) and in coinci-dence with social and political upheavals – that led to famine and to people's responses. This chapter shows how those responses shaped the formation of a 'tribe' in ethnographies and in indirect rule from the 1920s.

Influenza and the making of the Nyakyusa

Historians and anthropologists know of the Nyakyusa at the northern end of Lake Nyasa largely through Monica and Godfrey Wilson's ethnographic research, conducted between 1934 and 1938.[4] Today the Nyakyusa are one of the largest ethnic groups in Tanzania, numbering approximately 800,000. Yet the Wilsons initially proposed fieldwork among the 'Konde', the common reference among Europeans to people of the area during the 1920s. At a finer level than the European-imposed 'Konde', those people claimed identity by reference to the names of sacred groves where chiefs sacrificed for rain and crop fertility, the names of mothers of particular chiefs or of long-deceased founding chiefs, the names of ancestral homes, and the names of regions or villages. A relatively small number of those people spoke of themselves as 'Nyakyusa'. The Wilsons interpreted cultural similarities across the region to indicate historical connections. Thus, although they distinguished the Nyakyusa of Tanganyika from the Ngonde in Nyasaland, within the Nyakyusa they included Kisi, Kukwe, Lugulu, Mwamba, Ndali, Nyakyusa proper, Penja, Saku, Selya and Sukwa peoples. Central to Monica Wilson's criteria for a 'people' was ritual, 'for though the details differ, the values and attitudes expressed are identical'.[5] Nyakyusa age-villages, lineages and chiefdoms were integrated as people drew from a symbolic whole to perform individual rituals. Wilson felt that Nyakyusa informants shared a common knowledge of ritual; when individuals provided idiosyncratic interpretations, 'it was at least a Nyakyusa subconscious, and the interpretation is in terms of the culture'. In individual ritual acts, therefore, 'the values of a group (as opposed to those of individuals) are revealed'.[6]

Defining 'tribes' by cultural and linguistic variables resembled British colonial efforts elsewhere in Africa to establish indirect rule. Taking control of this part of German East Africa in 1916, the British knew of the people as 'Konde', a legacy of missionaries who had arrived through areas inhabited by Ngonde peoples. In 1926 the British lumped most of the people of the region into the Nyakyusa and Kukwe 'tribes', under eleven chiefs and two paramount chiefs. Appointed chiefs competed for authority in the colonial structure; some who were not appointed tried to discredit those who were, and others competed for or complained about the office of paramount. Some people resisted subservience to chiefs with whom they had no established relations of obligation, and they lobbied for different tribal definitions. In 1935 the government eliminated paramount chiefs in favour of a council of chiefs and redefined the 'Kukwe' as 'Nyakyusa'. Like the ethnographers, colonial government rationale included similar rituals and the common roles of chiefs in relation to their peoples. To Europeans, Nyakyusa political structure meant chiefs with shared ancestry, whose common rituals involved rainmakers (usually male kin) who provided community health and fertility.

The first British administrators in the district observed rituals directed at alleviating the crises surrounding the influenza pandemic. The 'famine of corms', a collective label for the crises in oral histories, resulted in two types of response: those directed from households, and those directed by individual chiefs. Government officers seldom witnessed household responses, whereas they noted the highly visible actions of chiefs. Responses by chiefs, in fact, shaped relations between the British and their subjects and partly determined the course of indirect rule. Among other results, by codifying the role of a presumed chiefly class and their rain-makers as the protection of human health and fertility of the land, government and colonial ethnographers displaced women healer/officiants from leading roles in community health and fertility and helped construct one of colonial Tanganyika's largest ethnic groups.[7]

The crises

By 1917, the war had convulsed all aspects of social and political life in occupied southwest German East Africa. Germans had conscripted porters and soldiers and requisitioned food and livestock. Fighting occurred throughout the countryside. The 1916 British invasion brought further requisitioning by a new European power and African forces from other territories. The British initially distrusted local people who had had obvious contacts with German missionaries, whom the British expelled, and the German regime, the remnants of which were at large. The British feared anti-European uprisings like those in Nyasaland, Northern Rhodesia and Portuguese East Africa, but saw only small millenarian gatherings. Some Africans were loyal to the Germans and acted against the British. A few were arrested, some executed.[8] Others, such as those traders and chiefs who hoped to gain power through the British, were glad to be rid of the Germans.

The British began collecting taxes in 1917, including crops necessary for feeding troops in the campaign, and used German record books to appoint chiefs.[9] They appointed some who had previously held no overrid-ing claim to rule, and they did not recognise, or removed from official positions, others whom they perceived as German allies. Thus, they 'wrote in' chief Mwaikambo because he had helped them, although he had no such position under the Germans. Similarly, it was said that Mwakalobo was not a chief through the 'coming out' ceremony (*ubusoka*), but that he was given a position by chief Mwakalukwa and his supporters.[10] In Selya, the British wrote in Mwaipopo as chief; Mwaipopo knew no German and was junior to Mwaihojo, who spoke German and was not 'written in'.[11]

In oral histories, people often associated the 1916 coming of the British with illnesses, in particular smallpox, and academics have therefore associ-ated famines in Eastern Africa between 1916 and 1920 with smallpox.[12] Rather than causing famine, smallpox more probably contributed to or exacerbated situations of hunger. Smallpox had existed in eastern Africa for generations, with minor epidemics continuing into the mid-1920s.[13] Epidemics occurred in dry seasons, along with intensive social interac-tions. The thousands of soldiers who traversed the region during the war carried mutating strains of smallpox into villages. When the war slowed during the dry season in mid-1917, people gathered for funerals, dances and feasts, at which smallpox spread easily.

Most accounts consider the German-led forces' trek through the region in October and early November 1918 a move to Northern Rhodesia rather than a significant moment in the history of southwest German East Africa.[14] Although the German-led forces left Portuguese East Africa with low rations, an officer among them noted, 'We again had good times in the area of Bena-Langenburg where the herds of cattle provided us with meat and where both the sick and well could be given milk.'[15] 'Good times' meant, of course, that they came into greater food stores in the agriculturally rich areas of the eastern and northern sides of Lake Nyasa. Many African porters and troops deserted as the German forces crossed the region. Some were from the area, but undoubtedly others only sought to escape war, hunger and illness. Deserters spilled into villages where people had prepared fields for planting and were anticipating the associated hunger and heavy labour of the season. Ironically, deserting troops and porters, who had survived smallpox in military camps and tested vaccines made by German field doctors, brought viruses to their sanctuary, creating epidemic conditions.[16] Several thousand people continued with the German-led forces, and they and the pursuing British forces engaged in the 'bulk acquisition of local African livestock'.[17] Pillaging was a critical blow to farmers who had prepared well for the rain and planting season.

It was during this pillage of October and November 1918 that tens of thousands were struck down by the rapidly spreading second wave of the Spanish influenza, whose full impact was felt by December. In a few short months perhaps 10 per cent of the population – mostly young adults – died.[18] As a result, the onset of rain was not met by enthusiastic planting, as masses of the population lay ill, many dying. For those who planted, the crucial work of weeding could not be done when entire households suffered from the flu. What followed was the most severe famine recalled in oral histories of the last century.[19] The district administration was ill-equipped to deal with the influenza and stopped work for 6 weeks in December and January.[20]

David Patterson suggested that the influenza pandemic 'was almost certainly the single greatest short-term demographic catastrophe in [Africa's] history'.[21] Alfred Crosby noted how the 1918–19 influenza differed from others: 'One, it killed more humans than any other disease in a period of similar duration in the history of the world. Two, it killed an unprecedently large proportion of the members of a group who, according to records before and since, should have survived it with no permanent injury.'[22] The influenza killed large numbers of people between the ages of 20 and 40 wherever it hit.[23] This mortality curve is radically different from that for other influenza epidemics, in which the very young and the very old perished.

The influenza was widespread at the northern end of Lake Nyasa by

November 1918. It had first arrived in Eastern Africa by Indian Ocean traffic: Mombasa by 23 September, Portuguese East Africa by 20 October and southern Nyasaland by 5 November. Late in October the disease had spread along the railway line from Kenya into Uganda, yet since August the German-led forces in Portuguese East Africa had been suffering from what their doctors identified as 'epidemic croupous pneumonia'.[24] The flu's arrival in the southwestern districts of British-occupied German East Africa therefore perhaps resulted from a convergence from the south and the east, which had made the Nyasa-Tanganyika region a sort of 'disease corridor'.

The death toll from the influenza is nearly impossible to measure accurately in even the best documented areas.[25] Based on little data, Patterson estimated that at least 100,000 people in Nyasaland and Tanganyika died in the pandemic.[26] In addition to the high death rate, recovery brought a post-flu fatigue characterised by mental apathy, depression, subnormal body temperatures and low blood pressure, which could last for weeks or months.[27] These post-flu conditions would have been devastating to agricultural communities desperately needing to plant and weed and who had already suffered substantial losses to the able-bodied population.

The pandemic brought varied local interpretations, beginning with accusations of witchcraft and sorcery. Tunyasye Ikofu recalled that several of her mother's relatives perished at this time, victims of sorcery.[28] The acting district political officer, Major Wells, noted increased crime and cattle theft related to witchcraft, which he attributed to the pandemic. He also wrote that chiefs were calling for poison ordeals to determine the practitioners of witchcraft.[29] People soon interpreted the illness as an *ikigwaja*, a generalised plague.[30] Kileke Mwakibinga, who survived the influenza, recalled in the 1990s that an *ikigwaja* claimed his sister and an aunt in Selya as the Germans fled. Some people attributed the illness to the British, others to the war in general.[31]

Faced with an *ikigwaja*, people worked with healer/officiants to treat their families. As the *ikigwaja* became tenacious, several chiefs called meetings at which they gave instruction about the illness and measures to avoid it. People saw illnesses as the results of acts by themselves, others or ancestors, and at mass meetings chiefs, headmen and healers sought to determine the responsible parties.[32] Kileke Mwakibinga recalled a meeting in Selya:

[Mwaipopo] called the entire country.... And there he said, 'My people, today we are starting to raise our voices about this disease, this *ikigwaja* which has happened. This *ikigwaja* which has come into our country, may it leave! And if they brought it, the British, then may they leave as well. They should go to their homes abroad.' That is it. Maybe it lasted a year. But it was like three or four months with people becoming ill and dying all over the place, and then the end came. The chiefs saw this and said, 'God too has heard. See today that this illness is over.' ... [Headmen then said] 'Now that is enough. Let's begin to depart.' And those leaves of banana plants, you know how we cut them to sit on in a meeting, not like they were bringing chairs and so on. Leaves. 'Each person take the leaf on which they sat and dispose of it away from here. They are not to be left here. Leaves that remain will stay with the witchcraft of those who sat there.' Ha. Everything there on which you sat you took away, or you took to throw into the river when you passed.... Maybe witches would be able to bewitch someone. They would leave it there where they sat, and someone else might come and sit right there and they would be afflicted with illness.[33]

Many chiefs introduced a radical policy limiting funerals. Funerals were sad times but were also occasions for the largest of public feasts and rituals, dancing, courting, flirting, fighting, sacrificing and discussing. Much sacrificing and feasting was directed towards ancestors and the deceased, but also to the living, among whom debt relations were continually renegotiated.[34] Failure to carry out a funeral properly, failure to notify relatives, to dance, to wail, to sacrifice and feast, all but guaranteed eventual illness and threatened crops. The decision to cease public funerals was therefore a serious step. Kileke Mwakibinga discussed the ramifications for his home:

[The chief said] 'When things settle, and the illness has decreased, then we can start to cry. We can have funerals for those who died.' At my father's place two people died. We buried without crying at all, not at all. You would go to dig there – not like [when] others would come to help to dig the grave; no, they would not come. You would dig, those in your own family there, at home, you would bury them, and then everyone would go to their home. We would not gather, not like now when people gather at the funerals to talk and what not, no. That we called the *ikigwaja*.[35]

In 1936 a man named Kalume told anthropologist Godfrey Wilson about a change in Kukwe and Penja burial practices during an epidemic. People of the village were normally obliged to dig graves, but with the fear of contagious illness, only immediate relatives handled a corpse. The particular illness they feared, Kalume explained, was that which 'killed the people terribly'. Asked if this meant sorcery, Kalume responded, 'yes indeed'.[36]

Chiefs stopping funerals provided new European patrons with a demonstration of unmistakable significance. Since precolonial times people have expressed group identity and difference through funerals. An ability to stifle the display of difference encouraged British officials to see essential sameness over the area and to see chiefs as a class who controlled what were in fact regionally particular practices. The moratorium on funerals and sacrifices blocked largesse and reciprocal feasting while focusing attention on chiefs.[37]

The famine and local responses

The 'famine of corms' that followed the flu lasted 2 years and went largely unrecorded in government papers. The name 'famine of corms' derives from women's use of banana corms as famine food to feed their families.[38] Local actions in the face of the famine fell into two categories, those directed by households and those involving chiefs. Households, where the most immediate impacts were felt, were the sites of first responses. People called on healer/officiants (usually women) and exploited known resources and networks. Chiefs, on the other hand, sacrificed with their rainmakers and called on foreign male healer/officiants to treat their villages, although across the northern end of the lake there was no overarching ethnic response to the crisis. There was no functioning, unified ethnic community, no paramount chiefs, no emphasis on common origins.

Chiefs took actions that were observed by important historical actors outside the villages – namely the British, who were recording African customs and political structure. Chiefs created obligations by taking in the destitute and feeding people who worked for them. Boys hoed for chiefs in exchange for cattle for bridewealth.[39] Many chiefs performed two other sets of rituals. One set of rituals was esoteric sacrifices to chiefly ancestors performed by chiefs' rainmakers and foreign healer/officiants in sacred groves. The Germans had suppressed such sacrifices, in part fearing mobilisation of anticolonial sentiment;[40] however, since the British came, 'we go [and sacrifice] at daylight'.[41] Chiefs and their headmen drew on historical ritual relations and the fame of particular healer/officiants to sacrifice to their ancestors to eliminate hunger. Those esoteric rituals scarcely involved the people of villages, most of whom neither saw the foreign healer/officiants nor knew details of the offerings. Although gossip was thick during such sacrifices, they were carried out in places to which most people never went.

Esoteric sacrifices concerned individual chiefs and their ancestors, emphasising a chief's control over an area, the chief as embodying the land and its fertility through ancestral ties, and the chief's connections with distant and powerful healer/officiants. Several chiefs in different areas referred to certain ancestors and god-like founding figures in common. To outsiders, like the anthropologists 15 years later, the esoteric sacrifices highlighted those commonalities and came to be seen as charter rituals that linked the people of chiefs in a coherent tribal unit, even though chiefs stated clearly that these sacrifices were not about tribal unity, and that different chiefs had their own sacrifices.[42]

The second set of rituals that chiefs sponsored did not emphasise sameness between various chiefs but stressed an individual chief's relations with his community and a chief's obligation to provide for local crop fertility. In years of scarcity or illness chiefs often recruited foreign healer/officiants to treat the land, houses, fields and banana plants.[43] Treating the land sometimes coincided with esoteric sacrifices,[44] but people in villages experienced the two rituals differently, and the rituals had different ramifications. Treating the land took place at people's homes and fields, not in sacred groves. Treating the land, widely performed during the 'famine of corms', was a matter felt by the local community only, not inclusive of members of wider groups signified by names like Saku, Nyakyusa, Kukwe, nor all who identified with the sacred grove of a chief.[45] But treating the land was also invisible to European observers.

People remember their houses rattling when healer/officiants splashed medicines, and physically reacting from fear and surprise despite advance warnings. Headmen and healer/officiants instructed people to go indoors and not to come out, not to interfere with the ritual, to be silent. Village nights, following instructions to be silent, were shaken by healer/officiants rushing about splashing medicines, shaking people out of sleep or night-time conversations.[46] In some cases people contributed to pay the healer/officiants. Treating the land was, after all, directed at their ancestors to bring fertility to the land.[47] People viewed these offerings to the ancestors, this splashing of medicine on houses, banana plants, cattle and crops, as so successful that memories often exaggerate the efficacy.[48] Headmen and chiefs obtained healer/officiants to treat the land at the urging of the people, and treating the land was not directed solely to the ancestors of the chiefs. Leonard Mwaisumo, one of the Wilsons' research assistants in the 1930s, said that by treating the land, foreign healer/officiants 'give something to the ancestors so that they do not come up and make trouble for the country'.[49]

Conclusion

As the 'famine of corms' abated in 1921, people found themselves with an entrenched new colonial ruler, to whom they were not 'Konde' but 'Nyakyusa'. When social anthropologists traversed the countryside a decade after the famine, Kukwe, Ndali, Ngonde, Penja, Saku and Selya people willingly told them about their Nyakyusa customs, but they also told of each other's differences. The Wilsons arrived at the end of the 1932–3 'famine of wheat' and people discussed their current troubles in the context of the previous 15 years' history. Chiefs had become government men. Women healer/officiants had no legitimacy in the eyes of African indirect rule authorities, Europeans in general, and educated Africans, while missionaries campaigned against their work. Working closely with these chiefs, the Wilsons learned how they and their rainmakers were responsible for community health and crop fertility.

Social anthropologists and colonial officials interpreted Africans' assessments of change and causality through knowledge of detribalisation in the face of European contact, effects the anthropologists had come to study. They misunderstood that recent historical experience with epidemic influenza and famine had shaped a new social and political landscape; already in the 1930s social analysts had forgotten the magnitude of the 1918–19 influenza. People in southwest Tanganyika were willing to become Nyakyusa in the aftermath of the crises surrounding the pandemic. African peasant farmers and labourers, social anthropologists and colonial officials were creating one of the largest ethnic groups in Tanganyika, but its history was already obscure and its internal organisation a matter for continued debate.

15 'The dog that did not bark'

Memory and the 1918 influenza epidemic in Senegal[1]

Myron Echenberg

The [influenza] epidemic is seldom mentioned, and most Americans have apparently forgotten it. This is not surprising. The human mind always tries to expunge the intolerable from memory, just as it tries to conceal it while current.

H.L. Mencken, 1956[2]

The world influenza pandemic of 1918–19 pounced upon the French colony of Senegal with a ferocity of biblical proportions in the first week of September of 1918. By the time the last case was noted in December in the remote *cercle* or province of Kédougou, situated near the border with Guinea and Soudan, influenza had touched every village, had probably infected over half the estimated population of one and a quarter million, and had left a total of roughly 47,000 dead.[3]

Unlike most places in the world, the 1918 influenza outbreak has left comparatively little trace in Senegal's written or oral history, despite its heavy death toll. This is all the more surprising, given the presence of an elaborate French colonial bureaucracy situated in Senegal's leading city, Dakar, the core of the colonial Federation of French West Africa. As for contemporary newspapers, they appeared sporadically if at all during the crucial months of 1918 and said little or nothing about the raging pestilence.[4] The silence is also unusual because the diverse peoples of Senegal have long preserved a rich and elaborate tradition of oral history. Recognising that it is always more difficult to determine why something fails to materialise, this chapter nevertheless seeks to explain why this particular dog did not bark.

Such silence is not typical. For many historical research projects, including those dealing with the history of health and disease, Senegal offers a rich collection of archival records. An extensive bibliographic survey in 1989 produced almost 3,000 entries, many of which were based in part on archival sources, but with only three entries on the 1918 flu pandemic.[5] Indeed, Senegal, quite untypically, offers three layers of archival documentation. Like the other French African colonies, Senegal possessed an administrative capital (Saint-Louis), where the Governor received the various reports of the respective *commandants de cercle*, or local administrators. Unlike the others, Senegal also housed the seat of French West Africa's capital in its largest city, Dakar, where the Governor-General of the federation maintained a relatively large central bureaucracy. Finally, at the municipal level, because Dakar's daily affairs were the concern of the Governor of Senegal, he appointed a Delegate, who regularly reported on political, economic and, of special interest to this chapter, sanitary matters. In order to seek out an African voice, I also conducted over twenty interviews with African informants selected because they were reputed for their memories in general and for their interest in medical questions in particular.

In the *Archives Nationales du Sénégal* (ANS) which house the records for Dakar, Senegal and French West Africa, only one thin dossier, H61, entitled 'La Grippe Brésilienne, Dakar, 1918', is a specifically classified source for the pandemic. It contains three valuable handwritten letters by senior health and administrative officials to the Governor of Senegal, and little else. A thorough search of other series, for example the D and G series for military and political matters, did provide some additional information. A visit to the French colonial archives in Aix-en-Provence proved even more disappointing. If they were ever written, none of the medical reports for Senegal in 1918 seem to have survived.

Fortunately, the historical legacy for influenza in Senegal is not completely blank. A fragmentary record of the influenza pandemic of 1918 has survived, and in published form. This main source is a compilation covering all of the French colonies, published 3 years after the pandemic by Dr Paul Gouzien, Medical Inspector General of the French Colonial Army.[6] France, along with other member nations of the *Office International d'Hygiène Publique* (OIHP), received a questionnaire from that body requesting data some time after the world influenza pandemic had abated. Gouzien, in turn, issued his own questionnaire to his medical staff in each French colony, and it was on the basis of these responses that he constructed his published report. Gouzien's publications aside, no scientific or popular writing has ever been devoted to the 1918 flu epidemic in Senegal.

The various regional reports in the Gouzien compilation were of uneven quality. The best of the French West Africa reports, by Dr Pezet for Guinea, was based on his more detailed annual medical report, and provided regional breakdowns and the qualitative and quantitative information that are completely lacking for most other regions. The section by Dr Burdin for Ivory Coast, for example, was poorly done, and Dr Thoulon's for Senegal, unfortunately, was little better.[7] It would appear that each medical officer, upon receiving instructions from Gouzien in Paris, responded with what he found at hand. In Senegal, with little available in his files, Dr Thoulon passed on what he himself had written and observed. That is why a thorough search of the Dakar archives simply repeats what Thoulon, and therefore Gouzien, knew in 1920. While the arrival of influenza in late 1918 itself was a contributing factor to its under-reporting, fortunes of war had also conspired to leave most officials so short of staff and material that even routine annual reports were not written in 1918.

The course of the influenza pandemic in Senegal followed the global pattern. The presence of foreign and domestic soldiers, and wartime over-crowding generally, provided the influenza virus with an unusually large number of potential hosts. All but twenty of the 1,380 Brazilian sailors in Dakar harbour were infected aboard the crowded ships. By the time flu had run its course, 108 had perished, a mortality rate of seventy-eight per 1,000 men.[8]

French officials were quick to blame the Brazilians and especially British officials in Freetown, Sierra Leone, for not having alerted them earlier.[9] Yet French public health officers delayed 2 days after being apprised of influenza aboard the Brazilian fleet before inspecting the ships and the patients. In reality, even the most diligent actions of public health authorities would not have made any difference. The airborne virus A of influenza was virtually impossible to stop by means of quarantine throughout the world, even when authorities had ample warning of its approach.

African soldiers constituted a second group of victims. The deadly virus jumped from the Brazilian ships to the town of Dakar, first manifesting itself in buildings nearest the wharf before quickly moving to the city centre and beyond. At the military base in Ouakam, a good 10 km from the port, the first truly catastrophic day was 18 September, some 10 days into the pandemic, when twenty-eight *Tirailleurs Sénégalais* died. All told, the military was to register 155 deaths at Ouakam by the end of the pandemic in November.[10]

Authorities' reactions to the first influenza cases varied widely. The Governor's Delegate in Dakar was so alarmed at the number of deaths and at the prospect of hundreds more among the African military that he asked the Army to bury its dead in Ouakam, rather than sending the corpses to the main native hospital in Dakar.[11] On the other hand, the chief medical authority in the colony, Dr Thoulon, seemed to have misread the seriousness of the epidemic, and erroneously assumed, like many medical people the world over, that this disease would place at risk only the weakest elements in the population. No doubt he would later regret his optimistic prognosis:

> The flu does not seem to be very serious. As always, it strikes the most vulnerable, people with low resistance who are in poor physical con-dition. Without prejudging events, I nevertheless think that we can face the future without too much concern.[12]

On the contrary, the immediate future was most disquieting. Making its way by means of infected human hosts travelling by rail, river and road, influenza reached every town, village and hamlet in Senegal. One of the last regions to be affected, the remote interior *cercle* of Kédougou, provided a rare glimpse of the flu's impact in a rural setting:

> The outstanding event of the month has been the appearance of an influenza epidemic brought in from the [west]; and in another direction from the *cercles* of Kayes and Bafoulabé. In some major villages such as Dioulafoundou, with the exception of the village chief and three women, everybody was infected at the same time, and at the precise moment when the fields most needed strong arms following the rainy season floods.[13]

A month later, the *cercle* commandant reported that his medical staff, consisting of only one auxiliary nurse in the entire *cercle*, was helpless to treat the epidemic, lacking such basic medicines as quinine, tincture of iodine and camphor oil. Such medicines might have made the patients more comfortable but they would not have countered the influenza virus. Without the means to treat victims, the commandant ordered the school at Kédougou closed in late November after two pupils had died and another eight were seriously infected. All the children, sick, incubating or healthy, were sent back to their villages.[14]

This detail from remote Kédougou stands in dramatic contrast to most of the French colonial administration in Senegal. In the Upper Senegal Valley, flu went entirely unremarked in the monthly reports from Matam and Bakel, and was only briefly mentioned for Saldé.[15] In the three political reports written for 1918 Governor Léveque of Senegal devoted not a single line to flu.[16] The Governor-General, Angoulvant, was almost as mute. In a letter to the Minister of Colonies in January of 1919 he implied that flu was being used as an excuse for a failure of Senegalese authorities to bring the lower Casamance region under firm political control.[17] Such denial at the highest levels of administration ignored what little detail the local man-on-the-spot in Casamance had provided. Almost the entire population was reported to have been infected, and an estimated 8 to 10 per cent to have perished.[18] All political, agricultural and commercial activity had ceased, and the commandant complained that he would not be able to meet his anticipated tax collections, thus apparently arousing the ire of his superiors.

French medical officials, while not maintaining the virtual silence characteristic of their civilian counterparts, were less than adequate in their reporting of the pandemic. To be fair, it should be said that normal medical procedures broke down in many parts of the world under the double impact of war and infectious disease. As Dr Thoulon noted, it had become impossible in Dakar or anywhere else in Senegal to insist upon obligatory reporting of morbidity and even of mortality figures.[19] Never-theless, when the physicians did report on flu, in their confusion they relied more on rumours and guesswork than on facts.

Their confusion showed up both for diagnosis and treatment of the new illness. Understandably concerned about the recurring cases of plague, which had first struck Senegal in 1914, and had returned in 1917, some French doctors at first misread the pulmonary complications of influenza, confusing it with pulmonary plague, the most virulent form of this disease.[20] Believing quinine, the malaria suppressant, to be a wonder drug, Dr Thoulon urged the population by means of public notices and handbills, to take daily doses of 'this invaluable alkaloid'.[21] While this therapy was of no benefit, his prescriptions did at least help make the patients more comfortable. He recommended large quantities of iced drinks, careful hygiene relative to the mouth, hands and nasal passages, and the disinfection of contaminated apartments. A year later, well after the epidemic, Thoulon continued to hold to some curious notions about effective treatment:

> Nothing special to say about treatment, except that alcohol in all its forms – Todd's potion, champagne for Europeans, wine for natives – was administered to patients and distributed as a preventative, in the form of rum, to the general public, including Muslims. To this tonic is attributed a certain amount of success, at least as a stimulant, with some observers going so far as to state that the habitual consumption of 'bangui', a fermented alcoholic beverage in Balante country (Casamance) would explain, to a certain extent, the benign impact of influenza in that region. Still, it should be remembered that the immoderate consumption of alcohol leads to intoxication, to liver dis-order, and to myocarditis, and influenza, we know, is particularly severe among alcoholics.[22]

While there was no evidence that alcoholic beverages were of any benefit, Thoulon's prescriptions undoubtedly received a mixed reaction. The French Army took the advice seriously and issued hot drinks and alcoholic beverages to all its military personnel.[23] For those Africans who had no objection to alcohol, the chief medical authority's prescription of rum for them while French tax-payers were given champagne was a ludicrous example of colonial discrimination, while for those who were Muslims, many would have resented the obligation to violate a religious precept.

Estimated mortality rates often amounted to sheer guesswork. For the Upper Senegal Valley Dr Thoulon guessed that in some villages as many as a third of the population may have died.[24] By contrast, in the same region the Commandant of Saldé, less given to hyperbole, and one of the few local officials anywhere in the colony even to mention flu, would say only that influenza had been responsible for 'many deaths'.[25] It was commonly assumed that the more remote corners of the colony, difficult to reach, and the last to be struck by influenza, were less seriously affected, but no evidence permitted such a conclusion.

Despite the absence of reliable details, medical officials confidently, if somewhat rashly, generalised about which elements of the population were more vulnerable to flu. Dr Thoulon was convinced that soldiers, for example, suffered less than the general population because they received better supervision.[26] A similar argument was made for low mortality among the African *Tirailleurs* at the posts of Dagana and Podor. It is always possible that Senegal was the exception, of course, but these opinions ran contrary to better evidence elsewhere in the world that men in their twenties who were confined to crowded areas, in other words young soldiers, experienced the highest mortality rates of any age group.

Medical and civilian officials held sometimes directly opposite notions of what had transpired. In Casamance, the civilian man-on-the-spot maintained that his region had suffered death rates up to 100 per 1,000 population, but Thoulon later claimed that Casamance was *less* severely affected than other areas. He even speculated, as we have seen, that the alcoholic palm wine favoured in Casamance may have been responsible for the relatively moderate death rates![27]

Several explanations can be advanced for the relatively silent historical memory in Senegal. One speculation argued at the time can be quickly discarded. Wartime shortages of equipment and personnel, which French officials in Senegal constantly invoked, were not unique to them. The same difficulties were experienced in other parts of Africa where the historical record for the influenza epidemic is richer. For example, equally hard-pressed officials in Dahomey and especially in Guinea found time to offer significantly more details on the impact of influenza in their jurisdictions.[28]

A more valid explanation, but not the primary one, has to do with the peculiarities of epidemic influenza. Modern populations have a degree of familiarity with common influenza strains, and they are rarely lethal. It is the emergence of new and dangerous variants which produces periodic pandemics. When the 1918 epidemic struck, medical authorities in Senegal, as elsewhere in the world, at first mistook the epidemic for yet another annual visitation of a benign strain of the disease. A second reason for this misreading may have been caused by flu's similarity to a bad cold. Then, as now, it was common practice to use the term 'flu' colloquially as a label for a wide variety of respiratory infections, in which the general symptoms were a runny nose, a sore throat, a cough and a fever.

Only after the influenza pandemic of 1918 had run its course did medical authorities become alarmed. The highest ranking physician in the French Colonial Army, Dr Paul Gouzien, estimated that the scourge had claimed at least a half million victims in one year in the French colonies alone, and described the flu unequivocally as 'the most deadly of the pestilences which have, from time immemorial, raged over the earth'.[29] Calling for a new Paris Conference to revise the International Sanitary Convention on contagious diseases of 17 January 1912, Gouzien not only wanted influenza placed beside cholera, plague and yellow fever, all of which had permanent sanitary measures associated with them. He even argued that influenza was the worst of the lot since its etiology remained unknown and its prevention extremely uncertain. From the vantage point of 1921, while he could confidently predict the virtual disappearance of yellow fever and total control of cholera in the near future, he could not be as sanguine about influenza.[30]

In spite of Gouzien's fears, the world was given a reprieve for an entire generation. Indeed, no serious pandemic developed until 1957, when the 'Asian' flu, so named because it had been first identified as being of pandemic magnitude in Singapore, spread around the world. By this time, however, the rapid availability of anti-influenza vaccines, and above all of antibiotics to treat secondary infections, meant far less mortality worldwide. As in 1918, Dakar and Senegal were the first French territories infected, but while three-quarters of the population of the Cape Verde peninsula were reported sick in August of 1957, the overall mortality was limited to 120 persons.[31] The consequence of this twentieth-century pattern has been, with the partial exception of the years immediately following 1918, to remove influenza from the list of scourges.

If the relatively benign history of influenza after 1918 explains why people in all walks of life are not alarmed at the mention of flu, it does not help us understand why the collective memory of 1918 is blank in Senegal but indelibly sharp in other parts of Africa. In Nigeria, Chad, Southern Rhodesia and South Africa the time of the flu is recalled in rich detail. For example, in Igbugo and other Igbo towns of Eastern Nigeria, so powerful was the impact of influenza that all men and women born between 1919 and 1921 named their age set the *Ogbo Ifelunza*, or 'Influenza Age Group'. In Kenya, on the other hand, Marc Dawson found that a famine which raged at the same time rather than flu was the catastrophe which dominated people's recollections.[32] Perhaps the Kenyan example provides the essential clue for understanding flu in Senegal. If it is the case that a society may accord priority of place in their recollections to another, emotionally more memorable catastrophe, as the Kenyans seemed to have done, then a strong argument can be made that in Senegal it was not influenza but bubonic plague (*Yersinia pestis*), which made the first of its many visits to twentieth-century Senegal in 1914. By 1918 plague seems to have acquired a local wild animal reservoir in Senegal and to have become endo-epidemic as well as endo-epizootic.

During the first and most serious ever epidemic of plague in Senegal in 1914, French health officials appeared more interested in political control than in African health needs, and clashed frequently with the people of Dakar. Africans resisted, often successfully, attempts by Europeans to use the epidemic to intensify their control over African property and lives.[33] Vaccinations were not always effective, and some who received these died of plague, so that Africans developed little confidence in French medical procedures. Coercion was used to force Africans to have the vaccinations, and to force people to obtain certificates in order to travel from Dakar to the interior.

Unlike influenza, however, bubonic plague remained confined to Dakar, the Cape Verde peninsula and its extension inland as far as the north–south Thiès-Saint-Louis rail line. In this concentrated area it killed an estimated 3,700 people in 1914.[34] Its return in 1918 cost Senegal another 3,000 lives, and roughly the same number again in 1919. While these figures were about 10 per cent of the influenza deaths of 1918, these were highly concentrated among the population of the 'plague zone'. Indeed, bubonic plague remained present in endemic or epidemic form either in Dakar or its immediate hinterland each year thereafter until 1945. While no single year's mortality rates ever matched those of 1914, the numbers were nevertheless frightening enough. In contrast, as we have seen, only one subsequent flu epidemic recurred in Senegal and it was no match for the catastrophe of 1918.

Several other contrasts between plague and flu in Senegal can be noted. Of the two diseases, plague has received far greater attention in the scholarly health literature, with over 100 articles devoted to it.[35] Similarly, partly because its timing was associated so closely with the election of a Black African Deputy in Senegal for the first time, the Senegalese plague epidemic of 1914 has received frequent mention in the political histories devoted to Blaise Diagne and his times.[36]

Nor should it be forgotten that plague had a powerful place in the collective memory of Europeans living in the colonies. The Black Death of the fourteenth century remains to our own day a vivid symbol of pestilential disaster. The high death rates of plague in Senegal surely frightened colonial officials in a manner not possible for influenza. Even if Africans did not share in this particular collective memory of the Black Death, their first-hand observation of the terrible suffering of plague victims alarmed them deeply. Taken together, the high death tolls, arbitrary official repression, and political linkages to the election of Diagne, combined to imprint the plague indelibly on the Senegalese collective memory. Similarly, the people of the 'plague zone' in Senegal have preserved vivid recollections of their years of suffering. Healers' accounts, praise poetry and funeral dirges speak of how even wealthy and powerful men were brought down by this dreadful disease. Older villagers still preserved rusty rat traps and cages that testified to plague control measures imposed on them by French health officials.[37]

The Senegalese memory of plague overriding influenza has parallels in other parts of the world. In Australia, and especially in Sydney, the influenza pandemic of 1918 has become telescoped with a bubonic plague invasion in 1900 as a single historical event in the memories of a consistent number of oral informants. As in Senegal, Australia's influenza pandemic was the bigger killer, but bubonic plague the more dreaded disease in memory. Newspapers contributed to this fusion of the two diseases by referring to influenza by the generic term of 'plague', but more importantly, the two diseases hit young adult males hardest, and took greater tolls among the working classes of the poorer districts. In both instances, victims were stigmatised, and their property, dwellings and persons subjected to arbitrary sanitary measures. The result was a good deal of layering of memory of these momentous days, and the unusual social, political and economic circumstances in which influenza occurred.[38]

As Alfred Crosby has noted, people fear diseases with high mortality rates that are difficult to contract more than diseases with low but quite real mortality rates that they are likely to contract eventually.[39] Senegal's experience with plague and with influenza confirms the point. Somewhat embarrassed that Senegal was the only sub-Saharan French colony where plague became endemic in the twentieth century, French medical authorities were to struggle with little success for the next 25 years to eliminate this scourge from their jurisdiction.[40] As for the African population, with the passage of time, plague and not flu came to dominate the collective memory of epidemic disease in Dakar and the Senegalese hinterland, and at the same time it erased the memory of influenza. Accordingly, the recent epidemiological history of Senegal provides a dramatic illustration of how collective memory can sometimes become selective memory.

Part VI

Epidemiological lessons of the pandemic

16 Transmission of, and protection against, influenza

Epidemiologic observations
beginning with the 1918
pandemic and their implications

Stephen C. Schoenbaum

Introduction

The influenza pandemic of 1918–19 is still remembered as a remarkable event. Yet, 80+ years later much that was learned about the epidemiology of influenza in the pre-virologic era of 1918–30 has been forgotten. This is particularly unfortunate, since much of that information can be reinterpreted with our growing knowledge of influenza virology and can add to our overall understanding of influenza and its control. This chapter will review some epidemiologic phenomena that were studied in the era following the 1918 pandemic and continue to have importance today. In particular, it will review and discuss epidemiologic information on short-term natural immunity, long-term natural immunity, and the role of children in transmission of influenza.

Short-term immunity

Both natural and acquired immunity can modify the ability of influenza viruses to infect us or to cause severe illness. There are some fascinating early observations of natural immunity: for instance, in the northern spring of 1918, there was a significant influenza pandemic, which appears to have presaged the events of the next autumn and winter, a so-called 'herald wave'. In the United States Navy and Army, the British Navy and the French Army, observations, unfortunately not formal studies, indicated that those troops who experienced influenza in the spring and summer of 1918 were mostly protected from the extensive epidemics in the autumn and winter.[1] In one such account, V.C. Vaughan reported that in a military camp housing a division with 26,000 men there was a mild influenza epidemic in April 1918, with 2,000 recognised cases. Subsequently, over the summer, 20,000 recruits were added to the division. When influenza struck the camp again in October 1918, 'it confined itself almost exclusively to the recruits of the summer and scarcely touched the men who had lived through the epidemic of April'.[2]

It is not easy to assess the effects of natural immunity on the occurrence

of influenza in specific individuals for several reasons, including the
following:

1   Reported past experience of clinical influenza is not necessarily an
    accurate indicator of all of the persons who have been infected. For
    example, Vaughan's observations were that the protection of being
    present in the military camp extended not just to the 2,000 recog-
    nised cases of influenza in April but to the other 24,000 persons who
    had been in the camp at that time.[3] This suggests that many of the
    24,000 may have had mild, unreported, infections or subclinical infec-
    tions that conferred some degree of immunity. Careful, ongoing clini-
    cal and virologic study of entire populations is necessary to obtain a
    comprehensive picture of which specific individuals in a population
    have actually been infected in a given time interval. Indeed, longitudi-
    nal, or prospective studies, have provided most of our knowledge of
    herald waves, the relatively small occurrences of a new type of
    influenza late in the season preceding their significant epidemic
    appearance, and much information about the relationship of natural
    protection against illness to antibody levels.[4]

2   The index of immunity that we commonly measure, serum anti-
    haemagglutinin antibody titres, may be only indirect, or partial, evi-
    dence of immunity, or lack thereof. Serum anti-neuraminidase
    antibody also appears to be related to protection against influenza.[5]
    Furthermore, for over 50 years there has been interest in the role of
    local respiratory tract IgA antibody. Yet, studying local protection has
    not been simple. Influenza vaccine has been shown to induce or
    enhance nasal neutralising activity against influenza virus. But nasal
    neutralising activity is not a direct measure of local IgA antibody.
    There is conflicting evidence about whether levels of nasal neutralis-
    ing activity correlate with serum antibody levels; and, in one study,
    nasal neutralising activity did not correlate with protection from clini-
    cal illness.[6] Our understanding of immunity in individuals would be
    much richer if we had routine, simple measurements of multiple para-
    meters of immunity, not just serum antibody.

3   The important issue for an individual is how much immunity that
    individual has to the exact strain that he or she encounters in the
    midst of an epidemic. There are continual antigenic changes in the
    virus. Thus, the natural immunity an individual acquired in a first epi-
    demic is, to some degree, heterologous immunity for the second epi-
    demic appearance of the virus, even though we commonly use the
    term 'heterologous' only when there is significant enough antigenic
    drift for us to consider changing our reference strains. The degree to
    which the virus has drifted is clearly a critical variable; and only
    recently, with virus mapping studies, is it becoming possible to quan-
    tify the drift accurately.

4   In the face of a specific antigenic challenge, individuals differ in the types and amounts of antibody they produce. Reasons for this variation, for example possible genetic variations in antibody response, have not been carefully delineated.

5   In addition, the occurrence of a second infection in the community setting may depend upon the dose of exposure or numbers of exposures to a subsequent virus strain. These are parameters that are impossible to quantify in non-experimental settings.

Despite the suggestion from the military studies cited by Shope that natural immunity between the spring and autumn of 1918 was nearly complete, at least one study from that era has shown that immunity, while apparently present, was not complete. Armstrong and Hopkins[7] performed a truly remarkable epidemiologic study of influenza in the winter of 1920 on an isolated island in Lake Erie, Ohio. They ascertained all of the clinical illnesses during a severe influenza epidemic that occurred among the 689 persons living on this island. In addition, they determined who had been ill in 1918, when there had been a less severe epidemic of influenza, apparently mitigated by quarantine of the island. The attack rate in 1920 was 77.2 per cent among those not affected in 1918, as against 48.2 per cent among those who had been affected. Thus, in this population, a history of infection in 1918 was associated with a protective effectiveness of 37 per cent 2 years later.

In 1957–60, Hayslett *et al.*[8] obtained multiple sera from Navaho school children and found evidence of at least 9 second rises in antibody among seventy-seven Navaho school children in the 2.5 year period after the first H2N2 (Asian influenza) pandemic. Hayslett reported that this 12 per cent re-infection rate, or failure of recently acquired natural immunity, was probably an underestimate. In contrast, Foy *et al.*,[9] who observed a group of school children from 1968 to 1972, the first 4 years after the H3N2 (Hong Kong influenza) pandemic, found only one re-infection out of 156 children.

We can conclude from these not entirely consistent observations, beginning in 1918, that there does appear to be short-term natural protection of individuals against influenza. The protection is probably partial, i.e. not complete. Longitudinal studies have provided some information on how this natural protection has varied by age, virus type and antibody level.[10]

Long-term immunity

The 1918 pandemic was associated with a magnitude of mortality that was extraordinary in comparison to anything occurring in the 80 years before or since. In the United States, the excess mortality rate in October 1918 was approximately seven times higher than it had been in January 1892, and twelve times higher than it would be in January 1929 – the two largest epidemics before and after 1918. Furthermore, in 1918, the pattern of excess mortality was extremely unusual. Usually, in influenza epidemics and pandemics the highest excess mortality rates are seen among the elderly. Yet, in 1918, persons aged 20–40 accounted for the bulk of the excess deaths; and compared to this bulge in mortality among younger people, the elderly were relatively spared.[11] Indeed, from comparative survey data in the USA, persons over the age of 60 had a lower incidence of illness in 1918 than in 1928–9 or in 1943.

This phenomenon of long-term natural protection of the elderly was observed during the A/Hong Kong (H3N2) influenza pandemic in 1968–9. Schoenbaum *et al.*[12] studied a retirement community population in California, USA. They found a relationship between year of birth and pre-epidemic antibody, such that 38 per cent of persons born between 1890 and 1894, and 93 per cent of persons born before 1890 had detectable anti-H3 HI antibody (Figure 16.1). More importantly, compared to persons born after 1899, the attack rates of influenza-like illness were 42 per cent lower among persons born between 1890 and 1894, and 66 per cent lower among persons born before 1890. In contrast, in an epidemic of Asian influenza (H2N2) in this same retirement community only 2 years earlier, there was no consistent relationship of attack rate and age (Figure 16.2). Overall, observations such as this suggest that childhood exposure to an influenza virus leads to a long-lasting type of natural

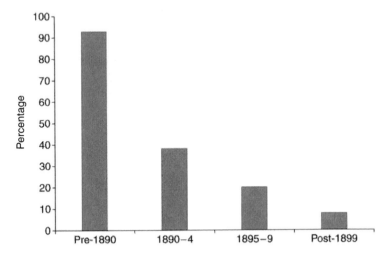

Figure 16.1 Prevalence of pre-epidemic antibodies to A/HK/68 (H3N2) at a Californian retirement community, by year of birth.

Source: S.C. Schoenbaum, M.T. Coleman, W.R. Dowdle and S.R. Mostow, 'Epidemiology of influenza in the elderly: Evidence of virus recycling', *American Journal of Epidemiology*, vol. 103, 1976, pp. 166–73. Reproduced here with permission of Oxford University Press.

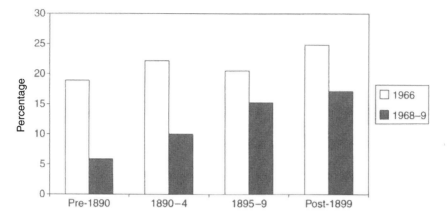

Figure 16.2 Age-specific attack rates of influenza-like illness in two epidemics at a
California retirement community.

Source: S.C. Schoenbaum, M.T. Coleman, W.R. Dowdle and S.R. Mostow, 'Epidemiology of
influenza in the elderly: Evidence of virus recycling', *American Journal of Epidemiology*, vol. 103,
1976, pp. 166–73. Reproduced here with permission of Oxford University Press.

immunity which can persist into adulthood and be manifest when a
similar virus re-enters the population. This immunity is likely to be related
to the phenomenon called 'original antigenic sin',[13] in which exposure to
various influenza A viruses leads to an anamnestic response, particularly to
the first influenza A virus infection during childhood. Marine and
Thomas[14] showed that the anamnestic response to H3N2 viruses, such as
the Hong Kong viruses of 1968–9, was likely to be stimulated by H2N2
infection, though not by H1N1 infection. The elderly in 1968–9 had exposure to H2N2 viruses in the preceding decade of Asian influenza infections; and those exposures were likely to have boosted the immunity to H3
viruses that they had first acquired in childhood.

Parenthetically, not only did there appear to have been natural protection of the most elderly members of the retirement community in California studied by Schoenbaum *et al.*,[15] but also there may have been sufficient
natural protection to reduce the attack rate in the community as a whole;
i.e. confer herd immunity. In this retirement community, as noted above
and in Figure 16.2, two epidemics of influenza were documented in a
short period of time. The first was an H2N2 (Asian) epidemic in 1966,[16]
the second was the H3N2 (Hong Kong) epidemic of 1968–9. Although
immunisation studies were being performed in the community throughout this period, a minority of residents received relevant vaccines in each
year. The attack rates in persons born between 1895 and 1899, and among
persons born after 1899 were significantly higher in the Asian influenza
epidemic of 1966 than in the Hong Kong influenza epidemic of 1968–9.
This observation is consistent with the notion of natural herd immunity. It

may, however, simply be due to a chance difference in the intensity of two epidemics in one population. Ideally, several populations would have been observed over the two epidemics and consistent differences would have been seen in each or most.

The phenomenon of protection against influenza in later life owing to childhood exposure to related influenza strains has occurred yet again: H1N1 epidemics occurred throughout the world prior to 1957, particularly up until about 1950, and then reappeared in 1977, as the so-called 'Russian influenza'. Glezen *et al.*[17] have made important observations of H1N1 epidemics in Houston, Texas, between 1978 and 1989. They followed adults prospectively between 1978 and 1989 through four H1N1 epidemics. In each epidemic, persons born between 1951 and 1960 had higher rates of infection, illness and recovery of virus than did those born between 1941 and 1950. Nonetheless, some persons born prior to 1950, who clearly had pre-existing exposure to H1N1 viruses, became infected, ill and virus positive.

Thus, armed with evidence obtained in the 'Hong Kong' and 'Russian' influenza eras indicating that childhood exposure to influenza virus leads to natural immunity that can persist into adulthood and be manifest when a similar virus re-enters the population, it is worth reconsidering the unusual pattern of morbidity and mortality in 1918, with its relative sparing of the elderly population. The most likely explanation is that the elderly in the 1918 pandemic had exposure to a virus with a similar haemagglutinin 60 or more years earlier.

The role of children in transmission of influenza

Although pre-school children and adults can serve as introducers of influenza into their households and families, there are many observations of influenza epidemics in which school children appeared to have been the first group attacked and the source of secondary infections in their families. In the beautifully studied epidemic in 1920 on Kelley's Island, Ohio,[18] an isolated community in Lake Erie, an outbreak first occurred in school children and then in the remainder of the community, with the epidemic curve for school children peaking 3 days before the community peak. Not surprisingly, then, there were two distinct epidemic curves for cases occurring among other family members in families with school children and cases in families with no school children. The curve for family members with school children peaked 3 days before the curve for families with no school children. This was an explosive epidemic in a confined population, and it gave a very sharp curve of secondary attack rates in family members, unlike ones deriving from studies in more open communities.[19]

The first community-wide epidemic of Asian influenza in the United States, which began in late July 1957, i.e. in the mid-summer, occurred in

Tangipahoa Parish, Louisiana, 2 weeks after the schools opened.[20] The schools had opened in that area earlier than elsewhere in the United States; and, as schools began to open in other parts of the country, epidemics began to occur first in the schools and then in the community.[21] In a study in England and Wales in 1957, it was claimed, erroneously I believe, that 'no consistent relationship was observed between the dates of re-assembly of schools and the establishment of epidemic conditions in the local communities' and that 'the aggregation of children in schools was not necessarily a decisive factor in the early stages of the influenza epidemic in England and Wales'. Nonetheless, in seventeen of twenty communities, the schools had reassembled one or more weeks before the beginning of community-wide outbreaks;[22] and in none of the seventeen had the schools reassembled for more than 3 weeks before the community-wide outbreaks.

In the 1970s there were several demonstrations of the role of school children as introducers of influenza infection into the broader community: in the Seattle Virus Watch study,[23] school-age children played the major role in introducing infection into their households in four epidemics (two A/H3N2, one A/H1N1, one B). The exact age-group of the introducers varied, with children 5–9 being more often introducers of the A/H3N2 epidemics and teenagers being the more frequent introducers in the A/H1N1 and B epidemics. Glezen and Couch[24] showed that in two A/H3N2 epidemics in Houston, the A/Port Chalmers and A/Victoria epidemics, there was a predominance of cases among school children in the early stages of each epidemic and there was a peak in school absenteeism before other community epidemic phenomena. Interestingly, the highest attack rates were seen in pre-school children. Finally, in Port Chalmers, New Zealand, itself a semi-isolated community, the principal introducers of the 1973 epidemic were school age children.[25]

Building upon the ideas that school children are a large, susceptible population for influenza within a community, that they often have high attack rates during influenza epidemics, and that they appear often to be introducers, Monto *et al.* performed a study[26] in which they immunised school children in Tecumseh, Michigan in the autumn of 1968. These children were the only ones in the community who had the opportunity to receive vaccine. When the A/Hong Kong/68 epidemic struck, there was three times as much illness in a neighbouring community as in Tecumseh. In the Novgorod study,[27] in a much larger community, large numbers of school children, in more than thirty schools, were immunised with live attenuated vaccine, inactivated vaccine, or placebo. The study was performed over multiple years, and there were epidemics in two of those years, 1989–90, and 1990–1. Efficacy of the vaccines varied from 20–50 per cent. There was some evidence of an 'indirect effect' or herd immunity: unvaccinated children in schools where more than 50 per cent of the students had received live vaccine were 27 per cent less likely to develop a clinical illness than unvaccinated children in schools where less than 50 per cent of the students had received live vaccine. There was no apparent differential protection of unvaccinated students in schools with greater or lesser use of inactivated vaccine. Staff in schools in which more than 50 per cent of the children were immunised were less likely to develop a clinical illness than staff in schools in which less than 50 per cent of the children were immunised – 37 per cent less likely for schools using live vaccine, and 27 per cent less likely for schools using inactivated vaccine.

In the Northern Territory of Australia an extensive immunisation programme had been planned in 1969 for the advent of Hong Kong influenza.[28] Vaccine was to be offered to the elderly, persons with chronic debilitating diseases, children 1–5 years of age, and pregnant women. Owing to the timing of the epidemic, the immunisation programme was almost completed in some communities and not in others. There was severe influenza in seventeen of the twenty communities that had not been given any vaccine before the disease appeared; whereas, there were mild outbreaks in only four of the twenty-nine partially immunised communities. No cases occurred in one community where 84 per cent of the total population had been immunised, despite the fact that in a neighbouring unimmunised community there was an outbreak with a clinical attack rate of almost 50 per cent.

Thoughts stimulated by the above observations

It is interesting to step back and think about the interdependent observations recounted above. Is there anything we might learn from our prior experiences that might lead to improved strategies for control of influenza?

We have seen that there is evidence for short-term and long-term natural immunity. Short-term immunity undoubtedly has epidemiologic significance. In the twentieth century, second and third waves of epidemic influenza have been observed just in the pandemics of 1918 and 1957–8, not in 1968–9 or 1977, and not in other large epidemics such as 1928–9 or 1943. Since the first wave of a new (antigenically shifted or significantly drifted) virus induces natural immunity in a sizeable percentage of the population, the ability of a virus to cause a second or third wave with minimal antigenic drift is likely to be a marker of its transmissibility. It is known that in 1957, and probably in 1918 too, the new viruses had new genes not only for the haemagglutinin but also for the neuraminidase. Monto and Kendal[29] have shown that the serologic rate of infection in the 1968–9 epidemic, among adults aged 20–45, was inversely related to the amount of pre-epidemic anti-neuraminidase antibody. In addition, they observed that the occurrence of clinical illness was less among those who were infected in the face of an anti-neuraminidase antibody. It is possible that the occurrence of second waves depends upon the population, prior to the pandemic, having very little natural immunity to both the haemagglutinin and the neuraminidase – the likely case in 1918 and 1957 as against other years cited above. Although the tendency has been to downplay the necessity for vaccines to induce anti-neuraminidase antibody, it may, in fact, be an important attribute of vaccines when a pandemic is anticipated.

Long-term natural immunity appears to occur and be important. The evidence suggests that the Hong Kong influenza pandemic of 1968–9 would have caused many more excess deaths among the most elderly persons in the United States had they not had natural protection. Relatively little vaccine was available to the general population of the United States by the time epidemics began to occur. It is not clear that we would consider the Russian influenza strains so benign, had most of the adult population been susceptible to them in 1977. Similarly, it is likely that the pandemic of 1918, as devastating as it was, would have been worse had the elderly not been relatively protected. Now that it has become possible to resurrect viruses from old pathologic specimens, it would be interesting to know if one could demonstrate that an influenza virus with a 1918-like haemagglutinin circulated for a limited time in the mid-nineteenth century.

The role of school children in transmission of influenza, and the possibility of inducing herd immunity by use of vaccines, opens a variety of speculative doors. An epidemic model developed by Elveback and Fox suggests that strategies, such as immunisation of 70 per cent of school children with inactivated or live-virus vaccines, should be effective in leading to much smaller community outbreaks than otherwise would be expected.[30] One might consider mass vaccination of children in some circumstances.

1   The first circumstance occurs when there is a limited amount of vaccine, such as was the case in the United States in the autumn of 1968. In such situations, the preferential vaccination of the group most likely to spread the infection, i.e. children, rather than the group at highest risk of complications of infection, i.e. the elderly, might delay or lessen the intensity of community epidemics. It fits with the results of epidemic modelling;[31] and ideally, a delay would allow sufficient time to make enough vaccine for the high-risk groups before they were infected in large numbers. Though this chain of reasoning seems logical, it is not likely to be adopted by vaccine policy-makers, who appear to have a strong bias towards direct protection of high-risk individuals. In times of vaccine shortage, policy-makers have tended to recommend selective vaccination of the high-risk population and 'essential community personnel'. Before recommending that a limited supply of vaccine be given to healthy children, policy-makers would probably want proof of just how much delay might occur or how much lower the attack rates would be in community epidemics. The

Novgorod study[32] is the only evidence on this subject so far. It provided evidence of some effect on unimmunised school children and school staff, but whether there was an effect on the general community, such as high-risk family members, was not studied.

2   In a second circumstance, since influenza vaccination is not 100 per cent effective, there is merit to considering strategies not only for protecting high-risk individuals with vaccine, but also for simultaneously reducing the overall attack rate in the community by more widespread immunisation of the populations most likely to introduce and transmit influenza, i.e. children. In other words, if there is enough vaccine to immunise multiple segments of the population, one can consider a strategy of immunising both the high-risk group and children. In the United States, there has been a significant barrier to adopting such a strategy, because only killed, injected, influenza vaccines have been available. It is unlikely that one could get widespread acceptance of the idea of annual vaccination of healthy children with such vaccines. The development of live vaccines for use in children in the United States, assuming their administration is well tolerated by children, should make it much more possible to test or adopt such a strategy.

There appears to have been insufficient experience with attempts to prevent or modify future pandemics of influenza by prior immunisation of the population with prototypes of the known influenza haemagglutinins. For a time, in the early 1960s, inactivated polyvalent vaccines were produced and used in the United States. They contained representatives of the haemagglutinins which had been isolated up until that time in humans and swine. Unfortunately, at the time these polyvalent vaccines were made, inactivated influenza vaccines were not highly purified enough; reaction rates were high; doses had to be limited to minimise reactions; and the amounts of the antigens contained in the preparations were quite small. Today, or in the near future, using live vaccines, it might be worth considering effective immunisation of people with the known human and animal haemagglutinins. This might even have the effect of producing the equivalent of 'original antigenic sin' for multiple types of haemagglutinins – a tantalising thought.

Despite the fact that we have learned an enormous amount about the epidemiology of influenza in the past century, our approaches to control of the disease are primitive and reactive. We wait until there is a new strain and a significant population has suffered from it before developing a control strategy for the rest of the world. It is always done under stress, as was the case in 1957, 1968 and 1977, and almost was the case in 1998, with the appearance of some human cases of H5N1 disease in Hong Kong. One can only speculate how different the epidemics of 1957 or 1968 might have been if much of the population had prior immunisation with prototypical H2N2 or H3N2 strains.

This chapter resurrects several epidemiologic issues. Indeed, some of the thoughts that derive from these issues, such as the role of anti-neuraminidase antibody, mass vaccination of school children, and use of vaccines representing prototypical haemagglutinins, have been raised in the past. With our present knowledge of influenza virology and ability to make and administer vaccines, it is time to re-examine these ideas and factor them into strategies for control of this important disease.

Notes

A virologist's foreword

1   Robert R. Edgar and Hilary Sapire, *African Apocalypse. The story of Nontetha Nkwenkwe, a twentieth-century South African prophet*, Ohio University Press, Athens, OH, and Witwatersrand University Press, Johannesburg, 1999.

Introduction

1   E.P. Cheyney, *The Dawn of a New Era 1250–1453*, New York and London, Harper, 1936, p. 35.
2   W.H. McNeill, *Plagues and Peoples*, Harmondsworth, Penguin Books, 1979, p. 12.
3   For example (in chronological order of publication): R.J. Morris, *Cholera 1832. The social response to an epidemic*, London, Croom Helm, 1976; M. Durey, *The Return of the Plague: British society and the cholera, 1831–32*, Dublin, Gill and Macmillan, 1979; F. Delaporte, *Disease and Civilization: The cholera in Paris 1832*, Cambridge, MA, MIT Press, 1982; R.S. Gottfried, *The Black Death: Natural and human disaster in medieval Europe*, New York, Free Press, 1983; P. Slack, *The Impact of Plague in Tudor and Stuart England*, Oxford, Oxford University Press, 1985; R. Evans, *Death in Hamburg: Society and politics in the cholera years*, Oxford, Oxford University Press, 1987; T.O. Ranger and P. Slack (eds), *Epidemics and Ideas. Essays on the historical perception of pestilence*, Cambridge, Cambridge University Press, 1992; C. Rosenberg, *Explaining Epidemics and Other Studies in the History of Medicine*, New York, Cambridge University Press, 1992; D. Arnold, *Colonizing the Body: State medicine and epidemic disease in 19th century India*, Berkeley, University of California Press, 1993; K. De Bevoise, *Agents of the Apocalypse: Epidemic disease in the colonial Philippines*, Princeton, NJ, Princeton University Press, 1995; F.M. Snowden, *Naples in the Time of Cholera, 1884–1911*, Cambridge, Cambridge University Press, 1995; D. Rosner (ed.), *Hives of Sickness*, New Brunswick, NJ, Rutgers University Press, 1995; C.J. Kucklick, *Cholera in Post-Revolutionary Paris: A cultural history*, Berkeley, University of California Press, 1996; D. Herlihy, *Black Death and the Transformation of the West*, Cambridge, MA, Harvard University Press, 1997; S. Watts, *Epidemics and History: Disease, power, and imperialism*, New Haven, Yale University Press, 1997; H. Markel, *Quarantine! East European Jewish immigrants and the New York City epidemics of 1892*, Baltimore and London, The Johns Hopkins University Press, 1997.
4   L. Garrett, 'Runaway diseases and the human hand behind them', *Foreign Affairs*, 1998, vol. 77, no. 1, p. 139.
5   K. David Patterson and Gerald F. Pyle, 'The geography and mortality of the 1918 influenza pandemic', *Bulletin of the History of Medicine*, 1991, vol. 65, no. 1, pp. 4–21.

6 R.G. Webster and W.G. Laver, 'Pandemic variation of influenza viruses', in E.D. Kilbourne (ed.), *The Influenza Viruses and Influenza*, New York, Academic Press, 1975, pp. 269–314.

7 E.A. Wrigley and R.S. Schofield, *The Population History of England, 1541–1871*, Cambridge, Cambridge University Press, 1981, pp. 336–7, suggest 5 per cent mortality; F.J. Fisher, 'Influenza and inflation in Tudor England', *Economic History Review*, 2nd ser., XVIII (1965), pp. 120–9, argues for 20 per cent; John S. Moore, '"Jack Fisher's 'flu": a visitation revisited', *Economic History Review*, XLVI, 2 (1993), pp. 280–308, using probate sources, revises the figure to 16 per cent.

8 K. David Patterson, *Pandemic Influenza, 1700–1900. A study in historical epidemiology*, Totowa, NJ, Rowman & Littlefield, 1986. See also *Encyclopaedia Britannica*, 11th edn, New York, The Encyclopaedia Britannica Company, 1910–11, vol. XIV, pp. 552–6.

9 Christopher W. Potter, 'Chronicle of influenza pandemics', in R.G. Webster, K.G. Nicholson and A.J. Hay (eds), *Textbook of Influenza*, Oxford, Blackwell, 1998, p. 3.

10 David Tyrrell, 'Discovery of influenza viruses', in Webster, Nicholson and Hay, *Textbook of Influenza*, ch. 2.

11 Sinn Féin papers. National Archives of Ireland, Dublin: 1094/1/2. *Ard-fheis* (Extraordinary Sinn Féin), 8th April, 1919. Report on Influluenza [*sic*] Epidemic, March 1919. We owe this reference to Dr Stephen Ball.

12 Alfred W. Crosby, *America's Forgotten Pandemic: The influenza of 1918*, Cambridge, Cambridge University Press, 1989, pp. 37–40. A recent popular account of the flu in the United States is by Lynette Iezzoni, *Influenza 1918: The worst epidemic in American history*, New York, TV Books, L.L.C., 1999, to accompany a television documentary film 'Influenza 1918' transmitted in PBS's documentary series *The American Experience*.

13 See Chapter 9: N.P.A.S. Johnson, 'The overshadowed killer: Influenza in Britain in 1918–19', has recalculated the official death rate figure of 169,000 up to 225,000.

14 See the arguments on the Indian origin of cholera in Sheldon Watts, *Epidemics and History. Disease, power and imperialism*, New Haven, NJ, Yale University Press, 1997, ch. 5, 'Cholera and civilization: Great Britain and India, 1817 to 1920'.

15 Such grief colours much of the writing of the American novelist William Maxwell, who was aged ten when his mother died in the pandemic; see *Ancestors: A family history*, 1971, Boston edn, 1985, chs 17–18.

16 K. David Patterson, 'The influenza epidemic of 1918–19 in the Gold Coast', *Journal of African History*, 1983, vol. 24, no. 4, pp. 484–502.

17 K. David Patterson and Gerald P. Pyle, 'The diffusion of influenza in sub-Saharan Africa during the 1918–19 pandemic', *Social Science and Medicine*, 1983, vol. 17, pp. 1299–1307.

18 Howard Phillips, *'Black October': The impact of the Spanish influenza pandemic of 1918 on South Africa*, Pretoria, The Government Printer, 1990.

19 Terence Ranger, 'Plagues of beasts and men: prophetic responses to epidemics in eastern and southern Africa', in Ranger and Slack, *Epidemics and Ideas*, particularly pp. 264ff.

20 See Chapter 7, Wataru Iijima, 'The Spanish influenza in China, 1918–20'.

21 G.W. Rice and E. Palmer, 'Pandemic influenza in Japan, 1918–19: mortality patterns and official responses', *Journal of Japanese Studies*, 1993, vol. 19, no. 2, pp. 389–420.

22 Colin Brown, 'The influenza pandemic of 1918 in Indonesia', in Norman G. Owen (ed.), *Death and Disease in Southeast Asia: Explorations in social, medical and demographic history*, Singapore, Singapore University Press, 1987, pp. 235–56.

23 D. Mills, 'The 1918–19 influenza pandemic: the Indian experience', *Indian Economic and Social History Review*, 1986, vol. 1, no. 23, pp. 1–40, reprinted in T. Dyson (ed.), *India's Historical Demography*, London, Curzon, 1989, pp. 222–60.

24 K. Wakimura, 'Famines, epidemics and mortality in northern India, 1870–1921', in R. Robb, K. Sugihara and H. Yanigisawa (eds), *Local Agrarian Societies in Colonial India: Japanese perspectives*, London, Manohar, 1996, pp. 280–319.

25 See further the debate over famine and disease in J.D. Post, *Food Shortage, Climate Variability and Epidemic Disease in Preindustrial Europe: The mortality peak in the early 1740s*, Ithaca, Cornell University Press, 1985.

26 Crosby, *America's Forgotten Pandemic*, p. 234.

27 Geoffrey W. Rice with Linda Bryder, *Black November. The 1918 influenza pandemic in New Zealand*, Wellington, Allen & Unwin and Department of Internal Affairs Historical Branch, 1988.

28 Sandra M. Tomkins, 'The influenza pandemic of 1918–19 in Western Samoa', *Journal of Pacific History*, 1992, vol. 27, no. 2, pp. 181–97; Phyllis Herda, 'The 1918 influenza pandemic in Fiji, Tonga and the Samoas', in Linda Bryder and Derek A. Dow (eds), *New Countries and Old Medicine*, Auckland, Pyramid Press for the Auckland Medical History Society, 1994, pp. 46–53.

29 See R.T. Ravenholt, 'Encephalitis Lethargica', in Kenneth Kiple (ed.), *A World History of Human Disease*, Cambridge, Cambridge University Press, 1993, pp. 708–13.

30 Besides the reports in scholarly academic journals, articles in news weeklies and also several popular books and television films have described these activities: e.g. Malcolm Gladwell, 'A reporter at large: The dead zone', *New Yorker*, 29 September 1997, pp. 52–64; the best book is by Gina Kolata, *Flu. The story of the great influenza pandemic of 1918 and the search for the virus that caused it*, New York, Farrar, Straus and Giroux, 1999, and London, Macmillan, 2000; and Pete Davies, *Catching Cold: 1918's forgotten tragedy and the scientific hunt for the virus that caused it*, London, Michael Joseph, 1999.

31 E. Larson, 'The Flu Hunters', *Time*, vol. 151, no. 11, 16 March 1998, pp. 51–8.

32 E.g. J.A.S. Grenville, *The Collins History of the World in the Twentieth Century*, London, HarperCollins, 1994, J.M. Roberts, *The Penguin History of the Twentieth Century*, Harmondsworth, Penguin Books, 1999, and Richard Overy (ed.), *The Times History of the 20th Century*, London, Times Books, 2000, all ignore the pandemic. A few lines are given by Clive Ponting, *Progress and Barbarism. The world in the twentieth century*, London, Chatto and Windus, 1998, p. 38, and by Michael Howard and Wm Roger Louis (eds), *The Oxford History of the Twentieth Century*, London, Oxford University Press, 1998, p. 70.

33 J. Müller, '"What's in a name?" Spanish influenza in Africa and what local names say about the pandemic', paper given to the conference on 'The Spanish Flu 1918–1998', Cape Town, September 1998.

34 J.M. Winter in *The Great War and the British People*, London, 1985, p. 104, examines, and rejects, the argument that influenza spread more rapidly and killed more people in Britain because it struck at a 'war-ravaged population'.

35 B. Croce, *History as the Story of Liberty*, London, Allen and Unwin, 1941, p. 19.

36 *These Eventful Years: The 20th century in the making . . . being the dramatic story of all that has happened throughout the world during the most momentous period in all history*, London and New York, Encyclopaedia Britannica, 1924, 2 volumes.

37 A. Macphail, *The Medical Services*, Ottawa, F.A. Acland by authority of Canadian Minister of National Defence in series on Official History of the Canadian Forces in the Great War, 1925, p. 271.

38 T.J. Mitchell and G.M. Smith, *Medical Services – Casualties and Medical Statistics of*

the Great War, London, HMSO in series on History of the Great War Based on Official Documents, 1931, p. 85.

39 H. Elias, 'Grippe', in C. Pirquet (ed.), *Volksgesundheit im Krieg*, Vienna, Hoelder-Pichler-Tempsky, and New Haven, Yale University Press, 1926; G.. Mortora, *La salute publica in Italia durante e dopo la Guerra*, Bari, Laterza e Figli, and New Haven, Yale University Press, 1925; L. Bernard, *La Guerre et la Sante publique*, Paris, Les Presses Universitaires de France, 1929; F. Bumm (ed.), *Deutschlands Gesundheitsverhältnisse unter dem Einfluss des Weltkrieges*, Stuttgart, Deutsche Verlaganstatt, and New Haven, Yale University Press, 1928.

40 Great Britain, Ministry of Health, *Report on the Pandemic of Influenza 1918–19*, London, Ministry of Health, Number 4 in series of Reports on Public Health and Medical Subjects, 1920, pp. iv and 3.

41 E.O. Jordan, *Epidemic Influenza: A survey*, Chicago, American Medical Association, 1927, p. 3.

42 F.M. Burnet and E. Clark, *Influenza*, Melbourne, Macmillan, 1942, Introduction.

43 A. Hoehling, *The Great Epidemic*, Boston and Toronto, Little Brown, 1961.

44 *San Francisco Chronicle*, 8 March 1961, p. 37.

45 C. Graves, *Invasion by Virus. Can it happen again?*, London, Icon, 1969, p. 7.

46 Graves, *Invasion by Virus*, p. 131.

47 A.C. de Gooijer, *De Spaanse Griep van '18: De epidemie die meer dan 20,000,000 levens eiste*, Amsterdam, Van Lindonk, 1968.

48 A.C. de Gooijer, *De Spaanse Griep van '18: De epidemie die meer dan 20,000,000 levens eiste*, Amsterdam, Tiebosch, 1978.

49 R. Collier, *The Plague of the Spanish Lady. The influenza pandemic of 1918–19*, London, Macmillan, 1974.

50 For example, D.C. Ohadike, 'The Influenza Pandemic of 1918–19 and the spread of cassava cultivation on the Lower Niger: a study in historical linkages', *Journal of African History*, 1981, vol. 22, no. 3; K.D. Patterson, 'The Demographic impact of the 1918–19 influenza pandemic in sub-Saharan Africa', in C. Fyfe and D. McMaster (eds), *African Historical Demography II*, Centre of African Studies, University of Edinburgh, 1981; B. Luckingham, *Epidemic in the Southwest, 1918–19*, El Paso, Texas Western Press, 1984; H. McQueen, 'The "Spanish" Influenza Pandemic in Australia', in J. Roe (ed.), *Social Policy in Australia*, Melbourne, Cassell, 1976; W. Nussbaum, 'Die Grippe Epidemie 1918/19 in der Schweizerischen Armee', *Gesnerus*, 1982, vol. 39, no. 2.

51 A.W. Crosby, *Epidemic and Peace 1918*, Westport and London, Greenwood Press, 1976.

52 A.W. Crosby, *Germs, Seeds and Animals: Studies in ecological history*, Armonk, NY and London, M.E. Sharpe, 1994, p. xiv.

53 T.M. Hill in *Annals of American Academy of Political and Social Science*, 1977, vol. 430, p. 213.

54 J.H. Cassedy in *American Historical Review*, 1977, vol. 82, no. 1, p. 202.

55 M.S. Pernick in *Journal of Interdisciplinary History*, 1977, vol. 8, no. 1, p. 162.

56 Crosby, *America's Forgotten Pandemic*, p. xii.

57 F.R. van Hartesveldt (ed.), *The 1918–19 Pandemic of Influenza. The urban impact in the western world*, Lewiston, NY and Lampeter, Edwin Mellen Press, 1992, p. 8.

58 Ibid.

59 Patterson and Pyle, 'The geography and mortality of the 1918 influenza'.

60 For instance, Rice, *Black November*; Phillips, *'Black October'*; M. Aman, *Spanska Sjukan. Den svenska epidemin 1918–1920 och dess internationella bakgrund*, Uppsala, Almqvist and Wiksell, 1990; B. Echeverri Davila, *La Gripe Española. La pandemia de 1918–19*, Madrid, Siglo XXI de España Editores, 1993; C.M. Langford and P. Storey, 'Influenza in Sri Lanka, 1918–1919. The impact of a new

disease in a pre-modern Third World setting', *Health Transition Review*, 1992, vol. 2, Supplement.
61 E. Le Roy Ladurie, *The Mind and Method of the Historian*, Brighton, Harvester, 1981, p. 2.
62 W.F. Bynum and R. Porter (eds), *Companion Encyclopedia of the History of Medicine*, London and New York, Routledge, 1993, p. 37.
63 J.M. Winter and J-L. Robert (eds), *Capital Cities at War – Paris, London, Berlin 1914–1919*, Cambridge, Cambridge University Press, 1997, p. 489.
64 Larson, 'The Flu Hunters'; Gladwell, 'A reporter at large'; Iezzoni, *Influenza 1918*; Davies, *Catching Cold*; Kolata, *Flu*.
65 Brian Abel-Smith, *The Hospitals*, London, Heinemann, 1964, p. 280, suggests that the diversion of medical resources to the military did lead to an increased death rate among civilians in Britain.

1 A virologist's perspective on the 1918–19 pandemic

1 K.D. Patterson, *Pandemic influenza, 1700–1900. A study in historical epidemiology*, New Jersey, Rowman and Littlefield, 1986.
2 J.K. Taubenberger, A.H. Reid, A.E. Krafft, K.E. Bijwaard and T.G. Fanning, 'Initial Genetic characterization of the 1918 "Spanish" influenza virus', *Science*, 1997, vol. 275, p. 1793.
3 E.D. Kilbourne, 'The severity of influenza as a reciprocal of host susceptibility', in Ciba Foundation Study Group, No. 4, *Virus Virulence and Pathogenicity*, Boston, Little, Brown and Co., 1960; D.D. Louria, H.L. Blumenfeld, J.T. Ellis, E.D. Kilbourne and D.E. Rogers, 'Studies on influenza in the pandemic of 1957–58. II. Pulmonary complications of influenza', *Journal of Clinical Investigation*, 1959, vol. 38, pp. 213–65.
4 F.X. Bosch, W. Garten, H.D. Klenk and R. Rott, 'Proteolytic cleavage of influenza virus hemagglutinins: Primary structure of the connecting peptide between HA1 and HA2 determines proteolytic cleavability and pathogenicity of avian influenza viruses', *Virology*, 1981, vol. 113, p. 725; R.G. Webster, Y. Kawaoka and W.R. Bean Jr., 'Molecular changes in A/chicken/Pennsylvania/83 (H5N2) influenza virus associated with acquisition of virulence', *Virology*, 1986, vol. 149, p. 165.
5 G.W. Both, C.H. Shi and E.D. Kilbourne, 'Hemagglutinin of swine influenza virus: A single amino acid change pleiotropically affects viral antigenicity and replication', *Proceedings of the National Academy of Sciences (USA)*, 1983, vol. 80, pp. 6996–7000.
6 E.D. Kilbourne, 'Perspectives on pandemics: A research agenda', *Journal of Infectious Diseases*, 1997, vol. 176 (Supplement 1), pp. 529–31.
7 T. Francis Jr., F.M. Davenport and A.V. Hennessy, 'A serological recapitulation of human infection with different strains of influenza virus', *Transactions of the Association of American Physicians*, 1953, vol. 66, pp. 231–9.
8 M. Dorset, C.N. McBryde and W.B. Niles, 'Remarks on "Hog Flu"', *American Veterinary Medicine Association*, 1922, vol. 62, pp. 162–71.
9 R.E. Shope, 'The epidemiology of the origin and perpetuation of a new disease', *Perspectives in Biology and Medicine*, 1964, vol. 3, pp. 263–78.
10 E.D. Kilbourne, 'Avian and human influenza: Which way does the gene pool flow?', in D.E. Swayne and R.D. Slemons (eds), *Proceedings of the Fourth International Symposium on Avian Influenza*, 1998, pp. 121–6.
11 Francis *et al.*, 'A serological recapitulation of human infection with different strains of influenza virus', pp. 231–9.
12 T. Francis Jr., J.E. Salk and J.J. Quilligan, 'Experience with vaccination against

influenza in the Spring of 1947', *American Journal of Public Health*, 1947, vol. 37, pp. 1013–16.

13 E.D. Kilbourne, C. Smith, I. Brett, B.A. Pokorny, Johansson, Cox, N. The total influenza vaccine failure of 1947 revisited; Major intrasubtypic antigenic change can explain failure of vaccine in a post-World War II epidemic. *Proceedings of the National Academy of Sciences (USA)*, 2002, Vol. 99, pp. 10748–52.

14 C. Scholtissek, W. Rohde, V. von Hoyningen and R. Rott, 'On the origin of the human influenza virus subtype H2N2 and H3N2', *Virology*, 1978, vol. 87, pp. 13–20.

15 E.D. Kilbourne in *New York Times*, 13 February 1976, p. 33 (OP-ed); E.D. Kilbourne, *Influenza*, New York, Plenum Medical Book Co., 1987, pp. 324–31.

16 *Weekly Compilation of Presidential Documents*, 29 March 1976, vol. 12, no. 3, pp. 483–4.

17 L.B. Schonberger, D.J. Bregman, J.Z. Sullivan-Bolyai *et al.*, 'Gullain–Barre syndrome following vaccination in the National Influenza Immunization Program, United States, 1976–1977', *American Journal of Epidemiology*, 1979, vol. 110, pp. 105–23.

18 P. Palese, M.B. Ritchey, J.L. Schulman and E.D. Kilbourne, 'Genetic composition of a high yielding influenza A virus recombinant: a vaccine strain against "swine" influenza', *Science*, 1976, vol. 194, pp. 334–5.

19 M. Pernis, K.Y. Yuen, C.W. Leung, K.H. Chan, P.L.S. Ip, R.W.M. Lai, W.K. Orr and K.F. Shortridge, 'Human infection with influenza H9N2', *Lancet*, 1999, vol. 354, pp. 916–17.

20 R.G. Webster, W.G. Laver and G.M. Air, 'Antigenic variation among type A influenza viruses', in P. Palese and D.W. Kingsbury (eds), *Genetics of Influenza Viruses*, New York, Springer-Verlag, 1983, pp. 127–68.

21 Ibid.; E.D. Kilbourne, 'Recombination of influenza A viruses of human and animal origin', *Science*, 1968, vol. 160, pp. 74–6.

22 Webster *et al.*, 'Antigenic variation among type A influenza viruses', pp. 127–68.

23 Kilbourne, 'Perspectives on pandemics', pp. 529–31.

24 See note 2.

25 N. Masurel and R.A. Heijtink, 'Recycling of H1N1 influenza A virus in man – a haemagglutinin antibody study', *Journal of Hygiene*, 1983, vol. 90, pp. 397–402.

26 H. Schleiblauer, M. Reinacher, M. Tashiro and R. Rott, 'Interactions between bacteria and influenza A virus in the development of influenza pneumonia', *Journal of Infectious Diseases*, 1992, vol. 166, pp. 783–91.

2 Genetic characterisation of the 1918 'Spanish' influenza virus

1 G.B. Kolata, *Flu: The Story of the Great Influenza Pandemic of 1918 and the Search for the Virus That Caused It*, New York City, Farrar Straus and Giroux, 1999, pp. 85–120, 255–66; A.H. Reid, T.G. Fanning, J.V. Hultin and J.K. Taubenberger, 'Origin and evolution of the 1918 "Spanish" influenza virus hemagglutinin gene', *Proceedings of the National Academy of Sciences (USA)*, 1998, vol. 96, pp. 1651–6; A.H. Reid, T.G. Fanning, T.A. Janczewski and J.K. Taubenberger, 'Characterization of the 1918 "Spanish" influenza virus neuraminidase gene', *Proceedings of the National Academy of Sciences (USA)*, 2000, vol. 97, pp. 6785–90. A.H. Reid and J.K. Taubenberger, 'The 1918 flu and other influenza pandemics: "Over there" and back again', *Laboratory Investigation*, 1999, vol. 79, pp. 95–101; J.K. Taubenberger, A.H. Reid, A.E. Krafft, K.E. Bijwaard and T.G. Fanning, 'Initial genetic characterization of the 1918 "Spanish" influenza virus', *Science*, 1997, vol. 275, pp. 1793–6.

2 N.J. Cox, 'Panel summary of international pandemic influenza plans', *Journal of Infectious Diseases*, 1997, vol. 176 (Supplement 1), S87–8; K.F. Gensheimer, K.

Fukuda, L. Brammer, N. Cox, P.A. Patriarca and R.A. Strikas, 'Preparing for pandemic influenza: the need for enhanced surveillance', *Emerging Infectious Diseases*, 1999, vol. 5, pp. 297–9; P.A. Patriarca and N.J. Cox, 'Influenza pandemic preparedness plan for the United States', *Journal of Infectious Diseases*, 1997, vol. 176 (Supplement 1), S4–7.

3 G. Marks and W.K. Beatty, *Epidemics*, New York City, Scribner, 1976; M.J. Rosenau and J.M. Last, *Maxcy-Rosenau Preventative Medicine and Public Health*, New York City, Appleton-Century-Crofts, 1980.

4 A. Crosby, *America's Forgotten Pandemic*, Cambridge, Cambridge University Press, 1989, p. 256.

5 Reid and Taubenberger, 'The 1918 flu and other influenza pandemics', pp. 95–101; L. Simonsen, M.J. Clarke, L.B. Schonberger, N.H. Arden, N.J. Cox and K. Fukuda, 'Pandemic versus epidemic influenza mortality: A pattern of changing age distribution', *Journal of Infectious Diseases*, 1998, vol. 178, pp. 53–60.

6 Crosby, *America's Forgotten Pandemic*, p. 206.

7 R.D. Grove and A.M. Hetzel, *Vital Statistics Rates in the United States: 1940–1960*, Washington, DC, US Government Printing Office, 1968.

8 O.T. Gorman, W.J. Bean and R.G. Webster, 'Evolutionary processes in influenza viruses: Divergence, rapid evolution, and stasis', *Current Topics in Microbiology and Immunology*, 1992, vol. 176, pp. 75–97; Y. Kanegae, S. Sugita, K. Shortridge, Y. Yoshioka and K. Nerome, 'Origin and evolutionary pathways of the H1 hemagglutinin gene of avian, swine and human influenza viruses: Cocirculation of two distinct lineages of swine viruses', *Archives of Virology*, 1994, vol. 134, pp. 17–28.

9 W. Beveridge, *Influenza: The Last Great Plague, an unfinished story of discovery*, New York, Prodist, 1977; J. Chun, 'Influenza including its infection among pigs', *National Medical Journal (of China)*, 1919, vol. 5, pp. 34–44; J.S. Koen, 'A practical method for field diagnoses of swine diseases', *American Journal of Veterinary Medicine*, 1919, vol. 14, pp. 468–70.

10 Reid and Taubenberger, 'The 1918 flu and other influenza pandemics', pp. 95–101; Reid, Fanning, Hultin and Taubenberger, 'Origin and evolution of the 1918 "Spanish" influenza virus haemagglutinin gene', pp. 1651–6.

11 R.G. Webster, W.J. Bean, O.T. Gorman, T.M. Chambers and Y. Kawaoka, 'Evolution and ecology of influenza A viruses', *Microbiological Reviews*, 1992, vol. 56, pp. 152–79.

12 R.G. Webster, S.M. Wright, M.R. Castrucci, W.J. Bean and Y. Kawaoka, 'Influenza – a model of an emerging virus disease', *Intervirology*, 1993, vol. 35, pp. 16–25.

13 S. Ludwig, L. Stitz, O. Planz, H. Van, W. Fitch and C. Scholtissek, 'European swine virus as a possible source for the next influenza pandemic?', *Virology*, 1995, vol. 212, pp. 551–61.

14 W. Bean, M. Schell, J. Katz, Y. Kawaoka, C. Naeve, O. Gorman and R. Webster, 'Evolution of the H3 influenza virus hemagglutinin from human and nonhuman hosts', *Journal of Virology*, 1992, vol. 66, pp. 1129–38; J.R. Schafer, Y. Kawaoka, W.J. Bean, J. Suss, D. Senne and R.G. Webster, 'Origin of the pandemic 1957 H2 influenza A virus and the persistence of its possible progenitors in the avian reservoir', *Virology*, 1993, vol. 194, pp. 781–8.

15 E.C. Claas, A.D. Osterhaus, R. van Beek, J.C. De Jong, G.F. Rimmelzwaan, D.A. Senne, S. Krauss, K.F. Shortridge and R.G. Webster, 'Human influenza A H5N1 virus related to a highly pathogenic avian influenza virus', *Lancet*, 1998, vol. 351, pp. 472–7 [published erratum appears in *Lancet*, 25 April 1998, vol. 351, p. 1292]; K. Subbarao, A. Klimov, J. Katz, H. Regnery, W. Lim, H. Hall, M. Perdue, D. Swayne, C. Bender, J. Huang, M. Hemphill, T. Rowe, M. Shaw, X.

Xu, K. Fukuda and N. Cox, 'Characterization of an avian influenza A (H5N1) virus isolated from a child with a fatal respiratory illness', *Science*, 1998, vol. 279, pp. 393–6.

16 Crosby, *America's Forgotten Pandemic*, pp. 305–6; Kolata, *Flu*, pp. 89–90, 98–112.

17 Crosby, *America's Forgotten Pandemic*, pp. 248–9; C. Fosso, 'Alone with death on the tundra', in R. Hedin and G. Holthaus (eds), *Alaska: Reflections on Land and Spirit*, University of Arizona Press, 1989.

18 A.E. Krafft, B.W. Duncan, K.E. Bijwaard, J.K. Taubenberger and J.H. Lichy, 'Optimization of the isolation and amplification of RNA from formalin-fixed, paraffin-embedded tissue: The Armed Forces Institute of Pathology Experience and Literature Review', *Molecular Diagnosis*, 1997, vol. 2, pp. 217–30.

19 Taubenberger, Reid, Krafft, Bijwaard and Fanning, 'Initial genetic characterization of the 1918 "Spanish" influenza virus', pp. 1793–6.

20 Reid, Fanning, Hultin and Taubenberger, 'Origin and evolution of the 1918 "Spanish" influenza virus haemagglutinin gene', pp. 1651–6.

21 Ibid.

22 Ibid.; Reid and Taubenberger, 'The 1918 Flu and other influenza pandemics', pp. 95–101.

23 Reid, Fanning, Hultin and Taubenberger, 'Origin and evolution of the 1918 "Spanish" influenza virus haemagglutinin gene', pp. 1651–6; Reid, Fanning, Janczewski and Taubenberger, 'Characterization of the 1918 "Spanish" influenza virus neuraminidase gene'.

24 Reid, Fanning, Hultin and Taubenberger, 'Origin and evolution of the 1918 "Spanish" influenza virus haemagglutinin gene', pp. 1651–6.

25 Reid, Fanning, Janczewski and Taubenberger, 'Characterization of the 1918 "Spanish" influenza virus neuraminidase gene'.

26 J.K. Taubenberger, 'Influenza virus hemagglutinin cleavage into HA1, HA2: No laughing matter', *Proceedings of the National Academy of Sciences (USA)*, 1998, vol. 95, pp. 9713–5.

27 Reid, Fanning, Hultin and Taubenberger, 'Origin and evolution of the 1918 "Spanish" influenza virus haemagglutinin gene', pp. 1651–6.

28 H. Goto and Y. Kawaoka, 'A novel mechanism for the acquisition of virulence by a human influenza A virus', *Proceedings of the National Academy of Sciences (USA)*, 1998, vol. 95, pp. 10224–8; Taubenberger, 'Influenza virus haemagglutinin cleavage into HA1, HA2, pp. 9713–5.

29 Reid, Fanning, Janczewski and Taubenberger, 'Characterization of the 1918 "Spanish" influenza virus neuraminidase gene'.

3 The plague that was not allowed to happen

1 All translations from German are via the author.

2 Generallandesarchiv Karlsruhe [henceforth GLA], Abt. 357, No. 34531.

3 *Freiburger Zeitung* and *Pforzheimer Anzeiger*, 29 May 1918.

4 *Freiburger Zeitung* and *Badische Landeszeitung*, 1 July 1918.

5 *Konstanzer Nachrichten* and *Pforzheimer Anzeiger*, 21 September 1918.

6 *Pforzheimer Anzeiger*, 23 September 1918.

7 GLA, Abt. 233, No. 11870.

8 *Badischer Geschäftskalender für 1919*, p. 116.

9 *Geschäftsbericht des Badischen Ministeriums des Innern für die Jahre 1913–1924*, vol. 1, Karlsruhe, Braun, 1926, p. 275.

10 GLA, Abt. 356, No. 4050, *Ministerium des Kultus und Unterrichts*, No. B. 15318, 15 October 1918.

11 GLA, Abt. 357, No. 30474, *Amtliches Verkündigungsblatt für den Großh. Bad. Amts- und Amtsgerichtsbezirk Karlsruhe*, No. 119, 20 November 1918.

12 *Badische Landeszeitung* and *Mannheimer Generalanzeiger*, 19 October 1918.

13 GLA, Abt. 235, No. 16238, 'Aktennotiz'. Information on a further meeting in *Freiburger Zeitung*, 29 October 1918.

14 *Heidelberger Tageblatt*, 11 October 1918.

15 Stadtarchiv Mannheim, *Ratsprotokolle 1918*, No. 4795.

16 *Mannheimer Generalanzeiger*, 18 October 1918.

17 *Mannheimer Generalanzeiger*, 19 October 1918.

18 *Mannheimer Generalanzeiger*, 21 October 1918.

19 Stadtarchiv Mannheim, *Ratsprotokolle 1918*, No. 4929.

20 Stadtarchiv Mannheim, *Ratsprotokolle 1918*, No. 5596, and *Mannheimer Generalanzeiger*, 2 November 1918.

21 According to Stahl, the second closure lasted no longer than 6 days (Ernst Leopold Stahl, *Das Mannheimer Nationaltheater*, Mannheim *et al.*, Bensheimer, 1929, p. 345).

22 *Anzeigeblatt für die Erzdiöszese Freiburg (Amtsblatt) 1918*, Ord. 5 December 1918, No. 11446.

23 Dr Anonymus Katholikus, 'Die Ruinierung der ärztlichen Landpraxis durch die katholischen Krankenschwestern in Baden', *Ärztliche Mitteilungen aus und für Baden*, 1920, vol. 74, p. 165. Cf. the comment by the editorial board following the article quoted.

24 For instance: A. Schittenhelm and H. Schlecht, 'Ueber eine grippeartige Infektionskrankheit (Pseudogrippe)', *Münchener Medizinische Wochenschrift* [henceforth *MMW*], 1918, vol. 65, p. 61.

25 Walter Hildebrandt, 'Blutuntersuchungen bei Influenza', Freiburger medizinische Gesellschaft, 22 July 1919, *Deutsche Medizinische Wochenschrift* [henceforth *DMW*], 1919, vol. 45, p. 1120.

26 For example *Konstanzer Nachrichten*, 19 July 1918. According to this article, the pathogen mentioned was said to be identical with the causative agent of conjunctivitis, the so-called *Pfeiferbazillus* (sic).

27 *MMW*, 1918, vol. 65, p. 890.

28 *MMW*, 1919, vol. 66, p. 140. Cf. Gustav von Bergmann, 'Die spanische Krankheit ist Influenza vera', *DMW*, 1918, vol. 44, pp. 933–5.

29 *MMW*, 1919, vol. 66, p. 169.

30 See for example *Berliner Klinische Wochenschrift* [henceforth *BKW*], 1919, vol. 56, p. 118; also *BKW*, 1920, vol. 57, p. 1128.

31 F. Neufeld and P. Papamarku, 'Zur Bakteriologie der diesjährigen Influenzaepidemie', *DMW*, 1918, vol. 44, p. 1181.

32 Otto Leichtenstern, 'Influenza und Dengue', in Hermann Nothnagel (ed.), *Specielle Pathologie und Therapie*, vol. 4, first half, Vienna, A. Hölder, 1896, pp. 2f.

33 Bernhard Möllers, 'Was hat uns die letzte Grippeepidemie gelehrt?', *BKW*, 1919, vol. 56, p. 1082.

34 Carl Fahrig, 'Grippe', in Otto von Schjerning (ed.), *Handbuch der Ärztlichen Erfahrungen im Weltkriege 1914/1918*, vol. 8: *Pathologische Anatomie*, ed. by Ludwig Aschoff, Leipzig, J.A. Barth, 1921, p. 145.

35 For example, *Grossh. Bezirksamt*, No. 41417, 15 October 1918.

36 A. Wolff-Eisner, 'Die Behandlung der Grippe mit Adrenalininhalationen', *MMW*, 1919, vol. 66, p. 15.

37 Heinrich Prell, 'Zur Ätiologie der pandemischen Grippe', *Zeitschrift für Hygiene und Infektionskrankheiten*, 1920, vol. 90, p. 128.

38 About A.W. Fischer see: G. Mollowitz, 'Albert Wilhelm Fischer 1892–1969', *DMW*, 1970, vol. 95, pp. 188f.; Heinz Grießmann, 'In memoriam Prof. Dr. med. h.c. Albert Wilhelm Fischer', *Zentralblatt für Chirurgie*, 1970, vol. 95, p. 489.

39 A.W. Fischer, 'Warum sterben an der Grippemischinfektion gerade die kräftigsten Individuen?', *MMW*, 1918, vol. 65, p. 1284.

40 A. Grabisch, 'Zur Frage, warum an der Grippeinfektion gerade die kräftigsten Individuen sterben', *MMW*, 1919, vol. 65, pp. 232f.

41 See for instance: E.J. Schmitz, 'Grippe und Gravidität', *DMW*, 1919, vol. 45, pp. 1328f.; Kurt Fränkel, 'Grippe und Gravidität', *MMW*, 1919, vol. 66, p. 614.

42 Ton van Helvoort, 'A bacteriological paradigm in influenza research in the first half of the twentieth century', *History and Philosophy of the Life Sciences*, 1993, vol. 15, pp. 3–21.

43 Karlheinz Lüdtke has recently described the complicated story of the early research in the field which nowadays we call virology: *Zur Geschichte der frühen Virusforschung*, Max Planck Institute for the History of Science, Berlin, 1999. Lüdtke does not talk about influenza in detail in his paper.

44 K. von Angerer, 'Ein filtrierbarer Erreger der Grippe', *MMW*, 1918, vol. 65, p. 1280.

45 See, for example, *MMW*, 1918, vol. 65, p. 1228. See also: H. Selter, 'Zur Aetiologie der Influenza', *DMW*, 1918, vol. 44, pp. 932f.

46 Heinrich Prell, 'Der Erreger der Influenza', *MMW*, 1918, vol. 65, pp. 1398f. Cf. Heinrich Prell, 'Zur Ätiologie der pandemischen Grippe', *Zeitschrift für Hygiene und Infektionskrankheiten*, 1920, vol. 90, pp. 135–40.

47 Hermann Sahli, 'Ueber die Influenza', *Correspondenzblatt für Schweizer Aerzte*, 1919, vol. 69, pp. 1–18.

48 For example Ferdinand Hueppe, 'Der bakteriologische Charakter der "Spanischen Krankheit"', *DMW*, 1918, vol. 44, p. 887; Peter Hanssen, 'Geschichte der "Spanischen Krankheit" in Schleswig-Holstein', *DMW*, 1918, vol. 44, p. 1030; F. Meyer, 'Die Behandlung der Grippepneumonie', *DMW*, 1919, vol. 45, p. 173.

49 For example, a sneering comment on the 'vornehmste Krankheit' ('noblest disease'), taken from 'Oeuvre', was published in *Badische Landeszeitung*, 1 July 1918. Cf. Wolfgang Eckart, '"Die wachsende Nervosität unserer Zeit". Medizin und Kultur um 1900 am Beispiel einer Modekrankheit', *Kultur und Kulturwissenschaften um 1900*, vol. 2, ed. by G. Hübinger *et al.*, Stuttgart, Steiner, 1997, pp. 207–26.

50 See also the publication on the latest epidemics of 'imaginary disease': Elaine Showalter, *Hystories. Hysterical Epidemics and Modern Media*, New York, Columbia University Press, 1997.

51 W. Hellpach, 'Die Nervengrippe', *Badische Landeszeitung*, 18 January 1919.

52 For instance: H. Siegmund, 'Zur pathologischen Anatomie der herrschenden Encephalitis epidemica', *BKW*, 1920, vol. 57, pp. 509–11.

53 C. von Economo, 'Ein Fall von chronischer schubweise verlaufender Encephalitis lethargica', *MMW*, 1919, vol. 66, pp. 1311–13.

54 *DMW*, 1918, vol. 44, p. 1271.

55 W. Alwens, 'Zur Therapie der Grippepneumonie', *DMW*, 1919, vol. 45, p. 626.

56 See *DMW*, 1918, vol. 44, p. 1446; *DMW*, 1919, vol. 45, pp. 156f.; *DMW*, 1920, vol. 46, p. 363; *MMW*, 1919, vol. 66, p. 914; *BKW*, 1920, vol. 57, pp. 329f.

57 For example H. Hohlweg, 'Zur Behandlung von Grippekranken mit Rekonvaleszentenserum', *MMW*, 1918, vol. 65, p. 1247.

58 E. Riese, 'Behandlung der bösartigen Grippe', *BKW*, 1918, vol. 55, pp. 1044f.

59 For a short summary see Martin Hahn, *Influenza, Genickstarre, Tetanus, Weilsche Krankheit*, in Franz Bumm (ed.), *Deutschlands Gesundheitsverhältnisse unter dem Einfluss des Weltkrieges*, half-volume 1, Stuttgart *et al.*, Deutsche Verlags-Anstalt, 1928, pp. 342f.

60 *Pforzheimer Anzeiger*, 28 October 1918.

61 *MMW*, 1919, vol. 66, p. 265.

62 *Freiburger Zeitung*, 22 October 1918.

63 A recommendation voiced by a Dr Joseph Häusle from Feldkirch in Austria

was published by several papers in Baden, e.g. *Mannheimer Generalanzeiger*, 17 October 1918.

64 Gustav Ramp (ed.), *Pforzheim im Weltkrieg – seine Söhne und Helden*, Pforzheim (Donatus Weber, 1914–20), p. 445.

65 Ignaz Zadek, 'Nil nocere! Zur Grippebehandlung', *BKW*, 1919, vol. 56, pp. 277–9.

66 'Zur Verhütung und Behandlung der Grippe – Eine Umfrage bei den deutschen Klinikern', *DMW*, 1920, vol. 46, pp. 326f.

67 Klaus-Dieter Thomann, *Alfons Fischer (1873–1936) und die Badische Gesellschaft für soziale Hygiene*, Cologne, Pahl-Rugenstein, 1980, p. 27; Alfons Fischer, *Gesundheitspolitik und Gesundheitsgesetzgebung*, Berlin, Leipzig, Sammlung Göschen, 1914, p. 34; Alfons Fischer, in Deutscher Verein für öffentliche Gesundheitspflege, *Bericht über die 40. Versammlung des Vereins in Weimar am 27. und 28. Oktober 1919*, Braunschweig, Vieweg & Sohn, 1921, p. 12.

68 Daniel S. Nadav, *Julius Moses (1868–1942) und die Politik der Sozialhygiene in Deutschland*, translated by Leo Koppel, Gerlingen, Bleicher, 1985.

69 Ernst Kürz, 'Zur Reform des badischen Gesundheitswesens', *Ärztliche Mitteilungen aus und für Baden*, 1920, vol. 74, pp. 102–5.

70 Alfred W. Crosby, *Epidemic and Peace, 1918*, Westport and London, Greenwood Press, 1976, ch. 15.

71 Walter Benjamin, 'Über den Begriff der Geschichte' (1940), point 9, in W. Benjamin, *Gesammelte Schriften*, vol. I.2, edited by R. Tiedemann and H. Schweppenhäuser, Frankfurt am Main, Suhrkamp, 1980, p. 697.

4 'You can't do anything for influenza'

1 Mabel Chilson, reporting on Fort Des Moines, Army School of Nursing, *Annual, 1921*, p. 177 (From the History of Nursing Archives General Collection, Department of Special Collections, Boston University).

2 Ibid.

3 A. Crosby, Jr., *Epidemic and Peace, 1918*, Westport, Connecticut, Greenwood Press, 1976, pp. 50–1, 71, 97, 108.

4 G. Kolata, *Flu: The Story of the Great Influenza Pandemic of 1918 and the Search for the Virus That Caused It*, New York, Farrar, Straus and Giroux, 1999, pp. 4, 6–8.

5 Ibid., pp. 12, 14, 18–21, 61.

6 Crosby, *Epidemic and Peace, 1918*, pp. 206–7.

7 Kolata, *Flu*, p. 12; L. Iezzoni, *Influenza 1918: The Worst Epidemic in American History*, New York, TV Books, 1999, p. 16.

8 Kolata, *Flu*, p. 4; Iezzoni, *Influenza 1918*, pp. 16, 49–51.

9 National Library of Medicine of the United States, History of Medicine Division, Oral memoir of Stanhope Bayne-Jones.

10 P. Starr, *The Social Transformation of American Medicine: The rise of a sovereign profession and the making of a vast industry*, New York, Basic Books, 1982, pp. 32–3, 39.

11 Ibid., pp. 39–40.

12 J. Cassedy, *Medicine in America: A Short History*, Baltimore, Johns Hopkins University Press, 1991, p. 30.

13 Ibid., pp. 33–9.

14 T.N. Bonner, *To the Ends of the Earth: Women's Search for Education in Medicine*, Cambridge, Massachusetts, Harvard University Press, 1992, pp. 15–16.

15 Cassedy, *Medicine in America*, pp. 87, 94, 96–7, 99–101; Starr, *The Social Transformation of American Medicine*, ch. 3, and pp. 117–24; M.R. Walsh, *Doctors Wanted – No Women Need Apply: Sexual Barriers in the Medical Profession, 1835–1975*, New Haven, Yale University Press, 1977, ch 6, and pp. 241–2; R.M.

Morantz-Sanchez, *Sympathy and Science: Women Physicians in American Medicine*, New York, Oxford University Press, 1985, ch. 9; Bonner, *To the Ends of the Earth*, pp. 139–56.

16 J.H. Warner, *The Therapeutic Perspective: Medical Practice, Knowledge, and Identity in America, 1820–1885*, Princeton, Princeton University Press, 1997, p. 15.

17 S.B. Lewenson, *Taking Charge: Nursing, Suffrage, and Feminism in America, 1873–1920*, New York, Garland Publishing, 1993, pp. xiii-xiv, chapters 1 and 2; Cassedy, *Medicine in America*, p. 75.

18 B. Melosh, '*The Physician's Hand': Work, Culture and Conflict in American Nursing*, Philadelphia, Temple University Press, 1982, p. 3.

19 Walsh, *Doctors Wanted*, p. 246.

20 *Daily Californian*, 15 October 1918, p. 2, 'The Spanish Influenza'; *Camp Dodger* (Des Moines, Iowa), 11 October 1918, p. 4, 'New Discovery Put[s] Check On Pneumonia'.

21 *Daily Californian*, 23 January 1919, p. 2, 'A Descending Curve'; *Wallace Press-Times* (Wallace, Idaho), 11 October 1918, p. 1, 'Wallace Under Influenza Ban – Only One Additional Case Reported'. See also Crosby, *Epidemic and Peace, 1918*, p. 74; Starr, *The Social Transformation of American Medicine*, pp. 134–42.

22 Iezzoni, *Influenza 1918*, pp. 89, 91; Columbia University Oral History Collection, Reminiscences of Dr William F. Draper (1976); William M. Donald, MD, 'Spanish Influenza', *Medical Review of Reviews*, 1919, vol. 25, p. 79; H.N. Street, MD, 'Personal Experience in Epidemic Influenza', *The Journal of the Arkansas Medical Society*, 1919, vol. 16, p. 100; I.P. Lyon, C.F. Tenney and L. Szerlip, 'Some Clinical Observations on the Influenza Epidemic at Camp Upton', *Journal of the American Medical Association*, 1919, vol. 72, p. 1726; S.J. McGraw, MD, 'Spanish Influenza', *The Journal of the Arkansas Medical Society*, 1919, vol. 16, p. 102.

23 National Archives of the United States of America [hereafter National Archives], Record Group 90, Box 146, File 1622, Letter of Surgeon General Rupert Blue to Senator Charles E. Townsend, 15 September 1919; W.H. Park, MD, 'Bacteriology of Recent Pandemic of Influenza and Complicating Infections', *Journal of the American Medical Association*, 1919, vol. 73, p. 321; 'Administrative Measures Against Influenza', *Journal of the American Medical Association*, 1919, vol. 73, p. 1547. For an account of the hunt for the virus, see Kolata, *Flu*, chs 3–10.

24 F.L. Gram, MD, 'The Influenza Epidemic and Its After-Effects in the City of Buffalo: A Detailed Survey', *Journal of the American Medical Association*, 1919, vol. 73, p. 887.

25 R.R. Elliott, 'The Influenza Epidemic of 1918–1919', *Halcyon*, 1992, vol. 14, p. 255.

26 Ibid.

27 Editorial in the *Journal of the American Medical Association*, 9 November 1918, quoted in *Literary Digest*, 1918, vol. 59, p. 25, 'Vaccination Against Influenza'.

28 Elliott, 'The Influenza Epidemic of 1918–1919', p. 255; National Archives, Record Group 90, File 1622, Letter of Surgeon General Rupert Blue to Dr W.E. Buck, Chief of Health Department, Pueblo, Colorado, 6 September 1919; 'Influenza Relative to a Possible Recurrence of the Epidemic During the Fall or Winter', *Public Health Reports*, 1919, vol. 34, p. 2105.

29 G.M. Price, MD, 'Influenza – Destroyer and Teacher', *The Survey*, 1918, vol. 41, p. 367.

30 Columbia University Oral History Collection, The Reminiscences of Dana W. Atchley (1964), p. 95.

31 Columbia University Oral History Collection, The Reminiscences of Benjamin Earle Washburn, MD (1971), pp. 11, 13–14.

32 Price, 'Influenza – Destroyer and Teacher', p. 368.
33 'Influenza Therapeutics in History', *New York Medical Journal*, 1918, vol. 108, pp. 778–9.
34 Price, 'Influenza – Destroyer and Teacher', p. 368.
35 Cassedy, *Medicine in America*, p. 46.
36 Major G.A. Soper, 'The Lessons of the Pandemic', *Science*, 1919, vol. 49, p. 501; H.M. Biggs, MD, 'The Recent Epidemic of Influenza', *American Review of Reviews*, 1919, vol. 59, pp. 69–70.
37 National Archives, Record Group 90, Box 145, File 1622, Letter of Carter Glass to Honorable Thetus W. Sims, House of Representatives, 1 March 1919; Price, 'Influenza – Destroyer and Teacher', p. 368.
38 Biggs, 'The Recent Epidemic of Influenza', p. 70.
39 W.L. Moss, 'Epidemiological Activities in Base Section No. 2', in *The History of U.S. Army Base Hospital No. 6 and Its Part in the American Expeditionary Forces 1917–1918*, Boston, Massachusetts General Hospital, 1924, p. 108 (From the History of Nursing Archives General Collection, Department of Special Collections, Boston University).
40 Colonel V.C. Vaughan, quoted in Price, 'Influenza – Destroyer and Teacher', p. 367.
41 V.C. Vaughan, *A Doctor's Memories*, New York, Bobbs-Merrill Co., 1926, pp. 383–4.
42 J.H. Means, 'Experiences and Opinions of a Full-Time Medical Teacher', in D. Igler (ed.), *A Dozen Doctors: Autobiographical Sketches*, Chicago, University of Chicago Press, 1963, p. 188; Lyon, Tenney and Szerlip, 'Some Clinical Observations on the Influenza Epidemic at Camp Upton', p. 1726.
43 A.C. Jamme, 'Conclusions Based on a Series of Inspections of Camp Hospitals in the United States', *Proceedings of the Twenty-fifth Annual Convention of the National League of Nursing Education Held at Chicago, Illinois, June 24 to June 28, 1919*, Baltimore, Williams and Wilkins Co., 1919, p. 188 (From the History of Nursing Archives General Collection, Department of Special Collections, Boston University).
44 Ibid., pp. 188–9.
45 E.H. Dyke, R.N., 'Influenza Experiences and What They Taught', *Public Health Nurse*, 1919, vol. 11, p. 891.
46 National Archives, Record Group 200, Box 521, File 494.2 – Div. Bulletins, Entry 27120D, 'How the Red Cross Met the Influenza Epidemic', Illustrated Supplement, *Potomac Division Bulletin*, 1918, vol. 1.
47 L.D. Wald, 'Influenza: When the City is a Great Field Hospital', *The Survey*, 1920, vol. 43, p. 579.
48 C.D. Noyes, Acting Director, Department of Nursing, American Red Cross, Washington, DC, 'The Red Cross Nursing Service At Home and Abroad', *Proceedings of the Twenty-fifth Annual Convention of the National League of Nursing Education*, p. 142 (From the History of Nursing Archives General Collection, Department of Special Collections, Boston University).
49 E.M. Lawler, 'How the Civil Hospitals and Nursing Schools Met the War Situation', *Proceedings of the Twenty-fifth Annual Convention of the National League of Nursing Education*, p. 161 (From the History of Nursing Archives General Collection, Department of Special Collections, Boston University).
50 Volunteer nurse quoted in B. Luckingham, *Epidemic in the Southwest, 1918–1919*, El Paso, Texas Western Press, 1984, p. 10.
51 National Archives, Record Group 200, Box 688, File 803.8 – Epidemics, Influenza – Reports and Statistics – Southern Division, 'Red Cross Care of Influenza Epidemic throughout Southern Division'.
52 G.W. Peabody, 'Report on Behalf of the Board of Managers', in *33rd Annual*

Report, The Instructive District Nursing Association, Boston, Year Ending December 31, 1918 (From the Visiting Nurses Association of Boston Collection, Department of Special Collections, Boston University).

53 See for example 'Hospital X-Ray', *Camp Jackson Click* (South Carolina), 16 November 1918, p. 4.

54 *Camp Sherman News* (Ohio), 9 October 1918, p. 1, 'Death Grip of Epidemic Broken, Following Toll of 483 Dead and 1438 Serious'; G.M. Price, MD, 'Mobilizing Social Forces Against Influenza', *The Survey*, 1918, vol. 41, p. 96; National Archives, Record Group 90, Box 144, File 1622, Letter of M.G. Parsons to the Surgeon General, 22 October 1918; Letter of Peter Reinberg, quoted in G.F. Schryver, *A History of the Illinois Training School for Nurses, 1880–1929*, Chicago, Illinois Training School for Nurses, 1930, pp. 108–9 (From the History of Nursing Archives General Collection, Department of Special Collections, Boston University); National Archives, Record Group 90, Box 146, File 1622, Letter of Assistant Attorney General Thomas Parran, Jr. to the Surgeon General, 19 October 1918, 'On the influenza control measures undertaken at this station since October 1, 1918'; *Camp Crane News* (Pennsylvania), 2 November 1918, p. 1, 'Wonderful Work Accomplished By Camp Crane Officers In Fight Against "Flu" In Hard Coal Regions of PA'.

55 Annual Report for Gardiner General Hospital, quoted in G.W. Kirkpatrick, 'Influenza 1918: A Maine Perspective', *Maine Historical Society Quarterly*, 1986, vol. 25, p. 170; National Archives, Record Group 90, Box 146, File 1622, Letter of Assistant Surgeon General Thomas Parran, Jr. to the Surgeon General, 19 October 1918, 'On the influenza control measures undertaken at this station since October 1, 1918'.

56 *Camp Crane News*, 2 November 1918, p. 1, 'Wonderful Work Accomplished By Camp Crane Officers In Fight Against "Flu" In Hard Coal Regions of PA'.

57 *Wallace Press-Times*, 6 November 1918, p. 2, 'Wear Your Mask'.

58 *Camp Jackson Click*, 16 November 1918, p. 4, 'Hospital X-Ray'.

59 *Literary Digest*, 1919, vol. 60, p. 62, 'War – Reports from the Influenza Front'.

60 National Archives, Record Group 200, Box 521, File 494.2 – Division Bulletins, Entry 27130D, 'The Epidemic Over', *Red Cross Clippings* (5 December 1918), p. 7. That this image of nurses as selfless was a powerful one is perhaps most clearly suggested by its persistence in the secondary literature of the epidemic. See for instance K.S. Allen, 'Plague on the Homefront: Arkansas and the Great Influenza Epidemic of 1918', *Arkansas Historical Quarterly*, 1988, vol. 47, p. 333; J.A. Blythe, 'The Great Flu Epidemic of 1918', *Panhandle – Plains Historical Review*, 1993, vol. 66, p. 13.

61 *Daily Californian*, 28 October 1918, p. 2, 'Doing Your Duty'; S.E. Parsons, 'The Nurses' Point of View', *The History of U.S. Army Base Hospital No. 6 and Its Part in the American Expeditionary Forces, 1917–1918*, Boston, Massachusetts General, 1924 (From the History of Nursing Archives General Collection, Department of Special Collections, Boston University); H. Lee, 'Night in the Hospital', *The Survey*, 1918, vol. 41, p. 214.

62 *Over-the-Top* (Camp Taylor, Kentucky), 22 January 1919, p. 2, '157 Nurses Give Healing and Spirit of Cheer'.

63 *New York Times*, 17 October 1918, p. 14, 'Science Has Failed to Guard Us'.

64 Ibid.

65 *New York Times*, 24 October 1918, p. 12, 'Prevention Seemingly Achieved'.

66 *Pittsburgh Leader*, quoted in K.A. White, 'Pittsburgh in the Great Epidemic of 1918', *The Western Pennsylvania Historical Magazine*, 1985, vol. 68, p. 225; *Wallace Miner*, 2 January 1919, p. 2, Editorial, 'Quarantine Does Not Prevent Spread of Flu'. See also untitled editorial, *Rathdrum Tribune* (Rathdrum, Idaho), 3 January 1919, p. 2.

67 For a basic introduction to the ideas of Christian Science, see J. Cassedy, *Medicine in America*, pp. 99–100.

68 US Army Military History Institute, Carlisle Barracks, World War One Research Project – Army Service Experiences Questionnaire Collection, Letter of V.W. Jones to his mother, 28 October 1918. For another example, see R. Collier, *The Plague of the Spanish Lady: The Influenza Pandemic of 1918–1919*, New York, Atheneum, 1974, p. 199.

69 Ibid.; L. Iezzoni, *Influenza 1918*, pp. 159–60.

70 National Archives, Letter of Miss Mary Theresia Fisher, Mascoutah, St Clair County, Illinois to Public Health Service, Washington, DC, 27 January 1920.

71 Collier, *The Plague of the Spanish Lady*, pp. 162–3.

72 Kirkpatrick, 'Influenza 1918', pp. 170–1; R.S. McPherson, 'Influenza Epidemic of 1918: A Cultural Response', *Utah Historical Quarterly*, 1990, vol. 58, p. 190; W.J. Doherty, 'A West Virginia County's Experience with the 1918 Influenza Epidemic', *West Virginia History*, 1977, vol. 38, p. 140; Elliott, 'Influenza Epidemic of 1918–1919', pp. 255–6. Before the epidemic herbal remedies may have suffered a declining popularity, and certainly did so among medical regulars – see Cassedy, *Medicine in America*, pp. 79–80.

73 National Archives, Record Group 393, Box 22, Decimal 710 – Influenza, Records of U.S. Army Continental Commands, 1821–1920, Camp Custer, Michigan, Correspondence 1918–1920, Letter from 'A lover of our Boys' to Head Surgeon, Camp Custer, 14 October 1918.

74 National Archives, Record Group 112, Box 394, Decimal 710, Entry 29 (Influenza, September 1918), Mrs. Ann Olds Woodson, 29 September 1918, 'Simple Influenza Remedy'.

75 National Archives, Record Group 112, Box 394, Decimal 710, Entry 29 (Influenza, September 1918), Letter of J.J.C. Elliott, Superintendent of Methodist Hospitle [sic] to Woodrow Wilson, 28 September 1918.

76 National Archives, Record Group 112, Box 394, Decimal 710, Entry 29 (Influenza, September 1918), Letter from Amarillo, Texas to Secretary Lane, 28 September 1918; National Archives, Record Group 112, Box 394, Decimal 710, Entry 29 (Influenza, September 1918), Letter of Mr Wm. B. Scott to Surgeon General, US Army, 27 September 1918; McPherson, 'Influenza Epidemic of 1918', p. 190; Doherty, 'A West Virginia County's Experience with the 1918 Influenza Epidemic', p. 140.

77 McPherson, 'Influenza Epidemic of 1918', p. 188; Kirkpatrick, 'Influenza 1918', p. 172; National Archives, Record Group 90, Box 146, File 1622, Ad for Allen Remedy Co.

78 National Archives, Record Group 112, Box 394, Decimal 710, Entry 29 (Influenza, September 1918), Letter of Julius C. Leve to Secretary of War Baker, 28 September 1918. See also Elliott, 'Influenza Epidemic of 1918–1919', p. 255; P.C. Ensley, 'Indiana and the Influenza Pandemic of 1918', *Indiana Medical History Quarterly*, 1983, vol. 9, p. 12.

79 'Sure Cures for Influenza', *Public Health Reports*, 1918, vol. 33, pp. 1931–1933; Kirkpatrick, 'Influenza 1918', p. 173.

80 Crosby, *Epidemic and Peace, 1918*, pp. 312–13.

81 As Gina Kolata notes, the eminent historian of the epidemic, Alfred Crosby, refers to the event as 'America's forgotten pandemic' (Kolata, *Flu*, p. 53). See A. Crosby, *America's Forgotten Pandemic: The Influenza of 1918*, New York, Cambridge University Press, 1989, pp. 314–25.

82 Crosby, *America's Forgotten Pandemic*, pp. 319–23; Kolata, *Flu*, pp. 53–4.

83 This idea may complement Crosby's suggestion that, 'On the level of organisations and institutions – the level of collectivities – the Spanish flu had little impact' (Crosby, *America's Forgotten Pandemic*, p. 323).

5 Japan and New Zealand in the 1918 influenza pandemic

1 This paper is based on my book, *Black November: The 1918 Influenza Epidemic in New Zealand* (Wellington, Allen & Unwin and Historical Branch, Internal Affairs, 1988), which is fully referenced, and three articles jointly authored with my wife, Dr Edwina Palmer: 'Pandemic Influenza in Japan, 1918–19: Mortality Patterns and Official Responses', *Journal of Japanese Studies*, 1993, vol. 19, pp. 389–420; '"Divine Wind versus Devil Wind": Popular Responses to Pandemic Influenza in Japan, 1918–1919', *Japan Forum*, 1992, vol. 4, pp. 317–28; 'A Japanese Physician's Response to Pandemic Influenza: Ijiro Gomibuchi and the "Spanish Flu" in Yaita-cho, 1918–1919', *Bulletin of the History of Medicine*, 1992, vol. 66, pp. 560–77.

2 For a short history, see Keith Sinclair, *A History of New Zealand*, Harmondsworth, Pelican, 1959; revised edition, 1988. For more comprehensive and detailed treatment, see Geoffrey W. Rice (ed.), *The Oxford History of New Zealand*, Auckland, Oxford University Press, revised second edition, 1992.

3 See Janet E. Hunter, *The Emergence of Modern Japan: an introductory history since 1853*, London, Longman, 1989, and the same author's *Concise Dictionary of Modern Japanese History*, Berkeley, University of California Press, 1984. Neither mentions the 1918–19 influenza pandemic, even though it killed more Japanese than the 1923 Kanto earthquake.

4 Official sources include the following: New Zealand: *Appendices to the Journal of the House of Representatives*, 1919, H-31, Annual Report of the Department of Public Health, pp. 23–40 (by Dr R.H. Makgill); ibid., H-31A, Report of the Influenza Epidemic Commission. Japan: *Annual Report, Central Sanitary Bureau of the Home Office*, 7th year of Taisho, 1918, pp. 46–50; ibid., 8th year of Taisho, 1919, pp. 56–63; *Ryukosei Kanbo*, Tokyo, Ministry of Internal Affairs, 1922. The New Zealand death rate for European population was 5.5 per thousand; the addition of soldiers who died from flu overseas raises the rate to 5.8 per thousand. See Rice, *Black November*, p. 143.

5 See J.H.L. Cumpston, *Influenza and Maritime Quarantine in Australia*, Melbourne, Government Printer, 1919.

6 *Asahi Shinbun* (Tokyo edition), 2 November 1918, p. 5.

7 Rice, *Black November*, chapter 7, 'Origins and Diffusion: was the *Niagara* to blame?', pp. 125–40.

8 *New Zealand Gazette*, 1919, Register of Medical Practitioners.

9 *New Zealand Official Yearbook*, 1919, pp. 203–21.

10 *Japan Year Book*, 1921–2, p. 162.

11 Derek A. Dow, *Safeguarding the Public Health: A History of the New Zealand Department of Health*, Wellington, Victoria University Press, 1995, p. 89.

12 *Ryukosei Kanbo*, 1922, Part III, p. 151.

13 For references see Rice and Palmer, 'Pandemic Influenza in Japan, 1918–19', pp. 389–420.

14 Dow, *Safeguarding the Public Health*, p. 89.

15 For this and the following paragraph, see Rice, *Black November*, pp. 32–4, 98–101.

16 See Rice and Palmer, 'Pandemic Influenza in Japan, 1918–19', pp. 401–3, citing *Ryukosei Kanbo* and newspaper sources in Japanese.

17 Ibid., pp. 403–6.

18 Rice, *Black November*, pp. 32–40, 72–3, 96–8 for these paragraphs.

19 Palmer and Rice, '"Divine Wind versus Devil Wind"', pp. 317–28.

20 Rice, *Black November*, pp. 102–24.

6 Coping with the influenza pandemic

1　This paper is based on work carried out with support from the Wellcome Trust, London.
2　See David Arnold, *Colonizing the Body*, Berkeley, University of California Press, 1993; Mark Harrison, *Public Health in India: Anglo-Indian Preventive Medicine 1859–1914*, Cambridge, Cambridge University Press, 1994.
3　Government of Maharashtra Archives, Mumbai, General Department volumes [henceforth GD], Part II, 232, 1919, Preliminary Report on the Influenza Pandemic of 1918 by the Sanitary Commissioner of the Government of India [henceforth PRI], p. 1, F. Norman White, IMS, Sanitary Commissioner, Government of India.
4　Ian D. Mills, 'The 1918–1919 Influenza Pandemic – The Indian Experience', *Indian Economic and Social History Review*, 1986, vol. 23, 1, p. 2; K. David Patterson and Gerald F. Pyle, 'The Geography and Mortality of the 1918 Influenza Pandemic', *Bulletin of the History of Medicine*, 1991, vol. 65, pp. 2–41.
5　GD 232, 1919, PRI, p. 3.
6　Ibid., p. 12.
7　GD 232, 1919, Health Officer [henceforth HO] to Municipal Commissioner, No. H/14B, 25 November 1918, pp. 1–4.
8　*Times of India*, 25 June 1918.
9　Government of Maharashtra Archives, Mumbai, Report on Native Newspapers, Bombay Presidency [henceforth RN], *Bombay Chronicle*, 3 February 1919; *Times of India*, 13 September 1919. Both of these were English dailies published from Bombay.
10　GD 232, 1919, Embarkation Commandant to Chairman, Bombay Municipality, 15 July 1918.
11　Mills, 'The 1918–19 Influenza Pandemic', p. 4.
12　GD 232, 1919, HO to Municipal Commissioner, 25 November 1918, p. 9.
13　Ibid., p. 12.
14　GD 232, 1919, Final Report on the Influenza Epidemic of 1918 in the Bombay Presidency by the Sanitary Commissioner, Government of Bombay [henceforth RBP], p. 3.
15　GD 232, 1919, PRI, p. 4.
16　*Report on the Administration of Bombay Presidency, 1918–19*, Bombay, Government Central Press, 1920, p. x.
17　Government of Maharashtra Archives, Mumbai, Government of Bombay Public Health Report [henceforth PHR], 1918, p.23.
18　Ibid., p. 2; GD 232, 1919, RBP, p.3.
19　GD 232, 1919, HO to Municipal Commissioner, 25 November 1918, p. 17.
20　Mills, 'The 1918–19 Influenza Pandemic', p. 24.
21　*Bombay Executive Health Officer's Report*, Third Quarter, 1918, p. 5, as quoted in Mills, 'The 1918–19 Influenza Pandemic', p. 35.
22　GD 232, 1919, Report of R.K. Mhatre, HO, Ahmedabad, 8 January 1919. The 'low castes' mentioned are the *vaghries*, fowlers, *thakardas*, of part-Rajput descent and cultivators, *dheds*, originally weavers but who, with the establishment of textile mills, had become labourers, and *bhangis*, bamboo splitters or scavengers.
23　GD 353, 1918, Sanitary Commissioner, Bombay to Government of Bombay [henceforth GOB], 2 November 1918.
24　*Times of India*, 7 October 1918.
25　GD 353, 1918, Memorandum of Surgeon-General, 5 October 1918.
26　*Annual Report on Civil Hospitals and Dispensaries, Bombay Presidency*, 1918, Bombay, Government Central Press, 1919, p. 2.

27 RN 1918, *Bombay Chronicle*, 16 October 1918; *Young India*, 16 October 1918; *Gujarati*, 6 October and 13 October 1918; *Praja Mitra and Parsi*, 28 September 1918; *Akhbar-e Islam*, 30 September 1918. *Young India*, a weekly started by the Home Rule party of Bombay, was then edited by P.K. Telang, and was destined to win world-wide renown in the hands of Mahatma Gandhi, who took it over in 1919. *Gujarati* was an English weekly, *Praja Mitra and Parsi*, an Anglo-Gujarati daily and *Akhbar-e-Islam*, a Gujarati daily; all were published in Bombay.

28 *Times of India*, 7 October 1918.

29 *Times of India*, 13 September 1918.

30 RN 1918, *Jam-e-Jamshed*, 5 October 1918; *Sunday Chronicle*, 20 October 1918. *Jam-e-Jamshed* was an English daily catering mainly to a Parsi readership.

31 *Proceedings of the Legislative Council of the Governor of Bombay, 1918*, vol. 1, vi, pp. 929, 935. Of the Rs. 1,000,000 allotted for sanitary works, Rs. 407,000 having been expended, Rs. 300,000 was surrendered in view of the directive to curtail expenses and Rs. 200,000 re-appropriated for purposes other than sanitation. Purshotamdas Thakurdas was a nominated member of the Council from 1916–20, and often voted independently. He had worked on the Famine Fund earlier in the decade.

32 GD 353, 1918, GOB to District Magistrate, Bijapur, 13 November 1918.

33 GD 232, 1919, Moroji Morarji and Vishanji Dossa, Proprietors Kohinoor cinema, Karachi to GOB, 26 October 1918.

34 Sandra M. Tomkins, 'The Failure of Expertise: Public Health Policy in Britain during the 1918–19 Influenza Epidemic', *Social History of Medicine*, 1992, vol. 5, p. 443.

35 GD 232, 1919, PRI, p. 12.

36 Ibid., p. 13. The constitution was 70 million influenza 'bacilli', 200 million *pneumococcus*, and 350 million *streptococcus*, for the first dose, to be repeated after an interval of seven days.

37 Ibid. This comprised 30 million influenza 'bacilli', 100 million *pneumococcus*, 40 million *streptococcus*, and doubling the dose the second time.

38 Ibid., p. 14.

39 GD 232, 1919, Government of India [henceforth GOI] to GOB, No. 441, 14 July 1919.

40 GD 232, 1919, HO to Municipal Commissioner, 25 November 1918, p.18

41 The Bombay Medical Union was an organisation of Western-educated Indian doctors established in 1884. Sir Cowasji Jehangir, who commenced his career as a warehouse keeper, rose to be a prominent industrialist and was noted for his philanthropy.

42 GD 232, 1919, HO to Municipal Commissioner, 25 November 1918, pp. 18–19. The pneumonia jacket, devised as a substitute for woollen clothing for the poor, was made of two pieces of cloth with an inch-thick layer of cotton between and sown like a quilt. It was fastened with tags sown on the side. Marathi and Gujarati were the languages most widely spoken in Bombay Presidency.

43 *Bombay Chronicle*, 19 November 1918.

44 GD 232, 1919, *Report of the Relief Work of the Hindu Medical Association*.

45 'Report of the Influenza Epidemic', *The Social Service Quarterly*, 1918, vol. iv, pp. 148–54. Donations were received from Wadia charities, Tata Sons & Co., Richardson & Cruddas, the Cotton Brokers Association, and the Cotton Merchants and Mukadams Association. A young co-worker, B.R. Bhende, described Joshi's tremendous drive in collecting funds and in organising relief in areas where it was most needed.

46 *Times of India*, 8 October 1918. Tragically, one of the young volunteers, Krishna Natarajan, succumbed to influenza.

47 The Gujarati-speaking Lohanas, the Bhatias and the Marwaris from Rajasthan were the trading and commercial castes, the Marathi-speaking Gaud Saraswat Brahmins and the Pathare Prabhus were traditionally the literate castes, while the Bhandaris, traditionally associated with the liquor industry, had taken to education. While all of these were Hindus, the Bohras and the Khojas, also commercial communities, were Islamic.

48 GD 232, 1919, pp. 34–8. There were 50 Parsi, 18 Gujarati Hindu, 19 Hindu, 15 Jewish and 26 other volunteers in the Overseas Cosmopolitan Division. This ambulance service had been founded in 1904.

49 GD 232, 1919, HO to Municipal Commissioner, 25 November 1918, p. 20.

50 Ibid., p.21. The mills were the Sir Shapurji Broacha, Century, Textile, Pearl and Fazulbhoy mills. A *vaid* is a practitioner of the *ayurvedic* system of medicine.

51 *Report on the Administration of the Bombay Presidency, 1918–1919*, Bombay, Government Central Press, 1920, p. xi.

52 RN, 1918, *Hindusthan*, 9 October 1918. This paper was an Anglo–Gujarati weekly from Bombay.

53 GD 232, 1919, HO to Municipal Commissioner, 25 November 1918, p. 23.

54 GD 232, 1919, President, Poona Municipality to Collector, 29 September 1918.

55 *Times of India*, 15 October 1918.

56 GD 232, 1919, Municipal Commissioner, Surat to Collector, 11 December 1918.

57 GD 232, 1919, A.E.L. Emmanuel Collector to Commissioner, Northern Division, 14 January 1919.

58 Ibid. Report by Dr E.D. Shroff, HO, Karachi, 2 September 1918. The other doctors were Drs Ahmed, Billimoria, Mirchandani, K.B. Patil, Lul, Bhatnakar, Lakoomal, Mahomedali, Faiz Mohammed, Tarachand, Ramchand, Balchand and Vishnoo.

59 PHR, 1918, p. 26.

60 'Gujarat Sabha Influenza Relief Committee', *The Social Service Quarterly*, 1918, vol. iv, p. 156.

61 *Praja Bandhu*, 20 October 1918. This weekly, which appeared every Sunday, had a circulation of 1,000 and was edited by Jagjivandas S. Trivedi.

62 *Praja Bandhu*, 13 October 1918 to 1 December 1918.

63 *Praja Bandhu*, 13 October 1918.

64 Mahadev Desai, *Day to Day with Gandhi*, vol. 1, Varanasi, Sarva Seva Sangh, 1968, p. 259.

65 *British Medical Journal*, 5 April 1919, p. 417.

66 *Social Service Quarterly*, 1918, vol. iv, pp. 126–7.

67 GD 232, 1919, Surgeon-General, Col. W.E. Jennings to GOB, 29 January 1919.

68 GD 232, 1919, PRI, p. 12.

69 Ibid.

70 *Indian Medical Gazette*, December 1918, p. 446. This journal was the mouthpiece of the Indian Medical Service, manned mainly by the British.

71 GD 232, 1919, HO to Municipal Commissioner, 25 November 1918, p. 22.

72 *Indian Medical Gazette*, February 1919, p. 68.

73 RN, *Gujarati*, 13 October 1918.

74 GD 232, 1919, *Report of the Relief Work of the Hindu Medical Association*.

75 GD 353, 1918, Opinions of Doctors Dadachanji, Surveyor and Abraham S. Erulkar, January 1919.

76 GD 232, 1919, GOI to GOB, 14 July 1919.

77 Ibid., GOI to GOB, 10 September 1919.

78 GD 353, 1918, Sanitary Commissioner, Bombay to GOB, 2 November 1918.

79 RN, *Deccan Ryot*, 31 October 1918.

80 *Kesari*, 22 October 1918. This Marathi weekly from Pune had been in the fore-
front of the agitation against the interventionist measures employed by the
British during the plague epidemic of 1896 in Bombay Presidency. The *hakims*
were practitioners of the *Unani* system of medicine. Indian medicine pre-
scribes powdered long pepper, mixed with ginger juice and honey and a light
diet. To prevent congestion and bronchitis, *tulasi (osimum sanctum)* and *turmeric
(curcuma longa)* with milk were recommended.
81 RN, *Praja Mitra and Parsi*, 1, 4 and 5 October 1918. The Medical Registration
Act was passed in 1912.
82 RN, *Praja Mitra and Parsi*, 25 October 1918.
83 RBP, p. 5.
84 RN, *Gujarati*, 13 October 1918.
85 *Young India*, 23 April 1919. The Jallianwala Bagh incident of 13 April 1919 is
an important event in the story of India's freedom struggle. General Reginald
Dyer ordered firing on an unarmed crowd which had gathered for a public
meeting at the Jallianwala Bagh, Amritsar, disobeying orders prohibiting
public assemblies. The Government estimate was 379 dead, while other estimates were higher. This incident led to the launch of a nation-wide struggle
the following year, by Gandhi.

7 Spanish influenza in China, 1918–20

1 C. Benedict, *Bubonic Plague in Nineteenth-Century China*, Stanford, Stanford UP,
1996; K.L. MacPherson, 'Cholera in China, 1820–1930: An Aspect of the Inter-
nationalization of Infectious Disease', in M. Elvin and T. Liu (eds), *Sediments of
Time: Environment and Society in Chinese History*, Cambridge, Cambridge University Press, 1998; W. Iijima, *Pesuto to Kindai Chuugoku (Plague and Modern China)*,
Tokyo, Kembun Shuppan, 2000.
2 K. Yip, *Health and National Reconstruction in Nationalist China*, Ann Arbor, Michigan, Association for Asian Studies, 1995; Iijima, *Plague and Modern China*.
3 K.D. Patterson, *Pandemic Influenza, 1700–1900*, Totowa, Rowman & Littlefield,
1986; K.D. Patterson and G.F. Pyle, 'The 1918 influenza pandemic', *Bulletin of
History of Medicine*, No. 65, 1991. In the latter study, they pointed out the necessity to research the basic situation in China from the local record (p. 5).
4 On the value of the CMC reports, see T. Hamashita, *Kindaichuugoku keiza-
ishikenkyu (Economic History of Modern China)*, Tokyo, Kyukoshoin, 1989.
5 On Japan see above, Chapter 5.
6 E.O. Jordan, *Epidemic Influenza – A survey*, Chicago, American Medical Association, 1927, p. 75.
7 *Shen-pao*, 19 January 1919, p. 10. This was the Chinese language newspaper
with the largest circulation, printed in Shanghai.
8 The *North-China Herald (NCH)*, 22 February, 1919, p. 448.
9 Patterson and Pyle, 'The 1918 influenza pandemic', p. 8.
10 Tangshan and Shanhaikwan were not treaty ports. The report on Chinwangtao
had information on the occurrence of Spanish influenza in those areas.
11 *The China Year Book 1919–20*, London, 1921, Routledge, p. 490.
12 CMC, *Decennial Report of Hankow*, 1912–1921, p. 327.
13 *NCH*, 2 November 1918, p. 267.
14 *NCH*, 28 December 1918, p. 785.
15 *NCH*, 23 November 1918, p. 460.
16 *NCH*, 23 November 1918, p. 455.
17 *NCH*, 2 November 1918, p. 275.
18 *NCH*, 23 November 1918, p. 459.
19 *NCH*, 16 November 1918, p. 399.

20 Shanghai Municipal Council, *Health Department Annual Report 1921*, Kelly and Walsh, Shanghai, 1922, p. 4.

21 *NCH*, 22 February 1919, p. 448.

22 *NCH*, 15 March 1919, p. 704.

23 *Shen-pao*, 10 March 1919, p. 10.

24 C. Wong and L. Wu, *History of Chinese Medicine*, National Quarantine Office, Shanghai, 1936.

25 For epidemiological transition and health conditions in Hong Kong before the Second World War, see D.R. Phillips, *The Epidemiological Transition in Hong Kong*, Centre of Asian Studies of Hong Kong University, Hong Kong, 1988, ch. 2.

26 Hong Kong Government, *Hong Kong Administrative Report*, 1918, 1919, 1920.

27 Taiwansoutokufu (Japanese colonial government in Taiwan), *Taiwanjinno seimeihyou (The Mortality of Taiwanese)*, Taipei, 1936, p. 2. See C.H. Chan and W.T. Liu, 'The evolution of influenza A/H1N1 in Taiwan', unpublished paper presented at 1998 Cape Town conference on 'The Spanish Flu 1918–1998: Reflections on the influenza pandemic of 1918 after 80 years', p. 2.

28 On malaria and Japanese colonial rule in Taiwan, see Iijima, *Plague and Modern China*, ch. 3.

29 Robert Perrins, 'Disease, doctors and development: Japanese colonial medicine in Southern Manchuria, 1905–1928', unpublished paper presented to the 74th Annual Meeting of the American Association for the History of Medicine, Charleston, SC, 21 April 2001.

30 E. Palmer and G. Rice, 'A Japanese Physician's Response to Pandemic Influenza: Jiro Gomibuchi and the "Spanish Flu" in Yaita-cho, 1918–1919', *Bulletin of History of Medicine*, No. 66, 1992.

31 Nihon koushueisei kyoukai (The Public Health Association in Japan), *Isei hyakunenshi (The development of public health in Japan for one hundred years)*, Tokyo, Gyousei, 1967, pp. 711–20.

32 Patterson and Pyle, 'The 1918 influenza pandemic', p. 18.

8 Flu downunder

1 The exact number who died in the epidemic is uncertain. The deaths section of the 1920 *Official Year Book of the Commonwealth of Australia* (pp. 190–3) put the national toll at 11,552, with a figure for New South Wales of 5,783. Later in the same volume, in a special report on the epidemic (pp. 1128–32), the national total was stated as 11,989 and the New South Wales figure as 5,980. Official New South Wales Government tabulations in the *New South Wales Statistical Register, 1919–20* (Table 108, p. 134), however, put the State's deaths at 6,387.

2 The *New South Wales Statistical Register, 1919–20*, Table 108, p. 134 gives the metropolis' toll as 3,484 (including 26 from Islands and Shipping and 70 Resident outside Metropolis). A closely approximating figure, 3,376 (excluding Islands and Shipping and Resident outside Metropolis), was published by the Medical Officer of Health in *Metropolitan Combined Sanitary Districts: Report of the Medical Officer of Health for the Year 1919*, Sydney, Government Printer, 1920, Table 16, p. 61. A figure several hundred more than these totals, however, was given by the Government Statistician in the official report on the epidemic: 'Report of the Director-General of Public Health to the Honourable Minister of Public Health on the Influenza Epidemic in New South Wales (Part II – Mortality Statistics)', in *Joint Volume of Papers Presented to the New South Wales Legislative Council and Legislative Assembly, First Session, 1920*, Sydney, Government Printer, 1920, p. 173. The Government Statistician's figures in the

'Report' cover the Metropolitan Combined Sanitary District, which comprised the Metropolis plus fourteen Extra Metropolitan Districts. The Statistician's figure for this area (for January–September 1919) was 3,902 influenza deaths. This total was broken down into three categories: Pneumonic Influenza (3,246 deaths), Influenza with Pneumonia (396 deaths) and Influenza (260 deaths). It seems that the Influenza with Pneumonia deaths were not included in the *Statistical Register* or Medical Officer of Health's tabulations. Deleting these deaths and those for the Extra Metropolitan Districts from the Statistician's figure gives a total for the Metropolis similar to those in the first two sources. Whatever the exact number of deaths, Sydney's death rate was certainly the highest of the country's metropolitan areas. The 1920 *Official Year Book of the Commonwealth of Australia* figures (p. 1129) gave the Metropolis a rate of 413 per 100,000 persons, followed by Melbourne with 329 per 100,000 and Brisbane 203 per 100,000. The estimated attack rate of 36–37 per cent was made by Dr W.G. Armstrong, the Deputy Director-General of Public Health, in 'Report of the Director-General of Public Health to the Honourable Minister of Public Health on the Influenza Epidemic in New South Wales', in *Joint Volume of Papers Presented to the New South Wales Legislative Council and Legislative Assembly, First Session, 1920*, Sydney, Government Printer, 1920, p. 144.

3   J.H.L. Cumpston, *Influenza and Maritime Quarantine in Australia*, Melbourne, Commonwealth of Australia Quarantine Service, Publication No. 18, 1919.
4   'Report of the Director-General of Public Health', p. 151.
5   F.M. Burnet and E. Clark, *Influenza*, Melbourne, Macmillan, 1942.
6   H. McQueen, 'Spanish 'Flu – 1919: political, medical and social aspects', *Medical Journal of Australia*, 1 (1975), pp. 565–70.
7   Government Statistician, *New South Wales Statistical Register, 1919–20*, Sydney, Government Printer, 1921.
8   Medical Officer of Health, *Metropolitan Combined Sanitary Districts: Report of the Medical Officer of Health for the Year 1900*, and *Metropolitan Combined Sanitary Report of the Medical Officer of Health for the Year 1918*, Government Printer, Sydney, 1919.
9   *Sydney Morning Herald*, 27 January 1919, p. 6.
10   *Sydney Morning Herald*, 28 January 1919, p. 7
11   *Sydney Morning Herald*, 25 June 1919, p. 12.
12   *Sydney Morning Herald*, 2 May 1919, p. 7.
13   Between 35–40 per cent of Sydney's population was estimated by the health authorities to have been inoculated. The public were cautioned not to be too optimistic about vaccination preventing them from getting the flu, but rather that its likely protective value would be in saving them from going on to develop severe complications. No data is available on the respective attack rates of inoculated and non-inoculated persons and so nothing can be said about the vaccine's effectiveness as a first-line defence preventing the disease. A post-epidemic analysis of the mortality and survival rates of patients in the metropolitan influenza hospitals by Dr Armstrong, however, indicated persons who had been inoculated prior to admission to hospital fared better than those who had not been inoculated. Inoculation did not offer complete protection against complications developing, but it seems to have lessened their severity and reduced the risk of death. Armstrong's figures show 10.7 per cent of the inoculated patients to have died, compared with 16.5 per cent of those who had not been inoculated. Patients who had had three or more inoculations had the lowest mortality (8.2 per cent). See 'Report of the Director-General of Public Health', p. 156.
14   For detailed coverage of weather and health relationships, see P. Curson, 'Human Health, Climate and Climate Change: An Australian Perspective', in

T.W. Giambelluca and A. Henderson-Sellers (eds), *Climate Change: Developing Southern Hemisphere Perspectives*, Chichester, Wiley, 1996, pp. 319–48; and S.W. Tromp, *Biometeorology*, London, Heyden, 1980.

15 'Report of the Director-General of Public Health', p. 151.

16 *Sydney Morning Herald*, 21 June 1919, p. 13.

17 *Sydney Morning Herlad*, 4 July 1919, p. 10.

18 See 'Report of the Director-General of Public Health', p. 153.

19 For example, in 1918, of the 91 non-pneumonic influenza deaths in the metropolis, 52 were of persons aged 65+, while in 1920 the figure was 49 out of 118. Proportionately, however, the 65+ age bracket comprised just over 4 per cent of the population.

20 See *New South Wales Statistical Register, 1919–20*, Table 113, pp. 138–9.

21 F.R. Van Hartesveldt (ed.) *The 1918–1919 Pandemic of Influenza: The Urban Impact in the Western World*, Lampeter, Edwin Mellen Press, 1992, p. 10.

22 See *New South Wales Statistical Register, 1919–20*, Table 113, pp. 136–7.

23 Part of the variation in these rates may reflect age-structure differences between the occupational groups. For example, the 'Labourers' group probably had more younger workers in the high risk 25–39 age range than did the 'Professional' group. The 1921 Census occupational tables, however, gave no breakdowns by age and so age standardisation of the rates was not possible.

24 In June the epidemic hit Post Office employees so badly that over 1,000 were absent from work at one stage and several postal services had to be temporarily halted. See the *Sydney Morning Herald*, 21 June 1919, p. 13.

25 For contemporary comments on Sydney's housing scene at the time of the epidemic see, for example, the *Sydney Morning Herald*, 11 April 1919, p. 6 and 16 April 1919, p. 10.

26 See *Metropolitan Combined Sanitary Districts: Report of the Medical Officer of Health for the Year 1919*, p. 54.

27 The *New South Wales Statistical Register, 1919–20*, Table 105, p. 129 lists a metropolitan influenza death as having occurred on 29 January 1919. The person, however, was not one of the early, positively diagnosed cases notified by the Board of Health to the daily press. In the eyes of the Board of Health, and as announced in the press, the first death in the epidemic was considered to be the 10 February case.

28 Persons dying from the disease in hospital were identified in the press by name and area up until 8 April. On 9 April it was announced that 'in future the names of patients who die from the effects of pneumonic influenza in the various metropolitan hospitals will not be made public by the Board of Health. The numbers only will be published.' *Sydney Morning Herald*, 9 April 1919, p. 11.

29 Death rates were age–sex standardised to control for the very marked age and sex patterning of mortality during the epidemic and differences in local area age and sex population compositions. Estimates of each area's 1919 age and sex composition were produced by applying the area's 1921 Census age and sex distribution to its mean estimated total population for 1919. The 1919 age–sex specific influenza death rates for the Metropolis as a whole were calculated as the standard and then applied to the local area age–sex population estimates to obtain expected death numbers in each area. A standardised mortality ratio above 100 indicates an area to have had mortality levels higher than the metropolitan average (i.e. worse than expected), while ratios below 100 represent lower than average (i.e. better than expected) mortality.

30 Close population contact in the work environment was obviously an important diffusive pathway, as witnessed, for example, by the very large numbers of

postal service and tramways employees going down with the flu, but no suitable areal data were available on this dimension to put into the correlation and regression models.

31 See 'Report of the Director-General of Public Health', p. 181.

32 Also, in retrospect, density might perhaps be expected to have been more closely associated with morbidity than mortality levels, on the basis that getting the flu was presumably a simpler, more direct spread process than the causal web determining who would go on to die from it. Metropolis-wide local area attack rate data, however, are not available to allow this hypothesis to be tested formally. The earlier cited *Sydney Morning Herald* report of the disease sweeping through the highly populated flats of Darlinghurst, Randwick and other inner suburbs, however, lends anecdotal support to this.

9 The overshadowed killer

1 *The Times*, 29 October 1918, p. 7.

2 Registrar-General, *Supplement to the Eighty-First Annual Report of the Registrar-General [ARRG], Report on the mortality from influenza in England and Wales during the epidemic of 1918–19*, London, HMSO, 1920.

3 Niall Philip Alan Sean Johnson, 'Aspects of the historical geography of the 1918–19 influenza pandemic in Britain', University of Cambridge, unpublished PhD thesis, 2001, pp. 214–18. This revision of the estimate of total mortality is based on a survey of the recent literature, figures provided by other researchers and recalculations of that mortality.

4 Sandra M. Tomkins, 'The Influenza Epidemic of 1918–19 in Western Samoa', *Journal of Pacific History*, 1992, vol. 27, no. 2, pp. 181–97.

5 Alfred W. Crosby, *America's Forgotten Pandemic: The influenza of 1918*, Cambridge, Cambridge University Press, 1989.

6 The RG noted in the *ARRG* for 1918 that this was 'the first time since the commencement of registration' that deaths exceeded births (p. xxvii).

7 Expressed as the equivalent annual rate.

8 Registrar-General, *Report on the mortality from influenza in England and Wales*, p. 3.

9 Registrar-General for Scotland, *Report on the Mortality from Influenza in Scotland*, p. 2.

10 *ARRG*, 1886, p. xx cited in Graham Mooney 'Professionalization in Public Health and the Measurement of Sanitary Progress in Nineteenth-Century England and Wales, *Social History of Medicine*, 1997, vol. 10, no. 1, pp. 53–78.

11 Registrar-General, *Report on the mortality from influenza in England and Wales*, p. 3.

12 Registrar-General, *Report on the mortality from influenza in England and Wales*, pp. 3–7.

13 Registrar-General, *Report on the mortality from influenza in England and Wales*, p. 7.

14 Registrar-General for Scotland, *Report on the Mortality from Influenza in Scotland*, p. 2.

15 Registrar-General for Scotland, *Report on the Mortality from Influenza in Scotland*, p. 5.

16 Despite a 1928 Ministry of Health report (Ministry of Health, *Report of an inquiry into the After-histories of persons attacked by encephalitis lethargica*, London, HMSO, 1928), it was largely Ravenholt and Foege's work that established the link between the two conditions; see R.T. Ravenholt and William H. Foege, '1918 Influenza, Encephalitis Lethargica, Parkinsonism', *The Lancet*, 16 October 1982, pp. 860–4).

17 Ministry of Health, *Report on the pandemic of influenza 1918–1919*, London, 1920, p. 40.
18 Ministry of Health, *Report on the pandemic of influenza 1918–1919*, p. xiv.
19 Registrar-General for Scotland, *Report on the Mortality from Influenza in Scotland*, p. 8.
20 Registrar-General for Scotland, *Report on the Mortality from Influenza in Scotland*, p. 12.
21 Crosby, *America's forgotten pandemic*, pp. 215–22.
22 Sandra M. Tomkins, 'Britain and the influenza pandemic of 1918–19', unpublished PhD thesis, University of Cambridge, 1989, p. 118 citing William H. Hamer, *Report on Influenza by the County Medical Officer of Health*, London, London County Council, 1919, and Ministry of Health, *Report on the pandemic of influenza 1918–1919*.
23 Registrar-General for Scotland, *Report on the Mortality from Influenza in Scotland*, pp. 10–11.
24 Discussions of elevated mortality among pregnant women associated with influenza include Aleck W. Bourne, 'Influenza: Pregnancy, Labour, the Puerperium and Diseases of Women', in F.G. Crookshank (ed.), *Influenza: Essays by Several Authors*, London, William Heinemann (Medical Books) Ltd., London, 1922, ch. XIV; Alan P. Kendal and William P. Glezen, 'Pandemic Influenza and Pregnancy: Lessons from the Past, and Considerations about use of Live Attenuated Vaccines', unpublished paper presented at *The Spanish 'Flu 1918–1998: Reflections on the Influenza Pandemic of 1918 after 80 Years* conference, Cape Town, 1998; J.H. Underwood, 'Effects of the 1918 influenza pandemic mortality experience on subsequent fertility of the native population in Guam', *Micronesica*, 1984, vol. 19, pp. 1–10; and Howard Phillips, *'Black October': the Impact of the Spanish Influenza Epidemic of 1918 on South Africa*, Archives Year Book for South African History, Pretoria, Government Printer, 1990, pp. 173–4.
25 Registrar-General for Scotland, *Report on the Mortality from Influenza in Scotland*, p. 11.
26 Registrar-General for Scotland, *Report on the Mortality from Influenza in Scotland*, p. 11.
27 Examples include Svenn-Erik Mamelund, 'Estimating the death toll of Spanish Influenza 1918–19: The case of Norway', unpublished paper presented at The Spanish 'Flu 1918–1998: Reflections on the Influenza Pandemic of 1918 after 80 Years conference, Cape Town, 1998; Svenn-Erik Mamelund, 'Spanskeskyen i Norge 1918–1920: Diffusjon og demografiske konsekvenser', unpublished Master's thesis, University of Oslo, 1998; Andrew Noymer and Michel Garenne, 'Long-term effects of the 1918 "Spanish" influenza on sex differentials of mortality in the USA: exploratory findings from historical data', Chapter 13 in this book; Phillips, *'Black October'*; Howard Phillips, 'South Africa's worst demographic disaster: the Spanish influenza epidemic of 1918', *South African Historical Journal*, 1988, vol. 20, pp. 57–73; and Geoffrey W. Rice (with assistance from Linda Bryder), *Black November: The 1918 influenza pandemic in New Zealand*, Wellington, Allen & Unwin, 1988.
28 Johnson, 'Aspects of the historical geography', pp. 385–8. The fertility rates used are from Barry Werner, 'Fertility statistics from birth registrations in England and Wales, 1837–1987', *Population Trends*, 1987, vol. 48, p. 8.
29 Registrar-General, *Report on the mortality from influenza in England and Wales*, p. 29.
30 Ministry of Health, *Report on the pandemic of influenza 1918–1919*, p. 48.
31 Ministry of Health, *Report on the pandemic of influenza 1918–1919*, pp. 164–72.
32 Sandra M. Tomkins, 'The failure of expertise: Public health policy in Britain

during the 1918–19 influenza epidemic', *Social History of Medicine*, 1992, vol. 5, p. 446.

33 Johnson, 'Aspects of the historical geography', pp. 361–74.

34 Registrar-General, *Registrar-General Decennial Supplement England and Wales 1921*, London, HMSO, 1921 – Part II. Occupational Mortality, Fertility, and Infant Mortality, p. xvii. It should be noted that in this report only influenza mortality in the period 1921–3 was being considered.

35 W.M. Frazer, *A History of English Public Health, 1834–1939*, London, Baillière, Tindall and Cox, 1950, p. 368.

36 F.R. Van Hartesveldt (ed.) *The 1918–19 Pandemic of Influenza: The urban impact in the western world*, Lewiston, Edwin Mellen Press, 1992, p. 92.

37 Ministry of Health, *Report on the pandemic of influenza 1918–1919*, pp. 471–520. Part III of the Ministry of Health report also contains a number of other MOH reports, including reports for Cambridge, Leicester, South Shields, Warrington, Newcastle-upon-Tyne, Wigan and Blackburn in addition to Niven's report. Further MOH reports are available at the Wellcome Library for the History and Understanding of Medicine, London. However, not all MOHs saw influenza as a problem or as a topic worthy of discussion. Tomkins discussed the variation among London MOHs in their views of the pandemic; see Tomkins, 'Britain and the influenza pandemic'.

38 *The Times*, 2 July 1918, p. 3.

39 *The Times*, 8 July 1918, p. 5.

40 *The Times*, 23 July 1918, p. 8.

41 Reports from *The Times* used include 19 October 1918; 24 October 1918, p. 3; 25 October 1918, p. 3; 26 October 1918, p. 7; 28 October 1918, p. 3; 29 October 1918, p. 7; 30 October 1918, p. 7; 1 November 1918, p. 7; 2 November 1918, p. 7; 5 November 1918, p. 3; 5 December 1918.

42 *The Times*, 5 November 1918, p. 3.

43 This view is found in much of the literature on the pandemic. It was first clearly stated in F. MacFarlane Burnet and Ellen Clark, *Influenza: A survey of the last 50 years in the light of modern work on the virus of epidemic influenza*, Monographs from the Walter and Eliza Hall Institute of Research in Pathology and Medicine, Melbourne – Number Four, London, Macmillan, 1942; but most completely expounded by Alfred W. Crosby, *Epidemic and Peace, 1918*, Westport, CN, Greenwood Press, 1976; reprinted as Crosby, *America's Forgotten Pandemic*. It is Crosby's version of events that has gained widespread acceptance.

44 J.S. Oxford, A. Sefton, R. Jackson, N.P.A.S. Johnson and R.S. Daniels, 'Who's that lady?', *Nature Medicine*, 1999, vol. 5, no. 12, pp. 1351–2.

45 Burnet and Clark, *Influenza: A survey* considered that the introduction of influenza into England was by way of troops returning from France, but suggested it may have occurred in June 1918.

46 *The Times*, 15 January 1920, p. 9.

47 Lisa Sattenspiel and D. Ann Herring, 'Modelling the influence of settlement structure on the spread of influenza among communities', *American Journal of Human Biology*, 2000, vol. 12, no. 6.

48 *The Times*, 18 December 1918, p. 5.

49 Registrar-General, *Report on the mortality from influenza in England and Wales*, p. 12.

50 *The Times*, 31 March 1919, p. 9.

51 Registrar-General, *Report on the mortality from influenza in England and Wales*, p. 24.

52 Mamelund, 'Spanskeskyen i Norge'.

53 Examples of shipping being identified as importing the disease include India, West Africa, South Africa, Argentina, Canada, Australia, New Zealand and

other parts of Oceania as documented in Clifford A. Gill, *The Genesis of Epidemics and the Natural History of Disease*, London, Baillière, Tindall and Cox, 1928; Juergen Mueller, 'Patterns of reaction to a demographic crisis. The Spanish Influenza pandemic (1918–1919) in sub-Saharan Africa. A research proposal and preliminary regional and comparative findings', Department of History Staff Seminar Paper No. 6, University of Nairobi, 1994–95; Phillips, *'Black October'*; *The Times*, 1 November 1918, p. 7; H. McQueen, 'The "Spanish" influenza pandemic in Australia, 1918–19', in Jill Roe (ed.), *Social Policy in Australia: Some Perspectives 1901–1975*, Melbourne, Cassel, 1976; Eileen Pettigrew, *The Silent Enemy: Canada and the Deadly Flu of 1918*, Saskatoon, Western Producer Prairie Books, 1983; Rice, *Black November*; and National Archives of Australia files A457/1 501/17; A457/1 501/19; A1/15 1919/287; A6006 1919/1/9, 1919/2/3; A2 1919/452, 1919/482 Part 2, 1919/701, 1919/742, 1919/887 Part 2, and 1919/852. In other instances the railways have been cited, for example Portugal as documented in Beatriz Echeverri, Chapter 11, in this book. Many of these works also illustrate the role of national transport networks in dispersing influenza across the country.

54 Hamer, *Report of the County Medical Officer of Health and School Medical Officer for the Year 1918*, p. 44.

55 *The Times*, 26 October 1918, p. 7.

56 Entries under 'influenza' in the index to *The Times* extended for half a column during July–September 1918, six columns for October–December 1918 and four columns for January–March 1919. Similarly, the *British Medical Journal* and *Lancet* both went from negligible numbers of influenza stories prior to 1918 to more than 120 in 1919, before dropping back to very low levels. An example of the impact on pharmacy sales can be seen in the registers from Savory & Moore, a Belgravia pharmacy (Wellcome Institute, CMAC GC/16/4/92 and GC/16/5/93) in which the number of customers sold medication peaked in the third wave.

57 Reports of all these events can be found in most newspapers of the period. For example *The Times'* reports of 21 October 1918, p. 5; 22 October 1918, p. 3; 23 October 1918, p. 3; 24 October 1918, p. 3; 25 October 1918, p. 3; 28 October 1918, p. 3; 31 October 1918, p. 7; 1 November 1918, p. 7; 7 November 1918, p. 3; 27 November 1918, p. 5; 29 November 1918, p. 3; 4 December 1918, p. 3.

58 Tomkins, 'The failure of expertise', p. 441.

59 *The Times*, 28 November 1918, p. 3.

60 Public Record Office (PRO), Kew. CAB 24/149.

61 *The Times*, 8 March 1919, p. 7.

62 *The Times*, 11 January 1919, p. 12.

63 *The Times*, 7 March 1919, p. 7.

64 Tomkins, 'The failure of expertise'.

65 PRO. MH 10/83 and MH 10/84.

66 Reports come from PRO files MAF 60/307; MH 79/7; NATS 1/797 and NATS 1/849, and *The Times*, 23 October 1918, p. 3; 25 October 1918, p. 3; 29 October 1918, p. 10; 30 October 1918, pp. 7 and 8; 10 December 1918, p. 5; 17 December 1918, p. 5

67 John M. Eyler, *Sir Arthur Newsholme and State Medicine 1885–1935*, Cambridge, Cambridge University Press, 1997.

68 For example, New Zealand (Rice, *Black November* and Linda Bryder, '"Lessons" of the 1918 Influenza Epidemic in Auckland', *New Zealand Journal of History*, 1982, vol. 16, no. 2, pp. 97–121) and South Africa (Phillips, *'Black October'*; Howard Phillips, 'The origin of the Public Health Act of 1919', *South African Medical Journal*, 1990, vol. 77, no. 10, pp. 531–2) are the clearest examples of the pandemic having a direct bearing on the (re)creation of the national

health administration. Such developments abroad were reported in *The Times*, 23 November 1918, p. 5; 7 December 1918, p. 7, and 7 February 1919, p. 7.
69 Virginia Berridge, 'Health and medicine', in F.M.L. Thompson (ed.), *The Cambridge Social History of Britain 1750–1950, Volume 3: Social Agencies and Institutions*, Cambridge, Cambridge University Press, 1990, p. 217.
70 Including *The Times*, 28 October 1918, p. 7; 29 October 1918, p. 7; 30 October 1918, p. 7.
71 Lynn Hollen Lees, *The Solidarities of Strangers: the English Poor Laws and the People, 1700–1948*, Cambridge, Cambridge University Press, 1998, p. 328.
72 Royal Society of Medicine, *Influenza: A discussion*, London, Longmans, Green and Co., 1918, p. 13.
73 Tomkins, 'The failure of expertise', p. 449.
74 Descriptions of the activities undertaken by MOHs can be found in Tomkins, 'Britain and the influenza pandemic'; Tomkins, 'The failure of expertise', and Van Hartesveldt (ed.) *The 1918–19 Pandemic of Influenza*.
75 Reports of school closures came in all three waves of the pandemic, for example *The Times* carried reports of school closures as early as 26 June 1918 (p. 7) and throughout July. From mid-October to early 1919 there was at least one report on school closures every week.
76 Tomkins, 'The failure of expertise', p. 443.
77 Christopher Lawrence, 'Edward Jenner's Jockey Boots and the Great Tradition in English Medicine 1918–1939', in Christopher Lawrence and Anna-K Mayer (eds) *Regenerating England: Science, medicine and culture in interwar Britain*, Amsterdam, Rodopi, 2000.
78 Tomkins, 'The failure of expertise'.
79 Gerry Kearns, 'Tuberculosis and the medicalisation of British society, 1880–1920', in John Woodward and Robert Jütte (eds), *Coping with Sickness: Historical Aspects of Health Care in a European Perspective*, Sheffield, European Association for the History of Medicine and Health Publications, 1995, pp. 147–70.
80 For example, *The Times*, 24 February 1919, p. 10.
81 Registrar-General, *Report on the mortality from influenza in England and Wales*, p. 29.
82 Tomkins, 'The failure of expertise'.
83 *The Times*, 24 December 1918, p. 3; 17 February 1919, p. 7.
84 Tomkins, 'The failure of expertise'.
85 Wellcome Institute. CMAC GC/21. Other accounts of the experiences of nurses, doctors and medical students include William Hyam, *The Road to Harley Street*, London, Geoffrey Bles, 1963; A.H. Mackie, *Memories of a Scotch Doctor*, Aberdeen, Aberdeen University Press, 1949; G. Morton, 'The pandemic influenza of 1918', *Canadian Nurse*, 1973, vol. 69, pp. 25–7; Gladys Mary Wauchope, *The Story of a Woman Physician*, Bristol, John Wright & Sons, 1963; and Alistair Wilson, 'Oddity remembered: 1918 influenza pandemic', *British Medical Journal*, 1981, vol. 282, p. 1766. The famous Will Pickles also worked through the pandemic, with his experiences told in John Pemberton, *Will Pickles of Wensleydale*, London, Geoffrey Bles, 1970. Pickles also made some comments in his well-known work on epidemiology: William N. Pickles, *Epidemiology in country practice*, Bristol, John Wright & Sons, 1939. An example of the impact on those treating the sick can be found in Nurse Nelly Stevenson's file in PRO. PIN 26/20251.
86 Crosby, *America's Forgotten Pandemic*.
87 *The Times*, 18 December 1918, p. 5.
88 Registrar-General, *Report on the mortality from influenza in England and Wales*; Ministry of Health, *Report on the pandemic of influenza 1918–1919*.

89 Tomkins, 'Britain and the influenza pandemic'; Sandra M. Tomkins, 'Colonial Administration in British Africa during the Influenza Epidemic of 1918–19', *Canadian Journal of African Studies*, 1994, vol. 28, no. 1, pp. 60–83; Tomkins, 'The failure of expertise'; Tomkins, 'The Influenza Epidemic of 1918–19 in Western Samoa'.

90 Richard Hugheson Collier, *The Plague of the Spanish Lady: The Influenza Pandemic of 1918–1919*, London, Macmillan, 1974; Charles Graves, *Invasion by virus: Can it happen again?* London, Icon Books Limited, 1969; A.A. Hoehling, *The Great Epidemic*, Boston, Little, Brown, 1961.

91 For example Jonathon Wilshere, *Leicester's Great Influenza Epidemic 1918–1919*, Leicester, Chamberlain Music and Books, 1986.

92 *The Times*, 12 November 1918, p. 5

10 Death in winter

1 J.P.D. McGinnis, 'The impact of epidemic influenza: Canada, 1918–1919', *Canadian Historical Association Historical Papers*, 1977, p. 122, and E. Pettigrew, *The Silent Enemy. Canada and the Deadly Flu of 1918*, Saskatoon, Sk, Western Producer Prairie Books, 1986, p. 8.

2 The westward spread of the epidemic might have been forestalled but for a decision by Canadian military officials to allow healthy soldiers in quarantine in Quebec City to proceed by Canadian Pacific Railway train to Vancouver. Having been exposed to the virus prior to departure, soldiers who fell sick during the journey were turned over to local health officials at various points en route. This proved to be an effective, if not the most effective means, of spreading the epidemic across the continent. See McGinnis, 'The impact of epidemic influenza', p. 123.

3 H. MacDougall, 'The fatal flu', *Horizon Canada*, 1985, Vol. 8, No. 8, p. 2089.

4 P. Wilton, 'Spanish flu outdid WWI in number of lives claimed,' *Canadian Medical Association Journal*, 1993, Vol. 148, No. 11, p. 2037.

5 *Manitoba Free Press*, 12 October 1918.

6 Ibid., 25 November 1918.

7 Ibid., 1 November 1918.

8 Ibid., 2 November 1918.

9 Ibid., 26 October 1918. The complete failure of medical and public health interventions to stop the spread of the epidemic led Dr J.J. Heagerty, Bacteriologist and Assistant Medical Officer at the Grosse Isle Quarantine Station, to remark that, 'Every weapon upon which the health officer has been accustomed to rely in his struggle against infectious disease failed him miserably when influenza made its appearance upon the scene. Isolation of the sick, segregation and quarantine of contacts, masks, disinfection, gargles and sprays, one and all proved either "totally ineffective" or only "moderately efficacious"'. J.J. Heagerty, 'Influenza and vaccination', *Canadian Medical Association Journal*, 1919, Vol. 9, No. 37, p. 227.

10 D.A. Herring, '"There were young people and old people and babies dying every week": the 1918–1919 influenza pandemic at Norway House', *Ethnohistory*, 1994, Vol. 41, pp. 85–6.

11 Ibid; and D.A. Herring, 'The 1918 influenza epidemic in the central Canadian subarctic', in A. Herring and L. Chan (eds), *Strength in Diversity: A Reader in Physical Anthropology*, Toronto, Canadian Scholars' Press, 1994, pp. 365–84.

12 *The Last Days of Okak*, a 23-minute National Film Board of Canada production,1985, is a terrifying and moving account of the destruction of an Inuit settlement in northern Labrador during the 1918 epidemic.

13 H.N. Everett, 'Memoirs', unpub., 1985, p. 1, copy in Department of Anthro-

pology, McMaster University, Hamilton, Ontario. Harry Everett refers to his first memories of Berens River, Manitoba, the community in which he lived most of his life. Berens River, an important HBC post on the east coast of Lake Winnipeg, was devastated by Spanish flu in November and December 1918. The *Wolverine*, a passenger steamer that criss-crossed Lake Winnipeg, brought its suffering crew and influenza to Berens River on its last trip of the year, just before freeze-up closed the lake to traffic. See Pettigrew, *Silent Enemy*, pp. 78–9; K.M. Beckett, 'Investigating Disease in Aboriginal Populations in Canada: The 1918 Influenza Pandemic in Berens River and Poplar River, Manitoba', unpub. M.A. thesis, Department of Anthropology, McMaster University, 1998, p. 100, estimates a mortality rate of 141 per 1,000 population there, yet it appears that the epidemic did not reach Poplar River, an outlying fur trade post.

14 Provincial Archives of Manitoba (PAM), Winnipeg, Canada (1902–1930), MG8 B47, Anna M. O'Reilly, 'Notes re. History of the past – Le Pas, Northwest Territories – Later Manitoba (Reminiscences re: The LaRose Family and the Pas)'.

15 E.L. Stone, 'Tuberculosis among the Indians of the Norway House Agency', *The Public Health Journal*, 1925, Vol. 16, No. 2, pp. 76–81; Hudson Bay Company Archives (HBCA), Winnipeg, Manitoba, A/95/53, fo. 6–33; E.L. Stone, 'Health and Disease at the Norway House Indian Agency', HBCA, A/95/53, fo. 6–33, 1926.

16 Cited in Pettigrew, *Silent Enemy*, pp. 25–7.

17 Provincial Archives of Manitoba (PAM), Winnipeg, Canada (1902–1930), MG8 B47, Anna M. O'Reilly, 'Notes re. History of the past – Le Pas, Northwest Territories – Later Manitoba (Reminiscences re: The LaRose Family and the Pas)', p. 8.

18 Interview with Nathaniel Queskekapow, Norway House, July 1992.

19 Population sizes for the three communities are derived from Government of Canada Sessional Paper No. 27 (1917), George V (9–10), pp. 18–19.

20 A.J. Ray, *Indians in the Fur Trade*, Toronto, Toronto University Press, 1974, p. 128.

21 A.I. Hallowell, *Culture and Experience*, Philadelphia, University of Pennsylvania Press, 1955, p. 114.

22 Only Norway House, Cross Lake and Berens River Posts were struck by the epidemic, according to the 'Annual Report for the Keewatin District, Outfit 1918', of the Hudson's Bay Company. The rest of the posts 'fortunately escaped', HBCA, B.154/1/87, 'Norway House Post Journal, 1918', p. 51.

23 The Jack River Mission parish registers are the only surviving church records for Norway House during the 1918 influenza pandemic. Anglicans represented approximately one-third of the total population at Norway House at that time. Government of Canada, Sessional paper No. 27, 1917, George V (9–10), pp. 18–19.

24 Herring, 'There were young people and old people and babies dying every week', p. 96.

25 One of us (Herring) conducted interviews with elders of the Norway House First Nation during the summer of 1992. Only a few of the informants had been alive during the epidemic and even fewer had stories or recollections to share that had been passed down to them.

26 The resident physician at Norway House, Dr Norquay, quickly instituted a quarantine when Spanish flu broke out. News of the epidemic travelled quickly and the Chief at Island Lake, for instance, prevented dog teams from proceeding to Norway House because of the sickness there. HBCA, B.156/a/44, 'Oxford House Post Journal, 1918', pp. 9–11.

27 Herring, "'There were young people and old people and babies dying every week'", p. 97; and Herring, 'The 1918 influenza epidemic', p. 378.
28 See J. Brown and M. Matthews, 'Fair Wind: Medicine and consolation on the Berens River', *Journal of the Canadian Historical Association*, 1994, Vol. 4, n.s. pp. 55–73; Beckett, 'Investigating Disease in Aboriginal Populations in Canada', p. 105–12.
29 We are grateful to K.M. Beckett for providing a copy of National Archives of Canada, Ottawa, documents from RG29, Vol. 2970, File 851-4-096, which summarises the number of deaths from the Spanish flu by Indian Agency.
30 Beckett, 'Investigating Disease in Aboriginal Populations in Canada', p. 43.
31 C. Graham-Cumming, 'Health of the original Canadians, 1867–1967', *Medical Services Journal*, February 1967, p. 149.
32 Herring, "'There were young people and old people and babies dying every week'", pp. 96–8; Herring, 'The 1918 influenza pandemic', pp. 378–81; L. Sattenspiel and D.A. Herring, 'Structured epidemic models and the spread of the 1918–1919 influenza epidemic in the central Subarctic', *Human Biology*, 1998, Vol. 70, No. 1, pp. 91–115; L. Sattenspiel, A. Mobarry and D.A. Herring, 'Modeling the influence of settlement structure on the spread of influenza', *American Journal of Human Biology* 2000, Vol. 12, No. 6, pp. 736–48.
33 Sattenspiel and Herring, 'Structured epidemic models', pp. 91–115; Sattenspiel, Mobarry and Herring, 'Modeling the influence of settlement'.
34 Trippers were men employed to freight mail and supplies from post to post.
35 R.C. Harris, *Historical Atlas of Canada, Volume 1*, Toronto, University of Toronto Press, 1987, p. 63.
36 Sattenspiel and Herring, 'Structured epidemic models'.
37 A.I. Hallowell (ed. J.B. Brown), 'The Ojibwa of Berens River, Manitoba: Ethnography into History' (Case Studies in Cultural Anthropology), Fort Worth, Harcourt Brace Jovanovich, 1992; J.J. Honigmann, 'West Main Cree', in J. Helm (ed.), *Handbook of North American Indians, Vol. 6, Subarctic*, Smithsonian Institution, Washington, D.C., 1981.
38 For a description of Cree social life in winter, see J.J. Honigmann, 'Foodways in a Muskeg Community', Department of Northern Affairs and National Resources, Ottawa, Canada, 1961, pp. 88–98.
39 Stone, 'Health and Disease at the Norway House Indian Agency'.
40 F. Beardy and R. Coutts (eds), *Voices From Hudson Bay: Cree Stories from York Factory*, Montreal and Kingston, McGill-Queen's University Press, 1996, pp. 79–84; R. Flannery, *Ellen Smallboy: Glimpses of a Cree Woman's Life*, Montreal and Kingston, McGill-Queen's University Press, 1995; Hallowell, *The Ojibwa of Berens River*; Honigmann, *The Attawapiskat Swampy Cree*; J.J. Honigmann, 'West Main Cree', in Helm, *Handbook of North American Indians, Vol. 6*; Ray, *Indians in the Fur Trade*; J.G.E. Smith, 'Western Woods Cree', in Helm, *Handbook of North American Indians, Vol. 6*; E.S. Rogers and J.H. Rogers, 'The yearly cycle of the Mistassini Indians', *Arctic*, 1959, Vol. 12, No. 3, pp. 131–8.
41 HBCA B.283/a/8, 'God's Lake Post Journal 1917–1922'; HBCA B.154/1/87, 'Norway House Post Journal, 1918–1923'; and HBCA B.156/a/44, 'Oxford House Post Journal 1918–1922'.
42 Fortunately, post journals sometimes contain general observations on community life, including thumbnail sketches of local characters, as well as narrative accounts of epidemics and other noteworthy occurrences. The Norway House post journal (HBCA, B.154/a/87), for instance, contains many observations on the 1918 influenza epidemic and constitutes an invaluable source of information on events there and elsewhere in the Keewatin District.
43 The Norway House post journal for the period of the epidemic begins in

October 1918 (HBCA, 1918–1922); the preceding volume is missing and is not part of the Hudson's Bay Company Archives collection.

44 We are grateful to Mariane Ciampini, Tracy Farmer and Todd Garlie for their invaluable assistance in carrying out the tedious process of extracting, checking and compiling all the instances of travel from the HBC post journals to create the mobility database.

45 HBCA, Map Collection, National Topographical series: G.3/369 (N13684), 'Territorial Map, Berens River, 1928'; G.3/372 (N13685), 'Territorial Map, Norway House, 1928'; RG1/87/o/2B (N13683), 'Territoral Map, Oxford House, Manitoba, 1929'; and G.3/373 (N13686), 'Territorial Map, Cross Lake, 1930'.

46 The seasons were defined as follows: Winter: December to February; Spring: March to May; Summer: June to August; and Fall: September to November.

47 Ray, *Indians in the Fur Trade*, pp. 94–116; A.J. Ray, 'Diffusion of diseases in the western interior of Canada, 1830–1950', *Geographical Review*, 1976, Vol. 66, pp. 139–57.

48 Ibid. This is a typical pattern for the fur trade and has been described in detail by Ray.

49 For details of the model see L. Sattenspiel and K. Dietz, 'A structured epidemic model incorporating geographic mobility among regions', *Mathematical Biosciences*, 1995, Vol. 128, pp. 71–91.

50 Sattenspiel and Herring, 'Structured epidemic models'.

51 All are pseudonyms.

52 Interview with Nathaniel Queskekapow, Norway House, July 1992.

53 McGinnis, 'The impact of the epidemic influenza', p. 134, cites some of the dreadful personal losses that occurred during the epidemic, including the large numbers of children orphaned, families that lost their primary wage-earner, and the tragic case of a soldier who survived influenza in Europe only to return home to discover the loss of three brothers and two sisters during the epidemic.

54 Cf. W.P. Glezen, 'Emerging infections: pandemic influenza', *Epidemiologic Reviews*, 1996, Vol. 18, No. 1, pp. 64–76.

55 There are other examples of the vagaries of exposure to the 1918 flu. The Wabauskang reserve in western Ontario, for instance, was essentially wiped out during the 1918 epidemic, prompting the survivors to relocate to a site considered to be sacred ground. 'Today the people think of themselves as the descendants of the ten families who were north on their traplines when the epidemic hit Wabauskang'; see A.M. Shkilnyk, *A Poison Stronger Than Love: The Destruction of an Ojibwa Community*, New Haven, CN, Yale University Press, 1985, pp. 7–58.

11 Spanish influenza seen from Spain

1 W.T. Vaughan, 'Influenza: An Epidemiological Study', *The American Journal of Hygiene*, Monographic Series, No. 1, 1921, p. 71; W.F. Frost, 'The Epidemiology of Influenza', *Public Health Reports*, No. 33, vol. 34, 1919.

2 A. Lama and L. Piga, *Infecciones de Tipo Gripal*, Madrid, 1919, vol. 1, p. 106.

3 A.W. Crosby, *Epidemic and Peace 1918*, Greenwood, Westport, 1976, pp. 17–32; 'La Grippe Espagnole, la mal nommée', *Population*, No.1, 1973, pp. 136–8.

4 For example by *ABC* and *El Sol*.

5 G. Marañón, G. Pittaluga and A. Ruiz Falcó, 'Informe sobre el actual estado sanitario de Francia y su identidad con la epidemia gripal en España', *El Siglo Médico*, LXV, 1918, p. 919.

6 J. Arango, 'Modernización demográfica de la sociedad española', in J. Nadal,

A. Carreras and C. Sudría (eds), *La Economía Española en el Siglo XX*, Ariel, Barcelona, 1987, p. 203.

7   *Boletín Mensual de Estadística Demográfica-Sanitaria, Ministerio de Gobernación,* Madrid, 1917, 1918 and 1919.

8   Piga and Lama, '*Infecciones de Tipo Gripal*' p. 66; J. Chabais, 'La epidemia reinante. Información científica mundial de la epidemia', *Revista de Higiene y Tuberculosis,* Valencia, October, 1918, pp. 111–12.

9   J. Nadal, *La Población Española,* Ariel, Barcelona, 1986, p. 200.

10   Anales de la Real Academia de Medicina, Madrid, May 1918.

11   V. Rasueros, *Datos sintéticos acerca de la epidemia de gripe desarrollada en la provincia de Ávila en los años de 1918–1919,* Imprenta Católica, Avila, 1919, p. 3; *El Noticiero Extremeño,* June 1918.

12   L. Rodrigo Lavín, 'La lucha contra la gripe', Asociación Española para el Progreso de las Ciencias, Congreso de Bilbao, 1919, p. 124; *La Medicina Ibera,* May 1918.

13   L. Contreras, 'Un testimonio sobre la mal llamada gripe española de 1918', *Revista de Sanidad e Higiene Pública,* September 1971, pp. 863–72.

14   Nadal, *La Población Española,* p. 199.

15   *Report on the Pandemic of Influenza,* Ministry of Health, London, 1920; F. Zambrano, 'La gripe asesina de 1918', *El Tiempo,* Bogota, 6 December 1987.

16   A. Sanchez Gozalbo, *Contribución al estudio de la grippe de 1918 en la provincia de Castellón,* Hijos de Armengot, Castellón, 1919, p. 11; Rasueros, *Datos sintéticos acerca de la epidemia de gripe en la provincia de Avila,* p. 5.

17   Contreras, 'Un testimonio sobre la mal llamada gripe española de 1918'.

18   *La Medicina Ibera,* 12 October 1918.

19   Rodrigo, 'La lucha contra la gripe', pp. 124–7.

20   *Le Medicina Ibera,* 26 October 1918.

21   B. Echeverri, *La Gripe Española. La Pandemia de 1918–19 en España,* CIS, Siglo XXI, 1993, pp. 111–13.

22   R. García Durán, *Memoria descriptiva y datos estadísticos de la epidemia gripal padecida en la provincia de Valladolid en el año 1918,* Valladolid, 1919, p. 19.

23   Durán, *Memoria descriptiva y datos estadísticos ... provincia de Valladolid,* pp. 1–63.

24   Marañon *et al.,* 'Informe sobre el actual estado sanitario de Francia', p. 920.

25   *La Medicina Ibera,* November 1918.

26   *Diario de Sesiones del Senado,* 1918, pp. 1471–6; *Anales de la Academia de Medicina,* pp. 410–12

27   Marañon, 'Informe sobre el actual estado sanitario de Francia', p. 920.

28   *Boletín Oficial de la Diócesis de Zamora,* 1918.

29   R. Jorge, *La Grippe,* Lisbon, 1919.

30   *Anales de la Academia de Medicina,* October 1918.

31   Rodrigo, 'La lucha contra la gripe', p. 130.

32   R. Gómez Redondo, *La Mortalidad Infantil Española en el Siglo XX,* CIC, Siglo XXI, Madrid, 1992, pp. 80–4.

33   J. Díaz Nicolás, 'La mortalidad en la guerra civil española', *Boletín de la Asociación de Demografía Histórica,* Barcelona, III, No. 1, 1985, p. 48.

34   W.F. Frost, 'The epidemiology of influenza', *Public Health Reports,* Vol. 34, No. 33, Washington, DC, 1919.

35   Frost, 'The epidemiology of influenza'.

36   J. Barnabeu Mestre, 'La ciutat davant el contagi. Alacant: la grip de 1918–1919', *Monographhies Sanitaires,* No. 4, 1991, Generalitat, Valencia; M.I. Porras, 'Las repercusiones de la pandemia de gripe de 1918–19 en la mortalidad de la ciudad de Madrid', *Boletín de la Asociación de Demografía Histórica,* XIV – I, 1996, pp. 75–116.

37 C.H. Stuart-Harris, G.C. Schild and J.S. Oxford, *Influenza. The Viruses and the Disease*, Edward Arnold, Oxford, 1991, pp. 166–8.
38 Vaughan, 'Influenza', p. 21; *Report on the Pandemic of Influenza*, p. 297.
39 M. Burnet, *Historia de las enfermedades infecciosas*, Madrid, 1967.
40 The indexes used for the first wave are the case specific death rates from influenza for May–July 1918. To avoid the overlapping of the second and third wave, and, due to the necessity of making heterogeneous indexes for all provinces, the second/third wave is represented by the specific death rates from influenza during September 1918–May 1919.
41 In order to exude, as much as possible, the influence of the immunity factor, the following correlation coefficients were carried out for the twenty-seven provinces where cause specific death rates from influenza during the first wave were below the national average.
42 In this case the index used is the average height of recruits enlisted between 1915–29 in R. Gómez-Mendoza and V. Peréz Moreda, 'Estatura y nivel de vida en la España del primer tercio del siglo XX', *Moneda y Crédito*, No. 174, 1965.
43 J. Wilmoth, J. Vallin and G. Caselli, 'Quand certaines générations ont une mortalité différant de celle qu'on pourrait attendre', *Population*, No. 2, 1989, pp. 335–76.

12 A holocaust in a holocaust

1 An earlier version of this chapter in French appeared in L. Murard and P. Zylberman, *L'hygiène dans la République. La santé publique en France ou l'utopie contrariée, 1870–1918*, Paris, Fayard, 1996, pp. 565–71. The English version has been prepared with the help of Noal Mellott, CNRS, Paris.
2 J. Toubert, *Le Service de santé militaire au Grand Quartier Général français (1918–1919)*, Paris, 1934, p. 100.
3 Typhoid fever: Ministère de la Guerre, *Aperçu statistique sur l'évolution de la morbidité et de la mortalité générales dans l'armée et sur l'évolution de la morbidité et de la mortalité particulières à certaines maladies contagieuses de 1862 à nos jours*, Paris, 1932, p. 30, fig. 13; Chavasse and Landouzy, 15 May 1916, Commission Supérieure d'Hygiène et d'Épidémiologie Militaires, 15 May 1916, Musée du Val-de-Grâce, box 360. Other epidemic outbreaks: F. Duguet, 'Le Service de santé dans la nation. Essai d'un plan de reconstruction de la défense sanitaire du pays', *La Grande Revue*, 1925, pp. 22–9 and 34; and also L. Mourier, under-secretary of the Military Health Service, 5 February 1919, Commission d'Hygiène de la Chambre des Députés [hereafter: Chambre], 1914–19, Archives Nationales, Paris, C7726. H. Doizy, Chambre, 4 August 1915; Malaria: J. Godart, under-secretary of the Military Health Service, Chambre, 7 November 1917; Duguet, 'Le Service de santé', pp. 28–9; J. Toubert, 'La collaboration des services d'hygiène publique et du Service de Santé Militaire en temps de guerre', *Bulletin Union fédér. méd. réserve et armée territ.*, 1925, p. 359. See also Ministère de la Guerre, *Statistiques médicales. I – Données de statistiques relatives à la guerre 1914–1918*, Paris, 1922, p. 147; and Commission Supérieure Consultative du Service de Santé [hereafter: CSCSS], 6 February 1917, Musée du Val-de-Grâce, box 574.
4 Duguet, 'Le Service de santé', pp. 39–40. Epidemics (other than typhoid, smallpox, measles, scarlet fever, diphtheria, pertussis and flu): rates calculated from Institut National de la Statistique et des Études Économiques [hereafter: INSEE], *Annuaire statistique de la France, résumé rétrospectif 1951*, vol. 58, Paris, 1952, p. 69; Toubert, *Le Service de santé militaire*, p. 100; also Ministère de la Guerre, *Statistiques médicales*, p. 33.
5 L. Bryder, 'The First World War: Healthy or hungry?' *History Workshop Journal*,

no. 24, 1987, p. 143; J. Winter, *The Great War and the British People*, London, Macmillan, 1985, pp. 17 and 23.

6 H. Zinsser, 'Manifestations of influenza during the earlier periods of its appearance in France', *Medical Record*, vol. 97, 1920, p. 459; A.W. Crosby, *Epidemic and Peace, 1918*, Westport, Greenwood Press, 1976, p. 19; K.D. Patterson and G.F. Pyle, 'The geography and mortality of the 1918 influenza pandemic', *Bulletin of the History of Medicine*, vol. 65, 1991, pp. 4–7. The possible American origin of the spring wave was suggested after the war by Delater, 'La grippe dans la nation armée de 1918 à 1921', *Rev. hyg.*, vol. 45, 1923, p. 409. Contemporary writers put forward the idea that Chinese labourers might have brought the disease to France: D.C. Ohadike, 'Diffusion and physiological responses to the influenza pandemic of 1918–19 in Nigeria', *Social Science and Medicine*, vol. 32, 1991, p. 1394; and today: C. Hannoun, *La grippe et ses virus*, Paris, Presses Universitaires de France, 1995, p. 13.

7 Patterson and Pyle, 'Geography', p. 14; W.I.B. Beveridge, *Influenza, the last great plague: An unfinished story of discovery*, London, Prodist, 1977, p. 21. On Brest see 'L'épidémie de grippe observée à Brest 13–27 septembre 1918', *apud* Office International d'Hygiène, WHO Archives, Geneva, 1918, microfiche A54. WHO Archives also contain questionnaires on the epidemic (microfiches F95 and T39); 'Swiss' wave: Médecin-Général Rouget, CSCSS, 9 September 1918, Val-de-Grâce, box 490; Delater, 'La grippe', p. 627.

8 For mortality see Patterson and Pyle, 'Geography', p. 14. Such a case/fatality rate 'related to the prevalence of concurrent bacterial epidemics' (E.D. Kilbourne, 'Influenza pandemics in perspective', *JAMA*, vol. 237, no. 12, 1977, p. 1227) makes any estimate of overall mortality highly speculative (Delater, 'La grippe', pp. 422–3). The deadliness of the infection is covered by J. Castaigne, 'Chronique', *J. méd. franç.*, vol. 8, 1919, p. 11; and M. Huber, *Cours de démographie et de statistiques sanitaires*, Paris, 1940, p. 7.

9 Combat zone: Mourier, Chambre, 6 November 1918; Delater, 'La grippe', pp. 413–16; Crosby, *Epidemic*, pp. 161 and 165. Health Service alarmed: see Crosby, *Epidemic*, p. 25. Complications: Médecin Principal Lafforgue, CSCSS, 14 October 1918, Val-de-Grâce, 490; Delater, 'La grippe', p. 421; E. Folly, 'Contribution à l'étude de l'épidémie de grippe observée dans la garnison de Strasbourg, durant l'hiver 1918–1919', *Bull. Acad. Méd.*, vol. 82, 1919, p. 164; J.F. Townsend, 'History of influenza epidemics', *Annals of Medical History*, vol. 5, 1933, p. 546.

10 Gas victims, burials: R. Dujarric de la Rivière, *Souvenirs*, Périgueux, Pierre Fanlac, 1962, pp. 110–11. Deaths/cases, rear/front: Guerre, *Aperçu statistique*, p. 80. According to Delater, 'La grippe', p. 420, influenza caused 33,321 deaths in the army. Morbidity was higher in the AEF: Crosby, *Epidemic*, p. 205, and table, p. 159; Zinsser, 'Manifestations of influenza', p. 459. For mortality and morbidity rates see M. Huber, *La population de la France pendant la guerre*, Paris, Presses Universitaires de France, 1931, p. 433. On the spread of the disease among armies see H. Emerson, 'The Argonne influenza epidemic', *Medical Record*, vol. 97, 1920, p. 461. American Services of Supply and Depots: Crosby, *Epidemic*, pp. 153–4. Frontwards: Delater, 'La grippe', p. 414.

11 For figures of civilian mortality see Huber, *La population*, pp. 269, 459 and 693; J. Dupâquier, *Histoire de la population française*, Paris, Presses Universitaires de France, 1988, vol. 4, p. 71, has taken this figure from Huber, *La population*, p. 283; INSEE, 1952, p. 69, table 4. For 1920, see INSEE, *Annuaire statistique de la France, résumé rétrospectif*, Paris, vol. 72, 1966, p. 124. Inaccurate statistics: Delater, 'La grippe', p. 634. Flu victim–doctor relationship: Delater, 'La grippe', p. 423. Emphasis was placed on the usual uncertainty of clinical findings; see Castaigne, 'Chronique', pp. 13–15.

12 Pneumonia more than 10 per cent: Defressine and Violle, 'La prophylaxie et le traitement de la grippe', *C. R. hébdo. séances Acad. Sci.*, vol. 167, 1918, p. 503; and Castaigne, 'Chronique', pp. 11–14.
13 Physicians' reports incomplete: P. Faivre, 'La lutte contre la grippe', *Paris-médical*, vol. 30, 1918, p. 366. Nowadays, we know that out of eight deaths due to the flu only one is notified as caused by influenza. Censorship: M. Péhu and E. Ledoux, 'Revue documentaire sur l'épidémie actuelle de grippe en France', *Ann. Méd.* (Paris), 1918, p. 579; Patterson and Pyle, 'Geography', p. 14. Britain: S.M. Tomkins, 'The failure of expertise: public health policy in Britain during the 1918–19 influenza epidemic', *Social History of Medicine*, vol. 5, 1992, p. 441. Prussia: J. Müller, 'Die Spanische Influenza 1918/19. Einflüsse des Ersten Weltkrieges auf Ausbreitung, Krankheitsverlauf and Perzeption einer Pandemie', in W.U. Eckart and C. Gradmann (eds), *Die Medizin und die Erste Weltkrieg*, Pfaffenweiler, Centaurus Verlag, 1996, p. 342. The national mortality rate (3.9) given by Patterson and Pyle verges on Armengaud's 3.2, as compared with 0.15 in the preceding years: A. Armengaud, *La population française au XXe siècle*, Paris, Presses Universitaires de France, 1977, p. 23.
14 Young adults: Delater, 'La grippe', p. 420; Hannoun, *La grippe*, p. 33. Troops: Leuret, 'La grippe à Bordeaux', *J. méd. franç.*, vol. 8, 1919, p. 23. Widespread pattern: Crosby, *Epidemic*, pp. 215–16; R. Martin du Gard, *Journal* I, Paris, Gallimard, 1992, p. 991. Strauss: CSCSS, 9 September 1918, Val-de-Grâce, box 490. Persons aged over 50: Beveridge, *Influenza*, p. 31. Nursing infants: Péhu and Ledoux, 'Revue documentaire', p. 582; K.D. Patterson, *Pandemic Influenza, 1700–1900, a study in historical epidemiology*, Totowa, Rowman and Littlefield, 1986, pp. 1 and 76–7.
15 Deaths in July and August, excess mortality due to pneumonia: Hannoun, *La grippe*, pp. 21–2; L. Cruveilhier, 'La grippe à Paris (statistique, bactériologie, hygiène)', *J. méd. franç.*, vol. 8, 1919, pp. 26–8; Leuret, 'La grippe à Bordeaux', p. 22; and see the discussion in *Bull. Acad. méd.*, vol. 87, 1922, pp. 132–41 and 143–51. Prefecture: *Epidémie de grippe à Paris, 30 juin 1918–26 avril 1919*, Préfecture de la Seine, Service de la Statistique Municipale, 1919, 2e année, no. 2, Paris, Imprimerie des Beaux-Arts, n.d., a collection that served as a source of data for H. Pottevin, 'Rapport sur la pandémie grippale de 1918–19', *Bull. Off. Intern. Hyg. pub.*, vol. 13, 1921, pp. 125–81; and Delater, 'La grippe', p. 424. Médecins-inspecteurs: Préfecture de la Seine, *Épidémie de grippe*, p. 42. Respiratory diseases: Préfecture de la Seine, *Épidémie de grippe*, p. 90. In 1920, the British Ministry of Health gave figures rather close to Pottevin's: Crosby, *Epidemic*, p. 181.
16 M.L. Hildreth, 'Lyon and Marseille', in F.R. Van Hartesveldt (ed.), *The 1918–1919 pandemic of influenza: The urban impact in the Western world*, Lewiston, NY, Edwin Mellen Press, 1992, p. 44 (Table 3.2), and p. 48 (Table 3.3); see also M.L. Hildreth, 'The influenza epidemic of 1918–1919 in France: Contemporary concepts of ætiology, therapy, and prevention', *Social History of Medicine*, vol. 4, 1991, p. 278. The Lyons rates have been calculated on the basis of an overall population of 557,000 in 1914, in line with the crude figures cited by Delater, 'La grippe', p. 424.
17 Confusion: K.R. Robinson, 'The role of nursing in the influenza epidemic of 1918–1919', *Nursing Forum*, vol. 25, 1990, pp. 21–2. Brutality: Delater, 'La grippe', p. 535; and Lafforgue, CSCSS, 14/10/1918, Val-de-Grâce, box 490. Dutch East Indies: C. Brown, 'The influenza pandemic of 1918 in Indonesia', in N.G. Owen (ed.), *Death and disease in southern Asia: Explorations in social, medical and demographic history*, Singapore, 1987, p. 241. New Zealand: G. Rice, 'Christchurch in the 1918 influenza epidemic, a preliminary study', *New Zealand Journal of History*, vol. 13, 1979, p. 112.

288 *Notes*

18 Horses/soldiers: G. Cahen, *L'autre guerre. Essais d'assistance et d'hygiène sociales 1905–1920*, Paris-Nancy, 1920, p. 31. 700 doctors: Maginot, Chambre, 26/2/1914.

19 22,000, 80 per cent: Toubert, *Le Service de santé militaire*, pp. 27 and 127. British army: Winter, *The Great War*, p. 170.

20 Peyroux (Seine Inférieure), Chambre, 8 December 1915; Coyrard (Groupe médical parlementaire), Chambre, 22/3/1917. Lille: N. Rogeaux, 'La lutte contre la tuberculose à Lille, 1895–1940', Paris, Écoles des Chartes, 1992, p. 418. 1916: Chambre, 4 October 1916. Guiraud (Tarn): Chambre, 22 March 1917. Le Havre: Hermann Biggs, interview with Adrien Loir, 25 January 1917, Rockefeller Archive Center, R.G.1.1, 500T, box 28. Gard: Cabrol (Aveyron), Chambre, 6 March 1918. Police: Cruveilhier, 'La Grippe à Paris', p. 31. Lack of medicine: in Loire, Merlin, Chambre, 23 October 1918; also in Paris, Vincent (Côte-d'Or) and Merlin, Chambre, 9 October 1918; and in Nancy, Prefect to the Minister of Commerce, cable, 12 October 1918, Etat synoptique des cas de grippe par âge, du 9 septembre au 18 octobre 1918, Archives Municipales de Nancy I⁵31 [hereafter A.M. Nancy].

21 Civilian health services in Normandy, isolation, notification: G. Dequidt, 'Rapport de l'Inspection Générale des Services Administratifs', 18 January 1919, A.N. F1a 4586; Leuret, 'La grippe à Bordeaux', p. 22

22 Drafting doctors and nurses: Delater, 'La grippe', pp. 632 and 624; Robinson, 'The role of nursing', p. 21. Statistics on nursing: J. Godart, *Pour le travail et pour la paix. Hommage de ses amis à Justin Godart à l'occasion de son élection à l'Académie de Médecine*, Paris, Quillet, 1939, p. 176. Wards filled with sick soldiers: Dr Tuffier (Saint Antoine Hospital in Paris), CSCSS, 10 March 1919, Val-de-Grâce, box 365; Siredey, CSCSS, 10 February 1919, Val-de-Grâce; and meeting of 26 March 1918, Val-de-Grâce, box 530. Hospital beds: Cruveilhier, 'La grippe à Paris', pp. 30–1.

23 Masks rarely used: Delater, 'La grippe', pp. 624–5; Hildreth, 'The influenza pandemic', pp. 283–5. Closing public places: C. Dopter and V. de Lavergne, 'Données récemment acquises sur la prophylaxie et le traitement de la grippe', *Arch. Méd. Pharm. Mil.*, vol. 76, 1922, p. 6; Faivre, 'La lutte contre la grippe', p. 366; and the report by the Académie de Médecine, 15 October 1918: Hildreth, 'The influenza epidemic', p. 282; however, Parisian schools were dismissed from 26 October to 4 November: D.A.V. Puklin, 'Paris,' in Van Hartesveldt (ed.), *The 1918–1919 pandemic of influenza*, p. 74. Prefects: Chauffard, CSCSS, 14 October 1918, Val-de-Grâce, box 490. Académie des Science: see *C. R. hebdo. séances Acad. Sci.*, vol. 167, 1918, and vol. 168, 1919; see also Puklin, 'Paris', in Van Hartesveldt, *The 1918–1919 pandemic of influenza*, pp. 78–9; Roux was at that time head of the Pasteur Institute.

24 Tomkins, 'Failure', p. 446.

25 Altered age-structure: Huber, *La population*, p. 277. Spain: B. Echeverri Dàvila, *La gripe española. La pandemia de 1918–1919*, Madrid, Siglo XXI de España Editores, 1993, pp. 125–7; M.I. Porras Gallo, *Un Reto para la sociedad madrileña: la epidemia de gripe de 1918–19*, Madrid, Editorial Complutense, 1997, p. 65. Universal characteristic: G. Rice with L. Bryder, *Black November: The 1918 influenza epidemic in New Zealand*, Wellington, Allen & Unwin, 1988, pp. 159–60; N. Hart, 'Sex, gender and survival: Inequalities of life chances between European men and women', in J. Fox (ed.), *Health inequalities in European countries*, Aldershot, Gower, 1989, p. 124.

26 Demographers: Huber, *La population*, p. 278; historians: Dupâquier, *Histoire de la population française*, p. 71. Meurthe-et-Moselle: Statistique Générale de la France, *Résultats statistiques du recensement général de la population effectué le 6 mars 1921*, Paris, Imprimerie Nationale, 1925, t. 2, p. 13/1.

27 D. Tabutin, 'La surmortalité féminine en Europe avant 1940', *Population*, 1978, no. 1, pp. 135–6; Marañon, Pittaluga, Ruiz Falcó, 'Informe sobre el actual estado sanitario de Francia y su identitad con la epidemia gripal en España', *Siglo Médico*, 1918, quoted in Echeverri Dàvila, *La grippe*, p. 51. Pregnant women: Leuret, 'La grippe à Bordeaux', pp. 23–4; Camescasse, 'Le taudis rural et l'épidémie de grippe de 1918', *Rev. Hyg.*, vol. 41, 1919, p. 89. Recent calculations: J. Wilmoth, J. Vallin and G. Caselli, 'Quand certaines générations ont une mortalité différente de celle que l'on pourrait attendre', *Population*, vol. 44, 1989, pp. 350–3. Stillbirths: M. Dubesset, F. Thebaud and C. Vincent, 'Les munitionnettes de la Seine', in P. Fridenson (ed.), *L'autre front*, special issue of *Cahier du mouvement social*, 1977, p. 199, footnote 48. Paris: *Ann. Stat. Ville de Paris*, Paris, 1954, p. 17; Wilmoth, Vallin and Caselli, 'Générations', pp. 354–5.

28 Camps: Delater, 'La grippe', pp. 417–18. Army doctors: Sous-Secrétariat d'État au Service de Santé, 1ère Division Technique, 'Étude comparée des maladies contagieuses pendant les sept premiers mois de service chez les jeunes soldats des classes 1917–1918', CSCSS, Val-de-Grâce, box 534; M.A. Gouget, 'Une épidémie de grippe chez de jeunes recrues', *Ann. Méd.* (Paris), vol. 5, 1918, p. 421.

29 Bertillon's study: referred to in Préfecture, *Épidémie de grippe*, p. 45. Nancy: Bureau de l'État-Civil, 'Décès survenus par suite de grippe', 1/10/1918–31/3/1919, A.M. Nancy. The rate was based on the municipality's population of 104,898 in 1921, Statistique Générale de la France, *Résultats statistiques du recensement général de la population effectué le 6 mars 1921*, Paris, Imprimerie Nationale, t. 1, p. 1, 1923. Social geography of Nancy: F. Valette, 'Être pauvre à Nancy entre les deux guerres mondiales', *Ann. de l'Est*, 1988, vol. 40, p. 27.

30 Préfecture, *Épidémie de grippe*, pp. 41, 45, 76–7 and 82. Overcrowding: Gouget, 'Une épidémie de grippe', p. 420; A.W. Hewlett and W.M. Alberty, 'Influenza at navy base hospitals in France', *J. Amer. Med. Assoc.*, vol. 71, 1918, p. 1058; H. Brooks and C. Gillette, 'The Argonne influenza epidemic', *Medical Record*, vol. 97, 1920, p. 460.

31 Harmless, devastating scourge: L. Hersch, 'La Guerre et la grippe', *Biblio. univers. Rev. Genève*, 1924, p. 471. Difficult to blame the war: Crosby, *Epidemic*, pp. 216–17; Patterson, *Pandemic influenza*, p. 83; Tomkins, 'Failure', p. 443. Transportation network: K.D. Patterson and G.F. Pyle, 'The diffusion of influenza in sub-Saharan Africa during the 1918–1919 pandemic', *Social Science and Medicine*, vol. 17, 1983, pp. 1299 and 1302–4; Patterson, *Pandemic influenza*, p. 49; D. Killingray, 'The influenza pandemic of 1918–1919 in the British Caribbean', *Social History of Medicine*, vol. 7, 1994, pp. 59–87. Soldiers on leave: J. Reinach, Lafforgue, CSCSS, 14 October 1918, Val-de-Grâce, box 490. Virally equalised: Delater, 'La grippe', pp. 528–9.

32 Contingency: S. Ryan Johansson, 'Welfare, mortality, and gender: Continuity and change in explanations for male/female mortality differences over three centuries', *Continuity and Change*, vol. 6, 1991, p. 171. Impact on military tactics: Dujarric de la Rivière, *Souvenirs*, p. 110; Crosby, *Epidemic*, p. 163; P. Wilton, 'Spanish flu outdid World War I in number of lives claimed', *Canadian Medical Association Journal*, vol. 148, 1993, p. 2036.

33 One-off historical events: Hart, 'Sex, gender and survival', p. 121. Female workforce: A. Klaus, *Every child a lion: The origins of maternal and infant health policy in the United States and France, 1890–1920*, Ithaca and London, Cornell University Press, 1993, p. 248. The workday: G. Hardach, 'La mobilisation industrielle en 1914–1918: Production, planification et idéologie', in Fridenson, *L'autre front*, p. 94. War factories medical inspection: hearing of Albert Thomas, minister of Armament and Ammunition, Chambre, 17 November 1915. Wages: G. Hardach, 'Guerre, État et main-d'œuvre', in L. Murard and P. Zylberman

(eds), 'Le soldat du travail. Guerre, fascisme et taylorisme', *Recherches*, vol. 32/33, 1978, p. 292. Malnutrition: P. Pinchemel, *La région parisienne*, Paris, Presses Universitaires de France, 1979, pp. 29–30. Free restaurants: Cahen, *L'autre guerre*, pp. 90 and 94; and M. Gourwitch, 'Les cantines maternelles', doctoral dissertation in medicine, Paris, 1909.

13 Long-term effects of the 1918 'Spanish' influenza epidemic on sex differentials of mortality in the USA

1 M.C. Sheps, 'An examination of some methods of comparing several rates or proportions', *Biometrics*, 1959, vol. 15, pp. 87–97. See also N. Keyfitz, 'Should we index death rate or survivorships?', *Applied Mathematical Demography*, New York, Spring, 2nd edn, 1985, pp. 60–2.

2 M.C. Sheps, 'Shall we count the living or the dead?', *New England Journal of Medicine*, 1958, vol. 259, No. 25, pp. 1210–12.

3 B.N. Berin, G.J. Stolnitz and A. Tenenbein, 'Mortality trends of males and females over the ages', *Transactions of the Society of Actuaries*, 1989, vol. 41, pp. 1–19, in a review of the evolution of sex differences of mortality, do not make any influenza connection, probably because they considered changes in the value of $e(0)$ for men and women for decennial census years only. An earlier book by R.D. Retherford, *The Changing Sex Differential in Mortality*, Westport, CT, Greenwood Press, 1975, on the same subject makes no mention of flu. J. Wilmoth, J. Vallin and G. Caselli, 'When does a cohort's mortality differ from what we might expect?', *Population* (English Selection), 1990, vol. 2, pp. 113–14, using French data, discuss the long-term effects of the influenza epidemic, but they do not explicitly touch upon the same effects discussed here.

4 J.W. Tukey, *Exploratory Data Analysis*, Reading MA, Addison-Wesley, 1977.

5 In 1979, the differential between women and men in $e(0)$ was also 7.8 years.

6 S.H. Preston, N. Keyfitz and R. Schoen, *Causes of Death: Life Tables for National Populations*, New York, Seminar Press, 1972.

7 Other measures, such as the (overall or cause-specific) crude death date are not appropriate, because they can change as a result of changes in population structure, even when the age-specific rates have not changed.

8 United States Department of Health, Education and Welfare, 'Death rates by age, race, and sex, United States 1900–1953: selected causes. *Vital Statistics – Special Reports*, 43 (1–31), 1956. All data presented here come from this source, unless otherwise indicated.

9 In general, life expectancy is more sensitive than the ASDR to changes in mortality at specific ages, particularly young ages: in the life table, even if the force of mortality increases at only one age, the life table survivor column becomes lower for that age and for all ages thereafter; on the other hand, with the ASDR, if the force of mortality changes at one age, only that age is affected.

10 For the data used herein, the correlation between ASDR and $e(0)$ is 0.9935 for males and 0.9949 for females. For the difference between male and female values, the correlation between the ASDR and $e(0)$ is 0.87.

11 War deaths were not included in the US vital statistics registrations system, because these occurred overseas.

12 The term 'gastritis' is used here for the cause listed as 'gastritis, duodenitis, enteritis, and colitis, except diarrhea of newborn'.

13 This cause was later called 'peptic ulcers'; its classification under chronic conditions is for convenience only – *Heliobacter pylorii* is now known to play a role in the etiology of this condition.

14 The official classification of stroke was 'vascular lesions affecting central

nervous system' in earlier published tables and 'cerebrovascular disease' in the later tables.

15 It is possible that the selecting effect on men of the 1861–5 American Civil War (620,000 deaths out of a total population of 35 million, with deaths concentrated among young males) played *some* role in the observed sex difference in stroke. Many war deaths occurred due to infectious diseases, so it is not unreasonable to suppose that the surviving male cohorts had lower than average frailty (somewhat counteracted by the sub-population which was not fit enough to serve). Since the population at risk of death due to stroke is elevated in age, we might reasonably expect to see lower stroke death rates for males when the veterans' cohorts reached older ages. Nevertheless, this is unlikely to account for all of the observed effect because the age spread of veterans combined with the 4-year period of the war means that a putative war-related cohort effect would be somewhat diffuse. Veterans who were age 17 to 24 when they served in the war were age 69 to 88 in 1917–25, and if the observed effects are war-related, it is not obvious why the onset of the reversal is so sudden, because, for example, in 1915 the same veterans were in the age range 67–78, which is also susceptible to stroke.

16 While it is strictly true that the sum of all the cause-specific ASDRs exactly equals the ASDR for all causes, the same is not so when both the components and the total have been subjected to a smoother such as 3RSSH, twice, but the difference in this case is negligible.

17 The choice of years is somewhat arbitrary. Since the declines in these causes began in 1918 in some cases, it makes good sense to start one year earlier, in 1917. The end date of the interval is more subjective, but looking at 1920 or 1922 would not give substantially different results.

18 In the sense of Tukey, *Exploratory Data Analysis.*

19 A.J. Mercer, 'Relative trends in mortality from related respiratory and airborne infectious diseases', *Population Studies*, 1986, vol. 40, No. 1, p. 131, provides a similar graph for England and Wales for 1851–1921; the peak in 1918 for TB follows the American data insofar as it is present in the British data and is higher for males than for females. However, the decline in the male–female difference was less dramatic in Britain than in the USA, at least up to 1921. Later British data on TB clearly merits further attention in this regard.

20 The disproportionately high male use of tobacco and its damaging effects on the lungs is one possibility.

21 Another factor could come into play as well. Only some TB cases – those which are 'esputum positive' – are responsible for the spread of tuberculosis. These contagious cases cause cavities in their lungs which allow the production of bacilli-laden sputum; if these patients were disproportionately likely to die in 1918 (either from TB, or because their condition made them susceptible to influenza-related pneumonia), then that could have a further suppressing effect on TB transmission in the years immediately after 1918 (and hence on deaths due to new infections – but not those due to reactivated cases), because only sputum-positive cases spread *M. tuberculosis*. This would help men lower their gap in TB mortality only if there was a lot of intra-sex transmission, but it is plausible, given that TB is mostly a disease of adulthood, and given the levels of occupational segregation of the sexes in the 1920s.

22 The sort of selection seen here is what mathematical ecologists call 'harvesting', because the susceptible population is harvested at a particular time, due to some shock, leaving behind a much less susceptible population. This is seen in large cities during summer heat waves: in the first such episode, there are heat- and air quality-associated deaths, mostly among the elderly, and in the

second such episode there are many fewer deaths, the reason being that most of the susceptibles died during the first wave.

23 It is not entirely fair to call chronic nephritis an infectious cause, because it covers renal disorders of a variety of etiologies, but it includes the long-term effects on the kidneys of many infections. S.H. Preston, *Mortality patterns in National Populations: with special reference to recorded causes of death*, New York, Academic Press, 1976, cautions that it is an imprecise code.

24 For the war's selective effects on males see N. Hart, 'Sex, gender, and survival: inequalities of life chances between European men and women', in J. Fox (ed.), *Health Inequalities in European Countries*, Aldershot, Gower Press, 1989, pp. 109–41.

14 'A fierce hunger'

1 'Fierce hunger' is a common summation of the famine that followed the pandemic in southwest Tanzania, e.g. Kileke Mwakibinga, 17 January 1996. Oral histories are here cited by the names of the sources and dates and are keyed to an index in J.G. Ellison, 'Transforming obligations, performing identity: making the Nyakyusa in a colonial context', PhD dissertation, University of Florida, 1999. This chapter is based on field and archival research carried out from September 1994 to December 1996 in Tanzania and South Africa, funded in part by a Fulbright fellowship, for which I am grateful. I remain indebted to many people in southwest Tanzania, the archivists at the University of Cape Town Manuscripts and Archives Department [henceforth UCT], and the Tanzania National Archives [henceforth TNA]. I owe gratitude to the participants in the 1998 conference, and especially to Howard Phillips, David Killingray and Terence Ranger for their help with this chapter. I also thank others whose comments improved this paper, especially Tim Cleaveland, Holly Hanson, Peter Schmidt and Jan Shetler. The eastern African country Tanzania took its name at independence with the unification of mainland Tanganyika with Zanzibar and Pemba islands. Under German colonial rule the mainland territory was known as German East Africa.

2 Sabela Kinula and Kristina Ngahilo Matandala biti Mwaikama, 26 September 1996. Earthquakes rocked the region in May 1919 and devastated buildings in the district capital; TNA, New Langenburg District Annual Report for year ending 31 March 1920, p. 13.

3 Elija Mwakikagile, 6 November 1996.

4 G. Wilson, 'Introduction to Nyakyusa society', *Bantu Studies*, 1936, vol. 10, pp. 253–91; M. Wilson, *Good Company: A Study of Nyakyusa Age-Villages*, London, Oxford University Press, 1951; M. Wilson, *For Men and Elders: Change in the Relations of Generations of Men and Women among the Nyakyusa-Ngonde People 1875–1971*, New York, African Publishing Company, 1977.

5 M. Wilson, *Rituals of Kinship among the Nyakyusa*, London, Oxford University Press, 1957, p. 11.

6 Ibid., pp. 7–8.

7 Male rainmakers and both male and female healers/ritual officiants shared the title *abanyago* in Nyakyusa.

8 Andulile Mwafingulu, 27 September 1996; UCT, BC 880, Wilson Papers, Godfrey Wilson's fieldnotes, vol. 9, pp. 36–40, Kissoule [name of informant], December 1934. Subsequent references to Wilson's ethnographic fieldnotes are signified by 'GW', followed by volume and page numbers.

9 TNA, New Langenburg District Annual Report for year ending 31 March 1920. Asagwile Mwambulile Mwaliambwile, 7 November 1996.

10 GW 9, p. 68, 13 December 1934. On 2 November 1934, however, Mwakalobo

explained to Godfrey Wilson that he had gone through the *ubusoka* in German times, although not with his siblings – see GW 6, pp. 43–4.

11 Jeki Mwakilembo, 2 October 1996.

12 G. Maddox, '*Mtunya*: famine in central Tanzania, 1917–1920', *Journal of African History*, 1990, vol. 31, pp. 181–97; J. Iliffe, *Africans: The History of a Continent*, Cambridge, Cambridge University Press, 1995, p. 209, summarised it this way: 'The First World War campaign created widespread famine in East Africa ... As usual, these famines killed chiefly through diseases, especially smallpox among those clustered together for food and water.' Other illnesses were also associated with the time, e.g. venereal disease, probably syphilis – GW 41, p. 10, Fibombe, 24 September 1936; Kristina Ngahilo Matandala biti Mwaikama, 26 September 1996; TNA, New Langenburg District Annual Report for the year ending 31 March 1920.

13 See, for example, Great Britain, *Annual Reports on Tanganyika Territory*, 1920 to 1925; P. Prein, 'Mission to Arcadia: difference and identity in Rungwe (Tanzania) during the German colonial period (1890–1914)', MA thesis, University of Hamburg, 1995, p. 64. I am grateful to Philipp Prein for bringing this to my attention.

14 'General von Lettow did not go [to the railway between Kigoma and Dar es Salaam] but we turned, after we had marched northwards above Nyassa, to the west and were soon in Northern Rhodesia' (M. Taute, 'A German account of the medical side of the war in East Africa, 1914–1918', *Tanganyika Notes and Records*, 1939, vol. 8, p. 2); 'In mid-October, therefore, he [Lettow-Vorbeck] veered westward, passed around the north end of Lake Nyasa, and invaded Northern Rhodesia' (B. Farwell, *The Great War in Africa, 1914–1918*, New York, W.W. Norton and Company, 1986, p. 350).

15 M. Taute, 'A German account of the medical side of the war in East Africa, 1914–1918', p. 6.

16 Ibid., pp. 18–19.

17 C. Miller, *Battle for the Bundu: The First World War in East Africa*, New York, Macmillan, 1974, pp. 319–20.

18 TNA, New Langenburg District Annual Report for the year ending 22 June 1919, noted that it was 'peculiar how fatal the epidemic was in some villages whilst in others the death rate was small'; men more often died than women, and the total dead in the central area must have reached between 15,000 and 20,000 of a population estimated at 180,000. The report also mentioned that there were 43,000 fewer people than the previous year due to influenza, which is ambiguous and may indicate deaths from other outbreaks of the flu in 1918 or 1919. Heeding David Henige, the point is not the numbers of people who died, but the magnitude of the crisis as reflected in the high estimates, oral histories of responses, and the changes that are traceable to these times (D. Henige, 'Their numbers became thick: Native American historical demography as expiation', in J. Clifton (ed.), *The Invented Indian: Cultural Fictions and Government Policies*, New Brunswick, NJ, Transaction Publishers, 1990, pp. 169–91.

19 Elija Mwakikagile, 6 November 1996; Kileke Mwakibinga, 17 January 1996; Ambilike Mwasakyeni, 14 September 1996; Sondasi Matai Mwailima, 8 December 1995.

20 TNA, New Langenburg District Annual Report for the year ending 22 June 1919.

21 K.D. Patterson, 'The demographic impact of the 1918–19 influenza pandemic in sub-Saharan Africa: a preliminary assessment', in *African Historical Demography – Proceedings of a seminar held in the Centre of African Studies, University of Edinburgh*, Edinburgh, Centre of African Studies, University of Edinburgh, 1977, p. 404.

22 A.W. Crosby, *America's Forgotten Pandemic: The Influenza of 1918*, Cambridge, Cambridge University Press, 1989, p. 215. Many deaths were caused by pneumonic complications after bouts of flu.

23 Ibid.

24 Taute, 'A German account of the medical side of the war in East Africa, 1914–1918', p. 19. He recalled that 'that which we had in the war had never yet been known to me … The clinical picture, with its sudden onset with high fever and pain in the side was usually quite characteristic and showed a critical fall of fever about from the seventh to the twelve [sic] day. The scanty tenacious sputum was tinged with blood and showed either a rusty brown or even a markedly red colour until resolution occurred' (pp. 19–20). Editors of this translation suggested the ailment was influenza; Taute witnessed the influenza in November 1918 and said it was different from what they had confronted in August.

25 The most accurate records are for soldiers and officials; however, their mortality and morbidity might not resemble those of the ordinary population (Patterson, 'The demographic impact of the 1918–19 influenza pandemic in sub-Saharan Africa: a preliminary assessment', p. 409).

26 Ibid., p. 412. He accepted the estimate for New Langenburg of 10 per cent, which may be accurate, although there are no adequate means to know with certainty the exact mortality.

27 G. Pyle, *The Diffusion of Influenza: Patterns and Paradigms*, Totowa, New Jersey, Rowman and Littlefield, 1986, pp. 1, 41, 51. He noted that the virus had a 'sledgehammer effect' in the USA, which brought a 'temporary flattening or indisposition and mandatory bedrest [to] approximately 25 per cent of the United States population' (p. 52).

28 Tunyasye Tupilike Ikofu, 23 November 1995.

29 TNA, New Langenburg District Annual Report for the year ending 22 June 1919; GW 34, pp. 77–83, Ambilikile, 18 October 1935.

30 See definitions by Kileke Mwakibinga, 19 January 1996, and T. Meyer, *Wakonde: Maisha, Mila na Desturi za Wanyakyusa*, Mbeya, Tanzania, Motheco Publications, 1993, p. 223.

31 Kileke Mwakibinga, 19 January 1996. People on the Makonde plateau to the east considered the flu a judgement on Europeans for the war (T.O. Ranger, 'Godly medicine: the ambiguities of medical mission in southeastern Tanzania, 1900–1945', in S. Feierman and J. Janzen (eds), *The Social Basis of Health and Healing in Africa*, Berkeley, University of California Press, 1992, p. 262.) In Uzigua people blamed the flu on the war, seeing that the flu was 'spread by howitzers' smoke' or brought home by malevolent spirits with returning porters (J. Giblin, *The Politics of Environmental Control in Northeastern Tanzania, 1840–1940*, Philadelphia, University of Philadelphia Press, 1992, p. 155). See too T.O. Ranger, 'The influenza pandemic in Southern Rhodesia: a crisis of comprehension', in D. Arnold (ed.), *Imperial Medicine and Indigenous Societies*, Manchester, Manchester University Press, 1988, pp. 172–88.

32 Likakola Kisenjele, 6 December 1995.

33 Kileke Mwakibinga, 19 January 1996; D.R. Mackenzie, *The Spirit Ridden Konde*, London, Seeley, Service and Co. Ltd, 1925, p. 104, referred to the notion of contagions on the leaves where one sat during a case. Chiefs may have been told about the infectious nature of the flu by British officers, but these meetings had precedents.

34 See G. Wilson, 'Nyakyusa conventions of burial', *Bantu Studies*, 1939, vol. 13, pp. 1–31; Wilson, *Rituals of Kinship among the Nyakyusa*, ch. 2 and pp. 234–50.

35 Kileke Mwakibinga, 19 January 1996.

36 GW 43, pp. 31–3, Kalume, 16 October 1936. Before the war, perhaps in 1912

during a smallpox epidemic, Penja chiefs including Mwalukasa called for a cessation of funerals and told people not to attend funerals in other chiefs' areas (M. Wilson, *Communal Rituals of the Nyakyusa*, London, Oxford University Press, 1959, pp. 111–12).

37 The moratorium also checked actions by women healer/officiants at households to rectify past ritual failures, which some saw as a possible cause of the catastrophe.

38 E.g. Bilina Ifugwa Kalinga, Mbumi Lubange and Yusta Lukange kana Kalinga, 20 July 1996; Jeki Mwakilembo, 2 October 1996; Kileke Mwakibinga, 17 January 1996.

39 GW 68, p. 91, Fibombe, 7 October 1937. It was reported that, at times of scarcity, chiefs, who 'insist on their natives treating them with great respect . . . run what might be termed "soup kitchens" at their chief village, [and] during times of hunger any native under them has the right to call on his chief and be fed at least once per day provided he is of industrious habits' (TNA, New Langenburg District Annual Report for the year ending 31 March 1920).

40 Chief Polokoto described to Godfrey Wilson episodes in which the German administration hunted down officiants (GW 29, pp. 41–52, Polokoto, 15 August 1935). See too R. Kalindile, M. Mbilinyi and T. Sambulika, 'Grassroots struggles for women's advancement: the story of Rebeka Kalindile', in M.K. Ngaiza and B. Koda (eds), *Unsung Heroines: Women's Life Histories from Tanzania*, Dar es Salaam, WRDP Publications, 1991, pp. 112–13.

41 GW 33, pp. 48–50, Kikungubija and Nsyanigwa, 26 September 1935.

42 For example, see GW 29, pp. 30–3, Polokoto, 15 August 1935. That chiefs were expected to provide offerings was a point of contention in later famines, whereas during the 'famine of corms' chiefs tended to sacrifice.

43 Likakola Kisenjele, 6 December 1995; Tusaanege Mpuga, 10 December 1995; GW 34, pp. 77–83, Ambilikile, 18 October 1935; GW 25, pp. 23–4, Leonard Mwaisumo, 11 July 1935.

44 GW 28, pp. 91–9, Mwakasoule, 6 September 1935; GW 25, pp. 101–3, Kapetuka, 16 July 1935; Wilson, *Communal Rituals of the Nyakyusa*, p. 121.

45 GW 29, p. 29, Polokoto, 15 August 1935; Anyiambiliile Mwamaloba Mwasajonja, 27 June 1995; Tusaanege Mpuga, 10 December 1995.

46 GW 34, pp. 82–3, Ambilikile, 18 October 1935; Tusaanege Mpuga, 10 December 1995. Some people were fined for not remaining silent during the ritual: Tusaanege Mpuga, 10 December 1995; Ambilike Mwasakyeni, 14 September 1996.

47 Tusaanege Mpuga, 10 December 1995.

48 'Afterwards you would find *amatoki* [cooking bananas] when there had not been *amatoki*' (Likakola Kisenjele, 6 December 1995); 'And that's it. The next day you'd start harvesting food in the fields. It would be plentiful, not a little' (Ambilike Mwasakyeni, 14 September 1996); 'And they would pass and splash their medicines on the household. And many *amatoki* would come!' (Tusaanege Mpuga, 10 December 1995).

49 GW 25, pp. 23–4, Leonard Mwaisumo, 11 July 1935.

15 'The dog that did not bark'

1 Research for this chapter was undertaken with the help of a grant from the Hannah Institute for the History of Medicine, and from the Social Science and Humanities Council of Canada, whose support is gratefully acknowledged.

2 Cited in R. Collier, *The Plague of the Spanish Lady: The Influenza Pandemic of 1918–19*, London, Macmillan, 1974, p. 304.

3 Dr Thoulon, Chief of the Senegal Health Service, estimated the total dead at a

'minimum' of 19,000, but never indicated the basis for his calculation (P. Gouzien, 'L'Epidemie d'influenza de 1918–19 dans les colonies françaises', *Annales de Médecine et de Pharmacie Coloniale*, 1921–2, vol. 19, p. 273). It would appear he reached the figure by calculating 1.5 per cent of an overall Senegalese population estimated at 1.25 million. Accepting this total population figure, not because it is itself based on a formal census, but because we have no other choice, we would arrive at the very low mortality rate for Senegal of 15 per 1,000 from influenza in 1918. Patterson, for example, suggests an overall mortality of 37.5 per 1,000 for West Africa (K.D. Patterson, 'The demographic impact of the 1918–19 influenza pandemic in sub-Saharan Africa: a preliminary assessment', in *African Historical Demography – Proceedings of a seminar held in the Centre of African Studies, University of Edinburgh*, Edinburgh, Centre of African Studies, University of Edinburgh, 1977, p. 411). His rate would leave Senegal with just under 47,000 deaths, a number that, with all its problems, is far more probable than Thoulon's very low figure of 19,000.

4　The newspapers examined, *La Démocratie du Sénégal*, *L'A.O.F.* and *Le Petit Sénégalais*, seem to have been the only ones publishing in Senegal in the last quarter of 1918.

5　R. Collignon and C. Becker, *Santé et Population en Sénégambie des Origines à 1960: Bibliographie annotée*, Paris, Editions de l'I.N.E., 1989.

6　Gouzien wrote a general introduction, while the report for Senegal was written by Dr Thoulon (in Gouzien, 'L'Epidemie d'influenza de 1918–19 dans les colonies françaises', p. 273). During the same period, Gouzien also published a shorter version for the OIHP (P. Gouzien, 'La Pandémie grippale de 1918–19 dans les colonies françaises', *Bulletin Mensuel International d'Hygiène Publique*, 1920, vol. 12, pp. 686–724).

7　Gouzien, 'L'Epidemie d'influenza de 1918–19 dans les colonies françaises', pp. 289–91 and 270–6 respectively.

8　ANS, H61, Dr Thoulon to Governor of Senegal, 21 September 1918. A Brazilian researcher and a long-time resident of Dakar, Mme Isabel de Moraes, recently attempted to trace the Brazilian involvement in the Dakar pandemic. Although oral informants indicated to her that a small Brazilian cemetery near the present cathedral served as the burial site for the sailors, no trace of the site remains today (personal communication from Mme de Moraes, Dakar, 11 October 1990).

9　ANS, H61, Bernard to Governor of Senegal, 17 September 1918.

10　ANS, 4D 82, General Bonnier, Commander-in-Chief, Colonial Army in French West Africa, Report on Recruitment in 1918, Dakar, December 1918. Influenza continued to strike down African soldiers wherever it found them in 1918. One particularly disastrous episode involved the troop ship *Villaret Joyeuse*. It had left Douala in French Equatorial Africa with 974 new recruits aboard in September 1918, and had taken on another 732 at Cotonou in Dahomey. Before the ship reached Dakar, 80 per cent of the 1,706 men had contracted influenza, and when it docked, nine soldiers were dead on arrival as well as the French physician who had sailed with the men from Douala. The final death count was not recorded (ANS, 4D 81, Governor-General of French West Africa to General Bonnier, Dakar, 28 October 1918).

11　ANS, H61, Bernard to Governor of Senegal, 17 September 1918.

12　ANS, H61, Thoulon to Governor of Senegal, 21 September 1918. My translation here and elsewhere in the text.

13　ANS, 2G18 26, Monthly report for Kédougou, 20 November 1918.

14　ANS, 2G18 26, Report for December, 4 January 1919.

15　The monthly political reports for Podor stop in September 1918, too early for flu to have been reported, but other *cercle* reports were complete. See ANS

2G18 33 for Podor, 2G18 25 for Bakel, 2G18 27 for Matam and 2G18 28 for Saldé.

16 ANS, 2G18 1, Annual report for Senegal in 1918. The next year, when the Governor-General of French West Africa complained that he had received no political report for Senegal for 1919, the Governor excused himself on the grounds that he lacked sufficient personnel. ANS, 2G19 12, Governor-General Angoulvant to Minister of Colonies, undated, 1919.

17 ANS, 2G18 1, Angoulvant to Minister of Colonies, 17 January 1919.

18 ANS, 2G18 44, Monthly reports for Casamance, 1918. Such estimates were not based on solid data.

19 Gouzien, 'L'Epidemie d'influenza de 1918–19 dans les colonies françaises', p. 275.

20 See Thoulon for example, ibid., p. 272. The plague epidemic in the littoral was just beginning to abate when influenza struck. See ANS, 2G18 29, monthly political report for *cercle*, Diourbel, 30 September 1918. Like physicians the world over, many French doctors still believed that influenza was a bacterial rather than a viral disease. The viral agent for flu was not discovered until 1933.

21 ANS, H61, Thoulon to Governor of Senegal, Saint-Louis, 21 September 1918.

22 Gouzien, 'L'Epidemie d'influenza de 1918–19 dans les colonies françaises', p. 276.

23 ANS, 4D 82, General Bonnier, Report on recruitment in 1918, Dakar, December, 1918. While the question of whether the soldiers received free champagne cannot be ascertained, such a gesture by quartermasters in any national army would have been uncharacteristically generous.

24 Gouzien, 'L'Epidemie d'influenza de 1918–19 dans les colonies françaises', p. 273.

25 ANS, 2G18 28, Political report for Saldé, 1918. The entire *cercle's* medical staff consisted of one doctor and two aides, and indicates how ephemeral the French medical presence in the hinterland was.

26 Gouzien, 'L'Epidemie d'influenza de 1918–19 dans les colonies françaises', p. 271.

27 ANS, 2G18 44, Monthly reports for Casamance, 1918; Thoulon in Gouzien, 'L'Epidemie d'influenza de 1918–19 dans les colonies françaises', p. 276.

28 Ibid., pp. 284–8 and 291–4.

29 Ibid., p. 265.

30 Ibid., p. 269.

31 ANS, 1H89 163, Dr François Dieng, Head of Public Health, to the Delegate for Dakar, 2 October 1957.

32 Personal communication from Marc Dawson to David Patterson cited in Patterson, 'The demographic impact of the 1918–19 influenza pandemic in sub-Saharan Africa', p. 417.

33 E. M'Bokolo, 'Peste et société urbaine à Dakar: l'epidemie de 1914', *Cahiers d'études africaines*, 1982, vol. 22, pp. 27–44.

34 Ibid., p. 20.

35 See Collignon and Becker, *Santé et Population en Sénégambie.*

36 M'Bokolo, 'Peste et société urbaine à Dakar: l'epidemie de 1914', pp. 25–46; G.W. Johnson, *The Emergence of Black Politics in Senegal: The Struggle for Power in the Four Communes, 1900–1920*, Stanford, Stanford University Press, 1971.

37 M. Echenberg, *'Black Death, White Medicine': Bubonic Plague and the Politics of Public Health in Senegal, 1914–1945*, Portsmouth, N.H., Heinemann, 2002.

38 L. Taksa, 'The Masked Disease: Oral History, Memory and the Influenza Pandemic, 1918–19', in K. Darian-Smith and P. Hamilton (eds), *Memory and History in Twentieth-Century Australia*, Melbourne, Oxford University Press, 1994.

39 A.W. Crosby, *America's Forgotten Pandemic: The Influenza of 1918*, New York, Cambridge University Press, 1989, p. xiii.

40 Plague finally disappeared from Senegal after 1944 when the American Army medical corps helped French authorities exterminate the fleas which carried the deadly bacteria by spraying the infected areas with DDT.

16 Transmission of, and protection against, influenza

1 R.E. Shope, 'Influenza: history, epidemiology, and speculation', *Public Health Reports*, vol. 73, 1958, pp. 165–78.

2 V.C. Vaughan, 'Discussion of paper by F.C. Gram, "The influenza epidemic and its after-effects in the city of Buffalo"', *Journal of the American Medical Association*, vol. 73, 1919, pp. 890–1.

3 Ibid.

4 J.P. Fox, C.E. Hall, M.K. Cooney and H.M. Foy, 'Influenza virus infections in Seattle families, 1975–1979. I. Study design, methods and the occurrence of infections by time and age', *American Journal of Epidemiology*, vol. 116, 1982, pp. 212–27; W.P. Glezen, H.R. Six, A.L. Frank, L.H. Taber, D.M. Perrotta and M. Decker, 'Impact of epidemics upon communities and families', in A.P. Kendal and P. Patriarca (eds), *Options for the Control of Influenza*, New York, Alan R. Liss, 1986, pp. 63–73.

5 W.R. Dowdle, M.T. Coleman, S.R. Mostow, H.S. Kaye and S.C. Schoenbaum, 'Inactivated influenza vaccines. 2. Laboratory indices of protection', *Postgraduate Medical Journal*, vol. 49, 1973, pp. 159–63; A.S. Monto and A.P. Kendal, 'Effect of neuraminidase antibody on Hong Kong influenza', *Lancet*, vol. 1, 1973, pp. 623–5.

6 W.R. Dowdle, M.T. Coleman, S.C. Schoenbaum, S.R. Mostow, H.S. Kaye and J.C. Hierholzer, 'Studies on inactivated influenza vaccines. II. Effect on subcutaneous dosage on antibody levels in nasal secretions and protection against natural challenge', in D.H. Dayton Jr, P.A. Small Jr, R.M. Chanock, H.E. Kaufman and T.B. Tomasi Jr (eds), *The Secretory Immunologic System*, Washington, DC: US Department of Health, Education and Welfare, US Government Printing Office, 1970, pp. 113–27.

7 C. Armstrong and R. Hopkins, 'An epidemiological study of the 1920 epidemic of influenza in an isolated rural community', *Public Health Reports*, vol. 36, 1921, pp. 1671–702.

8 J. Hayslett, J. McCarroll, E. Brady, K. Deuschle, W. McDermott and E.D. Kilbourne, 'Endemic influenza. I. Serologic evidence of continuing and subclinical infection in disparate populations in the post-pandemic period', *American Review of Respiratory Disease*, vol. 85, 1962, pp. 1–8.

9 H.J. Foy, M.K. Cooney and R. McMahan, 'A/Hong Kong influenza immunity three years after immunization', *Journal of the American Medical Association*, vol. 226, 1973, pp. 758–61.

10 J.P. Fox, M.K. Cooney, C.E. Hall and H.M. Foy, 'Influenza virus infections in Seattle families, 1975–1979. II. Pattern of infection in invaded households and relation of age and prior antibody to occurrence of infection and related illness', *American Journal of Epidemiology*, vol. 116, 1982, pp. 228–42.

11 S.D. Collins, 'Trend and age variation of mortality and morbidity from influenza and pneumonia', in *A review and study of illness and medical care with special reference to long-time trends*, Public Health Monograph, No. 48 (Public Health Service Publication No. 544), Washington, DC, US Government Printing Office, 1957, pp. 51–73.

12 S.C. Schoenbaum, M.T. Coleman, W.R. Dowdle and S.R. Mostow, 'Epidemiol-

ogy of influenza in the elderly: Evidence of virus recycling', *American Journal of Epidemiology*, vol. 103, 1976, pp. 166–73.

13 T. Francis Jr, F.M. Davenport and A.V. Hennessy, 'A serologic recapitulation of human infection with different strains of influenza virus', *Transactions of the Association of American Physicians*, vol. 66, 1953, pp. 231–9.

14 W.M. Marine and J.E. Thomas, 'Antigenic memory to influenza A viruses in man determined by monovalent vaccines', *Postgraduate Medical Journal*, vol. 55, 1979, pp. 98–108.

15 Schoenbaum, Coleman, Dowdle and Mostow, 'Epidemiology of influenza in the elderly', pp. 166–73.

16 W.H. Stuart, H.B. Dull, L.H. Newton, J.L. McQueen and E.R. Schiff, 'Evaluation of monovalent influenza vaccine in a retirement community during the epidemic of 1965–1966', *Journal of the American Medical Association*, vol. 209, 1969, pp. 232–8.

17 W.P. Glezen, W.A. Keitel, L.H. Taber, P.A. Piedra, R.D. Clover and R.B. Couch, 'Age distribution of patients with medically-attended illnesses caused by sequential variants of influenza A/H1N1: Comparison to age-specific infection rates, 1978–1989', *American Journal of Epidemiology*, vol. 133, 1991, pp. 296–304.

18 Armstrong and Hopkins, 'An epidemiological study of the 1920 epidemic of influenza in an isolated rural community'.

19 T.D.Y. Chin, J.F. Foley, I.L. Doto, C.R. Gravelle and J. Weston, 'Morbidity and mortality characteristics of Asian strain influenza', *Public Health Reports*, vol. 75, 1960, pp. 149–58; R.E. Hope Simpson and I. Sutherland, 'Does influenza spread within the household?' *Lancet*, vol. 266, 1954, pp. 721–6.

20 F.L. Dunn, D.E. Carey, A. Cohen and J. Martin, 'Epidemiologic studies of Asian influenza in a Louisiana parish', *American Journal of Hygiene*, vol. 70, 1959, pp. 351–71.

21 Chin, Foley, Doto, Gravelle and Weston, 'Morbidity and mortality characteristics of Asian strain influenza'.

22 W.D.T. Brunyate, G.M. Fleming, A. Llopis and A.T. Roden, 'The early stages of the 1957 influenza epidemic in England and Wales in relation to the re-assembly of schools', *Monthly Bulletin of the Ministry of Health and the Public Health Laboratory Service*, vol. 20, 1961, pp. 88–91.

23 Fox, Cooney, Hall and Foy, 'Influenza virus infections in Seattle families, 1975–1979. II. Pattern of infection'.

24 W.P. Glezen and R.B. Couch, 'Interpandemic influenza in the Houston area, 1974–76', *New England Journal of Medicine*, vol. 298, 1978, pp. 587–92.

25 L.C. Jennings and J.A.R. Miles, 'A study of acute respiratory disease in the community of Port Chalmers. II. Influenza A/Port Chalmers/1/73: Intrafamilial spread and the effect of antibodies to the surface antigens', *Journal of Hygiene (Cambridge)*, vol. 81, 1978, pp. 67–75.

26 A.S. Monto, F.M. Davenport, J.A. Napier and T. Francis Jr, 'Modification of an outbreak of influenza in Tecumseh, Michigan by vaccination of schoolchildren', *Journal of Infectious Diseases*, vol. 122, 1970, pp. 16–25.

27 L.G. Rudenko, A.N. Slepushkin, A.S. Monto, E.P. Grigorieva, A.R. Rekstin, V.E. Bragina, A.P. Kendal, N. Cox, Y.Z. Gendon and G.I. Alexandrova, 'Comparative studies of the efficacy of live attenuated and inactivated vaccines in children in Novgorod', in C. Hannoun *et al.* (eds), *Options for the Control of Influenza II*, Amsterdam, Elsevier Science Publishers B.V., 1993, pp. 85–90.

28 M.F. Warburton, D.S. Jacobs, W.A. Langsford and G.E. White, 'Herd immunity following subunit influenza vaccine administration', *Medical Journal of Australia*, vol. 2, 1972, pp. 67–70.

29 Monto and Kendal, 'Effect of neuraminidase antibody on Hong Kong influenza'.

30 L.R. Elveback, J.P. Fox, E. Ackerman, A. Langworthy, M. Boyd and L. Gate-wood, 'An influenza simulation model for immunization studies', *American Journal of Epidemiology*, vol. 103, 1976, pp. 152–65.
31 Ibid.
32 Rudenko, Slepushkin, Monto, Grigorieva, Rekstin, Bragina, Kendal, Cox, Gendon and Alexandrova, 'Comparative studies of the efficacy of live attenuated and inactivated vaccines in children in Novgorod'.

Bibliography

Compiled by Jürgen Müller

There are two early bibliographies: D. and T. Thomson's *Influenza Biblio-graphy* (2 volumes, Baltimore, 1933–4), with 4,500 entries on Spanish Influenza, and C.G. Loosly, Bernard Portnoy and Edna Myers, *International Bibliography of Influenza 1930–1959* (Los Angeles, 1978) which added some 8,000 titles. Serial medical, historical and national bibliographies and recently published books and articles, unpublished theses and papers provided references to further titles. Contemporary European, US, other American, and South African medical journals were also checked for studies on Spanish influenza. Many of these articles were written by doctors summarising their experience in the pandemic, and therefore often began with comments on the aetiology and pathology of Spanish influenza, but without offering any new information to help in understanding the pandemic. The report written by the Ministry of Health of Great Britain (see entry under 'World') and the monographs written by E.O. Jordan and W.T. Vaughan (see entries under 'USA') superseded most of the earlier studies; thus, many of those earlier studies are not listed here. At the time of the influenza pandemic, the major US, French, British and German medical journals had correspondents in several countries; their often anonymous columns have not been included in the bibliography if regional studies have subsequently appeared.

As a result of the conference in Cape Town further titles, suggested by participants, were added to the bibliography, for which help I am grateful. All bibliographies are, in a sense, work in progress, and I would be pleased to receive further suggestions for inclusion. This bibliography includes published and some unpublished works. Most entries are in English or French. Some titles in other languages have been translated into English with the English title given in square brackets. It has not been possible to check all original titles, thus for a few entries only the translated title is known. The bibliography is intended as a guide to existing literature, which also indicates areas where significant research has been undertaken and those areas where little has been done. For example, there are very few studies on eastern Europe, most of Asia and several Latin American states.

The bibliography begins with a 'Global Studies' section, which includes international and inter-continental studies, and then is organised alphabetically by continents, and the countries within them. When an entry refers to two countries, the title is included in the first country mentioned and cross-referenced to the second country. Frontiers have changed but the references are to the boundaries as they were in 1918–19, e.g. the articles by Lemke and Lubinski, on the pandemic in the German region of Oppeln and the town of Breslau respectively, are under 'Germany', although today that region and city are Opole and Wrocław in Poland. Studies on United States and British troops in France have been included under that country's name.

Each entry provides the following information:

monograph: author(s), date of publication, title of book [translation of title into English where necessary], place of publication, publisher, and, where appropriate, the monograph series;
articles and chapters in books: author(s), date of publication, title of article [translation of title into English where necessary], name of journal or editor(s), and title of book, volume number, pages of article or chapter. Some entries are followed by an annotation in square brackets highlighting pages concerned with the Spanish influenza, original sources or special aspects covered. A few monographs are marked as 'reference work', and can be consulted for any regional study.

The following abbreviations are used:

AMédPhC = *Annales de Médecine et de Pharmacie Coloniales*
Anon. = Anonymous author(s)
J = Journal
JAMA = *Journal of the American Medical Association*
PHR = Public Health Reports

Global studies

Anon. (1927) *Quatrième Congrès International de Médecine et de Pharmacie Militaires*, 2 vols, Warsaw. [A conference section was on the influenza pandemic; text in French and English]
Collier, R. (1974) *The Plague of the Spanish Lady: The Influenza Pandemic of 1918–1919*, London and New York: Macmillan and Atheneum: 376 pp. (republished 1996, London: Allison & Busby). [Reference work; based on personal recollections by hundreds of people]
Davies, P. (1999) *Catching Cold. 1918's Forgotten Tragedy and the Scientific Hunt for the Virus*, London: Michael Joseph. [Popular account based on secondary sources]
Fouquier, A. (1922) 'La Pandémie Grippale dans les Colonies Françaises', Paris: Legrand, 42 pp. [Dissertation]

Frost, W.H. and Sydenstricker, E. (1919) 'Epidemic influenza in foreign countries', *PHR* 34, 25: 1361–76. [Also PHR Reprint No. 537]

Gouzien, P. (1920) 'La pandémie grippale de 1918–1919 dans les colonies françaises', *Bulletin Mensuel de l'Office International d'Hygiène Publique* 12: 686–724.

Gouzien, P. (1921) 'L'épidémie d'influenza, en 1918–1919 dans les colonies françaises. Note préliminaire', *Annales de Médecine et de Pharmarcie Coloniales* 19, 3: 264–70. [Gouzien was Médicin Inspecteur Général des Troupes Coloniales]

Graves, C. (1969) *Invasion by Virus. Can It Happen Again?*, London: Icon Books. [Episodic account based on newspaper reports]

Great Britain (1919) *Memoranda on Medical Diseases in the Tropical and Sub-Tropical War Areas*, London: HMSO, 280 pp.

Great Britain, Ministry of Health (1920) *Report on the Pandemic of Influenza, 1918–1919* (Reports on Public Health and Medical Subjects No. 4), London, 577 pp. [Reference work]

Hartesveldt, Fred R. Van (ed.) (1992) *The 1918–1919 Pandemic of Influenza. The Urban Impact in the Western World*, Lewiston: Edwin Mellen Press, 204 pp.

Hoehling, Adolph A. (1961) *The Great Epidemic*, Boston: Little Brown, 217 pp.

Johnson, Niall P.A.S. and Mueller, Juergen (2002) 'Updating the accounts: global mortality of the 1918–1920 "Spanish" influenza pandemic', *Bulletin of the History of Medicine* 76, 1: 105–15.

Jordan, Edwin Oakes (1927) see USA.

Killingray, David (1996) 'A new "Imperial Disease": The influenza pandemic of 1918–19 and its impact on the British Empire', unpublished seminar paper, University of London.

Kolata, Gina Bari (1999) *Flu. The Story of the Great Influenza Pandemic of 1918 and the Search for the Virus that Caused It*, New York: Farrar, Straus and Giroux, 330 pp. [Popular account]

Müller, Jürgen (1996) 'Die Spanische Influenza 1918/19. Der Einfluß des Ersten Weltkrieges auf Ausbreitung, Krankheitsverlauf und Perzeption einer Pandemie' [The influence of the First World War on the spread, course of disease and perception of a pandemic], in Wolfgang U. Eckart and Christoph Gradmann (eds), *Die Medizin und der Erste Weltkrieg* (Neuere Medizin- und Wissenschaftsgeschichte 3), Pfaffenweiler: Centaurus-Verlagsgesellschaft, pp. 321–42. [Based on newspapers, Prussian statistics]

Office Internationale d'Hygiène Publique (1919) Pandémie grippale de 1918–1919, *Bulletin Mensuel de l'Office International d'Hygiène Publique* 11, 8: 888–94. [Questionnaire that became basis for many national reports]

Oxford, J.S. (2000) 'Influenza A pandemics of the 20th century with special reference to 1918. Virology, pathology and epidemiology', *Reviews in Medical Virology* 10, 2: 119–33.

Patterson, K. David and Pyle, Gerald F. (1991) 'The geography and mortality of the 1918 influenza pandemic', *Bulletin of the History of Medicine* 65, 1: 4–21.

Pottevin, Henri (1921) Rapport sur la pandémie grippale de 1918–19, présenté au comité permanent de l'Office International d'Hygiène Publique, *Bulletin Mensuel de l'Office International d'Hygiène Publique* 13, 2: 125–81. [Reference work]

Royal Society of Medicine (1919) *Influenza. A Discussion*, London: Longmans, Green.

Africa

Cederquist, Karl (1919) 'Fran var mission i Ostafrika', *Missionstidning*, 12: 92. [Swedish missionary on influenza, probably in Ethiopia]

Huot (1921) L'Afrique Équatoriale française, l'épidémie d'influenza de 1918–1919, *Annales de Médecine et de Pharmacie Coloniales* 19, 4: 443–4.

Müller, Jürgen (1998) 'What's in a name? Spanish Influenza in Africa and what local names say about the perception of this pandemic', unpublished paper for Conference on 'The Spanish Flu 1918–1998', held in Cape Town. [Based on oral sources, African newspapers, colonial files and missionary journals]

Müller, Jürgen (1997) 'Marker und Beschleuniger der kolonialen Transformation. Regionale und komparative Hypothesen zur Spanischen Influenza in Afrika' [Marker and accelerator of colonial transformation. Regional and comparative hypotheses on Spanish influenza in Africa], in Andreas Eckert and Jürgen Müller (eds), *Transformationen der europäischen Expansion vom 16. bis zum 20. Jahrhundert* (Loccumer Protokolle 26/96), Loccum: Evangelische Akademie, pp. 198–207.

Patterson, K. David (1981) 'The demographic impact of the 1918–19 influenza pandemic in sub-Saharan Africa: A preliminary assessment', in Christopher Fyfe and David McMaster (eds), *African Historical Demography II. Proceedings of a Seminar held in the Centre of African Studies*, Edinburgh, University of Edinburgh, pp. 401–33.

Patterson, K. David and Pyle, Gerald F. (1983) 'The diffusion of influenza in sub-Saharan Africa during the 1918–1919 pandemic', *Social Science & Medicine* 17, 17: 1299–307.

Ranger, Terence O. (1992) 'Plagues of beasts and men: prophetic responses to epidemic in eastern and southern Africa', in Terence O. Ranger and Paul Slack (eds), *Epidemics and Ideas: Essays on the Historical Perception of Pestilence* (Past and Present Publication), Cambridge: Cambridge University Press, pp. 241–68.

Tomkins, Sandra M. (1994) 'Colonial administration in British Africa during the influenza epidemic of 1918–19, *Canadian J African Studies* 28, 1: 60–83.

Algeria

Daigre, J. (1933) 'Une Épidémie de Grippe dans le Sahara Central', Djanet, Janvier 1933, *Archives de l'Institut Pasteur d'Algérie* 11, 3: 445–54. [Probably a trailer epidemic to 1918 or 1933(?) in a remote oasis with a mortality rate of 7 per cent, mainly young adults]

Angola

Ribas, Oscar Bento (1952) 'Die Plage' [The plague], in Marie-Louise Lüscher (ed.) *Tam Tam und andere Erzählungen aus Ost-, West- und Zentralafrika*, Zürich: detebe 1980, pp. 211–28. [Short story about an epidemic in Angola in 1920, probably influenza. First published in 1952 as 'A praga' in Ribas, *Ecos da Minha Terra. Dramas Angolanos*, Luanda: Lello & Ca., pp. 125–42]

Benin

Bouffard, Gustave (1921) 'Dahomey, l'épidémie d'influenza de 1918–1919', *Annales de Médecine et de Pharmacie Coloniales* 9, 3: 291–4.

Botswana

Munshingeh, A.C.S. (1984) A history of disease and medicine in Botswana, 1820–1945, unpublished PhD thesis, University of Cambridge. [Chapters 4–5 on disease patterns, including influenza, in the colonial period]

Spears, John V. (1979) 'An epidemic among the Bakgatla: The influenza of 1918', *Botswana Notes and Records* 11: 69–76.

Burkina Faso

Delrieu (1921) 'Haut-Sénégal et Niger, l'épidémie d'influenza de 1918–1919', *Annales de Médecine et de Pharmacie Coloniales* 19, 3: 280–2.

Burundi

Botte, Roger (1985) see Rwanda.

Cameroon

Martin, Gustave (1921) 'Cameroun, l'épidémie d'influenza de 1918–1919', *Annales Médecine et de Pharmacie Coloniales* 19, 3: 294–303.

Central African Republic

Ricau (1921) 'Oubangui-Chari, l'épidémie d'influenza de 1918–1919', *Annales de Médecine et de Pharmacie Coloniales* 19, 4: 448–55.

Chad

Azevedo, Mario Joaquim (1978) 'Epidemic disease among the Sara of southern Chad, 1890–1940', in Gerald W. Hartwig and K. David Patterson (eds), *Disease in African History*, Durham: Duke University Press, pp. 118–52 [pp. 139–43 on influenza].

Grosfillez (1921) 'Territoire militaire du Tchad, l'épidémie d'influenza de 1918–1919', *Annales de Médecine et de Pharmacie Coloniales* 19, 4: 455–8.

Congo (Brazzaville)

Marzin, G. (1921) 'Moyen-Congo, l'épidémie d'influenza de 1918–1919', *Annales de Médecine et de Pharmacie Coloniales* 19, 4: 444–8.

Democratic Republic of Congo

Anon (1919) 'La grippe au Haut-Congo', *Missions d'Afrique des Pères Blancs*, pp. 26–8.

Janssens, Peter-Gustaf and Halet, J. (1992) 'Maladies respiratoires non tuberculeuses', in P.G. Janssens, M. Kivits and J. Vuylsteke (eds), *Médecine et hygiène en Afrique Centrale de 1885 à nos jours*, Bruxelles, pp. 767–89. [pp. 770–5 history of influenza]

Kivilu, Sabakinu (1984) 'Population and health in Zaire during the colonial period from the end of the 19th century to 1960', in *TransAfrican J History* 13: 92–109. [p. 97 influenza created labour shortage]

Van Den Branden, Jan Frans Fritz (1919) 'La grippe espagnole au Stanleypool', *Congo Belge*. 6.

Van Nitsen, R. and Walravens, P. (1922) 'Sur une épidémie de manifestations broncho-pulmonaires et leur traitement', *Annales de la Société Belge de Médecine Tropicale Bruxelles* 2, 2–3: 147–50. [Influenza trailer epidemic in Likasi in 1921]

Vincke (1919) 'De l'epidémie de grippe au Katanga. Ses principales formes cliniques. Sa prophylaxie et traitement. 11 pp.

Côte d'Ivoire

Burdin (1921) 'Côte d'Ivoire, l'épidémie d'influenza de 1918–1919', *Annales de Médecine et de Pharmacie Coloniales* 19, 3: 289–91.

Djibouti

Cozanet (1921) 'Côte française des Somalis, l'épidémie d'influenza de 1918–1919', *Annales de Médecine et de Pharmacie Coloniales* 19, 4: 476–8.

Egypt

Benjafield, J.D. (1919) 'Notes on the influenza epidemic in the Egyptian expeditionary force', *British Medical Journal* II (9 August): 167–9.

Garner, Cathcart (1921) 'Annual report for the year 1918: Colonial Medical Reports, No. 126, Egypt', *J Tropical Medicine and Hygiene* 24, Supplement, pp. 75–88.

Garner, Cathcart (1922) 'Annual report for the year 1919: Colonial Medical Reports. No. 133 Egypt', *J Tropical Medicine and Hygiene* 25, Supplement, pp. 17–25.

McWalter, J.C. (1919) 'On the influenza epidemic in Egypt', *The Medical Press*, London, n.s., 107, 2: 24–5.

Ethiopia

Pankhurst, Richard (1975) 'The "Hedar Basita" of 1918', *Journal of Ethiopian Studies* 13, 2: 103–31. [Based on Italian and British colonial files, Ethiopian diaries, oral sources and Ethiopian church records]

Pankhurst, Richard (1977) 'A historical note on influenza in Ethiopia', *Medical History* 21: 195–200.

Pankhurst, Richard (1989) 'The Great Ethiopian Influenza (Ye Hedar Beshita) Epidemic of 1918', *Ethiopian Medical Journal* 27, 4: 235–42.

Gabon

David (1921) 'Gabon, l'épidémie d'influenza de 1918–1919', *Annales de Médecine et de Pharmacie Coloniales* 19, 4: 458–62.

Ghana

Addae, Stephen (1996) *Evolution of Modern Medicine in a Developing Country: Ghana 1880–1960*, Edinburgh: Durham Academic Press, Chapter 19.
Dunn, John and Robertson, A.F. (1973) *Dependence and Opportunity. Political Change in Ahafo* (African Studies Series No. 9). Cambridge: Cambridge University Press. [pp. 100–1 on influenza]
Patterson, K. David (1983) 'The influenza epidemic of 1918–19 in the Gold Coast', *J African History* 24, 4: 485–502, and also in *Transactions of the Historical Society of Ghana* (1995), XVI, 2, n.s., 1: 205–25.
Scott, David (1965) *Epidemic Disease in Ghana, 1901–1960*, London: Oxford University Press. [pp. 188–91 on influenza]

Guinea

Pezet (1921) 'Guinée Française, l'épidémie d'influenza de 1918–1919', *Annales de Médecine et de Pharmacie Coloniales* 19, 3: 284–8.

Kenya

Dawson, Marc Harry (1983) 'Socio-economic and epidemiological change in Kenya: 1880–1925', unpublished PhD thesis, University of Wisconsin-Madison, 330 pp. [pp. 163–89 on influenza, based on medical and administrative records and interviews in Murang'a District, Kikuyu]
Müller, Jürgen (1995) 'Patterns of reaction to a demographic crisis. The Spanish influenza pandemic (1918–1919) in sub-Saharan Africa. A research proposal and preliminary regional and comparative findings', University of Nairobi, Department of History. Staff Seminar Paper No. 6, 1994–95, Nairobi, 18 pp.
Ndege, George Oduor (1996) 'Disease and socio-economic change: The politics of colonial health care in western Kenya, 1895–1939', unpublished PhD thesis, West Virginia University, Morgantown, 357 pp. [pp. 208–14 on influenza]

Liberia

Harley, George Way (1970) *Native African Medicine. With Special Reference to its Practice in the Mano Tribe of Liberia*, London: Frank Cass. [pp. 43–4 and 76–7 on treatment of Spanish influenza by healers]

Madagascar

Camail (1921) 'Madagascar, l'épidémie d'influenza de 1918–1919', *Annales de Médecine et de Pharmacie Coloniales* 19, 4: 463–74.
Gale, W. Kendall (1919) 'The reign of the terror', *The Chronicle of the London Missionary Society*, n.s., 27 (19 October), p. 163. [Notes from a missionary at the village of Anjozorobe on epidemic of May 1919]

Malawi

Gelfand, Michael (1957) *Lakeside Pioneers: Socio-Medical Study of Nyasaland (1875–1920)*, Oxford: Basil Blackwell. [pp. 296–7 on influenza]
Musambachime, Mwelwa Chambikabalenshi (1998) 'Consequences of the influenza pandemic of 1918 on Zambia and Malawi', unpublished paper for the 'Conference on the Spanish flu 1918–1998', held in Cape Town, 23 pp.
Page, Melvin (1998) 'The 'fluenza on the road to Vua: A Nyasaland case study of a medical crisis and colonial politics', unpublished paper for the 'Conference on the Spanish flu 1918–1998', held in Cape Town, 25 pp.
Stuart, M. (1919) 'The influenza in Nyasaland', *The Record of the Home and Foreign Mission Work of the United Free Church of Scotland* 19, 224 (19 August): 177.

Mauritania

Combe (1921) 'Mauritanie, l'épidémie d'influenza de 1918–1919', *Annales de Médecine et de Pharmacie Coloniales* 19, 3: 276–80.

Mauritius

Fokeer, A.F. (1921) *The Spanish Influenza in Mauritius*, Port Louis: Mauritius Indian Time, 54 pp.
Reddi, Sadasivam J. (1998) 'A case study of the influenza of 1919 in Mauritius', unpublished paper for the 'Conference on the Spanish flu 1918–1998', held in Cape Town, 20 pp.

Morocco

Abbatucci, Severin (1920) 'Considérations cliniques sur l'épidémie de grippe de 1918–1919. Observée à l'hôpital de Fez (Maroc)', *Annales de Médecine et de Pharmacie Coloniales* 18, 1: 76–80.
Nicaud, P. (1919) 'La grippe à Fez', *Bulletins et Mémoires de la Societé Médicale des Hôpitaux de Paris*, 3 serie, 43: 356–66.

Namibia

Kriele, Johannes (1923) 'Die Verbreitung der Influenzaepidemie des Jahres 1918 in Süd-Afrika und dem früheren Deutsch-Südwest-Afrika, ihre Erscheinungsform und Bekämpfung' [Spread of influenza epidemic in South Africa and former German Southwest Africa in 1918, form and treatment], unpublished dissertation, Friedrich-Wilhelm-Universität, Berlin, 63 pp. [Based on medical reports, newspapers and own experience as nurse in Swakopsmund]

Musambachime, Mwelwa Chambikabalenshi (1999) 'Kapitohanga: The disease that killed faster than bullets.' The impact of the Influenza Pandemic in the South West Africa Protectorate (Namibia) from October 1918 to December 1919', Basler Afrika Bibliographien Working Paper No. 4: 1999, Basel, 36 pp.

Wallace, Marion Elizabeth (1997) 'Health and society in Windhoek, Namibia 1915–1945', unpublished PhD thesis, University of London. [pp. 128–49 on influenza]

Niger

Delrieu (1921) see Burkina Faso.

Néel (1921) 'Territoire militaire du Niger, l'épidémie d'influenza de 1918–1919', *Annales de Médecine et de Pharmacie Coloniales* 19, 3: 282–3.

Nigeria

Amadi, Elechi (1970) *The Great Ponds* (African Writers Series No. 44), London: Heinemann. [A novel – see final chapter]

Isichei, Elizabeth (1976) *A History of the Igbo People*, London: Macmillan Press. [pp. 223–4 on influenza in Igboland, Nigeria]

Isichei, Elizabeth (1983) *A History of Nigeria*, London: Longman. [pp. 413–15 on influenza]

Ohadike, Don C. (1981) 'The influenza pandemic of 1918–19 and the spread of cassava cultivation on the lower Niger: a case study in historical linkages', *J. African History* 22, 3: 379–91. [Based on colonial reports and oral sources]

Ohadike, Don C. (1991) 'Diffusion and physiological responses to the influenza pandemic of 1918–19 in Nigeria', *Social Science & Medicine* 32, 12: 1393–9.

Peel, J.D.Y. (1983) *Ijeshas and Nigerians. The Incorporation of a Yoruba Kingdom 1890s–1970s*, Cambridge: Cambridge University Press. [pp. 165, 170 on influenza]

Schram, Ralph (1971) *A History of the Nigerian Health Services*, Ibadan: Ibadan University Press. [pp. 189–90 on influenza]

Willams, Luke (1989) 'Nigeria and the great influenza pandemic of 1918–1919: a conceptual challenge for the history of medicine', unpublished MA thesis, African Research Institute, La Trobe University.

Williams, Luke (1997) 'Nigeria and the great influenza pandemic of 1918', unpublished paper for AFSAAP Conference, Canberra.

Réunion

Auber, Léon (1921) 'Réunion, l'épidémie d'influenza de 1918–1919', *Annales de Médecine et de Pharmacie Coloniales* 19, 4: 474–6.

Ozoux, Leon (1919) 'Note sur la grippe à la Réunion', *La Presse Médicale* 27, 76, Supplement: 1086–8.

Rwanda

Botte, Roger (1985) 'Rwanda and Burundi, 1889–1930: Chronology of a slow assassination, Part 2', *International J African Historical Studies* 18, 2: 289–314. [pp. 304–5 missionary records on epidemiology of influenza]

Senegal

Echenberg, Myron (1993) 'L'historie et l'oubli collectif: L'épidémie de grippe de 1918 au Sénégal', in Dennis D. Cordell *et al.* (eds), *Population, réproduction, societés: Perspectives et grijeux de démographique sociale. Mélange en l'honneur de Joel W. Gregory*, Montreal: Les Presses de l'Université de Montréal, pp. 283–95. [Memory of influenza covered by experience of bubonic plague]

Lunn, Joe Harris (1993) 'Memoirs of the maelstrom. A Senegalese oral history of the First World War', unpublished PhD thesis, University of Wisconsin-Madison. [Based on 87 interviews, pp. 462–6 on influenza]

Maximo Prates, Manuel (1918) 'Una epidemia a bordo da canhoneira "Beira"' [An epidemic on board the gunboat "Beira"], *Medicina Contemporânea* 36, 34: 265–7 (abstract *Tropical Disease Bulletin*, 13 (1919), 6: 348). [Probably early influenza outbreak in Dakar harbour]

Thoulon (1921) 'Sénégal, l'épidémie d'influenza de 1918–1919', *Annales de Médecine et de Pharmacie Coloniales* 19, 3: 270–6.

Sierra Leone

Cole, Festus (1992) '"Man-Hu": The influenza epidemic in Sierra Leone, 1918', unpublished paper African History Seminar, School of Oriental and African Studies, University of London, 14 October 1992, 27 pp.

Cole, Festus (1994) 'Sierra Leone and World War I', unpublished PhD thesis, University of London. [Chapter 6 on influenza]

Somalia

Mohamed, Jama (1999) 'Epidemics and public health in early colonial Somaliland', *Social Science & Medicine* 48, 4: 507–21.

South Africa

Anderson, A. Jasper (1919) 'Influenza in Cape Town', *South African Medical Record* 17, 3: 36–9.

Anon. (1919) 'Medical influenza victims in South Africa', *The Lancet* 1919/I:78. [Baboons, monkeys dying of influenza]

Ashe, E. Oliver (1919) 'Some random recollections of the Kimberley influenza epidemic', *South African Medical Record* 17, 1: 6–9.

Broom, R. (1918) 'Notes on the influenza epidemic – Herbert District', *South African Medical Record* 16, 23: 363–4.

Bruce-Bays, J. (1918) 'Notes on the influenza epidemic – East London', *South African Medical Record* 16, 24: 383.

Burman, C.E.L. (1919) 'A review of the influenza epidemic in Ladysmith and District, with clinical observations', *South African Medical Record* 17, 1: 3–6.

Burman, Jose (1972) 'Influenza epidemic', *Standard Encyclopaedia of Southern Africa*, 12 vols. (1970–76) vol. 6, pp. 94–5.

Cairns, P.T. (1919) 'Report on an outbreak of epidemic influenza, Philipstown and District, October and November, 1918', *South African Medical Record* 17, 2: 19–24.

Cairns, P.T. (1920) 'Notes on epidemic influenza', *South African Medical Record* 18, 3: 165–7. [3 epidemics at Philipstown]

Callaway, Godfrey (1919) 'Letter', *The Cowley Evangelist*, February 1919, pp. 36–9. [Tsolo District]

Cassidy, C.G. (1918) 'Notes on the influenza epidemic – Valkenburg Mental Hospital', *South African Medical Record* 16, 24: 382.

Chard, Augustine (1919) 'Letter', *The Cowley Evangelist*, March 1919, pp. 56–7. [Tsolo District]

Coetzee, C.H.H. (1919) 'The influenza epidemic at Edenburg, O.F.S.: An apparently successful routine', *South African Medical Record* 17, 7: 97–101.

Gear, James H.S. (1983) 'The 1918 influenza epidemic', *Adler Museum Bulletin*, Adler Museum of the History of Medicine, University of the Witwatersrand (Johannesburg) Vol. 9, Special Issue, November, pp. 13–20.

Graham, John A. (1919) 'Some observation on the influenza epidemic at Bethulie', *South African Medical Record* 17, 3: 39–41.

Graham, John A. (1919) 'Notes on influenza at Bethulie, O.F.S', *South African Medical Record* 17, 18: 282–3. [Second epidemic]

Hamilton, C.B. (1919) 'The native mind', *The Presbyterian Churchman* 17, January 1919, p. 7. [Transvaal]

Hamilton, C.B. (1919) 'War and influenza', *The Presbyterian Churchman* 17, April 1919, p. 39. [Transvaal]

Hay-Michel, A. (1919) 'Influenza on the Zaaiplaats Mine', *South African Medical Record* 17, 2: 24–6.

Hummel, H.C. (1990) 'Grahamstown 1914–1918: Four wartime themes', *Contree: Tydskrif vir Suid Afrikaanse Stedelike en Streekgeskiedenis* (Pretoria) 28: 21–9.

Jones, F.R. (1918) 'Notes on the influenza epidemic – Oliphant's Hoek, Cape Province', *South African Medical Record* 16, 24: 384.

Katzenellenbogen, J.M. (1988) 'The 1918 influenza epidemic in Mamre', *South African Medical Journal* 74: 362–4. [Moravian mission station]

Kriele, Johannes (1923) see Namibia.

Leigh, R. (1918) 'Notes on the influenza epidemic – Reitz, O.F.S', *South African Medical Record* 16, 23: 365.

Lister, Fredrick Spencer (1918) 'The Bacteriology of epidemic influenza on the Witwatersrand', *Medical J South Africa* 14, 4: 290–3.

Loeser, H.A. (1918) 'Epidemic influenza of the pulmonary type. With a review of 2,183 cases in South African native mine labourers', *Medical J South Africa* 14, 5: 322–7. [Johannesburg]

Malan, Marais (1988) *The Quest of Health. The South African Institute for Medical Research*, Johannesburg: Lowry Publishers. [Chapter 4 'Influenza and Newcastle disease']

Marais, D.P. and Daneel, J. (1918) 'Discussion on the Cape Town influenza epidemic', *South African Medical Record* 16: 353–9.

Parnell, Susan (1991) 'Sanitation, segregation and the Natives (Urban) Areas Act. African exclusion from Johannesburg's Malay Location, 1897–1925', *J Historical Geography* 17, 3: 271–88. [Influenza epidemic was an argument for eviction]

Phillips, Howard (1979) 'Black October. Cape Town and the Spanish Influenza epidemic of 1918', in Christopher C. Saunders (ed.), *Studies in the History of Cape Town, Vol. 1,* Cape Town: University of Cape Town – Centre of African Studies. [Based mainly on Cape Times newspapers 1918–20]

Phillips, Howard (1985) 'The impact of the Spanish 'Flu epidemic of 1918 on Cape Town', in 10th Biennial National Conference of the South African Historical Society, 15–18 January 1985, University of Cape Town. Conference Paper No. 12, 58 pp.

Phillips, Howard (1987) 'The local state and public health reform in South Africa: Bloemfontein and the consequences of the Spanish 'Flu Epidemic of 1918', *Journal of Southern African Studies* 13, 2: 210–33. [Based on Influenza Epidemic Commission evidence, newspapers, municipal files and oral sources]

Phillips, Howard (1987) 'Why did it happen? Religious and lay explanations of the Spanish 'flu epidemic of 1918 in South Africa', *Kronos:* 'n Geleentheidspublikasie van die Wes-Kaaplandse Instituut vir Historiese Navorsing (Bellville) Vol. 12, pp. 72–92.

Phillips, Howard (1988) 'South Africa's worst demographic disaster. The Spanish Influenza epidemic of 1918', *South African Historical Journal* 20: 57–73.

Phillips, Howard (1990) *'Black October'. The Impact of the Spanish Influenza Epidemic of 1918 on South Africa* (Archives Year Book for South African History, 53rd year, vol. 1) Pretoria: The Government Printer, 281 pp. [published version of a PhD thesis, University of Cape Town, 1984. [Reference work; based on all available written evidence plus oral sources]

Phillips, Howard (1990) 'The origin of the Public Health Act of 1919', *South African Medical Journal* 77: 531–2.

Phillips, Howard (1996) 'The bifurcated transmission of Spanish Influenza to South Africa in 1918 and its life and death consequences', in Jeanette Covacevich, John Pearn, Donna Case, Ian Chapple and Gael Phillips (eds), *History, Heritage and Health. Proceedings of the Fourth Biennial Conference of the Australian Society of the History of Medicine* (Occasional Papers on Medical History 7), Brisbane: Australian Society of the History of Medicine, pp. 153–5.

Shine, A.V. (1919) 'Notes on the influenza epidemic – Steynsburg', *South African Medical Record* 17, 3: 41–2.

Thompson, Kelly (1996) 'Spanish Influenza in Natal', unpublished BA history honours dissertation, University of Natal, Durban.

Turner, Charles H. (1919) 'Letter', *The Cowley Evangelist,* January 1919, pp. 17–18. [Cape Town]

Union of South Africa (1919) *Report of the Influenza Epidemic Commission,* U.G.15-'19, Cape Town: Cape Times Ltd.

Wirgman, A.T. and Mayo, Cuthbert Edward (1925) *The Collegiate Church and Parish of St Mary Port Elizabeth. A Record of Parochial History,* London: Longmans, Green. [pp. 141–3 on influenza]

Wood, E.E. (1918) 'Notes on the influenza epidemic – Tokai Prison and Porter Reformatory', *South African Medical Record* 16, 23: 364.

Sudan

Darley, Henry A.C. (1926) *Slaves and Ivory. A Record of Adventures and Exploration in the Unknown Sudan, and Among the Abyssinian Slave Raiders*, London: Witherly. [Influenza reduced slave raids]

Tanzania

Boell, Ludwig (1951) *Ostafrika im Weltkrieg 1914–1918 – Der Lettow-Feldzug* [East Africa in the 1914–1918 World War – The Lettow campaign], Hamburg. [pp. 421–4 on influenza and how it affected German soldiers; based on German biographies]

Clyde, David F. (1962) *History of the Medical Services of Tanganyika*, Dar es Salaam: Government Printer.

Deppe, Ludwig (1919) *Mit Lettow-Vorbeck durch Afrika* [With Lettow-Vorbeck through Africa], Berlin: Verlag August Scherl. [pp. 451–2, 459–61 on influenza, autobiographical]

Fischer, Otto (1932) 'Studien zur Pathologie und Epidemiologie Ost-Afrikas. Beobachtungen und Untersuchungen im Mandatsgebiet Tanganyika (Deutsch-Ost-Afrika)', *Beihefte zum Archiv für Schiffs- und Tropen-Hygiene* 36, Supplement 1: 1–98. [pp. 77, 95–6 on influenza and encephalitis lethargica]

Giblin, James L. (1992) *The Politics of Environmental Control in North-eastern Tanzania, 1840–1940*, Philadelphia: University of Pennsylvania Press. [pp. 153–4 on influenza based on oral sources]

Lettow-Vorbeck, Paul von (1920) *Heia Safari! Deutschlands Kampf in Ostafrika* [Germany's struggle in East Africa], Leipzig: von Hase & Koehler Verlag. [pp. 243–6, 272 on influenza]

Schnee, Heinrich (1919) *Deutsch-Ostafrika im Weltkriege. Wie wir lebten und kämpften* [German East Africa in the World War. How we lived and fought], Leipzig: Quelle & Meyer. [pp. 373–5 and 399–403 on influenza]

Steudel, Emil (1928) 'Die Gesundheitsverhältnisse bei den Schutztruppen im Kolonialdienst. 22. Grippe', in Franz Bumm (ed.), *Deutschlands Gesundheitsverhältnisse unter dem Einfluss des Weltkrieges* (Wirtschafts- und Sozialgeschichte des Weltkrieges. Deutsche Serie. Vol. 10), Stuttgart and New Haven: Deutsche Verlagsanstalt and Yale University Press, No. 2, pp. 269. [Carnegie report]

Tunisia

Barthélemy, E. (1920) 'La pandémie grippale de 1918–1919 à Bizerte', *Revue d'Hygiène et de police sanitaire*, 42: 41–51.

Scialom, D. (1920) 'La grippe chez les Israélites Tunisiens (1918–19)', *Revue de Médecine et d'Hygiène tropicales* (Paris) 12: 41–6.

Uganda

Cook, Albert Ruskin (1945) *Uganda Memories 1897–1940*, Kampala: Uganda Society. [p. 325 influenza in Kampala]

Zambia

Doke, Olive C. (1919) 'Letter', *Lambaland – a Record of Missionary Work Among the Lamba-Speaking People of Northern Rhodesia*, 13 October 1919, 2 pp.

Fisher, W. Singleton and Hoyte, Julyan (1948) *Ndotolu. The Life Stories of Walter and Anna Fisher of Central Africa*, Ikelenge, 1987 Reprint. [p. 179 on influenza and supposed origin in witchcraft]

Gelfand, Michael (1961) *Northern Rhodesia in the Days of the Charter: a Medical and Social Study, 1878–1924*, Oxford: Blackwell. [pp. 193–4 on influenza]

Musambachime, Mwelwa C. (1994) 'The influenza epidemic of 1918–1919 in Northern Rhodesia', *Zambia J History* 6/7: 46–73. [Based on colonial files, missionary records and oral sources]

Musambachime, Mwelwa C. (1998) see Malawi.

Phillips, W.A. (1919) 'Letter', *Lambaland – a Record of Missionary Work Among the Lamba-Speaking People of Northern Rhodesia*, 11 April 1919, 2 pp., and 13 October 1919, 3 pp.

Zimbabwe

Anon. (1919) 'Notes on the "Spanish Influenza" in Rhodesia', *Zambesi Mission Record* 6, 84: 142–4.

Baker, R.H. (1919) 'A time of sickness', *C.R. A Chronicle of the Community of the Resurrection* 66: 9–16.

Cripps, Arthur Shearly (1928) *Africans All*, London: Sheldon Press, 31 pp. [Short story by a missionary: pp. 9–10, 30–1 expressing the horror of the influenza experience on the mines]

Daignault, C. (1920) Reminiscences of the influenza plague at Chishawasha', *Zambesi Mission Record* 7, 89: 316–17.

Gelfand, Michael (1953) *Tropical Victory: an Account of the Influence of Medicine on the History of Southern Rhodesia, 1890–1923*, Cape Town and Johannesburg: Juta & Co. Ltd. [Chapter 16]

Ndava, Zvidzai (1987) 'A study of the 1918–19 Spanish Influenza pandemic in Southern Rhodesia (Zimbabwe)', unpublished BA Honours dissertation, University of Zimbabwe, Harare. [Based on colonial files and a few interviews]

O'Neill, J. (1920) 'Our native missions in the Chilimanzi Reserve', *Zambesi Mission Record* 7, 88: 273–8.

Phimister, Ian R. (1973) 'The "Spanish" influenza pandemic of 1918 and its impact on the Southern Rhodesian mining industry', *The Central African J Medicine* 19, 7: 143–8.

Phimister, Ian R. (1976) 'African labour conditions and health in the Southern Rhodesian mining industry, 1898–1953. Part III: Health', *The Central African J Medicine* 22, 9: 173–81.

Phimister, Ian R. (1994) *Wangi Kolia. Coal, Capital and Labour in Colonial Zimbabwe 1894–1954*, Harare: Baobab Books. [pp. 43–5 on influenza]

Ranger, Terence O. (1986) 'The influenza pandemic in Southern Rhodesia: a crisis of comprehension', *The Society for the Social History of Medicine Bulletin* 39: 38–43.

Ranger, Terence O. (1988) 'The influenza pandemic in Southern Rhodesia: a crisis of comprehension', in David Arnold (ed.), *Imperial Medicine and Indigenous Societies*, Manchester and New York: Manchester University Press, pp. 172–88.

Shelley, Wilfred Percy B. (1920) 'Mine work in Penhalonga', *C.R. A Chronicle of the Community of the Resurrection* 70: 32–4.

The Americas

Escomel, E. (1919) 'La grippe en Río de Janeiro, Montevideo y Buenos Aires; médicas profilácticas y terapéuticas', *La Crónica Médica* (Lima) 35: 367–75. [Abstract *JAMA* 72: 903]

Killingray, David (1994) 'The influenza pandemic of 1918–1919 in the British Caribbean', *Social History of Medicine* 7, 1: 59–87.

Argentina

Anon. (1918) 'Buenos Aires letter' [on Spanish influenza], *JAMA* 71, 24: 2009.

Anon. (1919) 'Buenos Aires letter' [on Spanish influenza], *JAMA* 72, 1: 56; 4: 292; and 11: 811.

Dessy, S., Grapiolo, F. and Spada, C. (1919) 'Observaciones sobre la epidemia de grippe en la República Argentina', *Revista Sudamericana de Endocrinologia, Immunologia y Quimioterapia* (Buenos Aires) 3: 65–91.

Gonzalez Carrizo, O.H. (1969) 'Epidemiología de la gripe', *Revista de la Sanidad Militar Argentina* (Buenos Aires) 68, 1: 55–62.

Herrera Rodríguez, Francisco (1992) 'Un texto argentino sobre la gripe en 1918–19', in *Anales de la Real Academia de Medicina y Cirugía de Cádiz* (1992) 28, 1: 283–99.

Tobias, José W. (1920) 'La Epidemia de Gripe de 1918–1919', Buenos Aires: Las Ciencas, 207 pp. [Dissertation, Universidad Nacional de Buenos Aires]

Bermuda

Benbow, C. (1971) 'A sidelight on the Spanish Flu', *Bermuda Quarterly* 28: 81–6.

Brazil

Abrão, Janete Silveira (1998) *Banalizaçao da morte na cidade calada. A Hespanhola em Porto Alegre, 1918*, Porto Alegre: Edipucrs (História No. 3), 157 pp.

Adamo, Sam C. (1992) 'Influenza in Rio de Janeiro', in Fred R. Van Hartsesveldt (ed.), *The 1918–1919 Pandemic of Influenza. The Urban Impact in the Western World*, Lewiston, pp. 185–200.

Anselmo Olinto, B. (1993) '"Uma epidemia sem importancia". A influenza espanhola e o colapso do sistema de saúde no Sul do Brasil, 1918' ["An epidemic without importance". Spanish Influenza and the collapse of the health system in southern Brazil, 1918], *Quipu: Revista Latinoamericana de Historia de las Ciencas y la Tecnología* (México City) 10, 3: 285–303.

Bertolli Filho, Cláudio (1986) 'Epidemia e sociedade, São Paulo', unpublished dissertation, Faculdade de Filosofia, Letras e Ciêcias Humanas, Universidade de São Paulo.

Bertolli Filho, Cláudio (1989) 'A gripe espanhola em São Paulo', *Ciência Hoje*. *Revista de Divulgação Científica da Sociedade Brasileira Para o Progresso de Ciência* (Rio de Janeiro) 10, 58: 30–41.

Brito, Nara Azevede de (1997) 'La dansarina. A gripe espanhola e o cotidiano na cidade do Rio de Janeiro' [The influenza epidemic and the daily report of the city of Rio de Janeiro], *Historia, Ciências, Saude – Manguinhos* (Rio de Janeiro) 4, 1: 11–30.

Meyer, Carlos Luiz and Teixeria, Joaquim Rabello (1920) *A grippa epidemica no Brasil e especialmente em São Paulo*, São Paulo: Estado do São Paulo, Directoria do Serviço Sanitario.

Murillo de Campos (1919) 'Disturbios mentaes na grippe na guarnição do Rio de Janeiro', *Arquivos Brasileiros de Medicina* 9: 341–3.

Puinto, O. (1919) 'A epidemia de grippe no Rio de Janeiro, seus prodomos, fórmas clinicas', *Arquivos Brasileiros de Medicina* 9: 331–40.

Canada

Andrew, M.W. (1977) 'Epidemic and public health. Influenza in Vancouver, 1918–19', *BC Studies* (Vancouver) 34: 21–44.

Beckett, K.M. (1998) 'Investigating disease experience in aboriginal populations in Canada. The 1918 influenza pandemic in Berens River and Poplar River, Manitoba', unpublished MA thesis, McMaster University, Hamilton, Ontario.

Belyk, R.C. and Belyk, D.M. (1988) 'The Spanish Influenza 1918–1919: No armistice with death', *Beaver* 68, 5: 43–9.

Braithwaite, Max (1953) 'The year of the killer flu', *MacLean's Magazine* (Toronto) 66 (February), pp. 10–11 and 43–4.

Brown, Jennifer and Matthews, Maureen (1994) 'Fair winds. Medicine and consolation on the Berens River', *J Canadian Historical Association*, New Series, 4: 55–73.

Clarkson, F.A. (1920) 'History of influenza', *Canadian Medical Monthly* 4: 59.

Cooper-Cole, C.E. (1919) 'Preliminary report on influenza epidemic at Bramshott in September–October 1918', *Canadian Medical Association J* 9, 1: 42ff.

Delaunais, R. (1991) *Le Camp de la Grippe Espagnole. La Grippe Espagnole dans la Matapédia*. Québec: Amqui. [Matapédia River Valley, Québec Province]

Drolet, A. (1959) 'L'epidémie de grippe espagnole à Québec en 1918. Une dispute medicale', *Laval Médical* (Quebec) 27, 5: 647–55.

Drolet, A. (1970) 'L'épidémie de grippe espagnole à Québec, 1918', *Trois Siècles de Médecine Québécoise*, Québec: La Société Historique de Québec (Cahiers d'histoire 22), 98–106.

Graham-Cumming, G. (1967) 'Health of the original Canadians, 1867–1967', *Medical Services Journal Canada* 23: 115–66.

Heagerty, John J. (1919) 'Influenza and vaccination', *Canadian Medical Association J* 9, 2: 226–8. [Quebec]

Herring, D.A. (1994) '"There were young people and old people and babies dying every week", The 1918–1919 influenza pandemic at Norway House', *Ethnohistory* 41, 1: 73–105.

Herring, D.A. (1994) 'The 1918 influenza epidemic in the Central Canadian Subarctic', in D.A. Herring and L. Chan (eds), *Strength and Diversity. A Reader in Physical anthropology*, Toronto: Canadian Scholar's Press, 365–84.

Herring, D.A. and Sattenspiel, L. (1996) 'Social contact and the spread of the 1918 influenza epidemic in the Central Subarctic', *American J Physical Anthropology – Supplement* No. 22: 123ff.

Johnson, N.P.A.S. (1993) 'Pandemic Influenza: An analysis of the spread of influenza in Kitchener, October 1918', unpublished MA thesis, Wilfrid Laurier University.

Johnson, N.P.A.S. (1998) 'Kitchener's forgotten struggle: The 1918 influenza pandemic experience', *Waterloo Historical Society* 85: 41–67.

Kelm, M.E. (1998) 'First Nations' perspectives on the influenza pandemic of 1918–1919', unpublished paper for the 'Conference on the Spanish flu 1918–1998', held in Cape Town. [British Columbia]

Kelm, Mary-Ellen (1999) 'British Columbia first nations and the influenza pandemic of 1918–19', *BC Studies. The British Columbia Quarterly* (Vancouver) 122: 23–47.

Lux, Maureen Katherine (1992) 'Prairie Indians and the 1918 influenza epidemic', *Native Studies Review* 8, 1: 23–33.

Lux, Maureen Katherine (1996) 'Beyond biology. Disease and its impact on the Canadian Plains native people, 1880–1930', unpublished PhD thesis, Simon Fraser University, Burnaby, 430 pp. [Case studies: impact of influenza, measles, whooping cough, tuberculosis on mortality]

MacDougall, H. (1985) 'The fatal flu', *Horizon Canada* 8, 8: 2089–95.

McCullough, John W.S. (1918) 'The control of influenza in Ontario', *Canadian Medical Association J* 8: 1084–6.

McDonald, J.C. (1967) 'Influenza in Canada', *Canadian Medical Association J* 97, 10: 522–7.

McGinnis, J.P.D. (1976) 'A city faces an epidemic', *Alberta History* 24, 4: 1–11. [Calgary]

McGinnis, J.P.D. (1977) 'The impact of epidemic influenza. Canada, 1918–1919', *Canadian Historical Association Papers* 19: 120–40.

McGinnis, J.P.D. (1981) 'The impact of epidemic influenza. Canada, 1918–1919', in S.E.D. Shortt (ed.), *Medicine in Canadian Society: Historical Perspectives*, Montreal: McGill-Queens's University Press, 471–83.

Morton, G. (1973) 'The pandemic influenza of 1918', *Canadian Nurse* 69, 12: 25–7.

Parsons, H.C. (1919) 'Official report on influenza epidemic, 1918', *Canadian Medical Association J* 9: 351–4.

Pettigrew, E. (1983) *The Silent Enemy. Canada and the Deadly Flu of 1918*, Saskatoon: Western Producer Prairie Books.

Ray, A.J. (1976) 'Diffusion of diseases in the western interior of Canada, 1830–1950', *Geographical Review* 66, 2: 139–57.

Rioux, D. (1993) *La Grippe Espagnole à Sherbrooke et dans les Cantons de l'Est*, Sherbrooke (Études Supérieures en Histoire Université de Sherbrooke. Collection Histoire des Cantons de l'Est 9).

Sattenspiel, L. and Herring, D.A. (1998) 'Structured epidemic models and the spread of influenza in the Central Canadian Subarctic', *Human Biology* 70, 1: 91–115.

Smillie, W.G. (1930) 'An epidemic of influenza in an isolated community – Northwest River, Labrador', *The American J Hygiene* 11: 392–8. [Epidemic of 1927–28 compared with 1918–19]

Wetmore, F.H. (1919) 'Treatment of influenza', *Canadian Medical Association J* 8: 1075–80.

Wilton, Peter (1993) 'Spanish flu outdid WW I in number of lives claimed', *Canadian Medical Association J* 148, 11: 2036–7.

Colombia

Zambrano Pantoja, Fabio (1988) *Historia de Bogotá, Vol. 3,* Fundacion Mision Colombia. [pp. 170–4 on influenza]

Costa Rica

Nunez, Solón (1926) 'The occurrence and non-occurrence of certain diseases in Costa Rica', *American J Tropical Medicine* 6, 5: 347–56. [pp. 348–9 influenza trailer epidemic of 1920]

Cuba

Anon. (1918) 'Cuba letter' [on Spanish Influenza], *JAMA* 71, 4: 297, and 23: 1928.

Ortega, L. (1918) 'La epidemia actual de grippe', *Crónica Médico-Quirúrgica* (La Habana) 44: 633–8.

Dominican Republic

Republica Dominicana (1921) [La pandémie grippale de 1918–1919 dans la République Dominicaine] (abstract *Bulletin Mensuel de l'Office International d'Hygiène Publique* 13: 863).

French Guiana

Leger, M. (1922) 'Guyane, l'épidémie d'influenza de 1918–1919', *Annales de Médecine et de Pharmacie Coloniales* 20, 1: 62–3.

Guadelope

Pichon (1922) 'Guadelope, l'épidémie d'influenza de 1918–1919', *Annales de Médecine et de Pharmacie Coloniales* 20, 1: 62.

Guatemala

McCreery, David (1992) 'Influenza in Guatemala City', in Fred R. Van Hartesveldt (ed.), *The 1918–1919 Pandemic of Influenza. The Urban Impact in the Western World,* Lewiston, pp. 161–84.

Guyana

Rose, F.G. (1919) 'The influenza epidemic in British Guiana', *The Lancet* 1919/I: 421.

Martinique

Henric (1922) 'Martinique, l'épidémie d'influenza de 1918–1919', *Annales de Médecine et de Pharmacie Coloniales* 20, 1: 59–62.

Mexico

Aguilar Palma, Lauro (1920) *Aviso importante. Estando en inminente peligro esta Capital de ser invadida por la terrible influenza española*, Villahermosa.

Anon. (1918) 'Mexico letter' [on Spanish influenza], *JAMA* 71, 16: 1332; 17: 1426; and 25: 2089.

Anon. (1919) 'Mexico letter' [on Spanish influenza], *JAMA* 72, 1: 55, and 2: 131.

Comisión Central de Caridad de Puebla (1919) *Memoria documentada de la campana contra 'La influenza española'*, Puebla, 83 pp.

Gambao Ojeda, Leticia (1991) 'La epidemia de influenza de 1918. Sanidad y política en la ciudad de Puebla' [Public health and politics in the city of Puebla], *Quipu: Revista Latinoamericana de Historia de las Ciências y la Tecnología* (México City) 8, 1: 91–109.

Salinas Cantú, Hernán (1975) *Sombras sobre la ciudad: Historia de las grandes epidemas de viruela, cólera morbus, fiebre amarilla e influenza española que ha sufrido Monterrey*, Monterrey: Editorial Alfonso Reyes, 158 pp.

Paraguay

Moreno, M.A. (1918) 'Influenza in Paraguay', *Semana médica* (Buenos Aires) 25: 785.

Peru

Anon. (1918) 'Lima letter' [on Spanish influenza], *JAMA* 71, 12: 990.

Anon. (1919) 'Lima letter' [on Spanish influenza], *JAMA* 72, 14: 1016.

Paz Soldan, C.E. (1919) 'La grippe à Lima', *Reforma Medica* (Lima) Vol. 5, No. 53, p. 5. [Abstract *Bulletin Mensuel de l'Office International d'Hygiène Publique* (1919) 11, 6: 639, and *JAMA* 72: 970]

Puerto Rico

Valle Atiles, F. del (1918) 'Anotaciones acerca de la influenza en Puerto Rico', *Boletín de la Asociación Medica de Puerto Rico* 12, 121: 279–85. [Abstract *JAMA* (1919) 72, 9: 688]

Saint Pierre and Miquelon

Dupuy-Fromy (1922) 'Iles Saint-Pierre et Michelon, l'épidémie d'influenza de 1918–1919', *Annales de Médecine et de Pharmacie Coloniales* 20, 1: 64–6.

Trinidad and Tobago

Anon. (1921) 'Medical report for the year 1918' (Colonial Medical Report No. 122 Trinidad and Tobago), reprinted *J Tropical Medicine and Hygiene* 24, Supplement: 48–56.

Anon. (1922) 'Medical report for the year 1919' (Colonial Medical Report No. 131 Trinidad and Tobago), reprinted *J Tropical Medicine and Hygiene* 25, Supplement: 6–8.

Uruguay

Etchepare J., Brusco, L.D. and González, J.F. (1920) 'Sobre epidemiología, patología, etiología y profilaxis de la pandemia de gripe de 1918–19, en el Uruguay', *Boletín del Consejo Nacional de Higiene*, 15, 162; 513–609. [Abstract *Bulletin Mensuel de l'Office International d'Hygiène Publique* (1921) 13: 401–2]

Uruguay, Consejo Nacional de Higiene (1920) *Sobre epidemiología, patología, etiología y profilaxis de la pandemia de gripe de 1918–1919, en el Uruguay.* Montevideo: Imp. El Siglo Ilustrado, 99 pp.

USA

Adams, H.G. (1964) 'A local chronicle of the influenza epidemic of 1918', *North Carolina Medical J* 25: 351–4 and 397–400.

Armstrong, C. (1923) 'The devil's grip in Virginia', *PHR* 38: 1964–5.

Armstrong, C. and Hopkins, R. (1921) 'An epidemiological study of the 1920 epidemic of influenza in an isolated rural community', *PHR* 36: 1671–702.

Arrington, L.J. (1988) 'The influenza epidemic of 1918–1919 in southern Idaho', *Idaho Yesterdays* 32, 3: 19–29.

Arrington, L.J. (1990) 'The influenza epidemic of 1918–19 in Utah', *Utah Historical Quarterly* 58, 2: 165–82.

Baldwin, F. (1919) 'The epidemic in Joliet', *Public Health Nurse* 11, 1: 45–50. [Illinois]

Biggs, H.M. (1919) 'Recent epidemic of influenza', *The American Review of Reviews* (New York) 59: 69–71.

Britten, R.H. (1932) 'The incidence of epidemic influenza, 1918–1919. A further analysis according to age, sex, and color of the records of morbidity and mortality obtained in surveys of 12 localities', *PHR* 47, 6: 303–39. [a list of preceding papers by the office of statistical investigations on the epidemiology of influenza in the USA]

Brox, J. (1995) 'Influenza 1918', *The Georgia Review* 49, 3: 687–97.

Bucki, D.B. (1997) 'A history of Buffalo's medical response to the great influenza pandemic of 1918–1919', in L. Sentz (ed.) *Medical History in Buffalo, 1846–1996*, Buffalo: School of Medicine and Biomedical Services, 209–31.

Buelow, P. (1992) 'Influenza in Chicago', in F.R. Van Hartesveldt (ed.) *The 1918–1919 Pandemic of Influenza. The Urban Impact in the Western World*, Lewiston: Edwin Mellen Press, 119–46.

Burch, M. (1983) '"I don't know only what we hear". The soldiers' view of the 1918 influenza epidemic', *Indiana Medical History Quarterly* 9, 4: 23–7.

Burrill, E.A. (1919) *The Story of Brockton's Fight against Influenza*, Brockton: Press of Nichols & Eldridge. [Massachusetts]

Bush, O.T. (1986) 'The flu epidemic of 1918–1919', *Faulkner Facts and Fiddlings* 28: 1. [Arkansas]

Carr, D.J. (1991) 'The Spanish Influenza epidemic of 1918 and Berkshire County', *Historical J Massachusetts* 19, 1: 43–62.

Charles, A.D. (1977) 'The influenza pandemic of 1918–1919: Columbia and South Carolina's response', *J South Carolina Medical Association* 73, 8: 367–70.

Clark, S.H. (1991) 'The impact of the 1918–1919 Influenza Pandemic on Fresno, California', unpublished MA thesis, California State University, Fresno. [Based on interviews with survivors]

Collins, Selwyn D. (1957) 'Trend and age variation of mortality and morbidity from influenza and pneumonia', *A Review and Study of Illness and Medical Care with Special Reference to Long-time Trends* (Public Health Monograph No. 48, Public Health Service Publication No. 544), Washington, DC; US Government Printing Office, pp. 51–73.

Collins, Selwyn D., Frost, Wade Hampton, Gover, Mary and Sydenstricker, Edgar (1930) 'Mortality from influenza and pneumonia in 50 large cities of the United States, 1910–1929', *PHR* 45, 39. [Also Public Health Reports Reprint No. 1415]

Cornwall, Edward E. (1918) 'Spanish Influenza. Cases of influenza and pneumonia taken off S.S. *Bergensfjord* arrived in New York, August 12, 1918, from Norway', *New York Medical J* 108: 330.

Crosby, A.W. (1976) *Epidemic and Peace, 1918*, Westport: Greenwood Press. [Reference work]

Crosby, A.W. (1977) 'The influenza pandemic of 1918', in J.E. Osborn (ed.), *Influenza in America, 1918–1976: History, Science and Politics*, New York: Prodist, 5–13.

Crosby, A.W. (1989) *America's Forgotten Pandemic – The Influenza of 1918*, Cambridge, New York: Cambridge University Press. [Reprint of Crosby 1976 with new introduction]

Crosby, Alfred W. (1998) 'The Spanish Influenza in perspective', unpublished paper for the 'Conference on the Spanish flu 1918–1998', held in Cape Town.

Cumberland, W.H. (1981) 'Epidemic! Iowa battles the Spanish Influenza', *Palimpsest* 62, 1: 26–32.

Daniel, T.M. and Gerstner, P.A. (1991) 'The 1918–1919 influenza pandemic', *J Laboratory and Clinical Medicine* (St Louis) 117, 3: 259–60.

Davidson, H.A. (1957) 'New Jersey and the great pandemic of influenza, 1918'. *J Medical Society of New Jersey* 54: 390–6.

Deming, Dorothy (1957) 'Influenza – 1918. Relieving the great epidemic', *American J Nursing* 57, 10: 1308–9. [New York]

Doherty, W.T. (1977) 'A West Virginia County's experience with the 1918 influenza epidemic', *West Virginia History* 38: 136–40.

Eichel, O.R. (1923) *A Special Report on the Mortality from Influenza in New York State during the Epidemic of 1918–19*, Albany: New York State – Department of Health.

Ellis, E.R. (1975) *Echoes of Distant Thunder. Life in the United States, 1914–19*, New York: Coward, McCann & Geoghegan. [Chapter 30: 462–77 on influenza]

Emerson, G.M. (1986) 'The "Spanish Lady" in Alabama', *The Alabama J Medical Sciences* 23, 2: 217–21.

Ensley, P.C. (1983) 'Indiana and the influenza pandemic of 1918', *Indiana Medical History Quarterly* 9, 4: 3–15.

Fanning, P.J. (1996) 'Disease and the politics of community: Norwood and the great flu epidemic of 1918', unpublished dissertation, Boston College. [Social behaviour as a fundamental predictor of epidemic curve and consequence in a town in Massachusetts]

Figura, S.Z. (1998) 'The forgotten pandemic. The Spanish Flu of 1918 was gravest crisis American hospitals had ever faced', *The Volunteer Leader* 39, 2: 5.

Fincher, J. (1989) 'America's deadly rendezvous with the "Spanish Lady"', *Smithsonian* 19, 10: 130–45 and 147.

Friedlander, A. *et al.* (1918) 'The epidemic of influenza at Camp Sherman, Ohio', *JAMA* 71: 1652–6.

Frost, Wade Hampton (1920) 'Statistics on influenza morbidity: with special reference to certain factors in case incidence and case fatality', *PHR Vol.* 35, 11: 584–98. [Also Public Health Reports Reprint No. 586]

Frost, Wade Hampton (1921) 'The epidemiology of influenza', *PHR* 36, 33. [Also Public Health Reports Reprint No. 550]

Frost, W.H. and Sydenstricker, E. (1919) 'Influenza in Maryland. Preliminary statistics of certain localities', *PHR* 34, 11: 491–505.

Galishoff, S. (1969) 'Newark and the great influenza pandemic of 1918', *Bulletin of the History of Medicine* 43, 3: 246–58.

Ganley, M.L. (1998) 'The dispersal of the 1918 influenza virus on the Seward Peninsula, Alaska. An ethnohistoric reconstruction', *International J Circumpolar Health* 57, Supplement 1: 247–51. [Based on oral history]

Geister, Janet (1957) 'The flu epidemic of 1918', *Nursing Outlook* 5, 10: 582–4.

Gerhard, William Paul (1922) 'Municipal sanitary precautions during epidemic influenza. Rambling thoughts of a civil engineer', *Municipal and County Engineering* (Chicago), April/May, 7 pp. [Indianapolis]

Gernhart, G. (1999) 'A forgotten enemy. PHS's fight against the 1918 influenza pandemic', *Public Health Reports* 114, 6: 559–61.

Gram, F.C. (1919) 'The influenza epidemic and its after-effects in the city of Buffalo', *JAMA* 73, 12: 886–90.

Greenberg, D. (1920) 'Influenza statistics of the Visiting Nurse Association of New Haven', *Public Health Nurse* 12: 209–17.

Gribble, B. (1919) 'Influenza in a Kentucky coal-mining camp', *American J Nursing* 19, 8: 609–11.

Gribble, C.J. (1997) '"We hope to live through it." Nursing and the 1918 influenza epidemic. Lessons for this century and the next.', unpublished MSc thesis, Gonzaga University. [Based on nursing journals and Red Cross bulletins]

Grist, N.R. (1979) 'Pandemic influenza 1918', *British Medical J* 1979/II, 6205: 1632–3. [Camp Devens, Boston]

Guilfoy, W.H. (1918) 'Statistics of the epidemic of influenza in New York City', *Monthly Bulletin of Department of Health of the City of New York*, New Series 13: 265–77.

Hamilton, D. (1992) 'Unanswered questions of the Spanish flu pandemic', *Bulletin of the American Association for the History of Nursing* 34: 6–7.

Harvey, Oscar Jewell (1920) *The Spanish Influenza Pandemic of 1918. An Account of its Ravages in Luzerne County, Pennsylvania, and the Efforts made to Combat and Subdue it*, Wilkes-Barre Publisher, 63 pp.

Heiser, Victor G. (1918) 'Barrack life and respiratory disease. Some epidemiologic observations on the recent outbreak of influenza', *JAMA* 71, 23: 1909–11.

Hernoff, A.K. (1941) 'The influenza epidemic of 1918–19 in San Francisco', *Military Surgeon* 89: 805–11.

Hoffmann, F.L. (1919) 'Some statistics of influenza', *Medical Record* (New York) 96: 229–33.

Holt, Luther Emmett (1920) 'Home vs. hospital care of cases of influenza', *Medical Record* (New York) 97: 731.

Howard, D.C., Chamberlain, W.P. and Love, A.G. (1926) 'The influenza epidemic of 1918', *Medical Department, US Army in the World War* 6: 349–71.

Hutchens, K.S. (1979) 'The Indianapolis influenza epidemic of 1918', *Indiana History Society* 5, 4: 4–16.

Iezzoni, L. (1999) *Influenza 1918. The Worst Epidemic in American History*, New York: HarperCollins Publisher. [Popular account]

Irwin, R.T. (1981) '1918 influenza in Morris County', *New Jersey Historical Commission Newsletter*, March, p. 3.

Ivy, Robert H. (1960) 'The influenza epidemic of 1918. Personal experience of a medical officer in World War I', *Military Medicine* (Washington) 125, 9: 620–2. [Transport to Europe]

Jackson, Thomas W. (1919) 'Influenza in military camps', *Medical Record* (New York) 96, 17: 696–8. [Camp Meade]

Jenkins, V.S. (1998) 'The 1918 Spanish Flu pandemic: What the American people knew', unpublished paper for the 'Conference on the Spanish flu 1918–1998', held in Cape Town. [Based on newspapers]

Jordan, E.O. (1927) *Epidemic Influenza: a Survey*, Chicago. [Includes figures for most territories of the world]

Katz, R.S. (1974) 'Influenza 1918–1919: a study in mortality', *Bulletin of the History of Medicine* 48, 3: 416–22. [Secondary sources only]

Katz, Robert S. (1977) 'Influenza 1918–19: a further study in mortality', *Bulletin of the History of Medicine* 51, 4: 617–9.

Keegan, J.J. (1967) 'The epidemiology and pathology of influenza based on experience with the 1918 pandemic', *Nebraska Medical J* 52: 266–70.

Keen-Payne, R. (2000) 'We must have nurses. Spanish Influenza in America 1918–1919', *Nursing History Review* 8: 143–56.

Kerson, T.S. (1979) 'Sixty years ago. Hospital social work in 1918', *Social Work in Health Care* 4, 3: 331–43.

King, F. (1992) 'Influenza in Atlanta', in F.R. Van Hartesveldt (ed.), *The 1918–1919 Pandemic of Influenza. The Urban Impact in the Western World*, Lewiston: Edwin Mellen Press, 105–18.

Kingsley, S. (1918) 'Cleveland and the "flu"', *Public Health Nurse* 10: 12: 314–16.

Kirkpatrick, G.W. (1986) 'Influenza 1918. A Maine perspective', *Maine Historical Society Quarterly* 25, 3: 162–77.

Knoll, K. (1989) 'When the plague hit Spokane', *Pacific Northwest* 33, 1: 1–7.

Koblenz, L.W. (1998) 'A judgement in time: Medical responses to the 1918–1919 influenza epidemic in the United States', unpublished paper for the 'Conference on the Spanish flu 1918–1998', held in Cape Town.

Kopf, E.W. (1919) 'Statistical study of the influenza epidemic', *Science* 49: 228–30.

Lautaret, R.L. (1986) 'Alaska's greatest disaster. The 1918 Spanish Influenza epidemic', *Alaska J* 16: 238–43.

Lent, M. (1918) 'The extent and control of influenza in Washington, D.C.', *Public Health Nurse* 10, 12: 296–304.

Levin, M.L. (1978) 'An historical account of "the influence" (influenza)', *Maryland State Medical J* 27, 5: 58–62.

Lloyd, Bolivar J. (1945) 'Influenza. Death and a streptococcus in the pandemic of 1918–19. A review', *J Tropical Medicine and Hygiene* 48, 5: 115–20.

Luckingham, B. (1984) *Epidemic in the Southwest, 1918–1919*, El Paso: Texas Western Press (Southwestern Studies: Monograph No. 72).

Luckingham, B. (1984) 'To mask or not to mask. A note on the 1918 Spanish Influenza epidemic in Tucson', *J Arizona History* 25, 2: 191–204.

Lupton, H.B. (1919) 'Influenza in Louisville, Kentucky', *Public Health Nurse* 11, 1: 47–9.

Marks, Harry M. (1998) 'Influenza 1918', *Philadelphia Magazine*, October.

Mason, R. (1998) 'Surviving the Blue Killer, 1918', *Virginia Quarterly Review* 74, 2: 343–56.

McCord, Carey P. (1966) 'The purple death. Some things remembered about the influenza epidemic of 1918 at one army camp', *J Occupational Medicine* 8, 11: 593–8. [Camp Sherman, Ohio]

McLaurin, A. (1982) 'The influenza epidemic of 1918 in Shreveport', *North Louisiana Historical Association J* 13, 1: 1–14.

McPherson, R.S. (1990) 'The influenza epidemic of 1918. A cultural response', *Utah Historical Quarterly* 58, 2: 183–200. [Moab and Navajo Area, Ohio]

McShane, K.C. (1968) 'The 1918 Kansas City influenza epidemic', *Missouri Historical Review* 63: 55–70.

Melzer, R. (1982) 'A dark and terrible moment. The Spanish Flu epidemic of 1918 in New Mexico', *New Mexico Historical Review* 57: 213–36.

Morton, C.A. (1919) 'How a city and a school met the epidemic: San Jose, California', *Industrial Arts Magazine* 8: 199–200.

Mullen, P.C. and Nelson, M.L. (1987) 'Montanans and "the most peculiar disease". The influenza epidemic and public health, 1918–1919', *Montana – The Magazine of Western History* 37, 2: 50–61.

Murphy, J.P. (1918) 'Meeting the Scourge: How Massachusetts organized to fight influenza', *The Survey* 41: 97–100.

Noyes, W.R. (1968) 'Influenza epidemic 1918–1919. A misplaced chapter in United States social and institutional history', unpublished PhD thesis, University of California, Los Angeles.

Nuzum, John W., Pilot, I. and Stangel, F.H. *et al.* (1976) '1918 pandemic influenza and pneumonia in a large civil hospital', *The Illinois Medical J* 105, 6: 612–16.

Oliver, Wade W. (1919) 'Influenza – the sphinx of diseases', *Scientific American* 120: 200, 212–13.

Olson, H.D. (1976) 'The 'flu, 1918', *Kansas Quarterly* 8: 35–40.

Pearl, Raymond (1919) 'Influenza studies. I. On certain general statistical aspects of the 1918 epidemic in American cities', *PHR* 34: 1743–83. [Also Public Health Reports Reprint No. 642]

Perret, J.M. and Shaar, C.M. (1919) 'Study of an epidemic of influenza at Pensacola', *US Naval Medical Bulletin* 13: 365–78. [Florida]

Persico, Joseph E. (1976) 'The great swine flu epidemic of 1918', *American Heritage* (New York) 27: 28–31 and 80–6.

Peterson, R.H. (1989) 'The Spanish Influenza epidemic in San Diego, 1918–1919', *Southern California Quarterly* 71, 1: 89–105.

Peterson, R.H. (1992) 'Influenza in San Diego', in F.R. Van Hartesveldt (ed.), *The*

1918–1919 Pandemic of Influenza. The Urban Impact in the Western World, Lewiston: Edwin Mellen Press, 147–60.

Pettit, D.A. (1976) 'A cruel wind. American experiences pandemic influenza, 1918–1920. A social history', unpublished PhD thesis, University of New Hampshire. [Based on letters, diaries, oral histories, reports and newspapers]

Porter, Katherine Ann (1939) *Pale Horse, Pale Rider*, New York: Harcourt, Brace and Co. [Spanish Influenza as a subject for a short novel]

Reagan, A.B. (1921) 'The influenza and the Navajo', *Proceedings of the Indiana Academy of Science* 29: 243–7.

Robertson, J.D. (1919) *A Report of an Epidemic of Influenza in Chicago in the Fall of 1918*. Reprinted from the Octennial Report, Department of Health, City of Chicago, 1911–1918 (Chicago, Department of Health, Educational Series No. 15).

Robinson, K.R. (1990) 'The role of nursing in the influenza epidemic of 1918–1919', *Nursing Forum* 25, 2: 19–26.

Rockafellar, N. (1986) '"In gauze we trust." Public health and Spanish Influenza on the home front, Seattle, 1918–1919', *Pacific Northwest Quarterly* 77, 3: 104–33.

Rodies, K.E. (1998) 'That great call. The pandemic of 1918', *Nurse Health Care Perspective* 19, 5: 204–5.

Ross, Irwin (1969) 'The great plague of 1918', *American History Illustrated* 1: 12–17.

Russell, F. (1958) 'A journal of the plague: the 1918 influenza'. *Yale Review* 47: 219–35.

Russell, S.C. (1985) 'The Navajo and the 1918 pandemic', in C.F. Merbs and R.J. Miller (eds), *Health and Disease in the Prehistoric Southwest*, Tempe: Arizona State University (Anthropological Research Paper No. 34) 382–5.

Sage, M.W. (1995) 'Pittsburgh plague – 1918. An oral history', *Home Healthcare Nurse* 13, 1: 49–54.

Sage, M.W. (1998) 'A nurse looks at the influenza pandemic of 1918 through the memories of aged individuals in Pittsburgh, Pennsylvania and environs', unpublished paper for the 'Conference on the Spanish flu 1918–1998', held in Cape Town.

Sánchez González, M. (1991) see Spain.

Sanford, W.L. (1983) 'The influenza epidemic of 1918 and its effect on the military', *Indiana Medical History Quarterly* 9, 4: 16–22.

Scott, K.A. (1988) 'Plague on the homefront: Arkansas and the great influenza epidemic of 1918', *Arkansas History Quarterly* 47, 4: 311–44. [Also *Research Papers/ History of Medicine Associates*, Charlotte, North Carolina (1990) 1: 121–47]

Snape, W.J. and Wolfe, E.L. (1987) 'Influenza epidemic. Popular reaction in Camden 1918–1919', *New Jersey Medicine* 84, 3: 173–6.

Soper, George A (1918) 'Influenza pneumonia pandemic in the American army camps during September and October, 1918', *Science* 48: 451–6.

Springer, J.K. (1991) '1918 flu epidemic in Hartford, Connecticut', *Connecticut Medicine* 55, 1: 43–7.

Starr, I. (1976) 'Influenza in 1918: Recollections of the epidemic in Philadelphia', *Annals of Internal Medicine* 85, 4: 516–18.

Steele, V.W. (2000) 'The 1918 Influenza Epidemic in Montana', *Montana. The Magazine of Western History*.

Straight, W.M. (1981) 'Florida and the Spanish Flu', *J Florida Medical Association* 68, 8: 644–54.

Street, H.N. (1920) 'Personal experience in epidemic influenza', *J Arkansas Medical Society* 16: 100–2.

Sydenstricker, Edgar (1921) 'Variations in case fatality during the influenza epidemic of 1918', *PHR* 36, 36: 2201–10. [Also Public Health Reports Reprint No. 692]

Sydenstricker, E. (1931) 'The incidence of influenza among persons of different economic status during epidemic of 1918', *PHR* 46, 4: 154–70.

Sydenstricker, E. and King, M.L. (1920) 'Difficulties in computing civil death rates for 1918, with especial reference to epidemic influenza', *PHR* 35, 7: 330–45.

Tamarin, J.S. (1959) 'The Boston Influenza Epidemic of 1918', unpublished bachelor's thesis, Harvard College.

Thomson, J.B. (1978) 'The 1918 influenza epidemic in Nashville', *J Tennessee Medical Association* 71, 4: 261–70.

Tourscher, Francis Edward (1919) *Work of the Sisters During the Epidemic of Influenza, October, 1918, Gathered and Arranged from Reports of Personal Experiences of the Sisters and Contributed by Request of the Compiler*, F.E.T. Philadelphia, 114 pp. [Reprinted from the Records of the American Catholic Historical Society of Philadelphia 30, 1–3, 1919]

US Congress. House. Committee on Appropriations (1919) *Influenza in Alaska and Puerto Rico*, Washington.

US Congress. Senate. Committee on Appropriations (1919) *Influenza in Alaska*, Washington.

US National Office of Vital Statistics (1957) *The Pandemic of Influenza in 1918–19*, Washington.

Vaughan, V.C. (1919) 'The influenza epidemic and its after-effects in the city of Buffalo', *JAMA* 73, 12: 890–1.

Vaughan, W.T. (1921) *Influenza: An Epidemiologic Study*. (The American Journal of Hygiene – Monographic Series No.1) Baltimore: The American Journal of Hygiene.

Waldron, S. (1990) 'In-Flu-Enza: The epidemic of 1918', *Table Rock Sentinel – Southern Oregon Historical Society* 10, 1: 2–9.

Wallack, G. (1977) 'Waterbury Influenza Epidemic of 1918–1919', *Connecticut Medicine* 41, 6: 349–51.

Walters, J.H. (1978) 'Influenza 1918: The contemporary perspective', *Bulletin of the New York Academy of Medicine* 54, 9: 855–64.

Walters, K.A. (1981) 'McLean County and the influenza epidemic of 1918–1919', *J Illinois State Historical Society* 74, 2: 130–44.

White, K.A. (1985) 'Pittsburgh in the great epidemic of 1918', *Western Pennsylvania Historical Magazine* 68, 3: 221–42.

Winslow, C.E.A. and Rogers, J.F. (1920) 'Statistics of the 1918 epidemic of influenza in Connecticut. With a consideration of the factors which influenced the prevalence of this disease in various communities', *J Infectious Disease* 26: 185–216.

Wooley, I.M. (1963) 'The 1918 Spanish Influenza epidemic in Oregon', *Oregon Historical Quarterly* 64: 246–58.

Woolley, Alma S. (1994) 'America's forgotten pandemic', *Bulletin of the American Association for the History of Nursing* 42: 4–5.

Venezuela

Belloso H.N. (1961) 'La epidemica de influenza (gripe) de 1918 en Maracaibo', *Revista de la Sociedad Venezolana de Historia de la Medicina* 9, 23: 543–62.
Benchetrit, A. (1954) *La Pandemia del Año 1918 en Venezuela. Datos para la Historia Medicina en Venezuela,* Bogotà: Editorial Minerva.
Risquez, F.A. (1919) 'La epidemia de 1918 en Caracas', *Gaceta Medica de Caracas* 26, 2: 13–17. [Abstract *JAMA* 72: 1112–13]

Asia

Gouzen, P. (1922) 'Union Indochinoise, l'épidémie d'influenza, en 1918–1919', *Annales de Médecine et de Pharmacie Coloniales* 20, 1: 43–5.

Cambodia

Mathis, Constant (1922) 'Cambodge, l'épidémie d'influenza de 1918–1919', *Annales de Médecine et de Pharmacie Coloniales* 20, 1: 52–3.

China

Cadbury, W.W. (1919) *The 1918 Pandemic of Influenza in Canton, China,* Canton: Christian College.
Cadbury, W.W. (1920) 'The 1918 pandemic in Canton, China', *China Medical J* 34, 1: 1–17.
Cadbury, W.W. (1920) 'The pandemic of influenza as it affected Canton, China', *Medical Record* 97, 10: 391–5.
Chun, J.W.H. (1919) 'Influenza, including its infection among pigs', *National Medical J China* 5: 34–44.
Hsieh, E.T. (1920) 'The recent epidemic of influenza in Peking', *National Medical J China* 6: 129–32.
Stanley, A. (1920) 'Annual report of the Medical Officer of Health, Shanghai, for the Year 1918' (Colonial Medical Reports 113 Shanghai), reprinted *J Tropical Medicine and Hygiene* 23, Supplement, 91–6 and 24 (1921) Supplement, 1.
Stedeford, E.T.A. (1919) 'Public health of Wenchow, 1918–1919', *The China Medical J* 33, 4: 391–3.
Vallet, A.L.M. (1920) 'Rapport sur le functionnement du service médical du consulat de France à Tchong-King pendant l'année 1919', *AMédPhC* 18: 105–9.
Watson, Percy T. (1919) 'The epidemic in Shansi. Pneumonic plague or influenza?', *The China Medical J* 33, 2: 169–73.
Zhen, C. (1998) ['The pandemic of influenza eighty years ago']. *Zhong-yishi-zazhi* [*Chinese J Medical History*] (Beijing) 28, 4: 207–11. [In Chinese with English abstract]

India

Bhatt, J.C. and Hiramamdani, K.M. (1919) *Epidemic of Influenza 1918.* Hyderabad: Standard Printing Works. [Abstract *Tropical Disease Bulletin* 14, 4: 242]

Bose, K.C. (1920) 'Influenza in and around the city of Calcutta', *Indian Medical Gazette* 55: 169.

Gill, C.A. (1928) *The Genesis of Epidemics and the Natural History of Disease*, London: Baillière, Tindall and Co. [pp. 251–88 on influenza in India]

Government of Bombay – Sanitary Commissioner (1919) *Final Report on the Influenza Epidemic of 1918 in the Bombay Presidency*, Bombay.

Guérin (1922) 'Établissements français dans l'Inde, l'épidémie d'influenza de 1918–1919', *AMédPhC* 20: 56–8.

Influenza Epidemic Relief Committee (1918) 'Report of the Influenza Epidemic Relief Committee', *The Social Science Quarterly* 4.

King, H.H. (1921) 'Rapport sur l'Influenza dans l'Inde', *Bulletin Mensuel de l'Office International d'Hygiène Publique* 13: 806–48.

Mills, I.D. (1986) 'The 1918–19 Influenza Pandemic. The Indian experience', *Indian Economic and Social History Review* 23, 1: 1–40; also reprinted (1989) 'Influenza in India during 1918–19', in T. Dyson (ed.), *India's Historical Demography*, London: Curzon (Collected Papers on South Asia 8), 222–60.

Phipson, E.S. (1918) 'Influenza in Bombay', *Indian Medical Gazette* 53: 441–7.

Phipson, E.S. (1923) 'The pandemic of influenza in India in the year 1918 with special reference to the city of Bombay', *Indian Medical Gazette* 58, 11: 509–24. [Abstract *Tropical Disease Bulletin* 21, 6: 494–6]

Ramanna, M. (1998) 'Coping with the influenza pandemic, 1918–1919: The Bombay experience', unpublished paper for the 'Conference on the Spanish flu 1918–1998', held in Cape Town.

Sen, R.K. (1923) *A Treatise on Influenza, with Special Reference to the Pandemic of 1918*, Assam and London: Hurmutty Tea Estate and J. Bale.

Wakimura, Kohei (1997) 'Famines, epidemics and mortality in Northern India, 1870–1921', in Peter Robb, Sugihara, K. and Yanagisawa, H. (eds), *Local Agrarian Societies in Colonial India. Japanese Perspectives*, London: Manohar, pp. 280–319.

Wakimura, K. (1998) 'The Indian experience of influenza pandemic 1918–19: Why the mortality was so huge', unpublished paper for 'Conference on the Spanish flu 1918–1998', held in Cape Town.

Waters, H.G. (1920) 'A note on influenza in India, 1918–1920', *British Medical Journal* 1920/II: 591.

White, F.N. (1919) *A Preliminary Report on the Influenza Pandemic of 1918 in India*, Simla. [Abstract *Medical Press* 107, 12: 228]

Indonesia

Anon. (1920) 'Rapport over de influenza-epidemie in Nederlandsch-Indië 1918', *Mededeelingen van den Burgerlijken Geneeskundigen Dienst in Nederlandsch-Indië* (Batavia), 10: 76–153. [Abstract in *Tropical Disease Bulletin* 19, 7: 604] [Report of the Influenza Commission]

Brown, Colin (1987) 'The influenza pandemic of 1918 in Indonesia', in Norman G. Owen (ed.), *Death and Disease in Southeast Asia. Explorations in Social, Medical, and Demographic History*, Singapore: Oxford University Press, pp. 235–56.

Iran

Afkhami, A.A. (2000) 'Compromised constitutions. The Iranian experience with the 1918–1919 influenza pandemic', *The Bulletin of the History of Medicine* 74.

Japan

Fujikawa Yu (1922) *Yukosei Kanbo* [Influenza Epidemic], Tokyo: Central Sanitary Bureau. [Official report]

Palmer, E. and Rice, G.W. (1992) 'Divine winds versus devil winds. Popular responses to pandemic influenza in Japan', *Japan Forum* 4, 2: 317–28.

Palmer, E. and Rice, G.W. (1992) 'Japanese physician's response to pandemic influenza: Ijiro Gomibuchi and the "Spanish Flu" in Yaita-Cho, 1918–1919', *Bulletin of the History of Medicine* 66, 4: 560–77.

Rice, G.W. and Palmer, E. (1993) 'Pandemic influenza in Japan, 1918–19. Mortality patterns and official response', *J Japanese Studies* 19, 2: 389–420. [Morbidity and mortality figures for all prefectures]

Shimizu, K. (1997) ['History of influenza epidemics and the discovery of the influenza virus, Japanese epidemics 862 to 1933'], *Nippon Rinsho – The Japanese J Clinical Medicine* (Osaka) 55, 10: 2505–11.

Sugiura Yoshio (1977) 'Waga kuni ni okeru "Supein Kaze" no kukanteki kakusan ni kansaru ikkosatsu' [Spatial diffusion of Spanish Influenza in Japan], *Chirigaku-hyoron* [*Geographical Review*] (Tokyo) 50, 4: 201–15. [Japanese with English abstract]

Korea

Schofield, Frank W. and Cynn, H.C. (1919) 'Pandemic Influenza in Korea. With special reference to its etiology', *JAMA* 72, 14: 981–3.

Laos

Carayon (1922) 'Laos, l'épidémie d'influenza de 1918–1919', *Annales de Médecine et de Pharmacie Coloniales* 20, 1: 54–5.

Philippines

Coutant, A.F. (1918) 'An epidemic of influenza at Manila, P.I.', *JAMA* 71, 19: 1566–7.

Philippine Health Service (1919) *Report of the Philippine Health Service from the fiscal year from January 1 to December 31, 1918.* Manila. [Abstract on influenza in *Tropical Disease Bulletin* 16, 4: 301–2]

Sri Lanka

Langford, C.M. and Storey, P. (1992) 'Influenza in Sri Lanka, 1918–1919. The impact of a new disease in a pre-modern Third World setting', *Health Transition Review* 2, Supplement, 97–123.

Taiwan

Liu, Wu-Tse and Chan, Chi-Ho (1998) 'The evolution of influenza A/H1N1 in Taiwan', unpublished paper for the 'Conference on the Spanish flu 1918–1998', held in Cape Town.

Turkey

Mayer, K. (1919) 'Ueber Schutzkörpermangel bei Grippe nach Beobachtungen über die Grippe 1918 unter den deutschen Truppenteilen in Konstantinopel' [About reduced immunity during the influenza of 1918 based on observations in German troops in Constantinople], *Münchner Medizinische Wochenschrift* 66, 17: 461–4.

Weinberg, M. (1919) 'Malaria und Grippe' [Malaria and influenza], *Beihefte zum Archiv für Schiffs- und Tropen-Hygiene* 23, Supplement 4: 176–85.

Weinberg, M. (1919) 'Die Grippeepidemie von Oktober bis Dezember 1918 in der Türkei' [Influenza epidemic in Turkey between October and December 1918], *Beihefte zum Archiv für Schiffs- und Tropen-Hygiene* 23, Supplement 4: 186–96. [Fear of bubonic plague]

Vietnam

Gaide, L.J. (1922) 'Cochinchine, l'épidémie d'influenza de 1918–1919', *Annales de Médecine et de Pharmacie Coloniales* 20, 1: 47–9.

Garnier, M. (1922) 'Tonkin, l'épidémie d'influenza de 1918–1919', *Annales de Médecine et de Pharmacie Coloniales* 20, 1: 45–7.

Montel, M.L.R. (1919) 'La pandémie grippale de 1918 à Saigon', *Bulletin de la Société médico-chirurgicale de l'Indochine* (Hanoï) 10, 1: 1–6. [Abstract *Tropical Disease Bulletin* (1920), 16, 3: 220–1]

Montel, M.L.R. (1919) 'La pandémie grippale de 1918 à Saigon', *La Presse Médicale* 27: 770.

Thiroux, A. (1922) 'Annam, l'épidémie d'influenza de 1918–1919', *Annales de Médecine et de Pharmacie Coloniales* 20, 1: 49–52.

Europe

Rollet, C. (1997) 'The "other war" II. Protecting public health', in Jay M. Winter and Jean-Louis Robert (eds), *Capital Cities at War: Paris, London, and Berlin, 1914–1919*, Cambridge: Cambridge University Press. [pp. 480–6 on influenza].

Albania

Letulle, M. (1919) 'Influenza in Albania', *Bulletin de l'Académie de médecine* (Paris) 81: 58.

Andorra

Montaña i Buchaca, D. and Pujol i Ros, J. (1999) 'L'epidèmia de grip del l'any 1918 al Principat d'Andorra', *Gimbernat* 30: 237–45.

Austria

Elias, Herbert (1926) 'Grippe', in Clemens Peter Pirquet von Cesnatico (ed.), *Volksgesundheit im Krieg*, Wien and New Haven: Hölder-Pichler-Tempsky and Yale University Press (Wirtschafts- und Sozialgeschichte des Weltkrieges. Österreichische und Ungarische Serie Vol. 4, No. 2), pp. 54–66. [Carnegie report]

Frey, E. (1918) 'Studien zur Epidemiologie der Influenza 1918' [Studies on epidemiology of 1918 influenza], *Wiener klinische Wochenschrift* 31: 1370–3.

Pichler, J. (1918) 'Die spanische Krankheit' [Spanish disease], *Wiener klinische Wochenschrift* 31: 892.

Raffelt, F. (1920) 'Ein Rückblick auf die Influenza vom Jahre 1918' [Retrospective on the influenza of 1918], *Wiener klinische Wochenschrift* 33: 334–6.

Rosenfeld, S. (1921) *Die Grippeepidemie des Jahres 1918 in Österreich* [Influenza epidemic of 1918 in Austria] (Veröffentlichungen des Volksgesundsheitsamtes im österreichischen Bundesministerium für soziale Verwaltung No. 13). Wien, 55 pp.

Schmidt, L. (1918) 'Klinische, aetiologische und epidemiologische Beobachtungen über die spanische Krankheit' [Clinical, etiological and epidemiological observations on the Spanish disease], *Wiener klinische Wochenschrift* 31: 1450–3.

Wiesener, R. v. (1918) 'Zur Aetiologie der Grippe' [On etiology of influenza], *Mitteilungen des Deutsch-oesterreichischen Staatsamtes für Volksgesundheit.*

Belgium

Colard, A., Firket, J., Spehl, P. and Nolf, P. (1919) 'Epidémie de grippe à l'armée de campagne belge', *Revue d'Hygiène et de Police Sanitaire* 41: 702.

Nolf, P. and Spehl, P. *et al.* (1919) 'L'épidémie de grippe à l'armée de campagne belges (mai-décembre 1918)', *Archives Médicales Belges, 4 Series* (Bruxelles) 72, 1: 149.

Bulgaria

Kayser-Petersen, J.E. (1919) 'Zur Epidemiologie der Grippe [On epidemiology of influenza], *Münchner medizinische Wochenschrift* Vol. 66, No. 25 (20 June): 691. [Epidemic at Varna, Black Sea]

Croatia

Fatovíc-Ferencic, S. (1988) 'Epidemiologija najcescih infektivnih bolesti na podrucju grada Zagreba od 1850–1950' [Epidemiology of most frequent diseases in Zagreb district from 1850 to 1950], unpublished MA thesis, University of Zagreb, Department for History of Medicine of Croatian Academy of Sciences and Arts.

Fatovíc-Ferencic, S. (1992) 'Akutne zarazne bolesti na podrucju grada Zagreba u razdoblju od 1878–1950' [Acute infectious diseases in the Zagreb District in the period 1878–1950], *Rasprave i gradja za povijest znanosti,* Hrvatska Akademija Znanosti i Umjetnosti [Discussions and Sources on the History of Sciences, Croatian Academy of Sciences and Arts], Book No. 7, Zagreb, pp. 205–53.

Fatovíc-Ferencic, S. and Sain, S. (1991) 'Spanjolska gripa kao uzrok smrti u gradu Zagrebu 1918' [Spanish Influenza as the cause of death in Zagreb in 1918], *Lijecnicki Vjesnik* 113, 11–12: 444–6. [Based on autopsy records and other public records]

Gross, Mavro (1919) 'K evropskoj epidemiji 1918' [On European epidemic in 1918], *Lijecnicki Vjesnik* 41, 2: 29–35.

Hirsch, S. (1923) 'Prilog k pandemiji gripe 1918–20' [On pandemic of influenza 1918–20], *Lijecnicki Vjesnik* 45, 2: 39–45.

Robida, I. (1919) 'Zivcane in dusevne bolezni po gripi 1918–19' [On neuro and psychiatric diseases after influenza in 1918–19], *Lijecnicki Vjesnik* 41, 7 and 10: 2361–70 and 539–42.

Sain, S. (1992) 'Uzroci smrti u gradu Zagrebu od 1916 do 1918 godine prema podacima obdukcijskih zapisnika prosekture javnih zdravstvenih zavoda' [Causes of death in Zagreb in the period from 1916 to 1918 according to data from autopsy reports of the pathological department and public health institutions], *Rasprave i gradja za povijest znanosti,* Hrvatska Akademija Znanosti i Umjetnosti [Discussions and Sources on the History of Sciences, Croatian Academy of Sciences and Arts], Book No. 7, Zagreb, pp. 255–80.

Sain, S. and Fatovíc-Ferencic, S. (1991) 'A retrospective analysis of the autopsy reports of the Zagreb Pathological Department made during the First World War', *Acta Clinica Croatica* 30, 3–4: 155–63.

Stanojevic, L. (1919) 'Neobicne neuritide iza spanjolske bolesti sa klinickog gledista' [Unusual neurotides after Spanish Disease], *Lijecnicki Vjesnik* 41, 7: 368–72.

Zerjavic, V. (1993) 'Kretanje stanovnistva i demografski gubici Republike hrvatske u razdobju 1900 do 1991 godine' [Population displacement and demographic losses of the Republic of Croatia, 1900–1991], *Casopis za Suvremenu Povijest* [Magazine of Contemporary History] (Zagreb) 25, 2–3: 65–85. [Based on the census, Spanish influenza mortality was estimated at 73,000 Croats, 25,000 Serbs and 11,000 other nationals in Croatia]

Denmark

Ammentorp, L. (1919) [Influenza epidemic in the Danish army during 1918–19], *Hospitalstidende* 62: 1161–70.

Heidemann, H. (1965) 'Om "Den Spanske syge" 1918–1920', *Medicinsk Forum* 18, 1: 15–23.

Olsen, T. (1918) [Influenza epidemic in the army], *Ugeskrift for Laeger* 80: 1980–3.

Thomsen, O., Kristensen, M. and Thorberg, F. (1918) *Undersoegelser over Influenza-'ens (Den 'Spanske syge's') Årsaksforhold* [Studies of influenza (Spanish Influenza) and causality], Koebenhavn and Kristiania: Gyldendalske Boghandel and Nordisk Forlag.

Finland

Hagelstam. J. (1919) '"Spanska sjukan" och dess komplikationer enligt iakttagelser pae Maria sjukhus i Helsingfors' [Spanish Influenza and its complications according to observations in Maria hospital in Helsinki], *Finska Laekaresaellskapets Handlingar* 61: 113–23.

Hagelstam, J. (1919) 'Naegra erfarenheter fraen den senaste influensaepidemien (mars-april 1919)' [Experiences during the latest influenza epidemic], *Finska Laekaresaellskapets Handlingar* 61: 511–16.

Linnanmaeki, E. (1998) 'Spanish Flu in Finnish cities 1918–1920', unpublished paper for the 'Conference on the Spanish flu 1918–1998', held in Cape Town.

Macklin, A.H. (1920) 'Influenza among the Lapps', *British Medical J* 1920/I: 465.

Sundelius, H. (1922) 'Influensan i Helsingfors 1918–1921', *Finska Läkaresällskapets Handlingar* 64: 172–85.

Vahtola, J. (1994) 'Espanjantauti Suomessa 1918–1920' [Spanish Influenza in Finland], *Kulttuuri, politiikka, historia, koulutus ja lehdistö*, Oulu: Kirjapaino Osakeyhtiö Kaleva, 131–43.

Vuorinen, H.S. and Linnanmaeki, E. (1997) 'Spanska sjukan i Finland' [Spanish Influenza in Finland], *Svensk Medicinhistorisk Tidskrift* 1, Supplement 1: 211–18.

France

Bernard, L. (1929) *La Défense de la Santé Publique pendant la Guerre*, Paris: Les Presses Universitaires de France. [Medical and sanitary affairs during World War One]

Bouron-Navet, F. (1998) 'La censure de la presse en France en 1918', *Revue Historique des Armées* 3: 13–18. [News about the epidemic in France was censored]

Brooks, H. and Gillette, C. (1919) 'Influenza in Soldiers. Argonne influenza', *New York Medical J* 110: 925.

Camecasse (1919) 'L'Épidémie de grippe de 1918', *Revue d'Hygiène et de Police Sanitaire* 41: 89–90.

Carnwath, T. (1918) 'A report on the influenza epidemic in the British armies in France 1918', *British Medical J* 1918/II: 505.

Chesney, A.M. and Snow, F.W. (1921) 'A report of an epidemic of influenza in an army post of the American Expeditionary Forces in France', *J Laboratory and Clinical Medicine* 6: 78–95.

Cruveilhier, L. (1919) 'La grippe à Paris en 1918. Statistique, bactériologie, hygiène', *Le Journal Médical Français* 8: 26–31.

Delater (1923) 'La Grippe dans la nation armée de 1918 à 1921', *Revue d'Hygiène* 45: 409–634.

France, Ministère de la Guerre (1922) *Statistique médicale*, Paris. [Part III Pandémie de grippe du 1er mai 1918 au 30 avril 1919]

Folly, E. (1919) 'Contribution à l'étude de l'épidémie de grippe observée dans la garnison de Strasbourg durant l'hiver 1918–19', *Bulletin de l'Académie de Médecine* (Paris), 3 Series, 82: 163–5.

Great Britain. National Health Insurance Joint Committee. Medical Research Committee (1919) *Studies of Influenza in Hospitals of the British Armies in France, 1918*, London (Special Report Series. Medical Research Committee No. 36).

Guillaume, P. (1978) 'La grippe à Bordeaux en 1918', *Annales de Démographie Historique*, 167–73.

Harris, D.T. (1918) 'Some observations on the recent influenza epidemic at a base hospital in France', *The Lancet* 1918/II: 877.

Hewlett, A.W. and Alberty, W.M. (1918) 'Influenza at Navy Base Hospital in France', *JAMA* 71, 13: 1056–8.

Hildreth, M.L. (1991) 'The influenza epidemic of 1918–1919 in France: Contemporary concepts of aetiology, therapy, and prevention', *Social History of Medicine* 4, 2: 277–94.

Hildreth, M.L. (1992) 'Influenza in Lyon and Marseille', in F.R. Van Hartesveldt (ed.), *The 1918–1919 Pandemic of Influenza. The Urban Impact in the Western World*, Lewiston: Edwin Mellen Press, 33–68.

Ichok, G. (1923) 'Les Epidémies de grippe à Paris dans les années 1900–1920 et la mortalité par tuberculose pulmonaire', *Revue d'Hygiène* 45: 123–8.

Jacquet, P. (1919) 'La grippe a Bourges. Contribution à l'étude épidémiologique, clinique, anatomique et bactériologique de la grippe épidémique de 1918 dans le centre de la France', Paris. [Dissertation]

Jouanin, C. (1987) 'Le "bon plaisir" des pharmacies en octobre 1918', *Revue d'Histoire de la Pharmacie* 34, 273: 121–3.

Leuret (1919) 'La grippe à Bordeaux', *Le Journal Médical Français* 8: 21–6.

Longcope, W.T. (1919) 'Survey of the epidemic of Influenza in the American Expeditionary Forces', *JAMA* 73, 3: 189–91.

MacNeal, W.J. (1919) 'The influenza epidemic of 1918 in the American Expeditionary Forces in France and England', *Archives of Internal Medicine* 23, 6: 657–88.

Menetrier, P. (1922) 'Influenza in 1918–1919', *Bulletin de l'Académie de médecine* (Paris) 87: 143–51.

Merklen, P. (1918) 'Deuxième note sur l'épidémie de grippe en Bretagne', *Bulletins et Mémoires de la Société Médicale des Hôpitaux de Paris*, 3 serie, 42: 924–8.

Morel, P. and Quetel, C. (1977) 'La grippe (espagnole) de 1918 à Caen et son impact au Bon-Sauveur', *Annales de Normandie* 27, 2: 205–18.

Murard, L. and Zylberman, P. (1996) 'The nation sacrificed for the army? The falling French public health, 1914–1918', in W.U. Eckart and C. Gradmann (eds) *Die Medizin und der Erste Weltkrieg*, Pfaffenweiler: Centaurus-Verlagsgesellschaft, pp. 343–64.

Péhu, M. and Ledoux, E. (1918) 'Revue documentaire sur l'épidémie actuelle de grippe en France', *Annales de Médecine* (Paris) 5: 579–81.

Préfecture de la Seine. Direction de l'Hygiène, du Travail et de la Prévoyance sociale (1919) *Recueil de Statistiques de la Ville de Paris et du Départment de la Seine, Epidémie de grippe à Paris, 30 Juin 1918 – 26 Avril 1919*, Paris.

Puklin, D.A.V. (1992) 'Influenza in Paris', in F.R. Van Hartesveldt (ed.), *The 1918–1919 Pandemic of Influenza. The Urban Impact in the Western World*, Lewiston: Edwin Mellen Press, pp. 69–90.

Sale, L. (1919) 'Influenza in France (in A.E.F., 1918)', *J Missouri State Medical Association* 16, 11: 373–4.

Zinsser, H. (1920) 'Manifestations of influenza during the earlier periods of its appearance in France', *Medical Record* (New York) 97, 11: 459–60.

Germany

Anon. (1918) 'Die Grippe-Epidemie im Sommer und Herbst 1918' [Influenza epidemic in summer and autumn 1918], *Schmidts Jahrbuch der gesamten Medizin* 85, 328: 177.

Anon. (M.K.) (1920) 'Die Grippe in Berlin' [Influenza in Berlin], *Münchner medizinische Wochenschrift* 67, 9: 273.

Bahrdt, R. (1919) 'Influenzatodesfälle. Vortrag Medizinische Gesellschaft zu Leipzig 6.5.1919' [Death from influenza], *Münchner medizinische Wochenschrift* 66, 38: 1097. [Leipzig; no relationship between war-related hunger and influenza mortality]

Bogusat, H. (1923) 'Die Influenza-Epidemie 1918/19 im Deutschen Reiche', *Arbeiten aus dem Reichsgesundheitsamte* 53: 443–66.

Brandt, W. (1919) 'Zur Epidemiologie der Grippe' [Epidemiology of influenza], *Münchner medizinische Wochenschrift* 66, 50: 1439–40. [Aschaffenburg]

Brasch, W. (1918) 'Über die Influenza-artige Epidemie im Juli 1918' [On the influenza-like epidemic in July 1918], *Münchner medizinische Wochenschrift* 65, 30: 809–11. [Munich]

Creischer, L. (1919) 'Grippe und Lungentuberkulose' [Influenza and tuberculosis], *Deutsche Medizinische Wochenschrift* 45, 12: 323.

Decker, N. (1996) 'Die "Spanische Grippe" 1918–1920 in Leipzig', *Archiwum Historii Filozofii Medycyny* 59, 1: 67–72.

Dörbeck, F. (1919) 'Die Influenzapandemie des Jahres 1918', *Deutsche Medizinische Wochenschrift* 45, 26: 716–18, and 27: 743–5.

Fassbender, C. (1921) 'Das epidemische Auftreten der Grippe und der Encephalitis lethargica in Preußen im Jahre 1920 und die gegenseitigen Beziehungen der beiden Krankheiten. Nach den amtlichen Berichten bearbeitet', *Veröffentlichungen aus dem Gebiete der Medizinalverwaltung* 13, 8: 565–602.

Federschmidt, H. (1919) 'Nürnbergs Grippeepidemie in statistischer Hinsicht', *Münchner Medizinische Wochenschrift* 66: 359–60.

Fikentscher, A. (1928) 'Die Gesundheitsverhältnisse bei der Marine', in Franz Bumm (ed.), *Deutschlands Gesundheitsverhältnisse unter dem Einfluss des Weltkrieges* (Wirtschafts- und Sozialgeschichte des Weltkrieges. Deutsche Serie. Vol. 10) Stuttgart and New Haven: Deutsche Verlagsanstalt and Yale University Press, No. 2, pp. 217–35. [Influenza 224–6; Carnegie report]

Fritz, S.G. (1992) 'Influenza in Frankfurt', in F.R. Van Hartesveldt (ed.), *The 1918–1919 Pandemic of Influenza. The Urban Impact in the Western World*, Lewiston: Edwin Mellen Press, pp. 13–32.

Fromme, A. (1918) 'Zur Influenzaepidemie', *Deutsche medizinische Wochenschrift* 44: 1416–18. [Epidemiology of influenza in a battalion]

Gins, M.A. (1918) 'Über die Grippe', *Die Ortskrankenkasse* (Dresden) 5: 629.

Gottstein, A. (1918) 'Zur Grippeepidemie', *Deutsche Medizinische Wochenschrift* 44, 41: 1128–9.

Graaz, H. (1920) *Die pandemische Grippe im Jahre 1918/19* [Pandemic influenza in 1918–1919], Berlin: Ebering, 41 pp. [Dissertation]

Grasmann, K.W. (1918) 'Über die Grippeepidemie an der Front in den Sommermonaten 1918', *Münchner Medizinische Wochenschrift* 65, 51: 1437–8.

Gruber, G.R. and Schädel, A. (1918) 'Zur pathologischen Anatomie und zur Bakteriologie der influenza-artigen Epidemie im Juli 1918' [On pathological anatomy and bacteriology of the influenza-like epidemic of July 1918], *Münchner medizinische Wochenschrift* 65, 33: 905–6.

Hahn, M. (1928) 'Krankheitsverhältnisse. G. Influenza, Genickstarre, Tetanus, Weilsche Krankheit', in Franz Bumm (ed.), *Deutschlands Gesundheitsverhältnisse unter dem Einfluss des Weltkrieges* (Wirtschafts- und Sozialgeschichte des Weltkrieges. Deutsche Serie. Vol. 10) Stuttgart and New Haven: Deutsche Verlagsanstalt and Yale University Press, No. 1, pp. 327–51. [Influenza pp. 327–43; Carnegie report]

Hesse, W. (1918) 'Die sogenannte "spanische Krankheit"' [So-called "Spanish disease"], *Münchner medizinische Wochenschrift* 65: 814.

Koenen, E. (1970) 'Die Grippepandemie 1918/19', unpublished medical dissertation, Universität Köln, Institut für Geschichte der Medizin.

König, W. (1920) 'Die Grippe-Epidemie im Regierungsbezirk Arnsberg Herbst 1918', *Veröffentlichungen aus dem Gebiete der Medizinalverwaltung* 10, 6: 29–46.

Lachmann, E. (1976) 'The German influenza of 1918–19: personal recollections and review of the German medical literature of that period', *Oklahoma State Medical Association J* 69: 517–20.

Lemke, M. (1920) 'Die Grippe-Epidemie des Jahres 1918 im Regierungs-Bezirk Oppeln', *Veröffentlichungen aus dem Gebiete der Medizinalverwaltung* 10, 6: 47–65.

Lubinski, H. (1924) 'Statistische Betrachtungen zur Grippepandemie in Breslau 1918–1922', *Centralblatt für Bakteriologie Parasitenkunde und Infektionskrankheiten* 91, 6: 372–83.

Mandelbaum, M. (1918) 'Epidemiologische und bakteriologische Untersuchungen über die pandemische influenza' [Epidemiological and bacteriological studies on pandemic influenza], *Münchner medizinische Wochenschrift* 65: 812.

Merkel (1928) 'Die Gesundheitsverhältnisse im Heer. 11. Influenza', in Franz Bumm (ed.), *Deutschlands Gesundheitsverhältnisse unter dem Einfluss des Weltkrieges* (Wirtschafts- and Sozialgeschichte des Weltkrieges. Deutsche Serie. Vol. 10) Stuttgart and New Haven: Deutsche Verlagsanstalt and Yale University Press, No. 2, pp. 181–2. [Carnegie report]

Müller, J. (1996) see Global.

Münter, F. (1921) 'Influenza', in L. v. Krehl (ed.) *Innere Medizin* (Handbuch der Ärztlichen Erfahrungen im Weltkriege 1914/1918, III) Leipzig, 322–6. [Influenza in German army]

Noll, H. (1953) 'Vergleichende Betrachtung über den Verlauf der Grippeepidemie in den Jahren 1918/20 und 1950/51 sowie 1952/53 [Comparative study about course of the influenza epidemics of 1918–1920, 1950–1951 and 1952–1953], unpublished medical dissertation, Universität Mainz, 349 pp.

Olm, K. (1998) 'The Spanish Flu in Saxony', unpublished paper for the 'Conference on the Spanish flu 1918–1998', held in Cape Town.

Ott, B. (1998) '"Die böse Spanierin treibt ihr Unwesen". Die Grippeepidemie von 1918/19, [The evil Spanish Lady is up to mischief. Influenza epidemic of 1918/19], *Schaffhauser Beiträge zur Geschichte* 75: 161–83.

Peiper, O. (1920) 'Bericht über die Grippe Epidemie in Preußen im Jahre 1918/19. Zusammengestellt nach amtlichen Berichten', *Veröffentlichungen aus dem Gebiete der Medizinalverwaltung* 10, 6: 1–28.

Prein, F. (1920) 'Zur Influenzapandemie 1918 auf Grund bakteriologischer, pathologisch-anatomischer und epidemiologischer Beobachtungen' [On influenza pandemic 1918. Based on bacteriological, pathological-anatomic and epidemiological observations], *Zeitschrift für Hygiene und Infektionskrankheiten* 90: 65–126.

Reichswehrministerium, Heeres-Sanitätsinspection (1934) 'Grippe', *Sanitätsbericht über das Deutsche Heer im Weltkriege 1914/1918*, III: 121–3 and supplement: 28–9. [Influenza in German army]

Roesle, E.E. (1928) 'Die Geburts- und Sterblichkeitsverhältnisse. B. Der Einfluß des Weltkrieges auf die Mortalität im Deutschen Reich', in Franz Bumm (ed.), *Deutschlands Gesundheitsverhältnisse unter dem Einfluss des Weltkrieges* (Wirtschafts- und Sozialgeschichte des Weltkrieges. Deutsche Serie. Vol. 10) Stuttgart and New Haven: Deutsche Verlagsanstalt and Yale University Press, No. 1, pp. 22–61. [Influenza passim; Carnegie report]

Rose, C.W. (1918) 'Die Influenzaepidemie in einem Festungslazarett im Juni/Juli 1918' [Influenza epidemic in a lazaretto June–July 1918], *Berliner klinische Wochenschrift* 55, 44: 1041–4.

Seligmann, E. and Wolff, G. (1923) 'Die Influenzapandemie in Berlin. Versuch einer statistischen Erfassung', *Zeitschrift für Hygiene und Infektionskrankheiten* 101, 1: 157–66. [Statistics on influenza pandemic in Berlin based on figures of health insurance societies]

Vasold, M. (1995) 'Die Grippepandemie in Nürnberg 1918 – eine Apokalypse', *Zeitschrift für Sozialgeschichte des 20. und 21. Jahrhunderts*, 10, 4: 12–37.

Vasold, M. (1996) 'Die Grippepandemie im Jahre 1918. Die Pflegenden waren doppelt betroffen', *Pflegezeitschrift* 49, 2: 112–15.

Vasold, M. (1998) 'The influenza pandemic of 1918/19 in Nuremberg', unpublished paper for the 'Conference on the Spanish flu 1918–1998', held in Cape Town.

Vaughan, V.C. (1919) 'Influenza in Germany', *J Laboratory and Clinical Medicine* (St Louis) 4: 142–5.

Greece

Filtzos, T.G. (1919) 'Epidemic influenza in Greece', *Public Health Reports* 34: 507.
Rondopoulos, P.J. (1919) 'Influenza in Greece', *JAMA* 72, 26: 1947.

Hungary

Henley, C. (1975) 'The toxic second period of the 1918–1919 influenza panepidemic in Hungary', *Medical J Australia*, 18: 570–1.

Iceland

Cliff, A.D., Haggett, Peter and Ord, J. K. (1986) *Spatial Aspects of Influenza Epidemics*, London: Pion Ltd, 280 pp. [133–67 on historical evidence]
Erlendsson, V. (1919) 'Influenzaepidemien paa Island', *Ugeskrift for Laeger* 81: 683–6. [Abstract *JAMA* 72: 1880]

Ireland

Crofton, W.M. (1918) 'The influenza epidemic', *Studies: Irish Quarterly Review of Letters, Philosophy and Science* 7, 28: 659–65.

Lynn, K. (1919) 'Report on influenza pandemic', *Ard-Fheis* (extraordinary) Sinn Fein (8 April).

MacNamara, D.W. (1954) 'Memories of 1918 and "the flu"', *J Irish Medical Association* 35, 208: 304–9. [Dublin]

Peacocke, G. (1918) 'Influenza', *Dublin J Medical Science*, 3 Series, 146: 249–53.

Speares, J. (1918) 'Influenza', *Dublin J Medical Science*, 3 Series, 146: 253–8.

Thompson, W.J. (1920) 'Mortality from Influenza in Ireland', *Dublin J Medical Science*, 4 Series, 4: 174–86. [Thompson was Registrar General for Ireland]

Thompson, W.J. (1921) 'Mortality from influenza in Ireland', *J Statistical and Social Inquiry Society of Ireland* 14: 1–14

Italy

Balduino, C. (1918) 'Note sulla recente epidemia di influenza', *Annali di Medicina Navale* (Roma) 1: 396–9.

Benussi, G. *et al.* (1985) 'Sequele neurologiche dall'influenza. Pandemia del 1918–19 ed encefalite letargica a Trieste', *Acta Medicae Historiae Patavina* 30: 11–19.

Cavina, G. (1959) '*L'Influenza Epidemica – attraverso secoli*, Rome: Edizioni Pozzi' [Chapter VIII Epidemia Influenzale degli anni 1918–19, 203–18].

Currado, C. (1993) *Epidemia di Influenza 'Spagnola' nell'Astigiano. Ricordi e Ricerche di un testimone*, Asti, Rotary Club di Asti, 115 pp.

Lutrario, A. (1922) *La Tutela dell'Igiene a della Sanitá pubblica durante la Guerra e dopo la Vittoria*, Rome: Artero. [Vol. III: 3–26 on influenza]

Mei, A. (1921) 'Per l'incremento degli studi di patologia esotica in Italia e nelle colonie italiane', *La Medicina Italiana* (Milano) 2: 478–89.

Mortara, G. (1925) *La Salute pubblica in Italia durante e dopo la Guerra*, Bari: Laterza. [259–64 on influenza and problems in estimating mortality figures]

Pancrazio, F. (1918) 'La febbre influenzale fra le truppe' [Influenza in soldiers in the Italian Army], *Gazzetta degli Ospedali e delle Cliniche* (Milano) 39: 688–91.

Netherlands

Gelderen, J. v. (1920) 'De invloed der Spaansche Griep op de Amsterdamsche Geboorte-Cijfers' [Influence of Spanish Influenza on birth figures in Amsterdam], *Nederlandsch Tijdschrift voor Geneeskunde* 64/I, 10: 791–4.

Gooijer, A.C. d. (1968) *De Spaanse Griep van '18. De Epidemie die meer dan 20,000,000 Levens eiste.* Amsterdam: Van Lindonk.

Mulder, J. and Hers, J.F.P. (1972) 'Influenza. Groningen', Chapter III 'A comparison of the severity and mortality of the influenza pandemics of 1889/90, 1918/19 and 1957/58 with respect to the incidence of fatal influenza virus pneumonia', pp. 239–46.

Quanjer, A.A.J. (1921) *De Griep in Nederland in 1918 tot 1920.* Den Haag: Staats Uitgeverij. [Abstract *Bulletin Mensuel de l'Office International d'Hygiène Publique* 13 (1921) 523–4].

Rhijn Jr, W.P. v. (1920) 'Spaansche griep te Leiden' [Spanish Influenza in Leiden], *Medisch Weekblaad voor Noord- en Zuid Nederland* 26: 119.
Straub, M. (1959) 'De influenza-epidemieën van 1918 en 1957' [Influenza epidemics of 1918 and 1957], *Nederlands Tijdschrift voor Geneeskunde* 103: 1208–14.

Norway

Aarhus, I. (1988) 'I Spanskesykens tegn. Ein rapport om epidemien i åra 1918–1919' [Sign of Spanish Influenza. Report from the epidemic], *Tidsskrift for Sunnmoere Historielag* 64: 57–118.
Barth, N. (1919) 'Den "Spanske Syke" i Arendal 1918' [Spanish Influenza in Arendal 1918], *Tidsskrift for Den Norske Laegeforening* (Kristiania) 39, 6: 221–9.
Davis, J.L., Heginbottom, J.A. and Annan, A.P. *et al.* (2000) 'Ground penetrating radar surveys to locate 1918 Spanish flu victims in permafrost', *J Forensic Science* 45, 1: 68–76.
Erichsen, S. (1919) 'Influenza, saerlig i 1890 – årene og 1918' [Influenza, particularly in the years 1890 and 1918], *Tidsskrift for Den Norske Laegeforening* (Kristiania) 39, 7: 265–8.
Gregersen (1918) '"Den Spanske" ["The Spanish"]. Norsk Forsikring', *Tidsskrift for Norsk Livsforsikring og Socialforsikring* (Kristiania) 9, 1.
Hansen, O. (1923) *Undersoekelser over Influenzaens optraeden specielt i Bergen 1918–1922* [Studies of Influenza, particularly in Bergen 1918–1922], Bergen (Arbeider fra Den medicinske Avdeling av Haukeland sykehus. Skrifter utgit ved Klaus Hanssens Fond. No. 3).
Hansson, R.S. (1919) 'Litt om influenza ("den spanske syke", la grippe, "catarrhus epidmicus") foer og nu' [A little bit about Influenza now and then], *Tidsskrift for Den Norske Laegeforening* (Kristiania) 39, 7: 268–72, and 9: 345–8.
Harboe, A. (1976) 'Spanskesyken 1918–1919 og svineinfluensavirus' [Spanish Influenza 1918–1919 and the swine influenza virus], *Tidsskrift for Den Norske Laegeforening* (Kristiania) 96, 16: 914.
Holst, H.B. (1919) 'Influenzaens smitteforhold' [Influenza and how it infects], *Medicinsk Revue* (Bergen) 36, 1: 1–7.
Keyser, G.W. (1918) '"Den spanske syke" – Pseudo-influenza' [Spanish Influenza – Pseudo-influenza], *Tidsskrift for Den Norske Laegeforening* (Kristiania) 39, 18: 801–5.
Keyser, G.W. (1919) 'Den "Spanske Syke"' [Spanish Influenza], *Norsk tidsskrift for militaermedicin* (Kristiania) 22: 172–7.
Mamelund, S-E. (1998) 'Diffusjon av influensa i Norge under Spanskesyken 1918–19' [The Diffusion of Influenza in Norway during the 1918–19 Pandemic], *Norsk Epidemiologi* 8, No. 1.
Mamelund, S-E. (1998) 'Estimating the death toll of Spanish Influenza: the case of Norway', unpublished paper for the 'Conference on the Spanish flu 1918–1998', held in Cape Town.
Mamelund, S-E. (1998) 'Spanskesyken i Norge 1918–20: Diffusjon og Demografiske Konsekvenser' [Spanish Influenza in Norway 1918–1920: Diffusion and Demographic Impact], unpublished MA thesis, University of Oslo, Institute for Sociology and Human Geography.
Mamelund, S-E. (1999) 'Spanskesyken i Norge: Kostnadene og konsekvensene' [Spanish Influenza in Norway: the costs and the consequences], *Samfunnsspeilet* 13, 6: 22–31.

Mamelund, S-E. and Iversen, B.G. (2000) [Morbidity and mortality in pandemic influenza in Norway], *Tidsskrift for den Norske Laegeforening* 120, 3: 360–3. [History of pandemics and calculation for future pandemics]

Mehn-Andersen, O. (1921) 'En isolert influenza-epidemi', *Medicinsk Revue* (Bergen) 38: 204–15.

Melby, F. (1955) 'Influenzaens Epidemiologi og problemet om spanskesyken 1918–19' [Epidemiology of Influenza and the problem of Spanish Influenza], *Kosthold og Helse* 1, 1: 177–80.

Neumann, T. (1919) 'Influenzaens indvirkning paa lungetuberkulosen' [Influenza and the impact on tuberculosis], *Tidsskrift for Den Norske Laegeforening* (Kristiania) 39, 22: 873–9.

Ormestad, M. (1919) 'Den spanske syke i 1918' [The Spanish Influenza of 1918], *Norsk Forsikring* (Kristiania) 2, 4: 22–3.

Ramberg, R. (1969) 'Spanskesyken i Norge 1918–1919' [Spanish Influenza in Norway 1918–1919], *Tidsskrift for Den Norske Laegeforening* (Kristiania) 89, 22: 1709–12.

Skajaa, K. (1921) *Om influenza og influenzapneumoni. En patologisk-anatomisk og bakteriologisk undersoekelse* [About influenza and influenza pneumonia. A pathological-anatomical and bacteriological study]. Skrifter utgit ved Klaus Hanssens fond. No. 2. Fra Dr. med. F.G. Gades patalogiske institutt, Bergen, 225 pp.

Solberg, M. (1919) 'Spanskesykens herjinger i Norge' [The ravage of Spanish Influenza in Norway], Norsk Forsikring, *Tidsskrift for Norsk Livsforsikring og Socialforsikring* 6, 2: 38–9.

Speilberg, T.T. (1919) 'Den spanske syke' [Spanish Influenza], *Norsk tidsskrift for militaermedicin* (Kristiania) 22: 179.

Ustvedt, Y. (1919) 'Iagttagelser under influenzaepidemien i juli 1918' [Observations during the influenza epidemic in July 1918], *Norsk Magazin for Laegevidenskaben* (Kristiania) 80, 1: 1–20. [Abstract *JAMA* 72, 15: 1115]

Utne, I. (1919) 'Influenzaens optraeden i Bergen' [Prevalence of influenza in Bergen], *Medicinsk Revue* (Bergen) 36: 120–3.

Poland

Lemke, M. (1920) see Germany
Lubinski, H. (1923) see Germany

Portugal

Fuerte, M.J. de la. (1994) *A gripe pneumónica em Portugal. Um olhar histórico sobre discriminação e solidariedade em tempo de epidemia*, Lisbon: M.J. de la Fuerte, 56 pp.

Lisbon. Direcção Geral dos Hospitais Civis (1920) *Relatórios e Notícias sôbre a Epidemia de Gripe Pneumónica*, Lisboa: Imprensa Nacional.

Martins, A.V.P de F. (1919) *A grippe*, Coimbra: Tip Popular de J. Bizarro, 76 pp.

Ricardo, J. (1919) *La Grippe*, Lisboa.

Serbia

Dragic, M. (1980) 'Zdravstvene prilike u Beogradu za vreme okupacije u prvom svetskom ratu i spanski grip 1918–1919 godine' [Health conditions in Belgrade during the occupation in World War I and the 1918–1919 Spanish Influenza epidemic], *Srpski Arhiv za Ceopkupno Lekarstvo* [Serbian Archives of Medicine] (Beograd) 108, 9: 969–74.

Gavrilovic, Z. (1995) 'Pandemija Spanske Groznice u Sajkaskoj 1918–1919. Godine' [The Spanish influenza pandemic in Sajkaska 1918–1919], *Medicinski Pregled* [Medical Review] (Novi Sad) Vol. 48, No. 7–8: 277–80.

Spain

Arias-Carvajal, P. (1918) 'Cosas del siglo pasado. La gripe de antano', *El Siglo Medico* (Madrid) 65, 3382: 817–19.

Artigues i Artigas, A. (1989) 'Pandèmia de grip de 1918–19. Evolució en la prensa de Lleida i el seu registre civil', *Gimbernat* 12: 9–22.

Bernabéu Mestre, J. *et al.* (eds) (1991) *La Ciutat devant el Contagi: Alacant i la Grip de 1918–19.* Valencia: Conselleria de Sanitat i Consum, Generalitat Valenciana (Monografies Sanitaries, Series B, No. 4).

Bernabéu Mestre, J. (1994) 'Les societats urbanes davant les crisis epidèmiques. Alacant i l'epidèmia de grip de 1918', in H. Capel Sáez, J. M. López Piñero and J. Pardo Tomás (eds), *Ciència e Ideología en la Ciudad. I Coloquio Interdepartamental* (II), Valencia: Conselleria d'Obres Públiques, Urbanisme i Transport.

Bernabéu Mestre, J. and Ramos Segura, J.R. (1995) 'Malaltia, poder i control social. El desallotjament de la barriada alacantina de Les Províncies amb motiu de la grip de 1918', in C. Puig-Pla *et al.* (eds), *Actes de les III Trobades d'Història de la Ciència i de la Tècnica,* Barcelona: Societat Catalana d'Història de la Ciència i de la Tècnica.

Cabezas Fernández del Campo, J.A. (1990) *Datos sobre las pandemias de 1889–90 y 1918–19 en Madrid y Salamanca y estudios sobre la sialidasa de los virus de la gripe A y B y la esterasa del virus C* [Data concerning the 1889–90 and 1918–19 pandemics in Madrid and Salamanca and studies on the A and B influenza viruses sialidase and the C virus esterase], Madrid: Real Academia de Farmacia, 93 pp.

Camino, J. (1919) 'Mis juicios clinicos y mi actuación terapéutica en los epidemiados de Laredo' [My clinical opinions and my therapeutic actions during the epidemics at Laredo], *Revista de Sanidad Militar*, 3 series, 9: 57–63.

Cardona Ivars, J.J. (1973) *La Epidemia de Gripe de 1918 en Benisa y Canarca,* Utiel: Cooperativa Utielana de Artes Graficas (Publicationes del Ayuntamiento de Benisa Serie Maior 2).

Carrillo, J.L., Castellanos, J. and Ramos, D. (1985) *Enfermedad y Crisis Social: la Gripe en Málaga, 1918.* Málaga: Universidad, Departmento de Historia de la Medicina.

Castillo Sáiz, E. (1919) *Nota sintética de la Epidemia de Gripe en esta Provincia durante los Años 1918–1919,* Cuenca.

Contreras Poza, L. (1971) 'Un testimonio definitivo sobre la mal llamada gripe española de 1918', *Revista de Sanidad e Higiene Pública* 45, 9: 863–72.

Echeverri Dávila, B. (1990) 'La pandemia de gripe de 1918–19 en España', unpublished dissertation, Facultad de Ciencias Politicas y Sociologia, Universidad Complutense de Madrid.

Echeverri Dávila, B. (1993) *La Gripe Española. La Pandemia de 1918–1919,* Madrid: Centro de Investigaciones Sociológicas: Siglo XXI de España Editores (Colección Monografias No. 132).

Eléxpuru Camiruaga, L. (1986) *La Epidemia de Gripe de 1918 en Bilbao. Estudio Demográfico y Estadistico,* Salamanca: Ediciones Universidad de Salamanca (Serie Resúmenes de tesis doctorales T-M 470).

Fernández Fernández, C.M. and Veiga Ferreira, X.M. (1995) 'La "gripe" de 1918–19 en Betanzos' [The "Influenza" of 1918–19 in Betanzos], *Anuario Brigantino* 18: 143–58.

Ferrán, Rincón de Arellano, Calvée y Pesset (1918) 'La epidemia reinante estudios experimentales practicados en el Instituto Provincial de Valencia' [The ruling epidemic. Experimental studies done in the Provincial Institute of Valencia], *Revista de Higiene y Tuberculosis* (Valencia) 11.

Galan i Urbano, A. (1994) 'L'epidèmia de grip de 1918 a la població de Sant Cugat del Vallés', *Gimbernat* 22: 129–35.

Garcia-Faria del Corral, J. (1995) *La Epidemia de Gripe de 1918 en la Provincia de Zamora. Estudio Estadistico y Social,* Zamora: Instituto de Estudios Zamoranos.

García Durán, R. (1919) *Memoria Descriptiva y Datos Estadísticos de la Epidemia Gripal Padecida en la Provincia de Valladolid en el Año 1918,* Valladolid.

Gómez Díaz, D. and Gómez Díaz, M.J. (1998) 'Anatomía de una crisis. Almería 1918, el año de la gripe' [Anatomy of a crisis. Almería 1918, the year of the flu], in J. Castellanos Guerrero *et al.* (eds), *La Medicina en el Siglo XX. Estudios Históricos sobre Medicina, Sociedad y Estado* [Medicine in the 20th century. Historical studies on medicine, society and the state], Málaga: Sociedad Española de Historia de la Medicina.

Herms i Berenguer, J. (1991) 'L'epidemia de grip de l'any 1918 a Avinyó (Bages). Segons les anotacions del metge Atilà Herms Jubany', *Gimbernat* 15: 165–8.

Herrera Rodríguez, F. (1992) 'Un texto argentino sobre la gripe de 1918–1919', *Anales de la Real Academia de Medicina y Cirugía de Cádiz* 28, 1: 283–99.

Herrera Rodríguez, F. (1996) 'Incidencia social de la gripe de 1918–1919 en la ciudad de Cádiz' [Social incidence of the 1918–1919 influenza in Cádiz], *Llull. Boletín de la Sociedad Española de Historia de las Ciencias* (Zaragoza) 19, 37: 455–70.

Herrera Rodríguez, F. (1996) '*La epidemia de gripe de 1918 en el Puerto de Santa María*' [The influenza epidemic of 1918 in the port of Santa María], *Revista de Historia de El Puerto* 17: 31–63.

Martín, C. (1919) *Notas histórica-clínicas de la epidemia de gripe del otoño de 1918 en el pueblo de Ventas con Péna Aguililera* [Historical-clinical notes on the influenza epidemic of autumn 1918 in the village of Ventas con Peña Aguililera], Toledo: Imp. Sebastián Rodríguez, 27 pp.

Martínez Pons, M. (1998) 'Debate médico en torno a la epidemia de gripe de 1918 a través de la prensa médica valenciana' [The medical debate concerning the influenza epidemic of 1918 as reported in the medical press of Valencia], in J. Castellanoes Geurrero *et al.* (eds), *La Medicina en el Siglo XX. Estudios Históricos sobre Medicina, Sociedad y Estado* [Medicine in the 20th century. Historical studies on medicine, society and state], Málaga: Sociedad Española de Historia de la Medicina.

Martínez Pons, M. (1999) 'València al limit. La ciutat de València davant l'epidèmia de grip de 1918', Simat de la Valldigna: La Xara (País No. 5), 207 pp.

Martínez Pons, M. and Arona Vilar, C. (1996) 'Repercusiones de la epidemia de gripe de 1918 sobre la mortalidad en la ciudad de Valencia' [Effects of the influenza epidemics of 1918 on mortality in the City of Valencia], in J.L. Barona and J. Mico (eds), *Salut i malaltia en els municipis valencians*, Valencia: Seminari d'Estudis sobre la Ciència.

Montaña i Buchaca, D. and Pujol i Ros, J. (1995) 'L'epidèmia de grip del l'any 1918 a Igualada', *Gimbernat* 24: 225–9.

Orellana (1918) 'La epidemia actual' [The current epidemic], *Andalucia Médica* (Nov 18).

Palazón Ferrando, J. (1991) 'La pandemia de gripe de 1918–1920 y sus repercusiones en la mortalidad de la provincia de Alicante' [The influenza pandemic of 1918–1920 and its effects on mortality in Alicante province], in Josep Bernabéu Mestre (ed.), *El papel de la mortalidad en la evolución en la población valenciana* [The role of mortality in the development of the population of Valencia], Alicante: Instituto de Cultura Juan Gil-Albert, pp. 89–98.

Parada Justel, G. (1919) *La gripe endémica y la epidemia grippal de 1918. Juicios clínicos. Conferencia pronunciada en el Ateneo de Madrid el 2 de mayo de 1919* [Endemic and epidemic influenza of 1918. Clinical opinions. Conference held in the Ateneo of Madrid, 2 May 1919], Orense: Impr. A. Otero, 16 pp.

Piga Pascual A. and Lamas, L. (1919) *Infecciones de tipo gripal. Con notas de terapéutica clínica y epidemiología de varios doctores* [Infections of the influenza type. With notes on clinical therapy and epidemiology by various physicians]. Madrid: Talleres Tip. (Los Progresos de la Ciencia), 2 Vol., 309 and 267 pp.

Porras Gallo, M.I. (1992) 'La epidemia de gripe de 1918–19 en la prensa obrera' [The influenza epidemic of 1918–19 in the workers' press], in R. Hiertase and R. Campos (eds), *Medicina Social y Clase Obrera en España (Siglos XIX-XX)* [Social medicine and the working class in Spain (19th–20th centuries)], Madrid: Fundación de Investigaciones Marxistas.

Porras Gallo, M.I. (1993) 'La profilaxis de las enfermedades infecciosas tras la pandemia gripal de 1918–19: Los seguros sociales' [Prophylaxis for infectious diseases after the 1918–19 influenza pandemic: Social security programmes], *Dynamis. Acta Hispanica ad Medicinae Scienticirumque Historiam Illustrandam* (Universidad de Granada) 13: 279–93.

Porras Gallo, M.I. (1993) 'La Real Academia Nacional de Medicina y la problemática sobre la etiología de la gripe en la epidemia de 1918–19' [Real Academia Nacional de Medicina and the problems surrounding the etiology of influenza in the 1918–19 epidemic], *Cuadernos Complutense Historia Medicina i de la Ciencia* 1993, 1: 103–28. [Review of medical thesis on the epidemic]

Porras Gallo, M.I. (1994) 'Una ciudad en crisis: la epidemia de gripe de 1918–19 en Madrid', unpublished thesis, Facultad de Medicina, Universidad Complutense de Madrid.

Porras Gallo, M.I. (1994) 'La lucha contra las enfermedades "evitables" en España y la pandemia de gripe de 1918–19' [The fight against 'avoidable' diseases and the 1918–19 influenza pandemic in Spain], *Dynamis. Acta Hispanica ad Medicinae Scienticirumque Historiam Illustrandam* (Universidad de Granada) 14: 159–83.

Porras Gallo, M.I. (1994) 'La diferente mortalidad por distritos durante la epidemia de gripe de 1918–19 en Madrid', in J.L. Carrillo and G. Olague de Ros (eds), *Proceedings of the XXXIII International Congress on the History of Medicine, Granada-Seville 1992*, Sevilla: Caja San Fernando: 753–82.

Porras Gallo, M.I. (1995) 'La prensa madrileña de informacíon general ante la epidemia de gripe de 1918–19', *Medicina e Historia* (Barcelona) 57: I–XVI.

Porras Gallo, M.I. (1995) 'La epidemia de gripe de 1918–19. Una oportunidad para evaluar la recepción de ideas científicas en el pensamiento médico español' [The influenza epidemic of 1918–19. An opportunity to evaluate the adoption of scientific ideas in Spanish medical thinking], in E. Arquiola and J. Martinez Perez (eds), *Ciencia en expansión. Estudios sobre la difusión de las ideas científicas y médicas en España (siglos XVIII–XX)* [Expanding science. Studies on the dissemination of scientific and medical ideas in Spain (18th to 20th centuries)], Madrid: Editorial Complutense.

Porras Gallo, M.I. (1995) 'Una ciudad en crisis. La epidemia de gripe de 1918–19 en Madrid' [A city in crisis. The influenza epidemic of 1918–19 in Madrid], *Quirón* 26, 3: 56–69.

Porras Gallo, M.I. (1996) 'Las repercusiones de la pandemia de gripe e 1918–19 en la mortalidad de la ciudad de Madrid' [The effects of the influenza pandemic of 1918–19 on mortality in the City of Madrid], *Boletín de la Asociación de Demografía Histórica* 14, 1: 75–116.

Porras Gallo, M.I. (1997) 'El Laboratorio Municipal de Madrid y la epidemia de gripe de 1918–19' [The municipal laboratory of Madrid and the influenza epidemic of 1918–19], *Anales del Instituto de Estudios Madrileños* 37: 585–91.

Porras Gallo, M.I. (1997) 'Atendiéndose al consejo de los "expertos". Los madrileños frente a la gripe durante las epidemias de 1889–90 y 1918–19' [Keeping the 'experts' advice. The inhabitants of Madrid confronted by the influenza epidemic of 1889–90 and 1918–19], in L. Montiel and M.I. Porras (eds), *De la Responsabilidad individual a la Culpabilización de la víctima. El papel del paciente en la prevención de la enfermedad* [From individual responsibility to the blaming of the victim. The patient's role in the prevention of disease], Madrid: Doce Calles.

Porras Gallo, M.I. (1997) *Un Reto para la Sociedad Madrileña: La Epidemia de Gripe de 1918–19*. Madrid: Editorial Complutense (Madrid en el Tiempo No. 5).

Porras Gallo, M.I. (1998) 'Popularizando la medicina en tiempos de crisis. Los médicos y la prensa madrileña durante la epidemia de gripe 1918–19' [Popularising medicine in times of crisis. Physicians and the Madrid press during the influenza epidemic of 1918–19], in R. Ballester Añon (ed.), *La Medicina en España y en Francia y sus Relaciones con la Ciencia, la Tradición y los Saberes Tradicionales (Siglos XVIII a XX). (IX Coloquio Francoespañol de Historia de la Medicina y Antropología 1994)*, [Medicine in Spain and France and its relation to science, tradition and traditional knowledge (18th–20th centuries) (9th Franco-Spanish colloquium on the history of medicine and anthropology 1994], Alicante: Instituto de Cultura Juan Gil-Albert.

Pumarola, A. and Rodríguez Torres, A. (1969) 'Investigación sobre la etiología y epidemiología de la gripe en Barcelona' [Investigations ino aetiology and epidemiology of the influenza in Barcelona], *Miscellanea Barcinonensia* 8: 65–79.

Rasueros Díez, V. (1919) *Datos Sintéticos acerca de la Epidemia de Gripe desarrollada en la Provincia de Avila en los Años 1918–1919*, Avila: Imp. de Sigirani Díaz.

Rico-Avello, C. (1964) 'La Epidemia de gripe, 1918–1919' [The influenza epidemic of 1918–19], *Gaceta Médica Española* 38, 1: 1–4.

Rodrigo y Lavin, C. (1919) *La Lucha contra la Gripe. Deducciones de una Campaña Epidémica*. Madrid: Imp. Clásica España.

Rodriguez Ocaña, E. (1991) 'La grip a Barcelona: un greu problema de salut pública. Epidèmies de 1889–1890 i 1918', in J.M. López Pinero *et al.* (eds), *Cent Anys de Salut pùblica a Barcelona*. Institut Municipal de Salut, Barcelona: Institut Municipal de la Salut, 131–56.

Rosado Fernández, J. (1918) *Instrucciones sobre la profilaxis colectiva e individual de la gripe* [Instructions on collective and individual prevention of influenza], Málaga.

Sàez i Aguello, J.L. *et al.* (1992) 'Anàlisi de la mortalitat al voltant de l'epidèmia gripal de 1918, en el municipi de Vandellòs-Hospitalet', *Gimbernat* 17: 343–50.

Sánchez González, M. (1991) 'Profesionalismo y sacerdocio en la requesta a la gripe de 1918 en España y los Estados Unidos', *Actas del IX Congreso Nacional de Historia de la Medicina, Zaragoza 21.–23.9.1989.* 1: 335–43.

Sánchez Gozalbo, Á. (1919) 'Contribución al estudio de la gripe de 1918 en la provincia de Castellón' [Contributions to the study of the influenza of 1918 in Castellón province], Castellón: Hijos de J. Armengot, 36 pp. [Medical dissertation Universidad Central]

Sena Espinel, M.P. (1992) 'La pandemia gripal de 1918 en Salamanca y provincia' [The influenza pandemic of 1918 in Salamanca and its environs], unpublished dissertation, Facultad de Medicina, Universidad de Salamanca.

Tomás i Monserrat, J. (1982) *El Grip de l'Any 18 a Llucmayor. Notes sobre l'Epidèmia.* Llucmayor: Impremta Moderna.

Urquia, J.M. (1986) La pandemia gripal de 1918 en Guipuzcoa, *Cuadernos de Historia de la Medicina Vasca* 4: 37–86.

Sweden

Åman, M.G.H. (1989) 'Spanska sjukan 1918 i et internationellt, svenskt och jämtlandskt perspektiv' [Spanish Influenza in an international, Swedish and Jämtlandskt perspective], *Jämten* 82: 74–86.

Åman, M.G.H. (1990) *Spanska Sjukan. Den Svenska Epidemin, 1918–1920, och dess Internationella Bakgrund* [Spanish Influenza. The Swedish epidemic 1918–20 and its international background], Uppsala: Almqvist & Wiksell International (Studia Historica Upsaliensia No. 160). [Dissertation, Uppsala University]

Henrikson, V. (1956) *Läkaren Berättar*, Stockholm: Lars Hökerbegs Bokförlag.

Lundström, B. (1965) 'Reyska snuvan och spanska sjukan. Ur influensaepidemiernas historia' [Russian cold and Spanish 'flu. On the history of influenza epidemics], *Medicinhistorisk Årsbok* – Yearbook of the Museum of Medical History (Stockholm).

Nordlander, O. (1932) 'Influensaen och des framträdande särskilt inom svenska armen under epidemierna 1918/19 samt 1920' [Influenza and its impact on the Swedish army during the epidemics of 1918/19 and 1920], *Tidskrift i Militär Halsovård* 57, 2: 63–187. [Large section on influenza among soldiers in many other countries]

Switzerland

Bettex, M. (1967) 'La grippe de 1918 à La Tour-de-Peilz', *Revue Medicale de la Suisse Romande* 87: 835–6.

Birchner, E. (1918) 'Zur Grippeepidemie', *Correspondenz-Blatt für Schweizer Ärzte* 48, 40: 1338–40. [Influenza in La-Chaux-de-Fonds]

Frey, F. (1920) 'Die Influenza-Epidemie 1918 bis 1919 im Kanton Aargau', unpublished dissertation, Universität Zürich.

Gemuseus, A. (1919) *Eine ignorierte Epidemie. Die nun erkannte Grippe.* Bern.

Gigon, A. (1919) 'Im Militärdienst gemachte Erfahrungen inbezug auf die Grippe' [Experiences with influenza in military service], *Correspondenz-Blatt für Schweizer Ärzte* 49: 558.

Hotz, A. (1918) 'Zur Prophylaxe der spanischen Grippe' [On prophylaxis of Spanish influenza], *Correspondenz-Blatt für Schweizer Ärzte* 48: 1372.

Hunziker, H. (1919) 'Epidemiologie der Grippe', *Correspondenz-Blatt für Schweizer Ärzte* 49, 16: 551–3. [Basel]

Hunziker, H. and Jenny, O.H. (1920) *Die Influenzaepidemie in Basel vom Juni 1918 bis Juni 1919.* Basel: Frehner (Statistische Jahresübersicht über die Bevölkerungsbewegung im Kanton Basel Stadt No. 8).

Imahorn, A. (1919) 'Epidemiologische Beobachtungen über die Grippeepidemie 1918 im Oberwallis' [Epidemiological observations on the influenza epidemic in Oberwallis region], unpublished dissertation, Universität Zürich.

Krafft, C. (1919) 'La grippe en 1918', *Revue Medicale de la Suisse Romande* (Lausanne) 39, 10.

Nussbaum, W. (1982) 'Die Grippe Epidemie 1918/19 in der schweizerischen Armee' [The Influenza epidemic in the Swiss Army 1918–19], *Gesnerus* 39, 2: 243–59.

Schinz, H.R. (1918) 'Die Influenza-Epidemie bei der Guiden-Abteilung 5. Ein Beitrag zur Epidemiologie und Symptomatologie' [Epidemiology and symptoms of the influenza epidemic in a military detachment], *Correspondenz-Blatt für Schweizer Ärzte* 48, 40: 1329–38 and No. 41: 1374–84.

Schönemann, A. (1918) 'Zur Prophylaxe der Influenza' [On prophylaxis of influenza], *Correspondenz-Blatt für Schweizer Ärzte* 48: 1125.

Service Suisse de l'Hygiène Publique (1919) *L'influenza en Suisse en 1918–1919* (Bulletin du Service Suisse de l'Hygiène Publique No. 31). [Abstract Bulletin *Mensuel de l'Office International d'Hygiène Publique* 11, 9: 994–1002]

Silberschmidt, W. (1919) 'Influenza', *Correspondenz-Blatt für Schweizer Ärzte* 49, 18: 626–9. [Zurich]

Sonderegger, C. (1991) 'Die Grippeepidemie 1918/19 in der Schweiz', unpublished licentatite dissertation, History Department, Universität Bern.

Staehelin, R. (1918) 'Einige Bemerkungen über die Influenzaepidemie' [Some observations on the influenza epidemic], *Correspondenz-Blatt für Schweizer Ärzte* 48: 1057.

Thalmann, H. (1968) *Die Grippeepidemie 1918/19 in Zürich.* Zürich: Juris Druck + Verlag (Zürcher medizingeschichtliche Abhandlungen. Neue Reihe No. 50). [Medical dissertation, medizinhistorisches Institut der Universität Zürich]

Wyss, E. (1977) 'Erinnerungen an die Grippeepidemie im Aktivdienst 1918', *Berner Zeitschrift für Geschichte und Heimatkunde* 39: 118–30.

United Kingdom

Bourne, A.W. (1922) 'Influenza: Pregnancy, labour, the puerperium and diseases of women', in F.G. Crookshank (ed.), *Influenza*, London: Heinemann.

Dudley, S.F. (1919) 'The epidemic of grippe as it was observed at Scapa Flow', *J Royal Navy Medical Service* 5: 359ff. [Orkney Islands]

Dudley, S.F (1921) 'The biology of epidemic influenza. Illustrated by naval experience', *Proceedings of the Royal Society of Medicine* 14 (Session 1920–1921. War Section): 42–50.

Dunlop, J.C. (1919) 'Notes on the influenza mortality in Scotland during the period July, 1918 to March, 1919', *Edinburgh Medical J* 22: 403, and 23: 46.

Gotch, O.H. and Whittingham, H.E. (1918) 'A report on the influenza epidemic of 1918', *British Medical J* 1918/II: 82–5.

Great Britain (1919) *Report on the Mortality from Influenza in Scotland during the Epidemic of 1918–19: A Supplement to the Annual Report of the Registrar-General for Scotland*, Edinburgh.

Great Britain (1920) *Supplement to the eighty-first Annual Report of the Registrar-General of Births, Deaths, and Marriages in England and Wales. Report on the Mortality from Influenza in England and Wales during the Epidemic of 1918–19*, London.

Hartesveldt, F.R. Van (1986) 'The government and the flu. British public response to the epidemic of 1918–1919', *Social Science Perspectives* 1: 35–49.

Hartesveldt, F.R. Van (1992) 'Influenza in Manchester', in F.R. Van Hartesveldt (ed.), *The 1918–1919 Pandemic of Influenza. The Urban Impact in the Western World*, Lewiston: Edwin Mellen Press, 91–104.

Johnson, N.P.A.S. (2001) 'Aspects of the historical geography of the 1918–19 influenza pandemic in Britain', PhD thesis, University of Cambridge.

League of Nations Health Organisation (1923) 'Scotland', *Epidemiological Intelligence* (Geneva) 8: 41.

London County Council (ed.) (1919) *Report on the Influenza by the County Medical Officer of Health*, London.

MacNeal, W.J. (1919) see France.

Meader, F.M., Means, J.H. and Hopkins, J.G. (1919) 'Account of an epidemic of influenza among American troops in England', *American J Medical Sciences*, New Series 158: 370–97.

Norrington, A.C. (2000) '"The Greatest Disease Holocaust in History". The British Medical Response to the Influenza Pandemic of 1918–19', unpublished BSc thesis, Wellcome Institute for the History of Medicine, London, 89 pp.

Tomkins, S.M. (1989) 'Britain and the influenza epidemic of 1918–19', unpublished PhD thesis, University of Cambridge. [Crises of medical administration; social impact of epidemic; historical amnesia in popular memory]

Tomkins, S.M. (1992) 'The failure of expertise: public health policy in Britain during the 1918–19 Influenza Epidemic', *Social History of Medicine* 5, 3: 435–54.

Wilshere, J. (1986) *Leicester's Great Influenza Epidemic 1918–1919*, Leicester: Chamberlain Music and Books.

Wilson, A. (1981) 'Oddity remembered. 1918 influenza epidemic', *British Medical J* 1981/I 282, 6278: 1766. [Aberdare]

Oceania

Allard (1922) 'Établissements français de l'Océanie, l'épidémie d'influenza de 1918–1919', *AMédPhC* 20: 66–72.

Crampton, H.E. (1922) 'On the differential effects of the influenza epidemic among native peoples of the Pacific Islands', *Science*, 55: 90–2.

Herda, P. (1995) 'The 1918 influenza pandemic in Fiji, Tonga and the Samoas', in L. Bryder and D.A. Dow (eds), *New Countries and Old Medicine: Proceedings of an International Conference on the History of Medicine and Health, 1994 Auckland, New Zealand*, Auckland: Pyramid Press: 46–53.

Herda, P. (1998) 'Disease and colonialism in the Pacific: The 1918 influenza pandemic in western Polynesia', unpublished paper for the 'Conference on the Spanish flu 1918–1998', held in Cape Town.

Knibbs, G.H. (1921) 'The influenza pandemic of 1918–19', *Transactions of the Australasian Medical Congress*, Brisbane, 321–8.

Australia

Blackwell, B. (1979) 'The 1919 influenza epidemic in Perth', unpublished BA Honours thesis, Murdoch University, Australia.

Briscoe, G. (1996) *Queensland Aborigines and the Spanish Influenza Pandemic of 1918–1919*, Canberra: Australian Institute of Aboriginal and Torres Strait Islander Studies (Research Discussion Paper No. 3).

Camm, J. (1984) 'The Spanish influenza pandemic: Its spread and patterns of mortality in New South Wales during 1919', *Australian Historical Geography Society Bulletin* 6: 13–25.

Cumpston, J.H.L. (1919) *Influenza and Maritime Quarantine in Australia*, Melbourne: Government Printer (Service Publication – Australian Quarantine Service No. 18). [Cumpston was founding director of Australian Department of Health]

Ferry, B. (1976) '1919 influenza in Australia', *New England J Medicine* 295, 9: 512.

Haines, G. (1998) 'The 1918–19 flu pandemic in Australia', *Pharmacy History Australia. The newsletter of the Australian Academy for the History of Pharmacy*, Issue 5: 15.

Hyslop, A. (1985) 'A plague on whose house? Ballarat and the Spanish Influenza of 1919', in H. Attwood and R.W. Home (eds), *Patients, Practitioners and Techniques: Second National Conference on Medicine and Health in Australia, 1984*, Melbourne: University of Melbourne, Medical History Unit (Occasional Papers on Medical History), 195–215.

Hyslop, A. (1995) 'Old ways, new means: fighting Spanish Influenza in Australia, 1918–1919', in L. Bryder and D.A. Dow (eds), *New Countries and Old Medicine. Proceedings of an International Conference on the History of Medicine and Health, 1994 Auckland, New Zealand*, Auckland: Pyramid Press: 54–60.

Hyslop, A. (1997) 'A question of identity. J.H.L. Cumpston and Spanish Influenza, 1918–1919', *Australian Cultural History* 16: 60–76.

McQueen, H. (1975) '"Spanish 'flu" – 1919: political, medical and social aspects', *Medical J Australia* 18: 565–70.

McQueen, H. (1976) 'The "Spanish" influenza pandemic in Australia, 1918–19', in Roe, J. (ed.), *Social Policy in Australia. Some Perspectives, 1901–1975*, Melbourne: Cassell Australia, 131–47.

Owen, D. (1919) *Pneumonic Influenza in Lithgow 1919. Report of the Lithgow Municipal Health Officer, 31st May 1919*, Lithgow, 17 pp. (Reprinted 1990 as *Papers of the Lithgow District Historical Society* No. 48). [Lithgow, west of Sydney]

Rice, G.W. (1990) 'Australia and New Zealand in the 1918–19 influenza pandemic', *Occasional Papers on Medical History Australia* 4: 67–74.

Taksa, L. (1994) 'The masked disease. Oral history, memory and the influenza pandemic 1918–1919', in K.D. Smith and P. Hamilton (eds), *Memory and History in 20th Century Australia*, Melbourne: Oxford University Press, pp. 77–91.

Thomas, C. (1998) '"All at sea" – Spanish Influenza, maritime quarantine and Australian troopships 1918–1919', unpublished paper for the 'Conference on the Spanish flu 1918–1998', held in Cape Town.

Victoria Board of Health (1919) *Spanish Influenza*, Melbourne.

Warburton, M.F. (1973) 'Epidemiology of influenza in Australia and Papua New Guinea', *Medical J Australia* 60, Supplement 1: 14–18.

Warburton, M.F. (1973) 'Epidemiology of influenza in Australia and Papua New Guinea', *Medical J Australia* 60, Supplement 1: 14–18.

Guam

Underwood, J.H. (1984) 'Effects of the influenza pandemic mortality experience on subsequent fertility of the native population in Guam', *Micronesia* 19: 1–10.

New Caledonia

Dhoste (1922) 'Nouvelle-Calédonie, l'épidémie d'influenza de 1918–1919', *AMédPhC* 20: 72–3.

Peltier (1922) 'L'Épidémie d'influenza qui a sévi en Nouvelle-Calédonie en 1921', *Bulletin Mensuel de l'Office International d'Hygiène Publique* 14: 676–85.

New Zealand

Bryder, L. (1980) 'The 1918 influenza epidemic in Auckland', unpublished MA thesis, University of Auckland.

Bryder, L. (1982) '"Lessons" from the 1918 Influenza Epidemic in Auckland', *New Zealand J History* 16, 2: 97–121.

Cuff, M. (1980) 'The great scourge: Dunedin in the 1918 influenza epidemic', unpublished research essay for postgraduate diploma in history, University of Otago, Dunedin.

Edwards, V. (1986) 'Pestilence from abroad? The 1918 influenza epidemic', *New Zealand Medical J* 99, 812: 809–12.

Firchett, F. *et al.* (1919) 'A report on the recent "influenza Epidemic" in Dunedin, New Zealand', *New Zealand Medical J* 18: 1–12.

Holcroft, M.H. (1973) 'The great epidemic', *New Zealand's Heritage* 6, part 76: 2123–8.

Jamieson, J.P.S. (1919) 'Notes on the recent epidemic of influenza in Nelson', *New Zealand Medical J* 18: 46–51.

Killick, E. (1919) 'Financing the influenza epidemic', *New Zealand J Health and Hospitals* 2: 6–12.

Lovell-Gregg. J. (1919) 'How Coromandel kept the influenza epidemic at bay', *New Zealand Medical J* 18: 46–51.

MacDiarmid, D. (1984) 'Influenza 1918', letter, *New Zealand Medical J* 97, 747: 23.

New Zealand, House of Representatives (1919) *Report of the Influenza Epidemic*

Commission (Appendices to the Journal of the House of Representatives No. H-31A), Wellington.

New Zealand, House of Representatives (1919) *Report of the Transport Epidemic Commission* (Appendices to the Journal of the House of Representatives No. 1–7), Wellington.

Pool, D.I. (1973) 'The effects of the 1918 pandemic on the Maori population of New Zealand', *Bulletin of the History of Medicine* 47, 3: 273–81.

Pool, D.I. (1983) 'The age–sex distribution of Maori mortality in the 1918 pandemic of influenza', *New Zealand Population Review* 9: 98–103.

Rice, G.W. (1979) 'Christchurch in the 1918 influenza epidemic, a preliminary study', *New Zealand J History* 13, 2: 109–31.

Rice, G.W. (1983) 'Maori mortality in the 1918 influenza epidemic', *New Zealand Population Review* 9, 1: 44–61.

Rice, G.W. (1984) 'Mapping mortality in the past: The diffusion of the 1918 influenza epidemic in New Zealand', unpublished paper for conference of New Zealand Historical Association, Dunedin August 1984.

Rice, G.W. (1985) 'Crisis in a country town: The 1918 epidemic in Temuka', *Historical News* [New Zealand] 51: 7–13.

Rice, G.W. (1988) *Black November: The 1918 Influenza Epidemic in New Zealand*, (with the assistance of Linda Bryder), Wellington: Allen & Unwin, Historical Branch, 230 pp.

Rice, G.W. (1988) 'The making of New Zealand's 1920 Health Act', *New Zealand J History* 22, 1: 3–22.

Rice, G.W. (1990) 'Microgeography of historical influenza mortality: A New Zealand example from the 1918 pandemic', *1990, One Thousand Years of New Zealand Population: Heeding the Past and Panning for the Future'*, Proceedings of the 1989 New Zealand Demographic Society Conference, Hamilton, pp. 35–43.

Rice, G.W. (1990) see Australia.

Rice, G.W. (1998) see Japan.

Richardson, G.M. (1948) 'The onset of pneumonic influenza in 1918 in relation to the wartime use of mustard gas', *New Zealand Medical J* 47, 257: 4–16.

Wright-St Clair, R.E. (1983) 'Influenza in New Zealand and the doctors who died from it', *New Zealand Medical J* 96:765–8.

Papua New Guinea

Warburton, M.F. (1973) see Australia.

Samoa

Anon. (1919) 'Stricken Samoa. The influenza plague in the islands', *The Chronicle of the London Missionary Society*, New Series, 27: 52–3.

Boyd, M. (1980) 'Coping with Samoan resistance after the 1918 influenza epidemic', *J Pacific History* 15: 155–74.

Grey, F.T. (1919) 'Notes on epidemic broncho-pneumonia (Spanish Influenza) in Samoa', *Medical J Australia*, 18: 359–61. [Abstract *Tropical Disease Bulletin* (1920) 16, 3: 221]

Hiery, H. (1992) 'West Samoans between Germany and New Zealand 1914–1921', *War & Society* (Australia) 10, 1: 53–80.

New Zealand, House of Representatives (1919) *Report of the Samoan Epidemic Commission* (Appendices to the Journal of the House of Representatives No. H-31C), Wellington.

Poleck (1925) 'Über einige bemerkenswerte in unserer ehemaligen Südseekolonie Samoa beobachtete Erkrankungen' [Observations on some diseases in our former colony Samoa], *Archiv für Schiffs- und Tropen-Hygiene* 29, 1: 16–35. [pp. 23–24 on influenza]

Tomkins, S.M. (1992) 'The influenza epidemic of 1918–19 in Western Samoa', *J Pacific History* 7, 2: 181–97.

Tonga

Webster, L.W. (ed.) (1996) *Malo Tupou. An Oral History*, Auckland: Pasifika Press, 175 pp. [Edited transcript of a tape recorded autobiography; personal influenza experience on Tonga]

Index

Use of the word *pandemic* without qualification refers to the 1918–19 outbreak

children: immunisation 247–8, 249–50; role in influenza spread 246–8
Chilson, Mabel 58–9
China, 1918–20 pandemic 101–5, 109; mortality 10, 109
Chinese Maritime Customs (CMC), treaty ports records 102–3, 104
Chinwangtao 103, 104
chiropractors 68
Christian Scientists 66–7
Chungking 103, 104
clinical features of Spanish influenza 5, 132–3
Collier, Richard, *The Plague of the Spanish Lady* (1974) 16
Cree Indians, Keewatin District *see* Keewatin District
Crosby, Alfred: *America's Forgotten Pandemic. The Influenza of 1918* (1989) 18; *Epidemic and Peace 1918* (1976) 17–18
crowding *see* population density
Cumpston, J.H.L. 110–11
cyanosis, blue-purple 5, 133

Dakar 231, 232, 237
de la Camp, Oskar 50, 51
De Spaanse Griep van '18: De epidemie die meer dan 20,000,000 lewens eiste (Gooijer) 16
diphtheria antitoxin 179–80
disinfection, internal 56
disinfection measures: New Zealand 82; Shanghai 105
doctors: Britain 152–3; response to pandemic 61–3, 68, 152–3, 179–80; shortage of, France 194–5; USA 61–3, 65–8

Eastern Samoa 10
encephalitis lethargica (choreatica) 55, 139
England and Wales: influenza mortality 133–6, 139, 141; vital statistics 1900–30 142, 143
Epidemic and Peace 1918 (Crosby) 17–18
Eukupin (isoamylhydrocupreine) 55
Europe, 1918–19 pandemic 7

Fahrig, Carl 53
famine and influenza epidemic, Tanzania 224, 227–8
Fiji 10
First World War *see* World War I

Fischer, Albert Wilhelm 54
Fischer, Alfons 56–7
folk remedies: New Zealand 83, 84; USA 67; *see also* traditional remedies
Fort Dix influenza outbreak 32, 33–4
fowl plague virus 45
France, 1918–19 pandemic 192–201; gender differences 197–8, 200; health services 194–7; military fatalities 192; mortality 7, 192–4, 197; origins and spread 192–4, 198–9; socio-economic distribution 198, 200–1
Freetown, Sierra Leone 6, 9
Freiburg 51

Gandhi, Mahatma 95
gastritis, gender differences in mortality 213, 216
gender: and life expectancy, effect of pandemic 202–17; mortality pattern and, 1918–19 pandemic 8–9, 121–3, 141, 183, 185–6, 197–8, 200
gender, healthcare workers: effect on public reaction to their work 65–6; effect on response to pandemic 63–4, 69; and healthcare role, USA 59–60, 69
geography of pandemic 4, 5–8, 39–40
Germany, 1918–19 pandemic: mortality 7; response to outbreak 49–57; suppression of information 49–50
God's Lake, Manitoba 159, 160, 161, 168
Gooijer, A.C. de, *De Spaanse Griep van '18: De epidemie die meer dan 20,000,000 lewens eiste* (1968) 16
Gore, Dr, researcher, Bombay laboratory 91
Gouzien, Dr Paul 231, 235–6
Grabisch, Alfons 54
Graves, Charles, *Invasion by Virus. Can it Happen Again?* (1969) 15
The Great Epidemic (Hoehling) 15
Grenfell Mission, Cartwright, Labrador 158–9

Haemophilus influenzae 6, 30, 50, 52
Hangchow 104
Hankow 103, 104
Harbin 103, 104
Hartesveldt, Fred Van, *The 1918–19 Pandemic of Influenza. The Urban Impact in the Western World* (1992) 19

Printed in Great Britain
by Amazon